You are requested NOT to mark this book IN ANY WAY

UNIVERSITY OF C
ENGLISH FACULTY LIBRARY
*Writing Religious Women*

4539L

# WRITING RELIGIOUS WOMEN

*Female Spiritual and Textual Practices in Late Medieval England*

Edited by

DENIS RENEVEY

and

CHRISTIANIA WHITEHEAD
University of Cambridge
English Faculty Library
9 West Road
Cambridge CB3 9DP
E-mail: efllib@hermes.cam.ac.uk

18·07·16

UNIVERSITY OF WALES PRESS
CARDIFF
2000

E 222
REN

© The Contributors, 2000

British Library Cataloguing-in-Publication Data.
A catalogue record for this book is available from the British Library.

ISBN 0–7083–1641–7 pb
       0–7083–1642–5 hb

*All rights reserved. No part of this book may be reproduced, sorted in a retrieval system, or transmitted, in any form or by any means, electronic, mechanical, photocopying, recording or otherwise, without clearance from the University of Wales Press, 6 Gwennyth Street, Cardiff, CF24 4YD.*
*Website: www.wales.ac.uk/press*

Cover illustration on paperback edition: The Assumption of the Virgin Mary, centrepiece of altar frontal (late fifteenth century) in St James's Parish Church, Chipping Campden. Reproduced by kind permission of the vicar and church wardens. Photo: Catherine Bates.

Cover design by Chris Neale

Typeset at Wyvern 21
Printed in Great Britain by Dinefwr Press, Llandybïe

# Contents

| | |
|---|---|
| Acknowledgements | vii |
| List of Abbreviations | viii |
| Notes on Editors and Contributors | ix |
| Introduction | 1 |

## Part One: The Influence of Anchoritic Spirituality upon Later Lay Piety

1. *Ancrene Wisse* and the Book of Hours  21
   BELLA MILLETT

## Part Two: Carthusian Links with Female Spirituality

2. Women in the Charterhouse? Julian of Norwich's *Revelations of Divine Love* and Marguerite Porete's *Mirror of Simple Souls* in British Library, MS Additional 37790  43
   MARLEEN CRÉ

3. Spirituality and Sex Change: *Horologium sapientiae* and *Speculum devotorum*  63
   REBECCA SELMAN

4. 'Listen to me, daughter, listen to a faithful counsel': The *Liber de modo bene vivendi ad sororem*  81
   ANNE MC GOVERN-MOURON

*Part Three: The Representation of Femininity in Anglo-Norman and Middle English Religious Poetry*

5. A Fortress and a Shield: The Representation of the Virgin in the *Château d'amour* of Robert Grosseteste     109
CHRISTIANIA WHITEHEAD

6. *Yate of Heven*: Conceptions of the Female Body in the Religious Lyrics     133
KARIN BOKLUND-LAGOPOULOU

*Part Four: Veneration, Performance and Delusion in* The Book of Margery Kempe

7. Measuring the Pilgrim's Progress: Internal Emphases in *The Book of Margery Kempe*     157
SAMUEL FANOUS

8. Veneration of Virgin Martyrs in Margery Kempe's Meditation: Influence of the Sarum Liturgy and Hagiography     177
NAOË KUKITA YOSHIKAWA

9. Margery's Performing Body: The Translation of Late Medieval Discursive Religious Practices     197
DENIS RENEVEY

10. Psychological Disorder and the Autobiographical Impulse in Julian of Norwich, Margery Kempe and Thomas Hoccleve     217
RICHARD LAWES

Bibliography     245

Index     263

# Acknowledgements

We would like to thank our contributors very warmly for the support, assistance and helpfulness they have all shown in bringing this volume to fruition. We would also like to thank Dr Vincent Gillespie of St Anne's College, Oxford, who originally suggested the idea of a series of oral sessions on the subject of female spirituality, and subsequently lent the book his generous support. We acknowledge the part of Leeds International Medieval Congress in providing the forum at which several of these papers could be initially presented; in addition, we would like to show our appreciation of the editors at the University of Wales Press for their help, tolerance and good nature throughout the duration of this project. Our English departments at the Universities of Fribourg and Warwick both went out of their way to support us in this project, upgrading IT facilities where necessary to help ease problems in electronic communication between England and Switzerland.

We are grateful to Jean-Michel Roessli for checking the Latin passages in Kukita Yoshikawa's article. In addition, particularly warm thanks must go to Anne Mc Govern-Mouron who spent many hours scrupulously proof-reading the draft version of the volume; to John Cullington, who generously solved various IT difficulties, and to Patricia Renevey Siffert, who provided personal and moral support with great gracefulness throughout.

DENIS RENEVEY
CHRISTIANIA WHITEHEAD

# List of Abbreviations

CCCM  Corpus christianorum. Continuatio mediaevalis (Turnhout, 1966–).

DS  *Dictionnaire de spiritualité: ascétique et mystique, doctrine et histoire*, ed. M. Viller et al. (Paris, 1937–95).

EETS  Early English Text Society; volume numbers in the Original Series are prefixed OS, those in the Extra Series are prefixed ES, those in the Supplementary Series are prefixed SS.

MED  *Middle English Dictionary*, ed. H. Kurath et al. (Ann Arbor, Mich., 1952–).

*MMTE*  M. Glasscoe (ed.), *The Medieval Mystical Tradition in England. Exeter Symposium*, 6 vols. (Exeter, 1980, 1982; Cambridge, 1984, 1987, 1992, 1999).

*PL*  *Patrologia latina*, ed. J.-P. Migne (Paris, 1841–64).

SC  Sources chrétiennes (Paris, 1941–).

SS  Surtees Society (1834–).

# Editors and Contributors

DENIS RENEVEY is Lecturer in Medieval English Literature at the Universities of Fribourg and Lausanne. Previously he held a Berrow Scholarship at Lincoln College, Oxford, and a Swiss National Foundation scholarship for post-doctoral work. He has published several articles on vernacular theologies in Middle English. He is currently working on the publication of a monograph on Richard Rolle and the commentary tradition of the Song of Songs. Other research projects include further research on the devotion to the Name of Jesus, an edition of Richard Rolle's Latin commentary on the Song of Songs, as well as work upon and a possible edition of the meditations of Eleanor Hull.

CHRISTIANIA WHITEHEAD is Lecturer in Medieval English Literature at the University of Warwick where she teaches medieval and Renaissance literature, and classical literature in translation. She completed her D.Phil. in medieval religious literature in 1995 at Magdalen College, Oxford, and held a short-term lectureship in Anglo-Saxon and Middle English at Balliol College between 1993–4. She has published various articles on allegorical and mystical literature, and is currently completing a book on architectural allegory in medieval religious literature. Future projects include editing a translation of *Piers Plowman* for Bloodaxe Books, in which the task of translation is divided between various contemporary poets. Christiania also writes poetry. Her first collection, *The Garden of Slender Trust*, was published in 1999, and was shortlisted for the Forward Prize for the Best First Collection.

KAREN BOKLUND-LAGOPOULOU is Professor of English Literature in the School of English Language and Literature at the Aristotle University of Thessaloniki, where she teaches medieval literature and literary theory. She received her Ph.D. in comparative literature in 1976 from the University of Colorado at Boulder. Her research interests focus on devotional literature and the lyrics. She has edited a number of volumes in Greek on literary theory and semiotics, and is currently completing a monograph on medieval popular poetry.

MARLEEN CRÉ is a teaching assistant at the University of Antwerp (UFSIA). After previous studies at the University of Antwerp and the University of Leuven, she obtained an M.Phil. from the University of Glasgow, and is currently studying at the Université de Fribourg (Switzerland) for her Ph.D. Her main research interest is the late medieval manuscript transmission of mystical texts in England. She has recently contributed to D. Mowbray et al. (ed.), *Authority and Community in the Middle Ages* (Stroud, 1999).

SAMUEL FANOUS was educated in France, England and the USA. His D.Phil. thesis 'Biblical and Hagiographical *Imitatio* in *The Book of Margery Kempe*' was completed in 1997 at Pembroke College, Oxford. Having lectured at the University of Bristol, he currently teaches at the Centre for Medieval and Renaissance Studies, Oxford. He is working on a volume on imitation in the Middle Ages and is adviser to the forthcoming Blackwell *Anthology of Christian Literature*.

NAOË KUKITA YOSHIKAWA is Associate Professor of English at the College of Medical Technology, Hokkaido University, Japan. She is preparing a Ph.D. dissertation on Margery Kempe at the University of Exeter, under the supervision of Marion Glasscoe. She has already written several articles in the field of religious literature, and has a special interest in Margery Kempe.

RICHARD LAWES is a Member of the Royal College of Psychiatrists. He is currently completing a D.Phil. in English at Magdalen College, Oxford, on the autobiography of religious experience among English Catholics 1450–1650, and he has been elected to a Junior Research Fellowship at Clare Hall, Cambridge. His research interests lie in the late medieval and Renaissance periods, and include the application of psychological theory to medieval and Renaissance texts, religious autobiography, the medieval and recusant mystics, and illness, both physical and mental, in texts of these periods. His paper, 'The Madness of

Margery Kempe', has appeared in M. Glasscoe (ed.), *The Medieval Mystical Tradition: England, Ireland and Wales* (Cambridge, 1999).

ANNE MC GOVERN-MOURON's Oxford doctoral thesis, 'An Edition of the *Desert of Religion* and its Theological Background', was completed in 1996. Since then she has been actively engaged in various research projects, notably in the editing of Middle English devotional texts. She is preparing an edition of the *Desert of Religion* for the Early English Text Society and one of the *Manere of Good Lyvyng* for Analecta Cartusiana. Her interests extend beyond the medieval period and she is also translating a seventeenth-century French text, Cyprien de Gamache's *Mémoires* with the Revd S. Innes of Greyfriars, Oxford.

BELLA MILLETT is a Reader in the English Department, University of Southampton. Her research interests lie in the early medieval period, with a particular focus on the early thirteenth-century rule for anchoresses, *Ancrene Wisse*, and the other Middle English works associated with it. In 1982 her edition of *Hali Meiðhad* was published by EETS; this was followed in 1990 by an anthology of 'AW Group' works, produced in collaboration with Jocelyn Wogan-Browne, and she is currently working on an edition of *Ancrene Wisse* for EETS.

REBECCA SELMAN is a part-time lecturer in English at the Universities of Exeter and Plymouth. She gained her Ph.D. in 1998 from the University of Exeter for a thesis upon the English translation of Henry Suso's *Horologium sapientiae*, and has recently published an article upon this topic in *The Medieval Translator 6*. Her research interests include devotional literature, translation, the status of the vernacular in the late Middle Ages, and lay and female spirituality.

# Introduction

DENIS RENEVEY and CHRISTIANIA WHITEHEAD

## Female Vernacular Theology

IN his groundbreaking essay entitled 'Censorship and Cultural Change in Late-Medieval England: Vernacular Theology, the Oxford Translation Debate, and Arundel's Constitutions of 1409', Nicholas Watson stresses the advisability of using the category heading of 'vernacular theology' to enable a far larger body of texts than the usual group of four or five Middle English mystics to be incorporated within the canon of Middle English religious literature in English departments.[1] The article, which aims to demonstrate the effect of Arundel's Constitutions on the production of vernacular writings after 1410–15, comes provided with an appendix containing a list of the vernacular theologies composed in the period 1300–1500. Commentaries, (poetic) biblical paraphrases, epistles, catechetic translations, didactic narratives, visionary writings and speculative theologies make up the various subgenres which Watson describes collectively as the canon of vernacular theology.

The texts on offer here all belong beneath this category heading and have been convened with two ends in mind. Our volume aims to participate in broadening knowledge of English medieval religious culture: first, by providing critical access to some texts which have attracted little previous attention but which nonetheless make a significant contribution to that culture; and second, by resituating certain better-known texts back within the continuum of vernacular textual practice and production from which they have often become detached. In addition, *Writing Religious Women* adds to our understanding of the 'situatedness' of vernacular theology *c.* 1220 to 1500, by turning its gaze specifically upon texts in which women play a significant role, as either author, recipient or subject.² Such texts can be said to belong to a new category heading of 'female vernacular theology'. If one is to be cautious in attributing too important a role to women in the spread of the vernacular as a universal language – witness, the insignificant role of women as authors or recipients of many of the pastoral and catechetical manuals which were written to support the clergy in its application of Archbishop Pecham's *Ignorantia sacerdotum* – nonetheless it remains possible to identify an important body of writings which can appropriately be grouped beneath this category heading.³ Texts such as *A Book to a Mother*, *A Talkyng of the Love of God*, *The Orchard of Syon* and Eleanor Hull's meditations and her translation of the *Commentary on the Penitential Psalms*, to mention just a few of the works which might have been included here, all belong beneath the category heading of female vernacular theology and deserve corresponding critical attention.

We will return to the issue of the relationship between spirituality and gender in due course. Initially, however, it seems appropriate to focus upon the variety of ways in which our texts reflect perceived characteristics of English vernacular theology. The texts selected for analysis within this collection reflect the distinctive trilingualism of many of the English vernacular theologies produced in the course of the Middle Ages. Certain texts, such as the *Speculum devotorum* and *Liber de modo bene vivendi*, manœuvre their way from Latin into English, exemplifying the linguistic phenomenon of fluidity, or *mouvance*. Grosseteste's *Château d'amour* responds to reading audiences with different expectations and social backgrounds by successively couching itself in Anglo-Norman and English in the course of its textual evolution. On another occasion, an undefined combination of source texts written in medieval French and Latin results in the formation of a further Middle English text (M.N.'s version of Marguerite Porete's *Mirror*). It is also characteristic for works of vernacular theology to move from the personal to the universal. Although *Ancrene Wisse* was originally addressed to three specific female recipients, nonetheless it participates in the spread of the vernacular and the interior life by adjusting to a newly expanded readership over a time-span of almost two centuries. Despite its peculiarities, *The Book of Margery Kempe* also shares in this tendency by inscribing itself in a liturgical mode which provides Margery's idiosyncrasies with a universalizing model accessible to the general Christian reader.⁴ The inclusion of *The Book of Margery Kempe*, together with two brief references to Julian of Norwich's *A Revelation of Love*, within this volume, is intended to query the presuppositions of certain older methodologies. Although such material has traditionally been assessed beneath the rather underexamined category headings of 'affective spirituality' or 'the female mystics', its re-emergence here, situated within the context of a wider textual milieu, is designed to show that mystical writings are not so hermetically sealed from the social and historical contingencies which shape medieval religious culture as may previously have been perceived.

Many of the texts discussed in this volume were not originally written in English. Those which were translated into Middle English after the first decade of the fifteenth century may be regarded as evidence of the vernacular religious output still considered acceptable in the wake of the implementation of Arundel's Constitutions. The sheer number of translations from Latin texts attests to the commanding influence of Latinate culture in the way in which it fed the emerging vernacular with a large body of material. However, this pragmatic process was only one ingredient within a larger project of *translatio studii et imperii* whose complexity escapes the narrow focus of this volume.[5] Suffice to say that we share in the view of medieval translation as a site of powerful cultural exchange, and that some of our texts serve as testimonies to that phenomenon in the late medieval period.[6] Different modes of *translatio studii* are to be seen at work in this collection of essays. Some texts, while not translations as such, are nonetheless the work of authors who would normally have written in Latin, but were prepared to resort to the vernacular when addressing specific recipients (see, Grosseteste's Anglo-Norman *Château d'amour* and, very probably, the *Ancrene Wisse*). Considered within the larger context of cultural exchange, such writings, composed using an author's second or third linguistic idiom, can suitably be regarded as acts of translation. Other theologies, which initially circulated solely in the Latin language, underwent a translation process several centuries after their composition. In such cases, with the exception of texts revealing authorial intentions in a prologue or elsewhere, translators were left without the original backdrop which would have facilitated the act of cultural transference in which they were engaged (*Liber de modo bene vivendi / The Manere of Good Lyvyng*; M.N.'s Middle English translation of Porete's *Mirror*). In view of recent appreciation of the broader phenomenon of *translatio studii*, there is perhaps a need to produce some more specialized translation categories which take such differences into consideration.

The sheer number of translations from Latin texts attests to the commanding influence of Latinate culture upon vernacular material. More broadly, the use of the term 'vernacular theology' invites an investigation of its relationship with medieval Latinate culture in general, and Latin theology in particular. Many of the vernacular texts which deal with the interior life, addressing a coterie audience of contemplatives, show disdain for the *litterati*, whose knowledge of Latin positioned them within the cultural élite of the medieval West. However, despite the efforts of Watson to dissociate this body of vernacular texts from Latinate culture, the origin of the term 'vernacular', from the Latin *verna*, 'a native slave',[7] considered together with other cultural parameters, suggests that attempts to separate the two theologies may prove complicated and misleading. Question after question springs to mind. How did religious vernacular authors perceive their work in relation to an imposing Latinate culture? Did they feel the sense of affiliation and continuation which the term 'vernacular theology' inevitably suggests? Despite their obvious knowledge of, and participation in, Latin religious culture, would authors like Rolle and the *Cloud* author have endorsed such an affiliation? Would they have regarded themselves as the heirs and propagators of a particular Latin theology? Once we move from the general to the specific, such a broad category heading fails to deliver the detailed context which enables a critical appreciation of the specificity of each text.

In addition to examining the impact of translation from Latin into the vernacular, it is also necessary to attempt to align 'vernacular theology' with a specific Latin theology. In the majority of instances, texts of vernacular theology function as part of the pastoral theology which was implemented in England in the wake of the decisions of the 1215 Fourth Lateran Council, rather than replicating the dogmatic and natural theologies which blossomed in the more hermetic contexts of the monastery and the university. We can observe the maturing of vernacular pastoral theology as it progressively severs ties with its imposing Latin counterpart, and begins to address a distinct audience composed both of *litterati* and *illitterati*. Nonetheless, texts such as the pastoral writings of Grosseteste (*Château d'amour* and the *Templum dei*) or the spiritual treatises of Bonaventure (*Incendium amoris* and *Itinerarium mentis in deum*), demonstrate how the advent of vernacular theology was often facilitated by individuals who held important academic positions at the universities of Oxford and Paris. Much vernacular theology can be categorized as post-Lateran pastoral theology. However, other works with a right to be included beneath this heading lack many of those didactic and evangelical qualities which characterize pastoral theology. Perhaps 'vernacular spirituality' might prove a suitable subcategory by which to distinguish those works of vernacular religious literature which remain predominantly dependent upon the classics of twelfth-century monastic spirituality. On occasion, both influences can be detected within the corpus of a single author. For, while some of the writings of Rolle are heavily marked by the influence of pastoral theology (*Judica me Deus, Super lectiones mortuorum*), others, such as his Latin commentary on the Song of Songs, and his Middle English letters of spiritual direction, seem to emerge primarily from the literary and spiritual practices of the monastery and the cathedral schools. Similarly, the heavy borrowing of love imagery from the Song of Songs by *The Manere of Good Lyvyng*, discussed in this volume, together with the text's overall tone, suggest the influence of a monastic literature of spiritual guidance.

It is not our aim to deny the usefulness of the terminology of 'vernacular theology'. We simply wish to draw attention to the fact that the term may require a more solid assessment, especially with regard to the necessity of arriving at a precise understanding of its difference from medieval Latin theology. While resisting a return to former concepts, we would like, nevertheless, to suggest the need for new subcategories to break down a paradigm which presently encompasses the entirety of medieval vernacular religious literature, from the pastoral manual to the visionary account. Our selection of the subcategory of 'female vernacular theology' seems an obvious choice, for reasons which will hopefully be clarified by reading this collection. Such a gender-based partitioning enables the inclusion of a wide range of medieval texts, both prose and verse, covering a multiplicity of medieval genres, from saints' lives to visionary literature. As our title suggests, this subcategory embodies religious works either written and performed by women, written for women, and/or, to a lesser degree, representing women. Perhaps it is inevitable that all these texts should have been affected to some extent by the 'structural misogyny' of the medieval period, yet, in one form or another, they all also contribute toward the shaping of a segment of textual religious culture marked with specifically feminine characteristics.[8]

DENIS RENEVEY

## Medieval Spirituality and Gender

Our use of the tag of 'female vernacular theology' would remain inadequately situated were it devoid of reference to the evolving discussions upon medieval spirituality and gender which have built up over the last twenty-five years. In addition, we would argue that it is only through attention to the pre-existing critical milieu that any essay collection can become properly aware of its own difference and the nature of its distinctive contribution.

The earliest volumes and edited collections to address the experience of medieval women, published in England and America during the late 1970s, found that, at that time, the theme of gender provided their material with a sufficiently coherent shape.[9] It is clear that, in their own decade, such collections played an important role: highlighting the presence of female literary activity within the Middle Ages, and challenging the exclusion of medieval women from the canons of syllabus and scholarship. The continued appearance of similar volumes in the mid-1990s is less justifiable. Twenty years on, the amassing of very disparate materials and approaches beneath the umbrella heading of gender can often seem an overly eclectic and insufficiently structured exercise.[10] As a consequence, the better collections which retain this general stance have, more recently, begun to project themselves from a polemic and feminist perspective which provides a theoretical unification. The collection edited by Ruth Evans and Lesley Johnson, *Feminist Readings in Middle English Literature: The Wife of Bath and All her Sect*, surveys the representation of the female in various canonical Middle English texts with the intention of providing undergraduates with models of feminist interpretation which may subsequently be applied to less well-known texts.[11] The volume by Linda Lomperis and Sarah Stanbury, *Feminist Approaches to the Body in Medieval Literature*, published one year previously, draws upon a mixture of secular and religious writings provenanced in England, France and Italy in the course of addressing its central theme of medieval corporeality in relation to feminist concerns.[12] Diane Watt's edited collection, *Medieval Women in their Communities*,[13] is similarly broad in scope, examining the nature and functioning of women's communities in northern Europe, from Wales to southern Germany. The introduction to the book elucidates Watt's wish to use the evidence drawn from the disharmonies, suppressions and hidden exclusion factors within such medieval communities as a means of problematizing the sixties ideal of the Utopian female collective.

All these collections are united by an explicitly theoretical agenda which lends them focus and direction. Their one (perhaps unavoidable) shortcoming is that, in the course of interrogating received attitudes within the medieval academy, the texts adopted as the site for feminist challenge tend to be picked from the canonical mainstream of the undergraduate syllabus. There is, for example, a preponderance of feminist essays upon Chaucer. By contrast, *Writing Religious Women* turns much of its attention toward the less studied narratives of female vernacular theology. In so doing, it acknowledges itself to be entering uncharted territories within which detailed historical and empirical research still remains the primary requirement. Any coherent collection of essays can only afford to juggle a limited number of emphases. Hence, given the nature of the research of our contributors, we have opted for a variety of close readings of specifically English spiritual material, in which texts are framed by their appropriate cultural and religious surround, set within their manuscript matrices, and probed to disclose the minute signs of engendering by which they become relevant to the requirements of female readers.

Our methodology is primarily historicist. In addition to this, and by contrast with the volumes discussed above, the essays which make up this collection have been deliberately sited at the intersection between two discursive fields: those of female *spiritual* practice and female *textual* practice. In other words, we are primarily interested in the relation of women to religious books, both as writers, as receivers, and as often contentious objects of representation within them. Exclusively historical approaches to the question of women's spirituality, and generically unrestricted examinations of issues of female literacy, book-owning and reading practice, obviously underpin much of the thinking which takes place here. Nonetheless, it is the case that few previous edited collections or monographs straddle this divide and that, in adopting these twin categories as our primary matrices, we are effectively presenting a new configuration of the defining features of women's vernacular spiritual and textual practices toward the close of the Middle Ages.

Many of the most remarkable books to have emerged upon the themes of spirituality and gender over the last twenty years fall toward the historical side of the intersection we have identified. The writings of Caroline Walker Bynum, which have had a very profound effect upon the medieval academy as a whole,[14] and Barbara Newman's magnificent book, *From Virile Woman to WomanChrist: Essays in Medieval Religion and Literature*,[15] stand out for their quality and breadth of perspective. Both writers navigate through a variety of religious genres (hagiography, formative literature, beguine writing) and into a number of continental women's communities, but the primary focus of interest remains historical and ideological rather than literary, and of necessity there is little close engagement with the specific circumstances of English spiritual behaviour. Two slightly older Cistercian collections hailing from the mid-1980s also turn their gaze toward medieval religious women. The first, *Distant Echoes*, contains essays on the historical and economic contexts surrounding female religious practice which are strongly biased in favour of monasticism.[16] The second, *Peace Weavers*, concentrates more closely upon the individual spiritual experience of exceptional figures but, again, its vision is panoramic – three of the four exceptional women chosen for elaboration are continental, one is situated in the mid-sixteenth century.[17]

While the majority of books upon medieval women generated during the 1980s project themselves from a primarily historical standpoint, several recent collections redress this balance in their pursuit of more *textual* areas of concern. Carol Meale's 1993 edited collection, *Women and Literature in Britain 1150–1500*, has attracted widespread attention for the impressive quality of its scholarship.[18] As the title suggests, the material assembled here focuses upon the British Isles. However, the collection's unifying theme is cogently defined by Meale as an investigation into the extent of 'women's access to written culture, and their ability, or lack of it, to use that culture to their own ends'. Female book-owning habits and the nature of female literacy both receive attention, but the essays are as much concerned with women's relation to romance literature as they are with religious texts, and the volume lacks any uniform preoccupation with spirituality.

Rosalynn Voaden's collection, *Prophets Abroad: The Reception of Continental Holy Women in Late-Medieval England*, has appeared yet more recently.[19] Compellingly specialized in focus, this volume examines the Middle English reception of the narratives and *vitae* of Hildegard of Bingen, Marguerite Porete, Mechtild of Hackeborn, Bridget of Sweden and Catherine of Siena, noting the 'common thread of acculturation' which governs the way in which these texts are adapted for an English readership. Voaden's volume has a clearly articulated set of objectives. Yet, although her concern with continental links is repeated briefly within several of the essays contained in this collection (Mc Govern-Mouron, Selman, Fanous), the themes which give structure to *Writing Religious Women* are sufficiently distinct to leave space for both volumes to breathe. The only other recent book to cover similar ground is the volume containing the selected proceedings of a 1993 conference at St Hilda's College, Oxford, edited by Jane Taylor and Lesley Smith, under the title, *Women, the Book and the Godly*.[20] This collection of detailed and scholarly essays, positioned at the same intersection of female spiritual and textual practice, contains a limited number of broad thematic threads, namely: the twelfth- and early thirteenth-century female reception of devotional texts, the circulation of books amongst women in the late Middle Ages, and the role of women in circles of heterodox literacy, together with some case studies of the continental female mystics.

We perceive our collection as a useful complement to *Women, the Book and the Godly*. For while the intellectual matrices of spiritual and textual interest obviously coincide, our collection, containing a smaller number of more extended essays, can be distinguished by its commitment to thematic areas of interest distinct from those explored in the Taylor–Smith compilation. We have grouped our essays beneath the general headings of (i) the influence of anchoritic spirituality upon later lay piety, (ii) Carthusian links with female spirituality, (iii) the representation of femininity in Anglo-Norman and Middle English religious poetry, and (iv) veneration, performance and delusion in *The Book of Margery Kempe*.

With one exception, we are not aware that any of these named subject areas have been the recipients of much contemporary critical attention. The most notable recent monographs upon thirteenth-century anchoritic spirituality have specific agendas concerned with subjectivity and empowerment through bodiliness, and do not examine the effect of that spirituality upon later lay practices.[21] Our three essays which focus upon Carthusian links with female spirituality in relation to specific vernacular translations all acknowledge the importance of Michael Sargent's book, *James Grenehalgh as Textual Critic*, in assisting their thinking;[22] but, apart from a few other intermittent articles published over the last fifteen years by Analecta Cartusiana,[23] little large-scale work has been undertaken within this field. The third section contains essays which examine a thirteenth-century Anglo-Norman poem by Bishop Robert Grosseteste and selected Middle English devotional lyrics. These unlikely textual partners are brought together through their common metaphorical representations of exemplary women; however, in terms of their critical inheritance, there is little that precedes them. Virtually no new material has been produced upon the devotional lyrics for quite some time, and the Grosseteste poem in question has never been extensively written about.

Our last section stands as the exception to the rule. Addressing issues connected with *The Book of Margery Kempe*, it confronts a woman who has moved toward the forefront of the higher educational mainstream in England and America over the last ten years. Margery's new-won popularity has been reflected by the flow of critical monographs seeking to interpret the significance of her controversial spiritual autobiography.[24] She has also been the focus of a recent essay collection edited by Sandra McEntire.[25] This collection, keenly aware of the earlier critical tendency to dismiss Margery out of hand, redresses the balance via a series of highly sympathetic readings. However, despite this abundance of available critical material, few contemporary studies pick up on the more *spiritual* side of Margery's activities. Among a wealth of interpretations which highlight Margery's personhood, her subjectivity, the use she makes of her body, and her appropriation by feminist critics, relatively little can be found regarding the specifically religious influences which determine her career. The essays situated in the fourth section of this volume help amend this gap. Focusing upon the anchoritic, hagiographic and liturgical influences which contribute to Margery's textual representation, they draw upon an expert knowledge of the prevailing religious culture to illuminate neglected facets in Margery's spiritual make-up.

CHRISTIANIA WHITEHEAD

# The Influence of Anchoritic Spirituality upon Later Lay Piety

Perhaps as a result of its fascinating idiosyncrasies, anchoritic culture is rarely assessed within the larger religious cultural milieu of the medieval period. Some of our contributions take issue with this unfortunate state of affairs. Mc Govern-Mouron places the *Liber de modo bene vivendi* alongside thirteenth-century anchoritic texts such as Aelred of Rievaulx's *De institutione inclusarum* and *Ancrene Wisse*, while Renevey draws material from the daily devotional routines of anchoresses to explicate the peculiar performative behaviour of Margery Kempe. However, the fullest investigation is carried out in Millett's essay, '*Ancrene Wisse* and the Book of Hours', in which Millett contributes to the debate regarding the origins of the 'breviary for the laity' by focusing upon the devotions so minutely described in *Ancrene Wisse*, Part One. The lay-anchoresses for whom *Ancrene Wisse* was written received instructions based on an existing model of institutional observance. It has often been argued that the devotions of the Book of Hours passed from monastic hands into those of the secular clergy, and then to the laity. Millett argues for an additional, intermediate stage: the anchoritic audience. Nonetheless, she is careful to note that other intermediaries may also have played a part in this process. During the late twelfth and early thirteenth century, it became necessary for the Church to provide prescriptions for devotional practice to groups practising new forms of quasi-religious and ascetic life, such as the communities who ran hospitals and leper-houses, beguinages, penitent confraternities and military orders. Since the mendicants were involved in drafting both the statutes and the devotions of those new groups which occupied the borderline territory between laity and cloistered religious, it is probable that they also encouraged the adoption of their own devotional practices by other members of the Christian laity.

## Carthusian Links with Female Spirituality

In a monograph of 1984, Michael Sargent commented that two of the most important extant Middle English compilations of contemplative texts, British Library, MS Additional 37790 and British Library, MS Additional 37049, were Carthusian products.[26] This, together with the Carthusian provenance of other manuscripts containing mystical and contemplative texts, raises important questions about the Carthusian role in the transmission and preservation of spiritual writing during the late Middle Ages, and the anticipated audience of such collections. Three of the essays in this collection focus closely upon texts and manuscripts copied or compiled within a Carthusian milieu with the intention of illuminating some of these issues.

Marleen Cré leads the way with a close textual investigation of BL MS Additional 37790 which includes extensive material by Rolle, the short text of Julian of Norwich's *Revelations*, translations of Ruusbroec's *Treatise of Perfection of the Sons of God* and Marguerite Porete's *Mirror of Simple Souls*. She analyses the reasons underlying Carthusian interest in these texts, and notes that the compilation acts as a testament to Carthusian openness toward many different styles of spiritual writing. The immediate audience of the compilation has been the subject of different theories in recent years. Cré investigates the plausibility of a readership of lay-brothers and novices within the Charterhouse itself, and goes on to consider the way in which such an audience would have engaged with the works of 'female spirituality' included in the manuscript.

Although MS Add. 37790 lacks any signs which might help elucidate the gender of its recipients, these omissions are made good in the Carthusian *Speculum devotorum*, a fifteenth-century Middle English life of Christ drawing upon the gospel commentaries of Nicholas de Lyra and Peter Comestor, which seems to have been written with a specifically female audience in mind. Selman's analysis of the *Speculum devotorum* concentrates upon the rhetorical mechanisms by which the text is made susceptible to female readership, and she examines how, through the interpolation of female voices of authority, the female reader is provided with easily identifiable models of percipience and response to the drama of the passion.

Our third essay focuses upon *The Manere of Good Lyvyng*, a unique Middle English translation of an early thirteenth-century Latin treatise, *Liber de modo bene vivendi*, which was addressed to the young aristocratic member of a female religious order. Unlike the *Ancrene Wisse*, with which it has various affinities, shamefully little work has been undertaken upon this substantial religious treatise which remained popular all over Europe until well into the seventeenth century. Mc Govern-Mouron makes good this scholarly neglect. She stages a thorough investigation, demonstrating that the translation has scribal links with the charterhouse at Sheen, and putting forward arguments which suggest that the initial author of the Latin *Liber* may well have been an Augustinian canon, a hypothesis which strengthens its already notable similarities to the *Ancrene Wisse*.

The *Liber*'s orientation toward a female religious, taken together with the fact that the translation was the product of the Sheen scriptorium, suggests that the Middle English version may well have been designed for a Bridgittine of Syon. Selman's work upon the *Speculum devotorum* also includes evidence demonstrating the likelihood that the text was translated and adapted for a Bridgittine at Syon. The obvious frequency with which Sheen Carthusians supplied and chose texts to be read within a Bridgittine milieu raises important closing questions concerning the nature of the affinity between Carthusian and Bridgittine spirituality, and the extent to which Carthusian compilers and adapters exercised control over the religious experience of the Syon nuns.

## The Representation of Femininity in Anglo-Norman and Middle English Religious Poetry

The textual construction of the feminine during the Middle Ages is a topic which has generated a sizeable secondary literature in recent decades. The two essays in the collection which engage with this topic limit themselves intentionally, focusing upon the representation of exemplary femininity located in vernacular religious verse. In such a context, the majority of representations tend to centre upon either the body of the Virgin Mary or that of the female believer. Both bodies are typically evoked at a level of almost unbroken metaphor. Prominent amongst these metaphors is the stock trope in which the exemplary female is written as a defensive habitation, presenting an inviolable surface of defiant virginity against the lures of the external world.

Whitehead's essay investigates the assumptions implicit in this trope using the example of a thirteenth-century Anglo-Norman poem by Bishop Robert Grosseteste in which the Virgin is allegorized as a fortress. Having reviewed the historical evolution of the metaphor, she analyses the way in which its increased elaboration during the early thirteenth century corresponds with contemporary advances in Marian doctrine. Whitehead notes that the feminized fortress proffers a picture of intact, untroubled bodily completion more conventionally associated with the male physique. This issue of gender inversion returns in the succeeding essay in which Boklund-Lagopoulou describes how the apparent erasure of the female body from the religious lyrics is belied by a subtext in which Christ is repeatedly evoked in feminine terms: 'the female body is not as absent from medieval literature as it would seem at first sight but ... is, as it were, disguised – in a body which is sexually male, but symbolically often female.' Boklund-Lagopoulou also turns her attention to the evocation of the bodily habitation within the religious lyrics. She identifies various areas of contradiction, including the way in which the metaphor of inhabitation, whereby the believer's body prepares itself for future indwelling by Christ, is suddenly abandoned in favour of poetic imagery in which the believer enters Christ's flesh through his wounds and through a dissolution of the will. The essay closes on a theoretical note, suggesting some models of interpretation through which these apparent contradictions may be combined and resolved.

## Veneration, Performance and Delusion in *The Book of Margery Kempe*

The ownership and annotation of the spiritual autobiography of a laywoman by the Carthusian monks of Mount Grace attests to its devotional quality. The first three essays of this section try to make sense of Margery's spirituality by considering the possible sources and influences which led to the couching of her experiences as we have them in *The Book*. Without in any way negating these spiritual aspects, the last essay in the volume reviews Margery, along with other medieval writers 'of the self', from a more psychiatric perspective.

Hagiographic elements form the chief concerns of Kukita Yoshikawa and Fanous. The apparent inattention to chronology and place in *The Book*, Fanous argues, conceals a high degree of selectivity on the part of Margery and her scribe. The care by which specific events are located and defined according to the liturgical calendar is demonstrated by a consideration of various key moments from her life. Fanous's essay emphasizes how Margery's desire for a sexual act on the eve of St Margaret's day casts her as a penitential figure in accordance with hagiographic tradition and sets her low upon the spiritual ladder. Her redemption as a type of the Magdalen is achieved through her mystical marriage and entry into the company of celestial virgins. Fanous argues that the extreme precision with which this event is detailed indicates the amanuensis's knowledge of the design and function of hagiographic convention, and shows his ability to apply the convention with remarkable skill.

Kukita Yoshikawa's essay investigates the influence of the Sarum liturgy and hagiography, paying special attention to Margery's veneration of three female saints, Katherine, Margaret and Barbara. The widespread devotion to these saints in the late medieval period helps account for some of Margery's more eccentric bodily performances. Kukita Yoshikawa focuses most closely upon Margery's veneration of St Katherine of Alexandria, tracing Margery's efforts to bring her life into line with this particular model of sanctity.

Margery's spiritual ambitions and her active involvement in the affairs of lay society create the dynamic tension at the heart of the third essay. Renevey asserts that Margery's primary text is her performing body. Its performance, triggered by Margery's imaginative re-enactment of the Passion incidents, fails to produce coherent meaning. Despite affiliations with some of the patterns characteristic of anchoritic spirituality and the affective meditations of the Passion, her performance is fraught with difficulties and is misinterpreted by her audience. Because of this partial failure, Margery provides her own hermeneutics on her performing body, *The Book*, which attempts to make sense of her peculiar mysticism.

The final essay in this section uses psychiatric expertise to illuminate the autobiographical information embedded in the writings of Margery Kempe, Thomas Hoccleve and Julian of Norwich. Having assessed the nature of the psychological disorders suffered by these writers, and discussed the typical behavioural patterns associated with such disorders, Richard Lawes makes an important case for the role played by psychological disorders in generating autobiographical impulses within medieval subjects.

## Notes

[1] N. Watson, 'Censorship and Cultural Change in Late-Medieval England: Vernacular Theology, the Oxford Translation Debate, and Arundel's Constitutions of 1409', *Speculum*, 70 (1995), 822–64.

[2] 'Situatedness' is used by the editors of *The Idea of the Vernacular* to discuss the status of the vernacular as part of an emerging culture in the context of other languages. We use it here to define vernacular theology in relation to other important theologies; see J. Wogan-Browne et al. (eds.), *The Idea of the Vernacular: An Anthology of Middle English Literary Theory 1280–1520*, Exeter Medieval Texts and Studies (Exeter, 1999).

[3] See N. Watson, 'The Middle English Mystics', in D. Wallace (ed.), *The Cambridge History of Medieval English Literature* (Cambridge, 1999), 553.

[4] See the essays in this volume by Fanous and Kukita Yoshikawa.

[5] See *The Idea of the Vernacular* for extensive discussions on this topic. See also *The Medieval Translator* volumes edited by Roger Ellis.

[6] See R. Evans, A. Taylor, N. Watson and J. Wogan-Browne, 'The Notion of Vernacular Theory', in *The Idea of the Vernacular*, 317.

[7] See J. M. Ziolkowski, 'Towards a History of Medieval Latin Literature', in F. A. C. Mantello and A. G. Rigg (eds.), *Medieval Latin: An Introduction and Bibliographical Guide* (Washington, 1996), 508.

8 For discussions on the structural misogyny of the medieval period, see A. Blamires, *The Case for Women in Medieval Culture* (Oxford, 1998), 236–8.
9 See, for example, D. Baker (ed.), *Medieval Women* (Oxford, 1978). Eileen Power's classic work, *Medieval English Nunneries: c. 1275–1535* (Cambridge, 1922) is, of course, an important exception to this rule.
10 Otherwise strong collections, such as J. Dor (ed.), *A Wyf Ther Was* (Liège, 1992), lend themselves to criticism on this front.
11 R. Evans and L. Johnson (eds.), *Feminist Readings in Middle English Literature: The Wife of Bath and All her Sect* (London and New York, 1994).
12 L. Lomperis and S. Stanbury (eds.), *Feminist Approaches to the Body in Medieval Literature* (Philadelphia, 1993).
13 D. Watt (ed.), *Medieval Women in their Communities* (Cardiff, 1997).
14 C. W. Bynum, *Jesus as Mother: Studies in the Spirituality of the High Middle Ages* (Berkeley, 1982) includes a section upon the mystical experience of the nuns of Helfta; *Holy Feast, Holy Fast: The Religious Significance of Food to Medieval Women* (Berkeley, 1987) focuses upon the dietary eccentricities of religious women; and *Fragmentation and Redemption: Essays on Gender and the Human Body in Medieval Religion* (New York, 1991) is primarily concerned with the cultural construction of the body during the Middle Ages and the relation of the parts to the whole.
15 B. Newman, *From Virile Woman to WomanChrist: Essays in Medieval Religion and Literature* (Philadelphia, 1995).
16 J. A. Nichols and L. T. Shank (eds.), *Distant Echoes* (Kalamazoo, 1984).
17 Idem (eds.), *Peace Weavers* (Kalamazoo, 1987). See also, from the same decade, M. B. Rose (ed.), *Women in the Middle Ages and the Renaissance: Literary and Historical Perspectives* (Syracuse, NY, 1986).
18 C. M. Meale (ed.), *Women and Literature in Britain 1150–1500* (Cambridge, 1993).
19 R. Voaden (ed.), *Prophets Abroad: The Reception of Continental Holy Women in Late-Medieval England* (Cambridge, 1996).
20 J. Taylor and L. Smith (eds.), *Women, the Book and the Godly* (Cambridge, 1995).
21 L. Georgianna, *The Solitary Self: Individuality in the Ancrene Wisse* (Cambridge, Mass. and London, 1981); E. Robertson, *Early English Devotional Prose and the Female Audience* (Knoxville, Tenn., 1990). A. Savage and N. Watson, *Anchoritic Spirituality: Ancrene Wisse and Associated Works*, The Classics of Western Spirituality (New York, 1991) has an admirably detailed introduction and critical apparatus, but is an anthology of translated texts rather than a collection of critical essays.
22 M. G. Sargent, *James Grenehalgh as Textual Critic*, 2 vols., Analecta Cartusiana 85 (Salzburg, 1984).
23 See, for example, A. I. Doyle, 'Carthusian Participation in the Movement of Works of Richard Rolle between England and Other Parts of Europe in the 14th and 15th Centuries', Analecta Cartusiana 55.2 (1981), 109–20; V.

Gillespie, 'Cura pastoralis in deserto', in M. G. Sargent (ed.), *De cella in seculum: Religious and Secular Life and Devotion in Late Medieval England* (Cambridge, 1989), 161–81.

[24] See K. Lochrie, *Margery Kempe and Translations of the Flesh* (Philadelphia, 1991), and L. Staley, *Margery Kempe's Dissenting Fictions* (University Park, Pa., 1994).

[25] S. McEntire (ed.), *Margery Kempe: A Book of Essays* (New York and London, 1992).

[26] Sargent, *James Grenehalgh*, 52.

# Part One

*The Influence of Anchoritic Spirituality upon Later Lay Piety*

# 1
# *Ancrene Wisse* and the Book of Hours

### BELLA MILLETT

THE early thirteenth-century Middle English rule for anchoresses, *Ancrene Wisse*, includes in the first of its eight parts a detailed set of prescriptions for the anchoresses' devotional routine. These prescriptions have already been fairly thoroughly investigated,[1] but most researchers have concentrated on the earlier history of the devotions described. I shall be looking instead at their relationship to later devotional practice, and in particular to the history of the Book of Hours.

Although most of the components of the devotional routine set out in *Ancrene Wisse* Part 1 are traditional, the routine itself is not. Its most notable feature is that the anchoresses do not say the full canonical Hours, the 'Divine Office' recited daily by religious and by secular clerics; instead, they use the much shorter and simpler Little Office of the Virgin. There is no precedent for this substitution in Aelred of Rievaulx's guide for anchoresses, *De institutione inclusarum* (c. 1160), on which the author of *Ancrene Wisse* drew. It is likely that the sister Aelred addresses was (like Eve of Wilton before her) a nun-anchoress, who had graduated from the convent to the anchor-house with a good reading knowledge of Latin and long practice in the recitation of the Divine Office. Aelred expects her to recite the full canonical Hours; he also recommends the Little Office of the Virgin, but only as a supplementary devotion.[2] He does make provision for other anchoresses who cannot cope with the Hours, but at a much lower level. The anchoress *quae litteras non intelligit* seems to be not only *illitterata* in the medieval sense (i.e. unable to read Latin easily) but illiterate in the modern sense as well. Aelred recommends that she should replace the Divine Office by manual work and frequent repetitions of the *Pater noster*, interspersed by psalms 'if she knows any' (*si quos psalmos noverit*).[3]

The recommendations in *Ancrene Wisse* Part 1 seem to have been designed for an audience occupying a middle ground between the extremes of *litteratura* and illiteracy assumed by Aelred. In the Preface to *Ancrene Wisse*, the author concedes that anchoresses may be either highly educated or uneducated, echoing Aelred's recommendations for the latter;[4] and provision is made in both the original and later versions of Part 1 for a much-simplified devotional routine based on repeated *Paters* and *Aves*.[5] The primary audience of *Ancrene Wisse*, however, falls into neither of these categories. The work seems to have been composed in the first instance for three well-born young women who had entered the anchor-house directly from the world; the revised version in Cambridge, Corpus Christi College, MS 402 addresses a group of anchoresses which had expanded to 'twenty or more', but not necessarily one which had changed its nature. The author assumes that at least some of the anchoresses can read, write and cope with a modest amount of liturgical Latin, but other Latin is translated for them, and their edifying reading is expected to be in English or French. The devotional routine that they are prescribed, although it remains fairly demanding,[6] is adapted to their capacities; it offers a shorter and less complicated substitute for the Divine Office, and includes a substantial vernacular element.

The routine is based on what Sitwell describes as 'semi-liturgical devotions':[7] that is, the supplementary devotions which had gradually accumulated in monastic usage around the Divine Office from the Carolingian period onwards. Its central component is the Little Office of the Virgin; the anchoresses are advised to recite its seven Hours at the times prescribed for the Hours of the Divine Office. They also say the Office of the Dead, and may, if they wish, add the Hours of the Holy Spirit, reciting each Hour before the corresponding Hour of the Virgin Mary. Their other 'semi-liturgical devotions' include the suffrages of the saints, the Commendation,[8] *Pretiosa*,[9] the Litany, the seven Penitential Psalms and the fifteen Gradual Psalms. In addition to these, the author includes a number of what could be called 'quasi-liturgical devotions': these incorporate elements from the liturgy (psalms, hymns, collects, antiphons and versicles), non-liturgical Latin hymns and prayers and, in some cases, prayers in English. They include devotions to be said on rising, at midday, on going to bed, and for the sick and prisoners; salutations and other devotions recited before the Cross, and at the raising of the Host at Mass; a devotional framework, including prayers in English, for the recitation of various numbers of *Paters*; and prayers in English on the Five Joys of the Virgin, accompanied by multiple *Aves* and further Latin material (including five psalms whose first letters spell out the name MARIA). The anchoresses are also encouraged to use their own devotions, reciting *Paters, Aves*, prayers and psalms, and to listen as far as possible to the Hours of the priest who serves the church their cell adjoins (though they are warned not to join in in such a way that he can hear them). Those who cannot say the Little Office of the Virgin are advised to recite multiple *Paters* and *Aves*. A few of these prescriptions are further modified or supplemented by later additions in some of the manuscripts.[10]

In 1955, Gerard Sitwell commented that the semi-liturgical and other devotions listed in Part 1 were of the kind that one would expect to find in a fifteenth-century Book of Hours,[11] and its links with the Book of Hours tradition have also been touched on by later scholars.[12] A typical Book of Hours of the fifteenth century would, like *Ancrene Wisse* Part 1, offer its reader a devotional routine including the Little Office of the Virgin, the Office of the Dead, the Litany, the suffrages of the saints and the seven Penitential Psalms. It might also add other votive Offices (such as the Hours of the Holy Spirit), the fifteen Gradual Psalms, and further devotions, sometimes extensive, in Latin or in the vernacular; frequently occurring features paralleled in *Ancrene Wisse* Part 1 include invocations to the Host, the Latin prayer to the Virgin *O intemerata*, and vernacular prayers on the Joys of the Virgin (although the number of Joys could vary, and in the later period was most often fifteen).[13] Books of Hours, however, are relatively rare before the late fourteenth century, so it is worth asking what light the devotional routine described in this early thirteenth-century work might shed on their earlier history.

The origins of the Book of Hours are poorly documented, and still not fully understood. As Victor Leroquais complained over seventy years ago, most researchers on the Books of Hours concentrate on the illustrations of the manuscripts rather than their content, and liturgists treat them as 'the poor relation' of the family of liturgical books.[14] The best general account of their early development is still that by Leroquais himself, in his 1927 catalogue of the Books of Hours in the Bibliothèque Nationale. He describes how certain semi-liturgical devotions, adopted in monastic use between the ninth and eleventh centuries as a supplement to the Divine Office,[15] spread first to the secular clergy and later (as a primary rather than a supplementary devotional routine) to the laity. Appended at first to the Psalter – still the commonest pattern in the twelfth and thirteenth centuries – they began increasingly to appear in a separate volume, which sometimes included additional devotions in Latin or the vernacular. There is some disagreement among scholars on when the 'Book of Hours' proper first appears: was it in the eleventh, the twelfth or the thirteenth century? This is to a great extent a problem of definition. By the fifteenth century the 'Book of Hours' had become a relatively well-defined (though never completely standardized) genre; but, for the early stages of its development, there is no scholarly consensus on what combinations of content, form, intended use and audience qualify a particular text to be described as a 'Book of Hours'. A helpful starting-point for the definition of terms is provided by Leroquais's treatment of the question, 'What is a Book of Hours?'[16] He concedes that liturgical manuscripts are not noted for clear delimitations of genre, and that the 'magnificent disdain' for uniformity which characterizes the Middle Ages means that no two Books of Hours are identical;[17] nevertheless, he identifies certain characteristics which distinguish the Book of Hours from other liturgical books. The 'Book of Hours' contains certain basic elements of content (a Calendar, the Little Office of the Virgin, the Litany, the Penitential Psalms, the suffrages and the Office of the Dead); it takes the form of a separate volume (although Leroquais treats the combined Psalter-Hours, where the Psalms are followed by the basic elements of the Book of Hours, as a 'special case'); it is designed for private devotion, voluntary and unofficial, rather than public recitation as part of the liturgy; and finally, it is for lay use:

> If the breviary is the book of the priest or the religious, the Book of Hours is the book of the faithful, of the layperson. What is a Book of Hours? It is a compilation of Offices and prayers for the use of the faithful: a breviary for the use of the laity.[18]

Leroquais here seems to be working back from the fully developed form of the genre, the 'mature' Book of Hours of the fifteenth century; the combination of characteristics that he lists is less often found in the earlier period, and not all the manuscripts which he catalogues meet his criteria in full. These criteria, however, can be usefully employed to distinguish various stages in the development of the 'Book of Hours', and to explain the widely different dates which have been suggested for its emergence. The late eleventh-century manuscript identified by Delaissé as 'a characteristic Book of Hours',[19] Oxford, Bodleian Library, MS Canonici Liturg. 277, although it meets Leroquais's criteria for both content and form, was designed for use in a community of Benedictine nuns. The point at which the Book of Hours acquired its function as a 'breviary for the laity' remains unclear. Leroquais saw it as a gradual process, taking place over the late twelfth and early thirteenth centuries, as the Psalter, the standard prayer-book of the laity from the Carolingian period to the thirteenth century, was increasingly supplemented by semi-liturgical devotions. 'In reality, the first Books of Hours are a combination of the Psalter and the Book of Hours. The first forms the most important part of the manuscript, the second is a sort of appendix which takes an increasingly large space, up to the point when it becomes detached from the psalter, as the fruit is detached from the tree.'[20] But the development of the form of the Book of Hours is a separate question from the development of its audience. The Psalter may have been the prayer-book of the laity in the early Middle Ages, but it was not used only by the laity; and, although compilations identifiable in form and content as Psalter-Hours or Books of Hours survive from the eleventh century onwards, clear evidence for their use by the laity before the early thirteenth century is difficult to find. Not all the late twelfth- and early thirteenth-century Psalter-Hours and Books of Hours catalogued by Leroquais have indications of ownership, but what indications there are suggest monastic users, even when the manuscripts include vernacular material.[21] Nigel Morgan, in his survey of manuscripts illuminated in the British Isles between 1190 and 1250, argues that the role of aristocratic laywomen 'in popularizing illuminated books of a devotional nature is not to be underestimated', but concedes that it is 'difficult to document', and that 'direct evidence for twelfth-century ownership of illuminated books by lay women in England is slight';[22] even in the early thirteenth century, the evidence for lay ownership (whether male or female) of Psalter-Hours in England is limited and mainly circumstantial.[23] The earliest surviving Book of Hours produced in England, the 'de Brailes Hours' (London, British Library, MS Add. 49999), may have been designed for a laywoman (if Morgan and Donovan are right in assuming that some of its illustrations represent its first owner); but this was not compiled until towards the middle of the thirteenth century, c. 1240.[24]

The detailed account of the anchoresses' devotional routine in *Ancrene Wisse* Part 1 may help to cast light on the otherwise poorly documented transition of the Book of Hours from monastic to secular use. The dating of *Ancrene Wisse* itself is uncertain, but it now seems likely that the original version was composed at some point between about 1216 and 1230, probably in the later 1220s.[25] Although *Ancrene Wisse* Part 1 describes a devotional routine closely similar to that found in later Books of Hours, it is not itself a Book of Hours (it provides texts only of some of the quasi-liturgical devotions), and there is no clear evidence that it refers to one. The author assumes that the anchoresses will have texts of the Little Office of the Virgin, apparently copied by themselves ('Each one should say her Hours as she has written them out'[26]), but they seem to be one element of an *ad hoc* library of books, booklets and scrolls rather than part of a single-volume devotional compilation. A reference to 'verseilunge of Sauter' ('reciting verses from the Psalter')[27] suggests that some anchoresses at least owned a Psalter, possibly brought with them to the anchor-house. Texts of the graces before and after meals have been copied out for them;[28] the author recommends the recitation of the hymn *Alpha et omega* to 'anyone who has it';[29] and they are told at one point, 'Texts of the prayers that I have only mentioned briefly are generally available, except for the last. Have anything that you do not know copied on to a scroll.'[30] The account of the anchoresses' devotions in *Ancrene Wisse* Part 1 does not necessarily point us towards a lost early Book (or Books) of Hours; its interest lies rather in the information it provides about how those devotions were used in a particular early thirteenth-century context, and what this might suggest about the adoption of the Book of Hours as the 'breviary of the laity'.

The lay-anchoresses for whom *Ancrene Wisse* was written are representative of a broader tendency in thirteenth-century anchoritism: because of a growing imbalance between the demand for the religious life and the supply of institutional places, women were increasingly entering the anchoritic life directly from the world, as an alternative (perhaps in some cases a second-best alternative) to life in a nunnery rather than as a progression from it.[31] Although the author of *Ancrene Wisse* describes his audience of lay-anchoresses as 'religiuse',[32] they appear to have felt, with some justification, that their status as religious was rather too marginal for comfort.[33] Although they had taken formal vows of chastity, obedience and stability of abode, and led a life of strict enclosure under episcopal supervision, they did not belong to a religious order, wear a habit, or follow a papally approved Rule; in the Preface to *Ancrene Wisse* we are told that they had complained of people asking them to which order they belonged, and whether it was 'black' or 'white'.[34] The author is firm that they must accept their relatively unofficial status, but he nevertheless makes some attempt to deal with their sense of exclusion, and the devotional routine which they are offered in Part 1 is at least partly based on an existing model of institutional observance. In his study of the origins of *Ancrene Wisse,* Dobson noted that both the Preface and the overall structure of the work were influenced by the constitutions adopted by the Premonstratensian canons in the mid-twelfth century and later taken over, with some modifications, by the Dominicans.[35] There is some evidence that the content and structure of Part 1 of *Ancrene Wisse* were also influenced by this model, and specifically by the Dominican version; the instructions for saying Matins which appear near the beginning of Part 1 are similar to those in a number of surviving Augustinian customaries, but their closest parallels are with the earliest Dominican Constitutions.[36] Two later additions to Part 1, modifying or supplementing its original prescriptions, refer explicitly to an existing institutional model. One, in the Corpus and Vernon manuscripts, suggests alternative times for the recitation of the Matins and Vespers of the Dead (*Dirige* and *Placebo*) based on the practice of the writer's own order.[37] The other, which is found only in one early manuscript, London, British Library, MS Cotton Nero A. xiv, recommends an alternative simplified routine, most closely paralleled in the earliest Dominican Constitutions,[38] for those who cannot recite the full Office: 'This is how our lay-brothers say their Hours ... If any of you wishes to do it in this way, she is following here, as in other observances, much of the practice of our order, and I strongly recommend it.'[39] The status of this addition is uncertain. Although Dobson thought it likely (on the grounds of its style, its early date and the presence in the Nero text of other, apparently authorized, additions found also in other manuscripts) that it was authorial,[40] it would be difficult to prove this conclusively. But, whether it is authorial or not, it is clear that whoever wrote it was a member of a religious order, probably a Dominican, and saw the anchoresses as following 'much of the practice of our order' in their other observances. These apparent links with mendicant devotional practice are complemented by two further additions to the original version (probably dating from some point after the beginning of the 1230s, when both orders of mendicants had established houses in the West Midlands) qualifying the author's original cautions against visiting religious by warm commendation of both Dominican and Franciscan friars,[41] and exempting their visits from the special permission required for other male visitors.[42]

The institutional context suggested by this internal evidence is less traditional than some earlier studies of *Ancrene Wisse* have suggested: the picture which emerges is of a group of women who, although leading an extra-monastic, relatively unstructured form of religious life, are being supported by unofficial legislative guidance and (in the later stages) pastoral care from members of the recently established mendicant orders, particularly the Dominicans. The devotional routine of Part 1 suggests careful adaptation of existing materials to the needs of an audience which was relatively well-educated and with religious aspirations, but not equipped to handle the full linguistic and liturgical demands of the Breviary; and its similarities in content to the later Books of Hours suggest that it may reflect a more widespread pastoral response to the needs of this new kind of user.

If *Ancrene Wisse* is placed in the context of thirteenth-century Europe, the situation it reflects can be seen as part of a broader contemporary process, the tendency towards breakdown of the sharp early medieval distinctions between religious and lay, *litteratus* and *illitteratus*.[43] The eleventh century had seen the emergence of lay-brothers and lay-sisters within the religious orders; and in the new military orders which appeared from the early twelfth century onwards, 'the majority of the members ... were laymen, and these held most positions of authority'.[44] But the twelfth-century Reformation also created a greater demand for the religious life than could be satisfied within traditional monastic structures. This led increasing numbers of the laity to adopt extra-monastic forms of religious life, some already established, some newly developed in the late twelfth or early thirteenth century. Kaspar Elm, surveying the new religious developments of the period as a whole, brings together a variety of groups under the general heading of *Semireligiosentum*, including lay-anchorites and hermits, lay-brothers and sisters working in hospitals, the Beguines of northern Europe, and the penitent confraternities of southern Europe – all groups described by contemporaries as occupying a *status tertius*, or following a *via media*, between lay and religious.[45] James of Vitry in his *Historia Occidentalis*, written in the early 1220s, noted the number of laymen and women renouncing the world to live in communities serving hospitals and leper-houses. These communities usually followed the (relatively brief and unspecific) Rule of St Augustine, but were not formally attached to any religious order; characteristically they included a fixed number of lay-brothers and sisters to look after the sick, served by a smaller number of priests and clerics in minor orders. In some cases the lay-brothers and sisters took no formal vows and might, if they wished, return to the world; but from the early thirteenth century onwards they were increasingly encouraged (particularly in the larger urban foundations) to live as religious, taking formal vows of poverty, chastity and obedience, adopting a habit and living *regulariter*, 'according to a rule'.[46] The Beguines, although they were often described as *mulieres religiosae*, followed no approved Rule, belonged to no religious order and took no formal vows; nevertheless, they observed a papally sanctioned *vita religiosa*, either in the world or (increasingly as time went on) in organized communities. The lay members of the penitent confraternities of southern Europe often lived in their own homes rather than communally, and many of them were married; but they led an ascetic life, wore distinctive habits and were accorded by long tradition a canonical status intermediate between lay and religious.[47]

The Church's concern that these extra-monastic ways of life should be effectively regulated led during the thirteenth century and later to the production of a substantial body of statutes, most of which (like *Ancrene Wisse*) include prescriptions for the devotional practice of the members of the group or community. A recurrent feature of these prescriptions is the requirement that all members, whether clerical or lay, should observe the canonical Hours. For *clerici*,[48] this involves the recitation of the full Divine Office; where the members are illiterate, they are expected, like the lay-brothers of the traditional Orders, to substitute multiple *Paters*, 'the Office of the Paternosters'. But some statutes also provide for an intermediate class of members who, although they are not expected to cope with the full canonical Hours, are capable of reciting the Psalter and/or the Little Office of our Lady. Although the language used to describe them can be ambiguous (*scientes psalterium, qui noverit horas Beate Virginis Marie*), there is some evidence in the surviving literature for the correlation of an intermediate degree of liturgical knowledge with an intermediate degree of literacy. In the *Memoriale propositi fratrum et sororum de penitentia* of 1228 (recording statutes adopted in 1221), those penitents 'who know the Psalter' (*scientes psalterium*) are distinguished from both the *clerici* and the *illitterati*,[49] a distinction also used in the 1285 rule for the Dominican 'third order' of penitents drawn up by Munio de Zamora.[50] The regulations drawn up by the Franciscan Rufo de Gurgone in 1261 for a new military order, the *Militia Beatae Virginis*, specify that *clerici* should recite the Divine Office, those brothers who are not *clerici* and know how to read (*qui non sunt clerici et sciunt legere*) may recite, if they wish, the Little Office of the Virgin, and those who are illiterate (*qui legere nesciunt*) should observe their Hours with repeated *Paters* and *Aves*.[51] It seems reasonable to assume that, like the lay-anchoresses addressed in *Ancrene Wisse*, these intermediate groups fell somewhere between illiteracy and *litteratura*, possessing 'comprehension literacy' in the vernacular but perhaps little more than 'phonetic literacy' in Latin.[52]

The most detailed provisions for this category of members, and also the earliest and most frequent mentions of the use of the Little Office of the Virgin as a substitute for the full Divine Office, can be found in some of the statutes for communities serving hospitals and leper-houses. A considerable number of these statutes were first drawn up in the thirteenth century; a major factor in their production was the stipulation of the councils of Paris (1212) and Rouen (1214) that all hospitals and leper-houses supporting a religious community should have written constitutions. The influential early statutes of the hospital of Montdidier (1207)[53] distinguish no fewer than six possible levels of liturgical knowledge: those (whether *clericus* or *laicus*) who can recite the full Divine Office, those who know the Hours of the Virgin, those who know only the seven Penitential Psalms, those who know only the psalm *Miserere*, those who know only the *Pater noster*, *Ave Maria* and Creed, and probationers who may need to be taught even the last four.[54] The 1239 statutes of the leper-house at Lille excuse anyone 'who knows the Hours of the Blessed Virgin and prefers to say them' (*qui horas beate Marie scierit et dicere maluerit*) from a simpler substitute Office of *Paters* and *Aves*.[55] The statutes of the hospital at Lille (c. 1250), based on the Dominican Constitutions of the late 1240s and adopted by a number of other hospitals, specify that *li frère clerc* should recite the Divine Office and the Office of the Virgin; 'the sisters and lay-brothers who know the Hours of Our Lady should say them every day' (*les sereurs et li frere lai ki sevent les heures Nostre Dame les doivent dire cascun jour*), and those who do not are given simpler alternatives (as at Montdidier).[56]

The statutes of Beguine communities, according to McDonnell, 'originally resembled the rules of the brothers and sisters who served hospitals and leper-houses'; but the earliest recorded legislation is from the mid-1240s, and most of the surviving statutes are from the fourteenth century or later.[57] They provide evidence for the use of the Little Office of the Virgin as a substitute Office from at least the early fourteenth century;[58] and there are other indications that devotional routines intermediate between the full canonical Hours and the 'Office of the Paternosters' were already being developed in the thirteenth century. Much of the early evidence is cited in a 1992 article by Judith Oliver, who examines in particular the rapid increase in the production of Psalters and Psalter-Hours in Liège from the mid-thirteenth century onwards, and the evidence for their connection with both the mendicants (who had settled in Liège around 1230) and the Beguine communities established in the 1240s and 1250s, in whose pastoral care the mendicants were closely involved.[59]

Although the statutes discussed above emerge from a variety of institutional contexts, reflecting a variety of forms of religious or semi-religious life, they demonstrate a common recognition of the devotional needs of those members occupying an intermediate position between *litterati* and the illiterate. In some cases, their alternative devotions were drawn from the traditional prayerbook of the laity, the Psalter; but the statutes also provide evidence, from the early thirteenth century onwards, for the use of the Little Office of the Virgin as a substitute for the full canonical Hours. Leroquais mentioned in passing the possibility of a link between the development of the Book of Hours and the penitent confraternities, 'whose rules prescribed the recitation of the Little Office of the Virgin, the Penitential Psalms, and the Office of the Dead on certain days fixed in advance.'[60] Their thirteenth-century statutes, however, make no mention of the Little Office of the Virgin; the evidence just reviewed suggests that it was first adopted as a substitute for the Divine Office by groups nearer to the 'religious' end of the continuum.

It would probably be going too far, on the existing evidence, to argue that the Book of Hours passed through a stage of being a 'breviary for the semi-religious' before it became a 'breviary for the laity'. There is some evidence for lay ownership of Books of Hours, particularly by members of the aristocracy, from the early thirteenth century onwards; Morgan suggests that in England this may have been encouraged by the Augustinian canons.[61] But it is likely that the spread of such devotions to the laity was accelerated, even if it was not initiated, by the new developments in extra-monastic religious life. The Dominicans and Franciscans took a leading role in the pastoral care of those groups occupying the borderline territory between laity and religious, and were sometimes directly involved in the drafting of their statutes;[62] they were in a position both to develop modified devotional routines suitable for semi-religious and to encourage their adoption more widely among the laity.[63] It may be significant that the earliest surviving English Book of Hours, the de Brailes Hours, compiled in Oxford *c.* 1240, has a mendicant connection; the vernacular devotions added at the end, in a near-contemporary hand, begin: 'I must pray for Friar Richard of Newark, and for Friar Richard of Westey, and for Friar Bartholomew of Grimston, and for all friars, Dominicans and Franciscans, so that God may grant me a share of their prayers and of their good works . . .'[64]

The interest of *Ancrene Wisse* Part 1 lies not only in its relationship to earlier devotional traditions, but in its relationship to later ones. Although much of its content is traditional, it anticipates in many respects the devotional routine of the later Books of Hours produced for a lay readership. Its early date makes it an important witness to the origins of that routine; and its parallels with the statutes of extra-monastic groups across thirteenth-century Europe suggest that it might provide not just an instance, but a paradigm of how the supplementary devotions of monastic practice evolved into the fully developed late medieval 'breviary for the use of the laity'.

## Appendix: The Instructions for saying Matins in *Ancrene Wisse* Part 1

In his discussion of the origins of *Ancrene Wisse* (in which he argued for Victorine authorship), Eric Dobson commented, 'Only an expert in medieval liturgical usage could say whether there are significant detailed resemblances between the instructions in Part 1 of *Ancrene Wisse* and those in the Augustinian ordinals, and distinguish what is remarkable from what is commonplace.'[65] It is true that, in this relatively poorly documented period, it is often hard to establish which liturgical observances were common practice and which distinctive of a particular order. However, there is one passage in Part 1 where the surviving evidence is full enough for a comparative study of sources, the instructions for the recitation of Matins. The anchoresses are being given instructions on how to say their Hours; when they have said their devotions on rising,

> Þer-efter ananriht ure Leafdi Uhtsong seggeð o þis wise. ȝef hit is wercdei, falleð to þer eorðe, ȝef hit is halidei, buhinde sumdeal dunward, seggeð *Pater noster* ant *Credo* ba stille. Rihteð ow up þrefter ant seggeð, *Domine,*

*labia mea aperies.* Makieð on ower muð a creoiz wið þe þume; ed *Deus, in adiutorium,* a large creoiz wið þe þume ant wið þe twa fingres from buue þe forheaued dun to þe breoste; ant falleð to þe eorðe, ʒef hit is wercdei, wið *Gloria Patri,* oðer buheð duneward, ʒef hit [is] halidei, aþet *Sicut erat.* Þus ed euch *Gloria Patri,* ant ed te biginnunge of þe *Venite,* ant i þe *Venite* ed *Venite, adoremus,* ant ed te *Aue Maria,* ant hwer-se ʒe eauer hereð Maries nome inempnet, ant ed euch *Pater noster* þet falle to ower Ures, ant to þe *Credo,* ant to þe collecte ed eauereuch Tide, ant ed te leatemeste vers of eauereuch ymne, ant ed te leaste vers wiðuten an of þe salm *Benedicite omnia opera Domini, Domino,* ed alle þes ilke, ʒef hit is halidei, buheð sumdel dunewart, ʒef hit is wercdei, falleð to þer eorðe. Ed te biginnunge of eauereuch Tide, wið *Deus, in adiutorium,* makieð Rode-taken as Ich ear tahte. Ed *Veni, creator* buheð oðer cneolið efter þet te dei is; wið *Memento, salutis auctor* falleð eauer adun, ant ed tis word, *Nascendo formam sumpseris,* cusseð þe eorðe; ant alswa i þe *Te Deum laudamus,* ed tis word, *Non horruisti uirginis uterum,* ant ed te Messe i þe Muchele *Credo,* | [fo. 6ʳ] ed *ex Maria uirgine, et homo factus est.*[66]

Similar instructions appear in a number of surviving Augustinian customaries, including the Victorine *Liber Ordinis,*[67] the Premonstratensian statutes,[68] and the earliest Dominican Constitutions[69] (in all these cases the Matins are those of the full Divine Office, not of the Virgin; the Victorines have a separate chapter on the recitation of the Hours of the Virgin, but the prescriptions are different from those in *Ancrene Wisse*[70]). The instructions in *Ancrene Wisse,* which were designed for a different kind of audience using a different Office, do not exactly parallel any of these regulations; however, the closest parallels in positioning, content, style and phrasing are with the instructions in the early Dominican Constitutions:

[the brothers, having risen and said the Matins of the Virgin, should enter the choir to recite the main Office and,] flexis genibus vel inclinati profunde pro tempore, dicant 'Pater noster' et 'Credo in Deum'. Et iterum facto signo a priore, surgant. Hora itaque devote incepta, versi ad altare, muniant se signo crucis. Et ad 'Gloria Patri' inclinet chorus contra chorum profunde vel prosternant se pro tempore usque ad 'Sicut erat'. Et hoc faciendum est quotiens 'Pater noster' et 'Credo in Deum' dicuntur ... Idem etiam faciendum est ... in singulis horis ad collectam et ad 'Gloria Patri', quotiens in inchoatione hore dicitur. Ad omnia autem alia 'Gloria Patri' et ad extremos versus hymnorum et ad penultimum versum cantici 'Benedicite' inclinamus usque ad genua ... et in 'Credo' in missa ad 'Homo factus est' ... item, in capitulo ad orationem 'Sancta Maria', et in omni oratione, quando nomen beate Virginis nominatur.[71]

The positioning of the prescriptions for Matins at the beginning of the first distinction (as in *Ancrene Wisse*) is found both in the Premonstratensian statutes and in the Dominican Constitutions, which used this chapter as a source; in the Victorine *Liber Ordinis,* however, the corresponding prescriptions are placed much later (chapter 54). The group of prescriptions *Idem etiam faciendum est . . . nominatur* is an addition to the Premonstratensian source chapter; similar prescriptions on bowing at the last verse of every hymn, and at the penultimate verse of *Benedicite,* are found at a later point in the Victorine chapter, but not together (as they are in the Dominican Constitutions and *Ancrene Wisse*). The passage in *Ancrene Wisse* is closer in style to the relatively concise chapters in the Premonstratensian and Dominican Constitutions than to the much longer and more elaborate Victorine prescriptions; and its closest verbal parallels are with the Dominican Constitutions.

## Notes

[1] See J. G. Cooper, 'Latin Elements of the "Ancrene Riwle"' (Birmingham University Ph.D. thesis, 1956), 9–53; G. Sitwell, 'Private Devotions in the *Ancrene Riwle*', in M. B. Salu (tr.), *The Ancrene Riwle* (London, 1955), 193–6; C. H. Talbot, 'Some Notes on the Dating of the *Ancrene Riwle*', *Neophilologus*, 40 (1956), 38–50 (on the later prayers); B. Raw, 'The Prayers and Devotions in the *Ancrene Wisse*', in B. Rowland (ed.), *Chaucer and Middle English Studies in Honour of Rossell Hope Robbins* (London, 1974), 260–71 (on the earlier prayers); R. W. Ackerman, 'The Liturgical Day in *Ancrene Riwle*', *Speculum*, 53 (1978), 734–44; R. Dahood, 'Design in Part 1 of *Ancrene Riwle*', *Medium Ævum*, 56 (1987), 1–11; R. W. Ackerman and R. Dahood (eds.), Ancrene Riwle: *Introduction and Part 1*, Medieval and Renaissance Texts and Studies 31 (Binghamton, 1984); also E. J. Dobson, *The Origins of* Ancrene Wisse (Oxford, 1976), ch. 2, and B. Millett, 'The Origins of *Ancrene Wisse*: New Answers, New Questions', *Medium Ævum*, 61 (1992), 206–28, on the evidence Part 1 provides for the origins of *Ancrene Wisse* as a whole.

[2] Aelred of Rievaulx, *De institutione inclusarum*, ch. 9, in A. Hoste and C. H. Talbot (eds.), *Aelredi Rievallensis: Opera omnia*, CCCM 1 (Turnhout, 1971), 644–5.

[3] Ibid., 645–6.

[4] 'Sum is clergesse, sum nawt, ant mot [te] mare wurchen ant on oðer wise seggen hire bonen' ['One may be well-educated, while another who is not must do more manual labour accordingly, and say her prayers differently'] (Cambridge, Corpus Christi College, MS 402, fo. 2ʳ/12–13; MS *moten* for *mot te*). All quotations from *Ancrene Wisse* are from this MS (hereafter cited

as Corpus 402), unless otherwise indicated, but emended and with modernized punctuation; for a diplomatic edition, see J. R. R. Tolkien (ed.), *The English Text of the Ancrene Riwle: Ancrene Wisse, edited from MS. Corpus Christi College Cambridge 402*, EETS 249 (London, 1962).

[5] For the original prescription, see Corpus 402, fo. 12ʳ/3–11; for the alternative recommendation found in London, British Library, MS Cotton Nero A.xiv, see below p. 27.

[6] 'Even after making allowance for optional acts of worship, one must conclude that the anchoress's liturgical day was a crowded one ... we can estimate that the anchoress spent not fewer than four hours daily in set prayers and acts of worship.' Ackerman and Dahood, Ancrene Riwle: *Introduction and Part 1*, 36.

[7] See Sitwell, 'Introduction', in Salu, *The Ancrene Riwle*, xxi–xxii. For discussion and definitions of the liturgical terms used below, see J. Harper, *The Forms and Orders of Western Liturgy from the Tenth to the Eighteenth Century* (Oxford, 1991).

[8] I.e. prayers and psalms appended to the Office of the Dead; see W. Maskell, *Monumenta ritualia ecclesiae Anglicanae* (Oxford, 1882), 3/161–79.

[9] I.e. the 'Capitular Office', prayers recited in Chapter after Prime by monastic orders.

[10] See, for example, below p. 27.

[11] Sitwell, 'Introduction', in Salu, *The Ancrene Riwle*, xxi–xxii.

[12] See, for example, Ackerman and Dahood, Ancrene Riwle: *Introduction and Part 1*, 33–4; C. Donovan, *The de Brailes Hours: Shaping the Book of Hours in Thirteenth-Century Oxford* (London, 1991), 135.

[13] For a fuller account of the components of the Book of Hours (divided into essential, secondary, and accessory), see V. Leroquais, *Les Livres d'Heures manuscrits de la Bibliothèque Nationale* (Paris, 1927), I, ch. 3.

[14] Ibid., I, i–ii.

[15] See above p. 22.

[16] Leroquais, *Les Livres d'Heures*, I, iii–vii.

[17] Ibid., I, iv, vi.

[18] 'Si le bréviaire est le livre du prêtre ou du religieux, le Livre d'Heures est le livre du fidèle, du laïque. Qu'est-ce qu'un livre d'Heures? C'est un recueil d'offices et de prières à l'usage des fidèles: un bréviaire à l'usage des laïques.' Ibid., I, vi.

[19] L. M. J. Delaissé, 'The Importance of Books of Hours for the History of the Medieval Book', in U. E. McCracken, L. M. C. Randall and R. H. Randall, Jr. (eds.), *Gatherings in Honor of Dorothy E. Miner* (Baltimore, 1974), 204.

[20] 'En réalité, les premiers Livres d'Heures sont une combinaison du psautier et du Livre d'Heures. Le premier forme la partie la plus importante du manuscrit, le second est une sorte d'appendice qui va prendre une place de plus en plus grande jusqu'à ce qu'il se détache du psautier, comme le fruit se détache de l'arbre.' Leroquais, *Les Livres d'Heures*, I, xi.

21 See Leroquais's entries for Paris, Bibliothèque Nationale, MS lat. 10526 (Book of Hours from Passau, early thirteenth century, including some German) and Paris, Bibliothèque Nationale, MS lat. 1073A (Psalter-Hours from Thérouanne, after 1220, including some French). Both seem to have been made for female religious; the first includes a reference to *nostram congregationem*, the second probably belonged to a house of Benedictine nuns.

22 N. Morgan, *Early Gothic Manuscripts [I], 1190–1250*, A Survey of Manuscripts Illuminated in the British Isles 4 (London, 1982), 12.

23 Ibid., 12.

24 See the detailed study by Donovan (n. 12 above).

25 For a discussion of the date of *Ancrene Wisse*, with full references, see B. Millett, *Ancrene Wisse, the Katherine Group, and the Wooing Group*, Annotated Bibliographies of Old and Middle English Literature 2 (Cambridge, 1996), 7–13.

26 'Euchan segge hire Ures as ha haueð iwriten ham' (Corpus 402, fo. 6ʳ/2); the word-order *haueð iwriten ham* (rather than *haueð ham iwriten*), shared by all the English MSS running, suggests that in this case the anchoresses did their own copying rather than having it done for them.

27 Corpus 402, fo. 11ʳ/22.

28 'Ower graces stondinde biuore mete ant efter as ha beoð iwriten ow' ['[Say] your graces standing before and after meals as they are written out for you']. Corpus 402, fo. 11ᵛ/5–6.

29 'Hwa-se hit haueð'. Corpus 402, fo. 7ʳ/14.

30 'Þe ureisuns þet Ich nabbe (buten ane) imearket beoð iwriten ouer al, bute þe leaste. Leoteð writen on a scrowe hwet-se ȝe ne cunnen.' Corpus 402, fo. 10ᵛ/21–2.

31 See P. J. F. Rosof, 'The Anchoress in the Twelfth and Thirteenth Centuries', in L. T. Shank and J. A. Nichols (eds.), *Peaceweavers: Medieval Religious Women*, Cistercian Studies 72 (Kalamazoo, 1987), 123–44; and, for statistical evidence on English anchoresses, A. K. Warren, *Anchorites and their Patrons in Medieval England* (Berkeley, 1985).

32 See, for example, Corpus 402, fos. 3ʳ/27, 17ʳ/24.

33 On the borderline status as 'religious' of hermits and recluses who were not members of a religious order, see J. Hourlier, *L'Âge classique 1140–1378: Les Religieux*, Histoire du Droit et des Institutions de l'Église en Occident 10 (Paris, 1974), 272–3.

34 Corpus 402, fos. 2ᵛ/28–3ʳ/2, 3ᵛ/5–15. White habits tended to be worn by the more austere Orders (e.g. Cistercian monks, Premonstratensian canons).

35 See Dobson, *Origins of* Ancrene Wisse, ch. 2, 55–113.

36 See the Appendix (below pp. 32–4) for a discussion of the evidence.

37 'In a-mel dei we seggeð ba *Placebo* ant *Dirige* efter þe mete graces, i twimel dei efter Non; ant ȝe alswa mote don' ['On a one-meal day we say both *Placebo* and *Dirige* after the grace after meals, on a two-meal day after

Nones; and you may do the same.'] Corpus 402, fo. 6ᵛ/7–9; also Oxford, Bodleian Library, MS Eng. poet. a. 1 (the 'Vernon Manuscript'), fo. 372ᵛᵇ/8–11 (with ȝe 'you' for Corpus 402 we).

[38] See Millett, 'The Origins of Ancrene Wisse', 211–2, 220–3.

[39] 'Vre leawede breþren siggeð þus hore Vres . . . ȝif ei of ou wule don þus, heo voleweð her ase in oþre obseruaunces muchel of vre ordre, and wel Ich hit reade.' M. Day (ed.), *The English Text of the Ancrene Riwle, edited from Cotton Nero A. XIV*, EETS OS 225 (London, 1952), 10/25–11/5 (fo. 6); my punctuation.

[40] Dobson, *Origins of* Ancrene Wisse, 6–9, 73–84.

[41] *Ancrene Wisse*, Part 2, Corpus 402, fos. 16ᵛ/13–17ʳ/2 (also in the earlier French translation: see J. A. Herbert (ed.), *The French Text of the* Ancrene Riwle, *edited from British Museum MS. Cotton Vitellius F. vii*, EETS 219 (London, 1944), 56/11–57/5).

[42] *Ancrene Wisse*, Part 8, Corpus 402, fo. 112ᵛ/11–12 (not in other MSS).

[43] See H. Grundmann, 'Litteratus-illitteratus: Der Wandel einer Bildungsnorm vom Altertum zum Mittelalter', *Archiv für Kulturgeschichte*, 40 (1958), 1–65.

[44] A. Forey, *The Military Orders from the Twelfth to the Early Fourteenth Centuries*, New Studies in Medieval History (London, 1992), 2.

[45] K. Elm, 'Die Stellung der Frau in Ordenswesen, Semireligiosentum und Häresie zur Zeit der heiligen Elisabeth', in *Sankt Elisabeth, Fürstin, Dienerin, Heilige* (Sigmaringen, 1981), 14–17.

[46] See J. F. Hinnebusch (ed.), *The Historia Occidentalis of Jacques de Vitry: A Critical Edition*, Spicilegium Friburgense 17 (Fribourg, 1972), ch. 29, 146–7.

[47] See G. G. Meersseman (ed.), *Dossier de l'ordre de la Pénitence au xiiiᵉ siècle*, Spicilegium Friburgense 7 (Fribourg, 1961), 2.

[48] The term *clerici* is not always used in the same sense in these regulations: it seems to mean sometimes 'cleric' as opposed to 'lay', sometimes 'in minor orders' as opposed to 'priest', and sometimes simply *litteratus* (i.e. fully literate in Latin, as opposed to literate in the vernacular or illiterate).

[49] Meersseman, *Dossier*, 99,§§122–3.

[50] Ibid., 99, §§12–12³, 105, §§23², 24 (*Memoriale propositi*, 1228), 156, §§39, 40 (*Regula fratrum et sororum ordinis de penitentia beati Dominici*, 1285).

[51] Ibid., 300, §33.

[52] For this distinction, see P. Saenger, 'Books of Hours and the Reading Habits of the Later Middle Ages', in R. Chartier (ed.), *The Culture of Print: Power and the Uses of Print in Early Modern Europe*, translated by L. G. Cochrane (Cambridge, 1989), 142. The earliest regulations of the Beguines at Bruges (c. 1290) include advice to those who 'niet ne verstaen dat si lesen ende horen lesen ende singhen' ('do not understand what they read and hear read and sung'); see R. Hoornaert (ed.), 'La plus ancienne règle du Béguinage de Bruges', *Annales de la Société d'Émulation de Bruges*, 72 (1929), 78.

⁵³ The earliest surviving MS, however, is from 1233, in the text adapted for use at Amiens.
⁵⁴ L. Le Grand (ed.), *Statuts d'Hôtels-Dieu et de léproseries: Recueil de textes du xii<sup>e</sup> au xiv<sup>e</sup> siècle* (Paris, 1901), §§10–15, 37–8.
⁵⁵ Ibid., §22, 202.
⁵⁶ Ibid., chs. 1–2, 65. Similar provisions, following those of Lille, are found in the statutes of the hospital of Vernon (ibid., 165).
⁵⁷ See E. W. McDonnell, *The Beguines and Beghards in Medieval Culture* (New Brunswick, NJ, 1954), 134–5; and W. Simons, 'The Beguine Movement in the Southern Low Countries: A Reassessment', *Bulletin de l'Institut Historique Belge de Rome*, 9 (1989), 63–101 (n. 125).
⁵⁸ The earliest statutes of the beguinage at Bruges (not later than c. 1290) required daily recitation of the Little Office of the Virgin (see Hoornaert, 'La plus ancienne règle', 8, 53); it is not absolutely clear from the wording of the regulation that these were a substitute for, rather than a supplement to, the full canonical Hours which were recited by some of the beguines, but the varying degrees of literacy in the beguinage make it possible (see above n. 52). The 1323 statutes of the beguinage at Antwerp required the Little Office of the Virgin to be read daily, and the 1401 statutes of the beguines at Lierre offered those who could read a choice of votive offices for the observance of the canonical hours: the Hours of our Lady, of the Holy Spirit, the Holy Trinity, or of the Holy Cross (see L. J. M. Philippen, *De Begijnhoven: Oorsprong, Geschiedenis, Inrichting* (Antwerp, 1918), 337–8, 341).
⁵⁹ J. Oliver, 'Devotional Psalters and the Study of Beguine Spirituality', *Vox Benedictina*, 9 (1992), 199–225.
⁶⁰ Leroquais, *Les Livres d'Heures*, I, xi, n. 1.
⁶¹ Morgan, *Early Gothic Manuscripts [I]*, 11. Morgan assumes, following Dobson, that *Ancrene Wisse* is of Victorine origin (see his comments on London, British Library, MS Egerton 1151 (Book of Hours, c. 1260–70), 155–7; but see also his notes on London, British Library, MS Arundel 157 (Psalter-Hours, c. 1200–10), 72–3, and Berlin, Kupferstichkabinett, MS 78.A.8 (Psalter-Hours, c. 1210–20), 84–5.
⁶² For detailed documentation of mendicant (especially Dominican) involvement with the hospitals, see Le Grand, *Statuts*; with the Beguines, McDonnell, *Beguines and Beghards*, Meersseman, 'Les Frères Prêcheurs et le mouvement dévot en Flandre au xiii<sup>e</sup> siècle', *Archivum Fratrum Praedicatorum*, 18 (1948), 69–130, and Simons, 'The Beguine Movement', 87–101; and with the penitential confraternities, Meersseman, *Dossier*.
⁶³ Humbert of Romans, master-general of the Dominicans, recommended in a model sermon for girls living in the world 'quod sciunt tempore opportuno dicere Psalterium, vel Horas de Beata Virgine, vel Officium pro mortuis, vel alias orationes Deo dicendas, vel fiunt aptiores ad hoc, ut fiant religiosae quandoque, si voluerint, vel intelligant melius Scripturas sacras, sicut accidit

de Paula, et Eustochio, et aliis, quae secum degebant virginibus, quae propter litteras, quas didicerant, profecerunt intantum, quod sacras Litteras intellexerunt profunde' ['that they know how to recite at the appropriate time the Psalter, or the Hours of Our Lady, or the Office of the Dead, or other prayers to be be recited to God, or become better equipped to do so, so that they may at some point enter the religious life, if they wish to, or understand the sacred Scriptures better, as happened with Paula and Eustochium and others, who led a virgin life at home, and because of their literary education made such progress that they developed a deep understanding of Holy Scripture'] (*De eruditione praedicatorum* (1266–77), Book 2, *Sermo* 97, in C. Casagrande (ed.), *Prediche alle donne del secolo xiii*, Nuova Corona 9 (Milan, 1978), 49).

[64] 'Io dei preir pur frere richart de neuerc. e pur frere richart de westey. e pur frere bartelmeu de grimistun. e pur tut frere prech[u]rs e menurs k[e] deus me dunt part de lur praers e de lur benfez . . .' London, British Library, MS Add. 49999, fo. 102$^v$.

[65] Dobson, *Origins of* Ancrene Wisse, 104. For a review of the case for Victorine authorship, see Millett, 'The Origins of *Ancrene Wisse*'.

[66] Corpus 402, fos. 5$^v$/5–6$^r$/1: 'Straight after that, say the Matins of our Lady as follows. Falling to the earth if it is a ferial day, bowing down to some degree if it is a festal day, say both the *Pater Noster* and the Creed quietly. Then straighten up and say, *O Lord, open my lips*. Make the sign of the Cross on your mouth with your thumb; at *O God, [come] to [my] help*, a large sign of the Cross with the thumb and with the two fingers from above the forehead down to the breast; and fall to the earth, if it is a ferial day, at *Gloria Patri*, or bow down, if it is a festal day, until *As it was [in the beginning]*. Similarly, at each *Gloria Patri*, and at the beginning of the *Venite* and in the *Venite* at *Come, let us adore*, and at the *Hail Mary*, and wherever you hear Mary's name mentioned, and at every *Our Father* that is part of your Hours, and at the Creed, and at the collect at every Hour, and at the last verse of every hymn, and at the last verse but one of the psalm *Bless all the works of the Lord, [praise] the Lord*; at all these, if it is a festal day, bow down to some degree, if it is a ferial day, fall to the earth. At the beginning of every Hour, at *O God, [come] to [my] help*, make the sign of the Cross as I instructed earlier. At *Come, creator [Spirit]*, bow or kneel according to what the day is. At *Remember, author of salvation* always fall down, and at these words, *Through birth you assumed [our body's] form*, kiss the earth; and also in the *Te Deum*, at these words, *You did not abhor the virgin's womb,* and at Mass in the Great Creed, at *[was born] of the Virgin Mary, and became man*.'

[67] L. Jocqué and L. Milis (eds.), *Liber ordinis Sancti Victoris Parisiensis*, CCCM 61 (Turnhout, 1984), ch. 54, *Quomodo fratres surgant vel qualiter se habeant ad Matutinas*. The version edited is from *c.* 1200.

[68] For the second version of the statutes, drawn up *c.* 1174, see Pl. F. Lefèvre

and W. M. Grauwen (eds.), *Les statuts de Prémontré au milieu du xii$^e$ siècle*, Bibliotheca Analectorum Praemonstratensium 12 (Averbode, 1978), Dist. 1, ch. 1, 4–5; for the third, see Pl. F. Lefèvre, *Les statuts de Prémontré, réformés sur les ordres de Grégoire IX et d'Innocent IV au xiii$^e$ siècle*, Bibliothèque de la Revue d'Histoire Ecclésiastique 23 (Louvain, 1946), Dist. 1, ch. 1, 4–5.

[69] A. H. Thomas (ed.), *De Oudste Constituties van de Dominicanen: Voorgeschiedenis, Tekst, Bronnen, Ontstaan en Ontwikkeling (1215–1237)*, Bibliothèque de la Revue d'Histoire Ecclésiastique 42 (Louvain, 1965), Dist. 1, ch. 1, *De matutinis*, 312–14. The parallels with *Ancrene Wisse* Part 1 cited below are all found in the earliest (1216) version of this chapter.

[70] *Liber ordinis*, ch. 55, *Qualiter se habeant fratres ad horas de sancta Maria*, 230–1; it is specified (line 6) that in the Hours of the Virgin there should be no bowing at the *Gloria Patri*.

[71] 'On bended knees or bowing deeply according to the time, they should say the *Pater noster* and the Creed. And when the prior gives the signal, they should stand up again. When Matins has been devoutly begun, they should turn to the altar and make the sign of the Cross. And at the *Gloria Patri* one choir should bow deeply to the other or prostrate themselves, according to the time, up to *As it was [in the beginning]*. And this should be done whenever the *Pater noster* and the Creed are recited . . . And the same is to be done at each Hour at the Collect and at the *Gloria*, whenever it is recited at the beginning of the Hour. But at all other *Glorias* and at the last verses of the hymns and at the second-to-last verse of the canticle *Benedicite* we bow down to our knees . . . and during the Creed at Mass at *And he was made man* . . . also, in Chapter at the prayer *Holy Mary*, and in every prayer, when the name of the Blessed Virgin is mentioned' (314–15).

# Part Two
*Carthusian Links with Female Spirituality*

# 2

# Women in the Charterhouse? Julian of Norwich's *Revelations of Divine Love* and Marguerite Porete's *Mirror of Simple Souls* in British Library, MS Additional 37790

MARLEEN CRÉ

BRITISH Library, MS Additional 37790 (Amherst)[1] is a mid-fifteenth-century anthology of texts about contemplation, containing Richard Misyn's translations of Richard Rolle's *Emendatio vitae* and *Incendium amoris*, the short text of Julian of Norwich's *Revelations of Divine Love*, a Middle English translation of Ruusbroec's *Vanden Blinckenden Steen*, entitled *The Treatise of Perfection of the Sons of God*, and a Middle English translation of Marguerite Porete's *Le Mirouer des Simples Ames*, as well as a number of short compilations and extracts from other works on the contemplative life, including fragments from Rolle's *Ego dormio* and *Form of Living*, Suso's *Horologium sapientiae*, Bridget of Sweden's *Revelationes* and material from the *Cloud* author.[2] Amherst has often been called an important manuscript, probably because many of the texts it contains are either single extant copies of a particular text, such as the short text of Julian of Norwich's *Revelations* and the Middle English translation of Ruusbroec's *Steen*, or one of a small number of extant copies of a particular text, such as the Middle English translation of Porete's *Mirouer*. The presence of these texts in the manuscript, together with the Misyn translations of Rolle's *Emendatio vitae* and *Incendium amoris*, seems to suggest that the editor of this anthology was a connoisseur of texts upon contemplation.[3] The unique character of Amherst explains why the manuscript has been extensively mined for editions of all of the main texts and some of the shorter texts.

The occurrence of these 'classics' of contemplative literature within one volume written in one hand must have had consequences for the way these texts were read. Julian of Norwich's short text and Marguerite Porete's *Mirror of Simple Souls*, both texts which are regarded by many scholars as expressions of a specifically female spirituality, constitute one another's context here; however, they also stand side by side with Rolle's and Ruusbroec's works. This contextual information needs to be supplemented with evidence of the provenance and early ownership of the anthology, as well as of early readers' reactions in the form of marginal annotations. Taken all in all, this context yields a picture of one specific fifteenth-century reading of the texts of Julian of Norwich and Marguerite Porete which does not attribute such a significant role to gender in spiritual writings as many modern critics and readers do. The present-day critical and interpretative angle that interprets all spiritual texts by women as expressing a typically *female* spirituality seems not to have been shared by the readers of Amherst.

## Formal Characteristics of the Manuscript

Even though there is no overt indication of any design to the anthology, and the medieval anthologist has not prefaced his selection with a prologue detailing his reasons for choosing the texts or how he believed his audience should read them,[4] the anthology does have some unifying formal characteristics which suggest that the manuscript was conceived in its present form. It is written in one hand[5] and is built up entirely from gatherings of eight folios, with the exception of folios 233 to 239, which are seven single leaves that have been added. Four of the texts in the anthology start on the verso side of a folio.[6] Ruusbroec's *Treatise of Perfection* is the only longer text that does not start on a new page; rather, it is copied immediately after the end of Julian's short text on folio 115$^r$.

Rolle's *Mending of Life*, Julian's *Revelations* and Porete's *Mirror* all start on the recto side of a folio, which is also the first folio of a gathering of eight. The texts beginning on the first folio of a quire mark the three parts into which the anthology divides. The first part contains the Rolle translations as the main texts, the second, Julian's *Revelations* and Ruusbroec's *Treatise of Perfection*, and the third, Marguerite's *Mirror*. The anthology was built around these longer, authorial texts. Two of the shorter texts come just before the start of a longer text that starts on the first page of a new quire, and can thus be regarded as quire-fillers.[7] The other short fragments come at the end of the manuscript and serve the same purpose.[8] The differences in the number of lines to the page may reflect the different times the scribe was working on one part of his text; they could also reflect the way in which the scribe laid out a particular text in the space allotted to it.[9]

The regularity of the quiring suggests that this manuscript was produced according to some kind of plan. Even though we can deduce from its layout that the shorter texts were put in to fill blank spaces, none of the three 'parts' of the manuscript we have distinguished earlier seems to have circulated as a separate booklet; all were most probably meant to be part of this anthology and were copied for that purpose.[10] Only at the end of the volume were single leaves added to accommodate other texts of interest.

Amherst is also an anthology with very strong thematic unity. Every single text contained in the manuscript deals with contemplation, teaches it, or describes its author's experience of it. Apart from the short compilations or quire-fillers which occur in the manuscript, the individual texts copied into it are mostly full versions of authorial texts. Some are translations, but there are no adaptations of existing Middle English or continental texts such as are to be found in the *Chastising of God's Children*, which incorporates fragments of *Ancrene Wisse*, Ruusbroec's *Die Gheestelike Brulocht*, Suso's *Horologium sapientiae* and Alphonse of Pecha's *Epistola solitarii*, or Nicholas Love's *Myrrour of the Blessed Lyf of Jesus Christ*, which is a translation and adaptation of (pseudo-)Bonaventure's *Meditationes vitae Christi*. This specific focus on authorial mystical texts makes Amherst a quite exceptional manuscript amid the host of devotional multi-text manuscripts of the period.

## Amherst and the Carthusians

The milieu in which Amherst originated and was read was almost undoubtedly Carthusian. The presence in Amherst of a translation of Ruusbroec's *Vanden blinckenden Steen* from the Latin translation by Willem Jordaens entitled *De calculo candido*, is particularly important in this respect. In their introduction to the edition of the *Treatise*, Bazire and Colledge point out that 'all the evidence we possess of the study and circulation in England of Ruysbroeck's writings in Latin translations points to the probability that they were introduced into [England] by the Carthusians, among many of whom an erroneous tradition persisted . . . that Ruysbroeck himself was a member of their order.'[11] Furthermore, it is assumed that the Carthusians, even though they were probably among the contemporary critics of Richard Rolle,[12] also played a part in the dissemination of his works in continental Europe.[13]

Another link between Amherst and the Carthusians is the presence of the Middle English translation of *Le Mirouer des Simples Ames*. Both Oxford, Bodleian Library, MS Bodley 505, and Cambridge, St John's College, MS 71, the two other manuscripts in which this translation occurs, originated in the London Charterhouse.[14] The presence of all extant copies of the Middle English *Mirror* in manuscripts that originated in or can be linked with one of the English Charterhouses led early *Mirror* scholars to speculate that the translator and commentator of *The Mirror*, M.N., might have been a Carthusian monk.[15] Since then, Nicholas Watson has argued that M.N. might well have belonged to a milieu outside the Charterhouse.[16] As there is no external evidence as to the translator's identity and the translation's origin, both views remain hypothetical.

The unique copy of *The Book of Margery Kempe*, which was owned by the Carthusian house of Mount Grace at the end of the fifteenth century,[17] and the short text of Julian's *Revelations* in Amherst are 'other examples of English Carthusian transmission and preservation of spiritual writings'.[18] The Carthusians evidently had a nose for such rarities and were probably also regarded as the ideal recipients of texts such as these. Though most of the texts in Amherst are only associated with the Carthusians in some way, and were also read in other circles, the absence of the Middle English *Mirror* in manuscripts outside the English Carthusian milieu does make it likely that Amherst was not bequeathed to a Carthusian house after its production, but was produced within a Charterhouse,[19] or commissioned by the Carthusians.[20]

Evidence for Carthusian readership of the anthology is both external and internal to the text. Carthusian ownership of Amherst during the fifteenth century can be proved through the identification of one of the annotators of the manuscript as James Grenehalgh, a Carthusian at Sheen Charterhouse, who also later stayed at the Charterhouses of Coventry, Hull, London and Mount Grace.[21] As the movement of both monks and books was not uncommon, it is difficult to assess where exactly Grenehalgh worked on the anthology.

The relatively few annotations in Amherst have been made by the same hands throughout the manuscript.[22] Most annotations mark passages of significance for the annotator himself, or perhaps for a subsequent audience. One annotator, roughly contemporary with the scribe, marks passages by writing the word 'nota' in the margin in a small neat hand, and in ink. Another annotator also writes 'nota' in the margin, but in a larger hand, and in plummet. A later hand writes catchwords in the margins. These annotations can be found in all of the major texts in the manuscript. The first part of Rolle's *Fire of Love* has been intensely marked by underlining and by the use of braces in the margins. However, this reader must soon have lost his enthusiasm, for the annotations become scarce and disappear altogether as the text progresses.

As with many manuscripts he annotated, Grenehalgh made both textual corrections (editorial work) and annotations marking the significance of a particular passage for his own spiritual life. His editorial work in Amherst was limited to Rolle's *Fire of Love* and Porete's *Mirror*.[23] Grenehalgh makes minor corrections in *The Fire of Love*, inserting missing letters or missing words. In only one instance is the missing phrase slightly longer.[24] In *The Mirror*, he provides missing phrases and emends erroneous readings.[25] All these corrections suggest Grenehalgh's meticulous work and the Carthusian zeal for accuracy in the texts they used.

Grenehalgh also marked three passages of personal interest in Rolle's *Fire of Love*, two with his monogram (J.G.) and one with a trefoil. The passages marked with the monogram deal with the clinging of the contemplative to God, and eternal rest in the beatific vision in the afterlife;[26] the passage marked with a trefoil deals with marriage (in the chapter on spiritual friendship).[27] Many of Grenehalgh's personal annotations – such as, perhaps, the marriage passage marked by the trefoil – relate to his own spiritual friendship with the Syon nun, Joanna Sewell. Sewell's monogram (J.S.) or the combined Grenehalgh-Sewell monogram (J.G.S.) do not occur in Amherst, making it highly unlikely that Grenehalgh annotated *The Fire of Love* for Joanna Sewell.[28] Grenehalgh's friendship with Joanna Sewell demonstrates the close contacts that existed between Sheen Charterhouse and the Bridgittine house of Syon. It is possible that Amherst was read by a Bridgittine audience at some point, but the manuscript itself does not yield any clues about a Bridgittine readership.

That Amherst might have been read within the Charterhouse is further corroborated by the contents of the texts themselves. The preoccupation of all the texts in the anthology with the solitary contemplative life makes it eminently suitable for a Carthusian audience. All the texts in the manuscript require that the true contemplative should withdraw from the world in a most radical way (*conversio*). In Rolle's *Fire of Love*, the contemplative chooses Christ as the only way to salvation and perfection:

> my saule now will not touche for bitterness before that was my fode. And my affeccion nowe is slyke [that] bot synne no thynge I hate, nought drede I bot to greue god. I ioye not bot in god. I sorowe not bot for my synne. no thynge I lufe bot god. no thynge I trist bot hyme. No thynge me heuys bot synne. no thynge me gladyns bot criste. (Amherst, fo. 38$^r$/9–15; *Fire*, 28/9–14)[29]

Rolle teaches his audience that the contemplative life is a slow process covering many years. He warns the audience that a person converting to the contemplative life will not immediately feel the burning of God's love: 'This mystery treuly fro many is hid and to fewe moste speciall it is schewyd for the hiar this degre is the fewer fynders has it in this warlde' (Amherst, fo. 22$^v$/1–4; *Fire*, 6/31–3). Both Ruusbroec's *Treatise* and Porete's *Mirror* describe the relationship of the soul with God as a series of different stages through which the soul ascends to perfection.[30]

The manuscript combines this emphasis on contemplation and perfect love for God with clear references to the solitary life as the ideal environment in which the soul can achieve these spiritual goals. In *The Fire of Love*, Rolle is adamant that the perfect soul is the soul of the solitary:

> In wyldyrnes more clerely thay meet for þer spekis the lufyd to the harte of the lufar als wer a schamefulle lufar that his lemman befor / men halsis not. nor frendely bot comonly and als a straungere he kissys. (Amherst, fo. 82$^v$/32–83$^r$/2; *Fire*, 87/21–4)

The soul can only experience *canor*, which marks the soul's participation in this life with the song of the blessed,[31] when it is seated in solitude, away from the physical sound of song. Rolle also invokes Psalm 54:8, a verse often cited in connection with discussions of the solitary life:[32] 'In anoþer place opinly he scheuys: *Elongavi inquit fugiens et mansi in solitudine*, þat is to say: ffleand myself I haue withdrawen and in wildyrnes I haue dwelt' (Amherst, fo. 40$^r$/11–13; *Fire*,

30/33–5). Other texts in Amherst also have a connection to the solitary life. Julian of Norwich was known as a recluse, and Ruusbroec wrote the *Vanden Blinckenden Steen* for a hermit who had asked him to write down some of the things they had been discussing.[33] Thus, the texts in the anthology share a common focus on radical contemplative life, which some of the texts associate with the solitary life.

The particular profile of the texts in Amherst fits a Carthusian audience perfectly. The Carthusians were an order of hermits who concentrated on contemplative prayer. There were some communal moments in the day-to-day life of the Charterhouse, but the monks would pray most offices in the solitude of their cells and would even cook some of their meals there. The references in Rolle's *Fire of Love* to the 'wyldyrnes' must have found double resonance amongst a Carthusian audience, as Carthusian houses were often referred to as '*heremi*', deserts, or the wilderness.[34]

A great deal of the evidence points to a Carthusian house as the environment in which Amherst originated and was read. However, an argument against this assertion would be the fact that all the texts but one in the anthology are in Middle English rather than in Latin, the ordinary language of texts intended for a monastic audience. The vernacular would be associated with a lay audience or an audience of female religious. Yet, recently, scholars have argued that, in the fifteenth century, the vernacular was increasingly used in monastic contexts as well. Novices and lay-brothers would have required instruction even though they were not Latinate, and the vernacular would have been seen as the obvious medium.[35] For instance, according to Kocijancic-Pokorn, *The Cloud of Unknowing*

> may have been written within the Carthusian order for their novices at the beginning of their studies, when they were not yet very strong in Latin, to avoid the possibility of misinterpretation caused by their relative mastery of the language. Some scholars also think that the text was written for novices coming from the class of *conversi* or *clerici redditi*, whose knowledge of Latin was undoubtedly meagre.[36]

The same argument has been advanced for *The Desert of Religion*, a didactic poem that might well have been used to instruct novices just after they had entered the Charterhouse, 'since it presents the monk in English with the likely shape of his future life'.[37]

However, the complex nature of the texts in Amherst might not have been deemed suitable for novices, at any rate not without proper guidance. Perhaps the anthology found an audience among the monks themselves – we have seen that one of them, James Grenehalgh, corrected Rolle and Porete's texts and put his monogram against passages which were meaningful to him. If this is the case, the anthology could be a landmark in 'the slow advance of the vernacular in sophisticated monastic writings'.[38] In Amherst we may be witnessing how written English 'passes from a language with which to target specific readers ... to being one which now connotes universality'.[39] Just as spiritual and devotional texts were brought to a wider audience outside the walls of the monasteries through the use of the vernacular, vernacular texts found their way into monastic settings. Thus not only the message was universalized – the medium was too.

## Women in the Charterhouse: The Textual Presence of Julian of Norwich and Marguerite Porete in BL MS Additional 37790

It is difficult to say why exactly the medieval anthologist of Amherst chose the particular texts which the manuscript contains. Whether he chose the texts from a larger available group of texts, or whether he copied only those that were available to him, will always be a case for conjecture. Whatever his principles of selection, the anthology is a homogeneous collection of texts in which the authors describe their experience of contemplation and teach their readers about the contemplative life. This suggests some process of selection, perhaps even some process of ordering of the texts in the anthology. *The Mending of Life*, the most systematically didactic text, opens the anthology; Marguerite Porete's *Mirror*, the most speculative text, comes at the end. As the anthology progresses, the complexity of the texts increases. The anthologist also seems to have had a preference for texts in which the authors could serve as a model for the audience. It is not an author's gender, but his or her reputation for sanctity and what could be learnt from their texts which seems to have been most significant. Julian of Norwich's and Marguerite Porete's texts did not find their way into Amherst because their spirituality was recognized as essentially feminine, but because it was considered useful for Amherst's Carthusian audience.

Apart from Porete, whose *Mirror* remains anonymous throughout the entirety of its manuscript tradition, the authors are identified in comparable ways. Julian of Norwich is identified as a woman in the scribal introduction to her text: 'Here es a vision Schewed be the goodenes of god to a deuoute woman and hir name es Julyan that is recluse atte Norwyche and ȝitt ys on lyfe. Anno d*o*m*i*ni mill*esi*mo CCCC xiij'[40] (Amherst, fo. 97ʳ/1–4; *Showings*, I, 201/1–3). In the introduction to the translation of Rolle's *Incendium amoris*, the author is also mentioned:[41] 'Therfore this haly man Richarde hampole his boke has namyd Incendium Amoris, That is to say the fyre of lufe' (Amherst, fo. 18ᵛ/11–13; *Fire*, 1/8–9). The *Treatise of Perfection* is identified as a text 'compiled bi Dan John Rusbroke the ffirst prior of the chartyr howse in valle viridi iuxta bruxellam' (Amherst, fo. 115ʳ/11–12; *Treatise*, 229/3–5).[42] Rolle is identified as a man, Julian as a woman – but perhaps more important than this indication of their gender is the qualifying adjective preceding the nouns. Rolle is 'this *haly* man'; Julian is 'a *deuoute* woman' [my italics]. Julian and Ruusbroec are also identified by reference to their status in life and their geographical location. Julian is 'recluse atte Norwyche'; Ruusbroec is 'ffirst prior of the chartyr howse in valle viridi iuxta bruxellam'. The function of this information is to authenticate the texts and the message they convey to the audience. It is interesting to see that the passages in which Julian herself could be said to 'gender' her text, such as the famous *captatio benevolentiae* passage (Amherst, fo. 101ʳ/4–10; *Showings*, I, 222/40–8) have not been marked by the scribe or an annotator in any way.

    *The Mirror of Simple Souls* is an altogether different case from Julian's *Revelations* as well as from Rolle's and Ruusbroec's texts. In its manuscript transmission, *The Mirror* is an anonymous text.[43] Marguerite Porete is not identified as the author of *The Mirror*, either in Amherst or in any other manuscript that contains a version of her text in French, Latin, English or Italian. In Amherst, the translator's introduction to the text reads as follows: 'This boke the which is called þe myrroure of symple soules, I mooste vnworþy creature and oute cast of alle oþ*er* many ȝeeris gone wrote oute of ffrenche . . .' (Amherst, fo. 137ʳ/3–6; *Þe Mirrour*, 1/4–6).[44] Throughout the text there are sustained references to 'this boke' rather than to the author's experience as the locus of teaching and authority. The author's voice is not clearly identifiable in *The Mirror* because the text takes the form of a dialogue between allegorical figures, of whom the main three are Lady Love, the Soul and Reason. As the Soul is the contemplative soul that completes its spiritual ascent throughout the book, and Lady Love is the figure of authority that teaches the Soul and Reason (in addition to other allegorical figures that make a brief appearance, such as Light of Faith, Temptation, Truth, Discretion, Holy Church and the Virtues), it is logical to look for the author's voice in the Soul's speeches, especially when one reads the book with one's own spiritual edification in mind. Yet it seems that the translator/commentator of the Middle English version did not ask himself who the author of *The Mirror* might have been, and even failed to identify the Soul with the authorial viewpoint 'for the sake of the authority inscribed in the figure of Amour',[45] thus focusing more on the teachings of Lady Love than on the author's experience as it is reflected in the speeches of the Soul.[46]

M.N.'s focus on Lady Love might have concealed *The Mirror*'s female authorship from him. Indeed, M.N. did assume that the text had been written by a man. In one of his explanatory passages, M.N. refers to the author as 'he':

> M. This worde perischid may nouȝt be taken as for perischynge of perdicion of saule, that they schulde not be saued: but it is to mene riȝt as loue sais. Thay leue so to thare awne werkis. Wenynge that it is beste: so thay kepe to followe none oþere: And therefore thay may not atayne to the hieste: but for the leste thay lese the beste. Therfore *he* calles tham perisched therfro: & nouȝt for the werkis: but for her sufficience. N. (my italics) (Amherst, fo. 176ᵛ/4–11; *Þe Mirrour*, 91/11–17)

The reference could be said to be ambiguous, as 'he' might also refer to 'Loue'. Yet Love is often addressed as 'Lady Love', a female allegorical figure, and – apart from in M.N.'s prologue[47] – is consistently referred to as 'she'.[48] In a later passage, M.N.'s text reads '*he . . . þat þis booke made*' (Amherst, fo. 201ʳ/25; *Þe Mirrour*, 145/8–12) where the French has '*celle* qui fist ce livre'.[49] M.N. overlooks this possible reference to the Soul and turns it into a reference to the anonymous author. This can be taken as proof that anonymous authors were (and are) generally taken to be male,[50] but it could also mean that the spirituality presented in the text did not strike the translator as being particularly 'feminine'. He did not conclude that this text could only have been written by a woman. It has been observed that *The Mirror* 'seems not to have circulated among the fifteenth-century women readers of Bridget of Sweden, Catherine of Siena, Elizabeth of Hungary and Mechtild of Hackeborn; at least, it did not circulate as a *woman's book*, if only because it was assumed to be by a man.'[51]

An intended audience of Carthusians, one of whose principal activities was contemplative prayer in the solitude of their cells, would have found in Amherst a collection of texts about contemplation (the mystical experience), all written in the same tradition. The texts share many characteristics as they all describe conversion, and the difficulties the contemplative will encounter during the process of ascent, as well as the joys of contemplative union with God. The anthology's appeal – and it is tempting to think that this was the anthologist's intention – is its diversity of voices taken in conjunction with its thematic unity. Amherst shows its Carthusian readers how different people experience contemplative union, the aim of the life that the monks themselves are leading. It also contains five literary texts that are generically quite different. Different genres make for different reading practices, and it is in this area that Julian of Norwich's and Marguerite Porete's texts can be seen to fulfil a specific function in the anthology.

Whereas women were normally forbidden from entering the bounds of the Charterhouse,[52] Julian of Norwich and Marguerite Porete may have been allowed access within the confines of Amherst (Julian in her anchoress's garb, Marguerite in drag[53]), due to certain generic characteristics within their texts which induced a specialized mode of reading (*lectio*) distinct from other texts within the anthology.

Whereas Rolle's and Ruusbroec's texts are treatise-like and straightforwardly didactic, the *Revelations* and *The Mirror* describe their authors' experiences within genres that necessitate a greater effort of interpretation on the part of the reader. Julian writes a visionary text, describing the revelations she was shown during a severe illness in which she thought she would die. The amount of text she devotes to providing the background against which her account of the visionary experience and her reactions to it have to be read is remarkable. She outlines her spiritual life preceding the illness and revelations, and the three gifts she desired: understanding of the Passion, a bodily illness, and the three wounds of contrition, compassion and true longing for God. She details her insistence that her desire for the first two gifts was contingent upon God's will, while her desire for the third gift was unconditional. Julian desires the first two gifts for her own spiritual edification: through the understanding of Christ's suffering and her imitation of it in her own illness, she aspires to grow closer to God: 'I hoped that it muȝt be to me a spede whenn I schulde dye, for I desyrede sone to be with my god' (Amherst, fo. 97ᵛ/7–8; *Showings*, I, 204/38–9). She describes her illness in great detail, stressing both its genuine nature and its severity. After having defined the illness and revelations as her personal experience by situating them in time and space, Julian moves away from a specific interpretation of her experience to a more general one. The vision she was given 'by the grace of God' was not shown to her as an individual, but as a representative of humankind: 'Alle that I sawe of my selfe, I meene in the p*er*sone of all myne evyn cristene' (Amherst, fo. 100ʳ/28–9; *Showings*, I, 219/1–2). She prays the audience to stop looking at the wretched and sinful creature that was shown the visions and to behold God, who 'of his curtays love and of his endles goodnes walde shewe gen*er*alye this vision in comforthe of vs alle' (Amherst, fo. 100ᵛ/2–4; *Showings*, I, 219/6–8 ). The text should be for the readers or listeners what the experience itself was for Julian: 'ȝe that hyerys and sees this vision and this techynge that is of Ih*es*u cryste to edificacion of ȝoure soule, it is goddys wille & my desyrere that ȝe take it with as grete ioye and lykynge as Ih*es*u hadde schewyd it ȝowe as he dyd to me' (Amherst, fo. 100ᵛ/4–7; *Showings*, I, 219/8–220/11). And later: 'for yt [ys] commo*n*n and gen*er*ale as we are alle ane. And I am sekere I sawe it for the profytte of many oder' (Amherst, fo. 100ᵛ/12–14; *Showings*, I, 220/16–18). She states that as an individual, she is nothing, but 'in gen*er*alle, I am in anehede of charyte with alle myne evyn cristene' (Amherst, fo. 100ᵛ/18–19; *Showings*, I, 220/22–3).

Julian thus invites the readers not just to read the text as the experience of someone else, but to try and make sense of it as if it had been their own experience. She tries to describe the revelations in terminology as detailed as possible, distinguishing between being taught 'be bodylye syght and be worde formede in myne vndyrstandynge & be gastelye syght' (Amherst, fo. 101ʳ/23–4; *Showings*, I, 224/2–3). Julian comments on her inability to do full justice to the 'gastelye' sight, but she trusts that her readers will receive divine assistance to understand it properly. Thus Julian explicitly urges her readers to interiorize and live the text, continually stressing the significance and validity of her own experience for all humankind.[54] Julian's guidance of her audience is so obvious that her Amherst readers cannot have missed it.

Marguerite Porete's *Mirror* can be placed within the secular and religious tradition of the dream-vision. In classic dream-vision texts, a dreamer (sometimes obliquely identifiable with the author, but often a persona) falls asleep and is transported to some other world where he meets a figure of authority (a saint, a deceased beloved, an allegorical figure), who tells the dreamer about the future, or who teaches him philosophical or religious truths.[55] However, *The Mirror* does not share all of the characteristics of classic dream-vision poems. There is no 'dreamer'; instead, after the introductory story of the princess who has the portrait of King Alexander painted,[56] the text immediately presents a monologue by the Soul which is followed by the teaching of Lady Love, the figure of authority whom the Soul encounters. After Love's complicated initial teaching, Reason steps in and starts to ask questions (Amherst, fo. 143ᵛ/4–5; *Þe Mirrour*, 16/6). It is the presence of allegorical figures, including figures of authority, which links Marguerite's text to the dream-vision tradition. During the Middle Ages, dreams and dream-vision texts would have been classified according to Macrobius' systematic description of different kinds of dreams in his commentary on Cicero's *Somnium Scipionis*.[57] *The Mirror* demonstrates some of the characteristics of the *oraculum*, a dream in which a figure of authority appears and gives advice, and of the *somnium*, the enigmatic dream, which Macrobius implies is the 'natural' equivalent to the artifice of allegory.[58] This would explain why allegorical fictions were often framed within dreams. The type of allegory often used in dream-vision texts is personification, a 'technique of explanatory power' very closely linked to the author's need to analyse 'the workings of the soul itself'.[59] In *The Mirror* the (author's) soul's ascent is described in its allegorical interchange with Reason and Lady Love. Through the rhetorical practice of personification the soul's ascent is dramatized; the otherwise mute players in this psychological, spiritual and mystical process have been attributed voice and language.[60]

Marguerite has stripped the dream-vision genre to its bare essentials: retaining the vision itself, while omitting the framework of the dreamer falling asleep. Yet she proves herself to be a master of the genre, evoking and simultaneously subverting courtly texts like the *Roman de la Rose*[61] and echoing Boethius' *De consolatione philosophiae* in its basic theme of spiritual ascent as her text describes 'an *anamnesis* in which the human mind returns to its divine origin'.[62]

One of the effects of the *somnium* or enigmatic dream tradition, with which Marguerite's text can be associated through her use of allegorical figures, relates to the need for reader interpretation, since the true meaning of the information offered lies concealed beneath the text's allegorical veneer.[63] Interestingly, M.N.'s translation of *The Mirror* is his second; in it he provides explanatory glosses which seem to have been motivated by the realization that the readers of his first translation had been unable to interpret the text correctly. Thus M.N.'s response to *The*

*Mirror* is largely characterized by his perceived need to interpret the text and the care he takes to alert his readers as to the enigmatic nature of the text. He concedes that the task at hand is daunting, even for him, as the text is 'of hiʒe diuine maters and of hiʒe goostli felynges, & kernyngli and ful mystili it is spoken' (Amherst, fo. 137ʳ/19–21; *Þe Mirrour*, 1/17–18), and interpretation is necessary.

> Therfore to þese soules þat ben disposed to þese hiʒe felynges, loue haþ made of him þis boke in fulfillynge of her desire, and often *he leieþ þe note and þe kernel wiþinne þe schelle vnbroke*. Þis is to seie, þat loue in þis boke leieþ to soules þe touches of his diuine werkis priuely hid vndir derk speche, for þei schulde taaste the deppere þe drauʒtes of his loue and drinke, and also to make hem haue þe more cleer insiʒt in diuine vndirstandinges to diuine loue & *declare it hemsilf.* (my italics) (Amherst, fo. 138ʳ/4–14; *Þe Mirrour*, 3/10–17)

Like Julian, M.N. directs the readers, describing in the glosses how they should understand the text, either by providing very definite interpretations, or sometimes by simply urging them to think about the text until they arrive at their own interpretation.

> M. O, þese wordis semen ful straunge to þe rederis, þat seiþ þe soule is lost in þe riʒt hiʒe bi plente of knowinge, and bicome nouʒt in hir vndirstandinge. And not oonli þese wordis, but also many mo oþir wordis þat ben writen before and aftir, semen fable or errour, or hard to vndirstande. But for þe loue of God, ʒe reders, demeþ not to soone, for I am siker þat who so rediþ ouer þis booke bi good avisement twies or þries and be disposid to þo same felynges, þei schulen vndirstonde it wel ynowʒ. And þouʒ þei be not disposid to þo felynges, ʒitt hem schal þenke it is al wel yseid. But who so takeþ þe nakid wordis of scriptures and leueþ þe sentence, he may liʒtli erre. N. (Amherst, fo. 143ᵛ/12–26; *Þe Mirrour*, 16/14–17/3)

Whether M.N.'s interpretation of the text is valid, whether it is an attempt to bring a heretical text into line, or whether it shows that he does not understand *The Mirror* as it was intended, his interpretative response (and the response of the readers of his first translation) was triggered by the dream-vision quality of the text. It is the reader's task to break the shell of the allegory and to find the sweet nut of the meaning of the text. Only then can the text become useful for his or her own spiritual development.

Thus Julian of Norwich's *Revelations* and Marguerite Porete's

*Mirror* bring to the anthology two texts that alert the reader to the need to understand them correctly. That monastic reading practices would have included both meditative reading and the interiorizing of what one read can only reinforce this invitation. In Marguerite's case, the demands she makes on her audience are embedded in the generic conventions of the allegorical dream-vision poetry tradition, which prove a suitable vehicle for her apophatic experience of God. M.N. responded to these demands, and provided his interpretation and reader guidance in the prologue and fifteen explanatory glosses. Julian's reader guidance is more explicit, yet it also derives from the visionary nature of her work, which she was aware required a careful approach.

It has been observed that a characteristic of affective English religiosity is its interest 'in the *rhetoric* of ecstasy, in the ability of words to convey the feelings which accompany elevated states of the soul, and ... on the subjective component of all religious language when it is used in an affective context'.[64] The Carthusians may have been interested in the *Revelations* and *The Mirror* for this very reason. The texts evoke an intense experience of God in intense language, to which the audience is given access by the guidance the texts include – direct authorial guidance in Julian's case, mediated guidance in the case of *The Mirror*. The evidence in Amherst suggests that the notion of female spirituality – or, for that matter, male spirituality – mattered little. What did matter is the author's message, which, as Amherst shows, the Carthusians largely passed on in the form in which it came to them. The manuscript shows Carthusian respect for authors and texts, and their openness to spiritual writings by men and women, English and continental. It also sheds light upon their enthusiasm for the preservation of spiritual teaching, and upon their desire to transmit these teachings to readers, places and times beyond the immediate orbit of the Charterhouse.

## Notes

[1] 'Amherst', the name often given to this manuscript, is the one I will use throughout this chapter. Lord Amherst was the last person to own the manuscript privately before it was acquired by the British Library in 1910.

[2] Amherst contains the following texts: (1) fos. 1$^r$–18$^r$: a Middle English translation by the Carmelite Richard Misyn of Richard Rolle's *Emendatio vitae*, dated 1435; (2) fos. 18$^v$–95$^r$: a Middle English translation by the Carmelite Richard Misyn of Richard Rolle's *Incendium amoris*, dated 1434;

(3) fos. 95ᵛ–96ᵛ: *The Golden Epistle of Saint Bernard*, an anonymous epistle wrongly attributed to Saint Bernard; (4) fos. 97ʳ–115ʳ: the short text of Julian of Norwich's *Revelations of Divine Love*; (5) fos. 115ʳ–130ʳ: a Middle English translation of Jan van Ruusbroec's *Vanden Blinckenden Steen* from the Latin *De calculo candido*; (6) fos. 130ᵛ–136ᵛ: fragments from Richard Rolle's *Form of Living*; fragments from Richard Rolle's *Ego dormio*; a fragment from ch. 4 of a Middle English translation of Heinrich Suso's *Horologium sapientiae*; (7) fos. 137ʳ–225ʳ: a Middle English translation of Marguerite Porete's *Le Mirouer des simples ames*; (8) fos. 226ʳ–233ᵛ: a Latin compilation 'which includes the greater part of chs. xxxi–xxxvii of the spurious *Liber soliloquiorum animae ad Deum*'; (9) fos. 234ʳ–236ʳ: a short tract on the contemplative life; (10) fos. 236ʳ⁻ᵛ: a separate tract on contemplation; (11) fos. 236ᵛ–237ʳ (cropped): a Middle English translation of Bridget of Sweden's *Revelationes*, II, 16 (incomplete). A description of the manuscript (with references to editions of the individual texts) can be found in E. Colledge and J. Walsh (eds.), *A Book of Showings to the Anchoress Julian of Norwich*, 2 vols. (Toronto, 1978), I, 1–5 (hereafter cited as *Showings*); in M. G. Sargent, *James Grenehalgh as Textual Critic*, 2 vols., Analecta Cartusiana 85 (Salzburg, 1984), II, 499–510, as well as in the British Museum, Department of Manuscripts, *Catalogue of Additions to the Manuscripts in the British Museum in the years MDCCCCVI–MDCCCCX* (London, 1912), 153–6.

[3] *Showings*, I, 2.

[4] This may suggest that the anthology was intended to be used in a small community where information on why these texts were put in, and how they could be read could be conveyed orally. See V. Gillespie, '*Lukynge in haly bukes: Lectio* in some Late Medieval Spiritual Miscellanies', Analecta Cartusiana 106.2 (Salzburg, 1984), 20.

[5] A very detailed study of the Amherst scribe has been carried out by Margaret Laing, 'Linguistic Profiles and Textual Criticism: The Translations by Richard Misyn of Rolle's *Incendium amoris* and *Emendatio vitae*', in A. McIntosh, M. L. Samuels and M. Laing (eds.), *Middle English Dialectology: Essays on Some Principles and Problems* (Aberdeen, 1989), 220 (n.10), 221 (n.20).

[6] Texts 2, 3, 6 and 11 in the list given in n.2.

[7] Texts 3 and 6 in the list given in n.2.

[8] Texts 8, 9, 10 and 11 in the list given in n.2.

[9] Laing suggests that the scribe of Amherst 'was very much influenced by his exemplars in matters of layout, spacing and script.' Laing, 'Linguistic Profiles', 220 (n.10).

[10] A. I. Doyle communicated to Julia Holloway that fos. 97–136ᵛ may have been intended as a separate booklet. Fo. 96ᵛ is smudged, but fo. 97 is not damaged, which might mean that the damage happened before the quires were bound together, except that the medieval quire signatures show that an

early decision was taken to bind the volume as it is now. This information was posted by Holloway on her Friends of God discussion list.

[11] J. Bazire and E. Colledge (eds.), *The Chastising of God's Children and the Treatise of Perfection of the Sons of God* (Oxford, 1957), 83 (hereafter cited as *The Treatise*). See also E. Colledge, 'The Treatise of Perfection of the Sons of God: A Fifteenth-Century English Ruysbroeck Translation', *English Studies*, 33 (1952), 54. For Ruusbroec's contacts with the Carthusians of Herinnes, see P. Verdeyen, *Ruusbroec and his Mysticism* (Collegeville, Ind. 1994), 70. From the foundation of Sheen onwards, the house had contacts with Charterhouses in the Low Countries. See Colledge, '*The Treatise of Perfection*', 55.

[12] Basset's defence of Richard Rolle is addressed to a Carthusian. See M. Sargent, 'Contemporary Criticism of Richard Rolle', Analecta Cartusiana 55.1 (Salzburg, 1981), 183.

[13] Interestingly, the Carthusians of Herinnes also possessed texts by Rolle; see A. I. Doyle, 'Carthusian Participation in the Movement of Works of Richard Rolle between England and other parts of Europe in the Fourteenth and Fifteenth Centuries', Analecta Cartusiana 55.2 (Salzburg, 1981), 111–12.

[14] See M. Doiron, '*Þe Mirrour of Simple Soules*: An Edition and Commentary' (Fordham University Ph.D. thesis, 1964), xii–xiv (hereafter cited as *Þe Mirrour*).

[15] In C. Kirchberger (ed.) *The Mirror of Simple Souls, by an Unknown French Mystic of the Thirteenth Century, Translated into English by M.N.* (London, 1927), xxxiii–xxxv, the suggestion is only obliquely made. M. Doiron explicitly states that the translator 'was probably a Carthusian', but does not provide further arguments for her claim. See *Þe Mirrour*, li.

[16] See N. Watson, 'Melting into God the English Way: Deification in the Middle English Version of Marguerite Porete's *Mirouer des simples âmes anienties*', in R. Voaden (ed.), *Prophets Abroad: The Reception of Continental Holy Women in Late Medieval England* (Cambridge, 1996), 32–3.

[17] S. B. Meech and H. E. Allen (eds.), *The Book of Margery Kempe*, EETS OS 212 (Oxford, 1940; repr. 1961), xxxii.

[18] Sargent, *James Grenehalgh*, 52.

[19] Laing identifies the Amherst's scribe as 'placeable in SW Lincs in the area of Grantham'. Laing, 'Linguistic Profiles', 208. A. I. Doyle suggested that the Charterhouse closest to this dialect area is Beauvale (in private correspondence).

[20] Charterhouses were often the recipients of books left to them in wills. V. Gillespie, 'Cura pastoralis in deserto', in M. G. Sargent (ed.), *De cella in seculum: Religious and Secular Life and Devotion in Late Medieval England* (Cambridge, 1989), 161.

[21] Sargent, *James Grenehalgh*, 79–80, 83–4.

[22] Of the quire-filling texts, only the Latin compilation has been annotated.

[23] Julian's *Revelations* have been thoroughly corrected by a hand contemporary

with the Amherst scribe. See F. Beer, *Julian of Norwich's Revelations of Divine Love: The Shorter Version* (Heidelberg, 1978), 4–6.
24 The corrections can be found on fos. 39$^r$, 40$^r$, 48$^r$, 75$^v$, 81$^v$; the longer phrase on 67$^v$. See also Sargent, *James Grenehalgh*, 509.
25 The corrections can be found on fos. 139$^r$, 143$^v$, 161$^v$, 166$^v$, 194$^v$, 210$^v$. See also Sargent, *James Grenehalgh*, 288–9.
26 See fos. 23$^r$, 33$^r$.
27 See fo. 87$^r$.
28 The only book annotated by Grenehalgh that was afterwards owned by Joanna Sewell is an early printed book, now Philadelphia, Rosenbach Foundation Museum and Library, Incunable H 491. Sargent suggests that the book may have been given by Grenehalgh to Sewell as a present on her profession. Sargent, *James Grenehalgh*, 86–7. The I.S. monograms, found in Amherst on fos. 96$^v$ and 225 cannot be Joanna Sewell's, as they are scribal and thus antedate Grenehalgh and Sewell's friendship by fifty years. Ibid., 69.
29 R. Harvey (ed.), *The Fire of Love and the Mending of Life or the Rule of Living: Translated from the Latin of Richard Rolle by Richard Misyn*, EETS OS 106 (London, 1896; repr. 1973) (hereafter cited as *Fire*).
30 Ruusbroec makes a distinction between the faithful servants, the secret friends and the hidden sons of God. The hidden sons of God are closest to God and therefore the most perfect. See Paul Mommaers's Introduction to the edition of Ruusbroec's *Vanden Blinckenden Steen*, in G. De Baere (ed.), *Jan van Ruusbroec. Opera omnia*, CCCM 110 (Turnhout, 1991), X, 11–33. Marguerite distinguishes between the perished, marred and free souls and describes spiritual ascent as consisting in seven estates. As the soul progresses through these states, she gradually sheds her own will and moves closer to God. See E. Babinsky, *Marguerite Porete: The Mirror of Simple Souls* (New York, 1993), 27–36.
31 N. Watson, 'The Middle English Mystics', in D. Wallace (ed.), *The Cambridge History of Middle English Literature* (Cambridge, 1999), 549.
32 This verse is also the opening quotation of the *Desert of Religion*, an anonymous poem likely to have originated with the Carthusians. A. Mc Govern-Mouron, 'The *Desert of Religion* in British Library Cotton Faustina B VI, pars II', Analecta Cartusiana 130.9 (1996), 152.
33 Verdeyen, *Ruusbroec and his Mysticism*, 27.
34 Mc Govern-Mouron, 'The *Desert of Religion*', 152.
35 Gillespie, '*Lukynge in haly bukes*', 23.
36 N. Kocijancic-Pokorn, 'Original Audience of *The Cloud of Unknowing* (In support of the Carthusian Authorship)', Analecta Cartusiana 130.1 (1995), 76–7.
37 Mc Govern-Mouron, 'The *Desert of Religion*', 156.
38 Ibid., 156. Mc Govern-Mouron also quotes Geert Grote on the directness and freshness of the mother tongue as opposed to the Latin acquired after

one's childhood, especially with regard to the effects of something holy being said. Ibid., 155.
39 Watson, 'The Middle English Mystics', 557.
40 The identification of Julian, the statement that she is still alive and the date must have been part of the exemplar that the Amherst scribe worked from, as the script of Amherst is usually dated c. 1450.
41 There is no translator's introduction to Rolle's *Emendatio vitae*, but Rolle is named as the author of the work (and Misyn as the translator) in the *explicit* of the work; see fo. 18ʳ/18–22. For the *explicit* of the *Incendium amoris*, see fo. 95ʳ/26–31.
42 The misunderstanding about Ruusbroec's status in life – he was actually an Augustinian canon – might have arisen because the name of the Augustinian Priory where Ruusbroec lived (Groenendaal or *Viridivalle* near Brussels) was confused with the Charterhouse of Valleviridi in the neighbourhood of Paris; see Colledge, '*The Treatise of Perfection*', 54.
43 One exception to this is Cambridge, Pembroke College, MS 221, in which Methley's Latin translation of the Middle English version of *The Mirror* is attributed to Ruusbroec; see Doiron, *Þe Mirrour*, l. Sargent argues that this erroneous attribution is the reason for the circulation of the text among the English Carthusians. See M. G. Sargent, 'The Annihilation of Marguerite Porete', *Viator*, 28 (1997), 262. However, the attribution of *The Mirror* to Ruusbroec is considerably later than the actual translation of *The Mirror* into Middle English and is therefore unlikely to have been the reason why *The Mirror* was translated. In 1946, Romana Guarnieri identified *The Mirror of Simple Souls* as the text that caused the Valenciennes beguine Marguerite Porete to be burned at the stake as a relapsed heretic in 1310; see R. Guarnieri, 'Lo *Specchio delle anime semplici* e Margharita Poirette', *L'Osservatore Romano*, 141, 16 June (1946), 3.
44 This translator also added fifteen passages of explanatory comments to the text, which he separates from Marguerite's text by putting the initial of his first name (M.) at the beginning of the passage he inserts, and the initial of his surname (N.) at the end.
45 Watson, 'Melting into God', 41.
46 M.N.'s reading of the texts seems to have been influenced by the generic conventions of dream-vision poetry, a genre with which *The Mirror* has close affinities as I shall go on to argue.
47 Amherst, fo. 138ʳ/8–10; *Þe Mirrour*, 3/10–12.
48 See Amherst, fo. 138/15 and fo. 140ᵛ/10; *Þe Mirrour*, 3/18 and 9/11.
49 See R. Guarnieri and P. Verdeyen (eds.), *Marguerite Porete: Le Mirouer des simples ames. Margaretae Porete. Speculum simplicium animarum*, CCCM 69 (1986), 270.
50 Clare Kirchberger, who translated the Middle English *Mirror* in 1927, nineteen years before Guarnieri published the hypothesis that *The Mirror* was Marguerite Porete's 'lost' text, also assumed its author was a man.

51 Watson's italics; see Watson, 'Melting into God', 26.
52 Sargent, *James Grenehalgh*, 91.
53 The joke is Nicholas Watson's; see Watson, 'Melting into God', 26.
54 When she writes how she believed she was dying, telling those around her that 'itt is to daye domesdaye with me' (Amherst, fo. 101ᵛ/5; *Showings*, I, 224/14–15), she describes her purpose in saying this to be the same as her purpose in writing her text: 'this I sayde for y walde thaye lovyd god mare & sette the lesse pryse be the vanite of the worlde forto make thame to hafe mynde that this lyfe es shorte as thaye myght se in ensampill be me' (Amherst, fo. 101ᵛ/7–10; *Showings*, I, 225/17–20).
55 Well-known dream visions include Boethius' *De consolatione philosophiae*, Guillaume de Lorris and Jean de Meun's *Roman de la Rose*, and, in the English tradition: *Pearl*, Chaucer's *Book of the Duchess*, *Parliament of Fowles* and *Legend of Good Women*, and Langland's *Piers Plowman*.
56 The likeness of King Alexander is a metaphor for *The Mirror*, Marguerite's book, which is a reflection of God as he is experienced by her.
57 For an account of Macrobius' commentary, see A. C. Spearing, *Medieval Dream-Poetry* (Cambridge, 1976), 8–11.
58 Ibid., 10.
59 See J. Whitman, *Allegory: The Dynamics of an Ancient and Medieval Technique* (Oxford, 1987), 24.
60 Ibid., 269.
61 See B. Newman, *From Virile Woman to WomanChrist: Studies in Medieval Religion and Literature* (Philadelphia, 1995), 137–67.
62 Whitman, *Allegory*, 112.
63 Spearing, *Medieval Dream-Poetry*, 10.
64 Watson, 'Melting into God', 46.

## 3
# Spirituality and Sex Change: *Horologium sapientiae* and *Speculum devotorum*

REBECCA SELMAN

IN her article, ' "A reasonable affection": Gender and Spiritual Friendship in Middle English Devotional Literature', Anne Clark Bartlett discusses a selection of religious texts written by men for female readers, usually nuns, which represent 'female and male religious as parallel partners in intellect, zeal, and worth before God, equal sharers in monastic labor'.¹ In the course of her discussion, Bartlett refers briefly to the *Speculum devotorum*, a meditative life of Christ translated and compiled from various Latin sources in the early fifteenth century by a Carthusian from Sheen for a nun, almost certainly one at the Bridgittine convent of Syon.² That text will form the focus of the discussion here. Using Bartlett's work as a starting-point, this chapter will address the *Speculum* as a work intrinsically concerned with the nature of female spirituality. The discussion is also indebted to Ian Johnson's characterization of the *Speculum* as a 'woman's work', and his argument that the author's concern to orientate his text towards woman as reader affects both his selection of material and his translation of sources.³ This analysis of the *Speculum* will begin by looking at how a quotation from one of the Latin source texts – the *Horologium sapientiae*, written in *c.* 1334 by the German Dominican Henry Suso for his fellow friars – is altered in one of the two extant manuscripts of the *Speculum* in order to suit a female audience.⁴ The implications of this will be developed in further discussion of the female spirituality of the *Speculum*. This will focus on the way the figures of Mary and Bridget are used in the text to engender identificatory practices in the reader. At the same time some additional comparisons will be drawn with the *Horologium* as a male-centred text.[5]

In the prologue to the *Speculum* the *Horologium* is used as a textual authority to support the author's statement that meditating on Christ's humanity is 'a trewe weye wythoute dysseyte to vertuys, & to the gostly knowynge, & trewe louynge of god, & suetnesse in grace to a deuot soule that canne deuoutly & dylygently occupye hym therinne'.[6] Three separate quotations from the *Horologium* are woven together at this point: the first comes from Book 1, chapter 3 of Suso's text, the other two from chapter 14 of the same book. The whole extract is reproduced below with the individual quotations labelled [1], [2] and [3]:

> Ferthyrmore ʒe schal vndyrstande þat the dylygent thynkynge of oure lordys manhede ys a trewe weye wythoute dysseyte to vertuys, & to the gostly knowynge, & trewe louynge of god, & suetnesse in grace to a deuot soule that canne deuoutly & dylygently occupye hym therinne, for euyrlastynge Wysedom seyt in the boke þat ys called the Orlege of Wysedom to hys dyscypyl thus: [1] *Be hyt knowe to the, that hyt ys not ʒeue to come to the hynesse of the godhede or vnvsyd suetnesse but to folke I drawe be a manyr meke affeccyon of feythe & loue be the byttyrnesse of my manhede & passyon. And þe hyer þat eny man goeth thys forsclewde the lower he falleth; for forsothe þys ys the weye be the whyche men goeth; thys ys the gate be the whyche an en / trynge ys grauntyd to the desyryd ende.* And in anothyr place of the same boke he seyt also to his disciples thus: [2] *The ofte thynkynge of my passyon makyth an vnlernyde man a ful lernyd man; & vnwyse men & ydyotys hyt makyth to profyte into maystrys not of the sciens that bloweth a man wythinne but of charyte that edyfyeth. Hyt ys a manyr boke of lyf in the whyche ben founden alle thyngys necessarye to helthe.* And sone aftyr he seyt thus: [3] *Blyssyd ys he* or sche *that sadly takyth hede to þe studye of hytt for he schal profyte in the dyspysynge of the worlde, & in þe loue of god & alle vertuys, and he schal take the encresyng of gracys.* (6/1–7/12)[7]

Quotation 3 is the object of concern here. In the *Horologium* it forms part of a similar discussion on the benefits of meditating on the Passion. The words in question are spoken by the figure of Eternal Wisdom who is instructing the Disciple, the questing figure of the text: 'Felix, qui eius studio seriose intenderit; quia proficiet in contemptu mundi et in amore Dei, cunctarumque virtutum et gratiarum sumet incrementum' (494/18–21).[8] In the Latin the fact that the person meditating on Christ's Passion is male is indicated by the use of the masculine singular relative pronoun 'qui'. However, in the Cambridge manuscript of the *Speculum*, when this sentence is either translated by the author or copied by a scribe, the activity of meditating on Christ's humanity is made gender-inclusive by the incorporation of the feminine pronoun 'sche': '*Blyssyd ys he* or sche *that sadly takyth hede to þe studye of hytt* . . .' Throughout the *Speculum* the author refers to both men and women: 'Now hyt were goode here I trowe to haue summe informacyon or techynge how a man or a womman mygthte knowe a goode vysyon fro a badde . . .' (45/6–9). 'Here as me semyth ys a fayre ensample to alle relygyus men & wymmen . . .' (111/12–14).[9] However, he tends to follow such instances with a male pronoun to represent both sexes: 'for whatsumeuyre eny man or woman doo or suffre for oure lorde god he schal haue hys mede therfore . . .' (291/7–9).[10]

Furthermore, in the extract from the *Speculum* reproduced above in which the three quotations from the *Horologium* come, there are repeated references to 'man', 'men' and 'he'. The use of the feminine pronoun in quotation 3 is thus striking and suggests a deliberate attempt to draw attention to the female reader of the *Speculum*.

As well as this adaptation of Suso's quotation, the female spirituality of the *Speculum* is reinforced in other ways, signalling its difference from the *Horologium*. The English writer prioritizes woman as reader in two specific ways which will now be addressed: the use of Mary as a model whose behaviour the reader is encouraged to emulate; and the use of St Bridget as a textual authority, specifically her role as an ideal spectator of the scenes she describes, whose 'seeing' the reader is invited to imitate.

The *Horologium* and the *Speculum* differ generally in both content and form. Suso's text is an account of the relationship between Wisdom, who is Christ, and the Disciple – a semi-autobiographical figure – and how that relationship, enacted through dialogue, leads the Disciple towards wisdom. The journey to wisdom is in two distinct stages, reflected in the *Horologium*'s division into a two-book structure. In Book 1, in which Wisdom speaks as the suffering Christ, the Disciple acquires knowledge of Christ in his humanity by learning to conform to his sorrows at the Passion. Book 2 focuses on the knowledge of the Godhead; this involves an ability to see and understand God and spiritual matters. Throughout the *Horologium* the Disciple functions implicitly as an identificatory figure for the reader; his questions and responses guide the reader through the text and encourage him also to participate in this search for wisdom. The *Speculum*, however, lacks an obvious textual figure with whom the reader can identify. This narrative account of Christ's life, divided into thirty-three chapters as a textual representation of the thirty-three years of Christ's life, is structured as a monologue with the authorial voice explicitly guiding the reader's responses.[11] These differences between the two texts have a bearing on their appeal and appropriateness for women readers.

In the *Horologium* Mary is the focus of discussion in the closing chapter of Book 1, entitled 'Commendatio singularis beatae virginis et de dolore eius inaestimabili, quem habuit in passione Filii' ('A singular commendation of the Blessed Virgin and of her incalculable sorrow, which she had at her Son's Passion'). At this stage in the text the Disciple has been instructed on meditation on the Passion and on conformity to Christ's sufferings. Now Mary is presented to him as an exemplar of *imitatio Christi*.[12] She speaks to the Disciple and describes how she felt at the Passion. The emphasis is on the reader learning to feel compassion for Mary's sorrows, motivated by gratitude for her help in bringing sinners to God's mercy. Through his responses to Mary the Disciple functions as a guide for the reader.

The chapter opens as a monologue – in the Disciple's voice – in which he praises Mary for her intercessory role. He ponders her sorrows as she stood under the Cross, and recognizes that mortals should empathize with her because of all she has done for them: 'Per quam enim miseri continue consolamur, iustum valde est, ut ei quoque patienti compatiamur' (513/14–16).[13] The Disciple then questions Mary about these sufferings. She describes her sorrow at seeing Christ on the Cross and relates how her physical response echoed His torments: 'Anima mea prae dolore cruciabatur, viscera materna sauciabantur, et commoriebantur omnia ossa mea' (514/30–31).[14] Her grief manifested itself physically as she swooned before the Cross, lifted up her hands to Christ and kissed the blood dripping from him. When the dead Christ was removed from the Cross she embraced His body, wept over it and was reluctant to release it. At the Resurrection, however, this sorrow turned to joy.

Responding to Mary's words, the Disciple bitterly criticizes those who do not feel sorrow for her: 'O quam induratum est cor, quod tibi ex intimis noncompatitur. Quam male exsiccati oculi, qui te sic flentem videntes nequaquam queunt lacrimari. Quam frigidum pectus, quod ex his non gemit' (516/26–9).[15] By the end of the chapter the Disciple, through the words and responses he articulates to the suffering Christ, shows how Mary has acted as a model of behaviour for him: 'tota anima mea ... vulnera sanguine cruentata crebrius perosculatur ...' (518/1–3).[16] Thus, from a starting-point of feeling compassion for Mary, the Disciple learns to imitate her behaviour. The reader, following the same journey through the narrative, will learn to do likewise.

Whereas in the *Horologium* compassion for Mary results in imitation of her behaviour, in the *Speculum* imitation is instead the logical continuation of the text's emphasis on the reader's identification with Mary. In the *Horologium* the imitation of Christ is encouraged in the Disciple, and hence in the intended reader of the text. For example, in chapter 4 Wisdom teaches the Disciple how to be spiritually crucified with him. By offering himself to Christ his hands will be pierced on the Cross; by enduring evils his feet will be nailed, and so on.[17] Through his spiritual actions the Disciple – and the male reader of Suso's text – will thus imitate Christ in his bodily sufferings and forge a resemblance with him. A Dominican friar, owing to his gender, has arguably a more immediate means of identification with Christ than a Syon nun. As Lochrie has suggested, the imitation of Christ's suffering humanity could be problematic for a woman.[18] Mary, however, as the author of the *Speculum* realizes, is an ideal model for a female reader.[19] The nun reader's bodily identification with Mary facilitates the imitation of her behaviour which the author encourages throughout the narrative.[20] He describes Mary as 'a parfyth example & a trewe merowre of perfeccyon to alle wymmen as oure lord Ihesu cryste to alle men', whom he urges the nun to 'folow aftyr as myche as god wole ȝeue ȝow grace & kunnynge' (53/2–6). For example, Mary's hasty journey to her cousin Elizabeth's house shows 'that a vyrgyne schulde not tarye loonge in opyn ne holde ne colloquyis in sueche placys' (51/1–3). Furthermore, one specific reference in the narrative makes even more explicit the identification between Mary and a Syon nun, not just any nun. In chapter 29, describing the risen Christ's first appearance to Mary, the author encourages the reader to imagine the scene:

> Beholdyth fyrste how the blyssyd lady syttyth alone in the same place þat oure lorde made hys laste sopyr inne, the whyche was in mount Syon for there ȝe maye thynke sche abode stylle aftyr sche was brought dethyr be seyint Ihon on goode frydaye at euyn tyl oure lorde apperyde to here there, alweye desyrynge the presence of here blyssyd sone wyth grettyr desyre thanne maye be seyde. (319/13–20)

For the nun sitting in Syon abbey reading the text, the reference to Mount Syon would have been an immediate point of identification, with the inference that if she, like Mary, desires the presence of the risen Christ, she too may experience it.[21] Moreover, Mary's importance for a Bridgittine nun is reinforced by the fact that the Syon liturgy, *The Mirror of Our Lady*, was translated from a service written in honour of Mary. As the translator writes in the prologue to this liturgical work:

> And for as muche as ye may se in this boke as in a myrroure, the praysynges and worthines of oure moste excellente lady therfore I name it. Oure ladyes myroure. Not that oure lady shulde se herselfe therin, but that ye shulde se her therin as in a myroure, and so be styred the more deuoutly to prayse her, & to knowe where ye fayle in her praysinges, and to amende: tyll ye may come there ye may se her face to face wythouten eny myrroure.[22]

But Mary's role as a model of behaviour is not just confined to nuns. As a wife and mother she offers another mode of bodily identification for female readers. All women, whatever their status, can identify with her. In chapter 10, when Mary and Joseph find Christ teaching the doctors in the temple in Jerusalem, Mary says to her son, 'Loo thy fadyr & I, sorowynge haue I softe the' (136/17–18). The author of the *Speculum* discusses how, in referring to Joseph before herself, Mary shows her awareness of the order of marriage. Through her humility she functions as a model for married women:

> & therfore be thys ensample of oure meke lady lett wymmen lerne to be meke & not to preferre hemselfe afore men in enythynge & namely sueche as haue hosebundys for oure lady ys a parfyth ensample to alle wymmen as oure lorde Ihesu cryste to alle men. (138/7–12)[23]

The imitation of Mary's behaviour is, however, most strongly advocated when she is a mourner at the Crucifixion. Whereas in the *Horologium* Mary speaks to the Disciple after the event, describing how she felt at the Crucifixion, in the *Speculum* Mary's sorrow is presented through the eyes of the author as part of the Passion narrative. In the *Horologium* the events leading up to the Crucifixion are all narrated from Christ's perspective, with no mention of Mary. But in the *Speculum* Mary's involvement is more extended as her reactions are described from the moment Christ leaves Jerusalem, bearing the Cross, to walk to Calvary. The events are effectively described through Mary's reactions to them which the reader is encouraged to imagine. For example, on first seeing Christ: 'ȝe maye thynke forsothe þat sche fylle downe in seyint Ihonys armys a suowne & mygthte nothyr stande ne speke to hym for passynge sorowe & heuynesse' (261/6–8). Not only an exemplary virgin, wife and mother, Mary is also presented, as in the *Horologium*, as the perfect reader of Christ's sufferings, identifying precisely with him at every moment. As his sufferings intensify, so too does her sorrow: 'And as ofte as hys paynys were encressyd, so ofte thynkyth wythoute eny dowte here heuynesse & sorowe were encressyd, & made more & more' (265/20–266/2). When Christ is hung on the Cross Mary's overwhelming sorrow is witnessed in her physical gestures which reflect Christ's: 'And thanne thynkyth how sche wepyth & waylyth & fallyth downe to the erthe for sorowe as half deed . . .' (270/2–3). Through her physical responses Mary thus demonstrates her ability to read and interpret Christ's suffering body.[24] She then functions as a model for the reader of the text.[25] Through reading Mary's reactions to Christ's sufferings, which are themselves a perfect reading of them, the nun reader learns to read Christ's body herself.[26] The author of the *Speculum*, having described to the reader what she should see as she reads, then draws a connection between this seeing and an appropriate emotional response:

> & / therfore wyth oure lady & seyint Ihon & othyr deuout folke þat were there hauyth inwardly pytee & compassyon of hym; for what deuout crystyn soule mygthte see hys lorde Ihesu cryste for hys euyrlastynge saluacyon in alle thys payne, & our lady so wepynge & waylynge & othyre deuout folke that were wyth here & not wepe wyth hem for pure pytee & compassyon. (262/4–11)

He takes this imaginative seeing one step further by encouraging the reader to imagine herself present at these scenes, emulating the behaviour of the mourners, specifically Mary. Having described how John and the women with Mary lament out of pity for both her and Christ, he then addresses the reader: '& so doeth ȝe wyth hem for ȝe muste thynke ȝowselfe in ȝoure ymagynacyon as thowgth ȝe were present wyth hem & one of hem' (261/11–13). Further on he states: 'Aftyr thys beholdyth also þat oure lady & seyint Ihon euangelyste & the deuout wymmen stondyn besyde the crosse of oure lorde wepynge & weylynge / for they see hym in so myche despyte & payne & so doeth ȝe wyth hem' (275/13–17). The reader's participation is pushed on to a higher level when the author encourages imagined interaction with

Mary. Describing Christ's journey to Calvary, the writer guides the reader to feel appropriate sorrow and to 'ymagynyth also what seruyse ȝe wolde haue doo to oure lady yf ȝe hadde be there present wyth hem' (263/18–19).[27]

Mary's suffering coexists with an understanding of the necessity of the Crucifixion and the promise of Resurrection. In this tension between sorrow and joy she functions as a model for the reader in a way that she does not in the *Horologium*, encouraging the nun to move towards a higher level of spiritual understanding. The author of the *Speculum* says of Mary at the Crucifixion that

> hyt was merueyle that sche mygthte lyue in alle þat sorowe saf þat the mygthte of god & the beleue þat sche hadde þat hyt was for the saluacyon of mankynde & also the hope þat sche hadde of hys resurreccyon for the feyth of holy chyrche abode þat tyme in here alone. (280/4–9)

On Holy Saturday the disciples have no hope of Christ's Resurrection, 'but oure lady alone, for in here abode the feyth of holy chyrche þat tyme' (307/9–11).[28] Through Mary, the reader of the *Speculum* thus learns both to identify with Christ's sufferings and to strive towards a glimpse of the divine plan.

In the *Horologium* Suso draws on many older writings, weaving them into his own material. Without exception all these texts are written by men – the Bible, the Desert Fathers, Augustine and Aquinas. The author of the *Speculum* also compiles much of his work from other sources. However, as well as drawing on the Bible and gospel commentaries by Nicholas of Lyra and Peter Comestor, he also consults 'sum reuelacyonys of approuyd wymmen' (9/20–10/1). In the course of the *Speculum* he refers to the writings of Bridget of Sweden, Catherine of Siena and Mechtild of Hackeborn and uses them as textual authorities. In so doing he orientates his work towards woman as reader.

Mechtild makes a fleeting appearance with the reference to her vision of the multitude of angels surrounding the tomb at Christ's resurrection drawn from her *Liber spiritualis gratiae*, translated into English in the Middle Ages as *The Booke of Gostly Grace*.[29] Catherine of Siena's *Dialogo* is consulted in chapter 3 of the *Speculum*, which relates the Annunciation, for a discussion on discerning spirits. The choice of Catherine as a textual authority is significant for two reasons. Firstly, the subject under discussion here – *discretio spirituum* – was one in which expertise was normally thought to lie with men.[30] Thus, by drawing on Catherine at this point in his text, the compiler of the *Speculum* grants her authority to speak on a topic normally out of bounds to women.[31] Secondly, her inclusion in the text reinforces the argument that the *Speculum* had a Bridgittine destination since the *Dialogo* was translated into Middle English in the early fifteenth century for the Syon nuns.[32]

The close connection between the choice of female textual authority and the destination of the *Speculum* continues with the use of Bridget of Sweden in the text. The Middle English author draws on her *Revelationes* to supplement the gospel accounts of Christ's life. Some of Bridget's material, specifically that concerning Christ's childhood, is communicated to her by Mary, who provides information about her son which is unknown to any man. Both Mary and Bridget are thus presented in the *Speculum* as authors, equivalent in status to the gospel writers. For example, in chapter 5 Mary is presented as the ultimate source of information for the evangelists. Referring to the shepherds' visit to the stable, the author notes, 'oure lady kepte wel alle in here herte, haply þat sche mygth the bettyr telle hyt to hem that schulde wryte hyt aftyrwarde' (82/16–19).[33] In chapter 11, which is translated from Book 6, chapter 58 of the *Revelationes*, Mary tells Bridget what Jesus did between the age of twelve and the time of his baptism.[34] In chapter 12 the author notes: 'Also oure lady tolde seyint Brygytte as hyt ys seyde in the fyrste chapetele of the viii boke of here reuelacyonys þat whenne sche noryischede hym he was so / fayre that hosoeuyre behelde hym he was confortyd of the sorowe of herte þat he hadde' (149/11–17).[35] However, it is not simply the information that Bridget provides that is important. Her mystical experience is primarily visionary, and she is thus privileged to see gospel scenes which she then describes in her text. Her manner of seeing, or beholding, is presented as having spiritual authority, and functions as a model for the reader who, throughout the *Speculum*, is invited by the author, using the verb 'biholden' – which covers both the physical action of seeing and spiritual contemplation[36] – to look upon the scenes he describes: 'Now thanne beholdyth deuoutly how the angil entryth in the forseyde cytee of Nazareth . . .' (40/1–2), and: '. . . thanne ȝe maye beholde how oure lorde stopyth downe & wrytyth wyth hys fyngyr in the erthe' (185/1–3). Having observed, the reader is encouraged to act, for example to feel compassion for the sight of Christ walking from Nazareth to the river Jordan to be baptized by John: 'Now thanne beholdyth hym wele & in ȝoure consyderacyon hauyth pytee & compassyon of hym how he goeth al that weye alone & merueylyth hys mekenesse & charytee' (148/11–15). As the author suggests in his prologue, seeing should be followed by action, imitation of what is seen. This will lead to spiritual rewards:

> & therfore hoso wole deuoutly & dylygently beholde oure lordys lyuynge & werkys & folow aftyr be hys powere as he byddyth hymself seyinge / thus: He þat seruyth me, lete hym folow me, & where I am there schal my seruaunt be; hosoeuyr do so he schal fynde in thys lyf grace, & aftyr thys lyf ioye wythoute ende ... (8/4–11)

Bridget's beholding is given authoritative status in the accounts of the Nativity and the Passion. In chapter 5 her description of her vision of Christ's birth, from Book 7, chapter 22 of the *Revelationes*, is reproduced in direct speech.[37] The author introduces her voice by noting that this scene was revealed 'more opynly' to Bridget, suggesting a superiority to the male-authored accounts of the Nativity (73/9). Bridget begins by describing what she saw: 'Whenne I was att oure lordys cracche in Bethleem I seygth a fayre mayde wyth chylde I clodyd in a whyte mantyl ...' (73/13–15). She sees all the preparations made by Joseph and Mary for the birth, including Mary laying out cloths on the stable floor on which to place the baby. The vision of the birth then follows:

> Whenne alle thys was thus aredy, thanne the vyrgyne knelyde downe wyth gret reuerence puttynge hereself to prayere, & forsothe sche helde vp here face to heuene I lefte vp to the estewarde. And thanne sche lefte vp here handys & eyen lokynge intently into heuenewarde, & sche stode as though sche hadde be lefte vp into the extasye or suownynge of contemplacyon filde wyth goostly suetnesse. And as sche stode so in prayere I seygth thanne þe chyld meuynge in here wombe & anone in a moment & the stroke of an eye sche brougth forth a sone of the whyche cam out so vnspekeable lyght & brygthnesse þat the sonne was not to be lykned therto ... (75/4–18)

Bridget does admit to not seeing everything, acknowledging that the birth happened so quickly, 'þat I mygth not perseyue ne dyscerne how or in what membyr sche browgth forth þe chylde' (76/4–6). However, she still provides many details about the spotless appearance of the newly born Christ, the immediate shrinking of Mary's womb and

Mary's wrapping Christ in swaddling clothes. At the end of the account the writer grants authority to this vision as a work of co-operation between Bridget and Mary which he encourages the reader to see in the same way as Bridget did:

> Thys ys seyint Brygytte ys reuelacyon how oure lady schewde here alle the manyr how sche bare oure lorde affermynge to here be reuelacyon also þat certaynely in the forseyde manyr sche brougth forth here blysful sone oure lorde Ihesu cryste & wyth so myche ioye & gladnesse of soule that sche felte no greuousnesse whenne he wente out of here body ne eny manyr sorowe;[38] the whyche ȝe maye thynke as thowgth ȝe were present & seygth hyt doo afore ȝow as sche dede. (79/2–13)

In chapter 22 Bridget's revelation of the Crucifixion is related. The author of the *Speculum* initially presents two versions of how Christ was nailed onto the Cross (horizontally and vertically), since the gospel writers do not specify exactly how Christ was crucified.[39] However, he grants greater authority to Bridget's version of Christ being nailed to an upright cross: 'Anothyr wyse ȝe may thynke hyt aftyr seyint Brygyttys reuelacyon & þat I holde sykyrer to lene to, & þat ȝe / maye thynke thus' (267/11–13).[40] Although, as the author notes, Bridget in her *Revelationes* 'tellyth hyt in here owen persone as sche seygth hyt doo' (267/16–17), he turns it into a meditation and addresses the reader, telling her how to see the scene according to the words Bridget has written: 'Beholdyth fyrste an hole I kytte out in þe mounte of Caluary & the crucyfyourys aredy as hyt ys wryte in the reuelacyon to doo creueltee ...' (267/13–16). He encourages her to see it as Bridget did: 'Now thanne beholdyth wyth the forseyde holy lady how the tormentorys fyx & make faste strongly the crosse in the forseyde hole ...' (267/19–268/2). There follows a long account of the Crucifixion in which Christ's physical sufferings are described in detail to the reader. Having been nailed to the cross, Christ's limbs were stretched out so 'þat alle the vaynys & synuys to braste' (269/5–6). When the crown of thorns was replaced on his head, it 'so strongly prykkyde hys reuerent heede þat hys eyen were fylde anone wyth flowynge blode, & hys erys were stoppyd, & hys face & berde were as hyt hadde be keueryd, & depte wyth that rede bloode' (269/9–13).[41] The amount of detail provided enables the reader to visualize the scene in her mind, making her party to Bridget's original vision. Throughout the passage the author switches between two verbs in his injunctions to the reader, telling her not only to 'beholden' the scene but also to 'thinken' it. Both terms cover a range of definitions and, in using them, the Middle English author encourages a variety of reactions from his reader, from seeing or imagining the scene to understanding it.[42] The action of seeing is not just confined to observation of an event or image; it also incorporates the possibility of insight or vision. By being constructed as an ideal viewer in the *Speculum*, Bridget functions as a model for the reader to emulate. By learning to see as she did, the reader will be brought closer to a sight of the truth.

In conclusion, the addition of the feminine pronoun to one of the quotations from Suso's *Horologium* by either a scribe or the compiler of the *Speculum* signals the way in which the Middle English work is orientated towards woman as reader. The priority accorded to women is substantiated in the figures of Mary and Bridget who, as models for the reader, empower women's spiritual status. Their modes of acting and seeing, if followed by the nun, will enable her to strive towards spiritual insights and understanding. However, despite the attention shown to woman as reader in the *Speculum*, men are not excluded from the text. As noted at the beginning of this discussion, the author frequently refers to both men and women. Women are not a special category with their own peculiar spirituality. Rather, they are presented as equal to men in spiritual experience, as is witnessed in the account of the Last Supper where the author anticipates the nun's anxiety about the effectiveness of receiving in one kind only, owing to her gender and non-clerical status, assuring her that her eucharistic experience is as valid as that of ordained males:

> Here as me semyth ȝe mygthte seye: Soth hyt ys þat prestys þat seye here massys resceyue oure lorde vndyr the forme of brede & wyne, but I þat am a woman & othyr commune peple whenne we be communyd we resceyue hym vndyr the forme of brede only & ȝytt I hope & beleue þat we resceyue oure lorde as wel as prestys þat resceyue hym vndyr bothe lyknesse. (214/16–215/1)

# Notes

[1] In A. Clark Bartlett, T. H. Bestul, J. Goebel and W. F. Pollard (eds.), *Vox Mystica: Essays on Medieval Mysticism in Honor of Professor Valerie M. Lagorio* (Cambridge, 1995), 137.

² The place of composition can be established from a Latin colophon at the end of the text which refers to the meadow of Bethlehem – 'Bethleem pratum' – since Sheen was the only Charterhouse dedicated to Jesus of Bethlehem (M. Sargent, 'Versions of the Life of Christ: Nicholas Love's *Mirror* and Related Works', *Poetica*, 42 (1994), 66). Elsewhere in her article Bartlett discusses the close pastoral friendship between a Syon nun, Joanna Sewell, and a monk from Sheen, James Grenehalgh ('a reasonable affection', 131–4). For further discussion of this relationship and of the textual practices of Grenehalgh see M. G. Sargent, *James Grenehalgh as Textual Critic*, 2 vols., Analecta Cartusiana 85 (Salzburg, 1984).

³ I. Johnson, 'The Late-Medieval Theory and Practice of Translation with Special Reference to Some Middle English Lives of Christ' (University of Bristol Ph.D. thesis, 1990), 364.

⁴ The two manuscripts of the *Speculum* are Cambridge University Library, MS Gg. I. 6 and the Foyle manuscript. The altered quotation comes in the Cambridge text.

⁵ Although Suso wrote his vernacular works primarily for nuns, in whose spiritual direction he was involved, the *Horologium*, being in Latin and dedicated to Hugo de Vaucemain, the Dominican Master General, is clearly intended for a male audience. On Suso's female audience see J. F. Hamburger, 'The Use of Images in the Pastoral Care of Nuns: The Case of Heinrich Suso and the Dominicans', *Art Bulletin*, 71 (1989), 20–46; C. W. Bynum, *Fragmentation and Redemption: Essays on Gender and the Human Body in Medieval Religion* (New York, 1992), 153.

⁶ J. Hogg (ed.), *The Speculum Devotorum of an Anonymous Carthusian of Sheen, Edited from the Manuscripts Cambridge University Library Gg. I. 6 and Foyle, with an Introduction and a Glossary*, 2 vols., Analecta Cartusiana 12–13 (Salzburg, 1973–4), 6/2–6. All references to the *Speculum* will be made to this edition and will be cited by page and line number in parentheses following the quotation.

⁷ Words in italics are translated from the *Horologium*.

⁸ P. Künzle (ed.), *Heinrich Seuses Horologium Sapientiae: Erste kritische Ausgabe unter Benützung der Vorarbeiten von Dominikus Planzer OP*, Spicilegium Friburgense: Texte zur Geschichte des kirchlichen Lebens 23 (Freiburg, 1977), 494/18–21. All quotations will be taken from this edition and will be cited by page and line number. 'Blessed is he who has seriously exerted himself to study it; because he will make progress in the contempt of the world and in the love of God, and will obtain an increase of all virtues and graces.' (All translations are my own.)

⁹ For other examples see 46/1, 47/1–2 and 53/20–55/14.

¹⁰ For other examples see 55/13–17, 57/12–16 and 60/16–20.

¹¹ On the structure of the *Speculum* see the author's comments in the prologue (1/16–20).

¹² For further discussion of the concept of *imitatio Christi* see K. Lochrie,

*Margery Kempe and Translations of the Flesh* (Philadelphia, 1991), 27–37.
13. 'It is indeed just that since we wretched ones are continuously comforted by her, that we also suffer with her in her torment.'
14. 'My soul was crucified through sorrow, my maternal heart was wounded, and all my bones were dying at the same time.'
15. 'O how hardened is the heart, which from its innermost parts does not feel pity for you. How wrongly dried up are the eyes, which seeing you weeping thus can in no wise shed tears. How cold the breast, which does not lament these things.'
16. 'My whole soul . . . kisses again and again your wounds spattered with blood . . .'
17. Suso, *Horologium*, 403/12–31.
18. Lochrie, *Margery Kempe*, 16.
19. In this he follows the author of the *Ancrene Wisse* who, as Renevey points out in his chapter in this volume, presents Mary as the model for all anchoresses (p. 202). Discussing silence, he notes, 'Our dear Lady St Mary, who ought to be the model for all women' (M. B. Salu (tr.), *The Ancrene Riwle*, Exeter Medieval English Texts and Studies (London, 1955; repr. Exeter, 1990), 33).
20. Johnson notes that the *Speculum* advocates '*compassio* (and *imitatio*) *Mariae* dealing with key events in the *vita* from Mary's point of view' ('Late-Medieval Theory', 335).
21. The two Syon locations are also noted by Johnson, 'Late-Medieval Theory', 364.
22. J. H. Blunt (ed.), *The Myroure of Our Lady*, EETS ES 19 (London, 1873), 4.
23. Elizabeth Scrope, who almost certainly owned the Foyle manuscript of the *Speculum*, was one such married woman reader. After the death of her husband – John, fourth Lord Scrope of Masham – she took vows and entered an unrecorded nunnery on 18 December 1455. Through her actions she thus emulates Mary as both wife and virgin. On Elizabeth Scrope see J. Hughes, *Pastors and Visionaries: Religion and Secular Life in Late Medieval Yorkshire* (Woodbridge, 1988), 123; A. I. Doyle, 'A Survey of the Origins and Circulation of Theological Writings in English in the 14th, 15th, and Early 16th Centuries with Special Consideration of the Part of the Clergy therein' (University of Cambridge Ph.D. thesis, 1954), I, 161; II, 267 n. 21. For Scrope's oath see J. Raine (ed.), *Testamenta Eboracensia: A Selection of Wills from the Registry at York*, *III*, SS 45 (Durham, 1865), 333.
24. For discussions of the medieval idea of Christ's suffering body as a book which requires reading and decoding see Lochrie, *Margery Kempe*, 167–8; V. Gillespie, 'Strange Images of Death: The Passion in Later Medieval English Devotional and Mystical Writing', in J. Hogg (ed.), *Zeit, Tod und Ewigkeit in der Renaissance Literatur*, III, Analecta Cartusiana 117 (Salzburg, 1987), 111–59.
25. Lochrie, in her fifth chapter, describes Mary as 'the primary reader of the

Crucifixion and the model for all subsequent mystical readings of the Christic body' (*Margery Kempe*, 177). She focuses in particular on the figure of Margery Kempe and argues that her reading of Christ's body, enacted in her hysterical weeping and physical gestures, is informed by accounts of Mary's behaviour at the Crucifixion (ibid., 167–202). On Kempe's empathetic response to Mary's feelings see also Renevey's discussion (p. 207).

[26] In Nicholas Love's *The Mirror of the Blessed Life of Jesus Christ*, a vernacular adaptation of Pseudo-Bonaventura's *Meditationes vitae Christi*, Mary's sorrow is also described as perfectly mirroring Christ's sufferings. For example when she sees how seriously wounded he is, she 'was also wondet in herte with a new wonde of sorowe' (M. Sargent (ed.), *Nicholas Love's Mirror of the Blessed Life of Jesus Christ: A Critical Edition Based on Cambridge University Library Additional MSS 6578 and 6686*, Garland Medieval Texts 18 (New York, 1992), 183/11–12). See similarly *Mirror* 178/17–19, 178/22, 183/13–15. However, unlike the author of the *Speculum*, Love does not explicitly invite the reader to respond to Mary's sorrow and imitate her behaviour.

[27] See similarly 66/9–13. Margery Kempe also participates in her visions. Meditating on Christ's death and burial she imagines herself going home with John and Mary, 'Than þe / creatur thowt, whan our Lady was comyn hom & was leyd down on a bed, þan sche mad for owr Lady a good cawdel and browt it hir to comfortyn hir' (S. B. Meech and H. E. Allen (eds.), *The Book of Margery Kempe*, EETS OS 212 (London, 1940; repr. 1961), 195/5–8). On Kempe's behaviour, see further Renevey's discussion and his argument that she 'inscribes her life into a history, sacred history, and into a particular story based upon the incidents of the Passion' (p. 198).

[28] Love makes the same point (*Mirror*, 193/5–10).

[29] For the reference in the *Speculum* see 316/11–17. For the reference in the Middle English translation of Mechtild see T. A. Halligan (ed.), *The Booke of Gostly Grace of Mechtild of Hackeborn*, Studies and Texts, Pontifical Institute of Mediaeval Studies 46 (Toronto, 1979), 181/2–5.

[30] Rosalynn Voaden points out that whereas generally women had the visions which required the discernment, the actual practice of discerning spirits was a male activity. R. Voaden, *God's Words, Women's Voices: The Discernment of Spirits in the Writings of Late-Medieval Women Visionaries* (York and Woodbridge, 1999), 48.

[31] Mc Govern-Mouron, in her essay in this volume, points out the similar case of the *Manere of Good Lyvyng* where, in a reversal of roles, the male writer of the text asks his female reader to instruct him and grants her the authority to expound Biblical verses (p. 92).

[32] For an edition of this text see P. Hodgson and G. M. Liegey (eds.), *The Orcherd of Syon*, EETS OS 258 (London, 1966). The material used in the *Speculum* comes from *Orchard*, part 4, ch. 1 (154–5).

[33] The same point is made in ch. 32 which narrates the Ascension. The author

describes how Mary, despite her desire to ascend to Heaven with her son, must remain on earth to comfort the disciples '*a also to the infor / mynge of the euangelystys of the incarnacyon. a the ʒougthe of oure lorde. for sche knewe þat best of alle othyre.*' Since Hogg's edition of the *Speculum* is incomplete, ending with ch. 29, I consulted an earlier edition for the final four chapters of the text; B. Wilsher (ed.), 'An Edition of *Speculum Devotorum*, a Fifteenth-Century English Meditation on the Life and Passion of Jesus Christ, with an Introduction and Notes' (University of London MA thesis, 1956), II, 378/1–3. Johnson also briefly discusses Mary's role as author in the *Speculum* ('Late-Medieval Theory', 364).

34  References to the *Revelationes* are noted by Wilsher in her notes for her edition of the *Speculum*. I confirmed them by consulting the Middle English translation of Bridget's text, R. Ellis (ed.), *The Liber Celestis of St. Bridget of Sweden: The Middle English Version in British Library MS Claudius Bi, together with a Life of the Saint from the Same Manuscript*, EETS OS 291 (Oxford, 1987), 446–7.

35  This material is actually from ch. 1 of Book 6 (not 8) of the *Revelationes* (Bridget, *Liber Celestis*, 397). Both manuscripts give Book 8 as the reference.

36  The MED includes amongst its definitions of 'biholden': to look (at), gaze (upon); observe, scrutinize; turn one's thoughts to something, consider, contemplate, see (in one's imagination) and understand; MED, 835–7.

37  See Bridget, *Liber Celestis*, 485–7.

38  To a greater extent than Bridget, the author of the *Speculum* negates the pain of childbirth. In so doing he sets Mary apart from other women. Whereas Bridget observes, 'And þe modir was nowþir chaungid in howe, ne sho had no seknes no febilnes of hir strengþe, and hir wombe was als smale as it was before sho had consaiued' (*Liber Celestis*, 486/36–8), in the *Speculum* an important addition is made to her words, 'Ne the vyrgyne thanne in that byrthe was chongyd in coloure or in sekenesse, ne ther fayklede eny bodyly strenthe in here *as hyt ys wonde to be in othyr wymmen whenne they brynge forth chylde* but that here wombe that was suolle wythdrew hytself into the fyrste state that hyt was in ere sche brought forth þe chylde' (78/9–17) (my italics). Despite the emphasis throughout the *Speculum* on Mary as the model for women, it seems that childbirth is one exception to the rule.

39  Love also refers to two versions of the Crucifixion but does not mention Bridget as a source for the upright Crucifixion, only noting, 'Þis is one maner of his crucifiyng after þe opinione of sume men' (*Mirror*, 177/23–4). This line is an addition by Love (*Mirror*, 292n.). The two ways of crucifying Christ upon the Cross are also mentioned in the *Meditationes* with no source given. This suggests that Bridget was drawing on a common tradition. See Johannis de Caulibus, *Meditaciones vite Christi: olim S. Bonauenturo attributae*, ed. M. Sallings-Taney, CCCM 153 (Turnhout, 1997), 271/20–272/52.

40  The Crucifixion account appears three times in the *Revelationes*: in Book 1,

ch. 10 (*Liber Celestis*, 17–22) and Book 4, ch. 70 (313–15), where Mary relates the episode to Bridget; and in Book 7, ch. 16 (479–81) where Bridget sees it for herself.

[41] See Julian of Norwich's similar description of 'the plentious bledeing of the hede' in M. Glasscoe (ed.), *A Revelation of Love*, 3rd rev. edn, Exeter Medieval English Texts and Studies (Exeter, 1993), 10.

[42] Among its definitions of 'thinken' the MED includes: to exercise the reason, to think about, to understand, to imagine, to have a vision, to remember; see MED, 507–21. For the definitions of 'beholden' see above n. 36.

# 4
# 'Listen to me, daughter, listen to a faithful counsel':[1] The *Liber de modo bene vivendi ad sororem*[2]

ANNE Mc GOVERN-MOURON

## Introduction

Omnes itaque nos Christi ancillae et in Christo filiae tuae . . . nunc a tua paternitate supplices postulamus . . . ut aliquam nobis regulam instituas, et scriptam dirigas quae feminarum sit propria et ex integro nostrae conversionis statum habitumque describat, quod nondum a Patribus sanctis actum esse conspeximus . . . Unam quippe nunc Regulam beati Benedicti apud Latinos feminae profitentur aeque ut viri. Quam sicut viris solummodo constat scriptam esse ita et ab ipsis tantum impleri posse tam subiectis pariter quam praelatis.[3]

IN these famous words, Heloise asked Abelard for a rule for herself and her companion-nuns living at the Paraclete. Heloise's situation is well known, but she is certainly not the only one to voice her concern about the lack of proper monastic regulations for the increasing number of *mulieres sanctae* in the twelfth and early thirteenth centuries.[4] As several studies have recently shown, the situation of religious women at this time was a thorny issue. The Cistercian attitude is a case in point, for it was not until a decree of the General Chapter in 1213 that the Cistercian Order finally addressed the woman question.[5]

It is hardly surprising, therefore, that Heloise's plea for specific and detailed instructions aimed at religious women was echoed elsewhere in Europe, in Latin and in the vernacular, as the following quotations demonstrate:

Iam pluribus annis exigis a me, soror, ut secundum modum vivendi quem arripuisti pro Christo, certam tibi formulam tradam, ad quam et mores tuos dirigere et necessaria religioni possis exercitia ordinare.[6]

Charissima mihi in Christo soror, diu est quod rogasti ut verba sanctae admonitionis scriberem tibi.[7]

ȝe mine leoue sustren habbeþ moni dei icrauet on me after riwle. Monie cunne riwlen beoð. ah twa beoð bimong alle þet ich chulle speoken of þurh ower bone wið godes grace.[8]

The first quotation comes from Aelred's *De institutione inclusarum*, the second from the *Liber de modo bene vivendi ad sororem*, or in its Middle English title, the *Manere of Good Lyvyng*, and the third from the *Ancrene Wisse*, Cambridge, Corpus Christi College, MS 402.[9] Unlike the *De institutione inclusarum*, the *Liber de modo bene vivendi ad sororem* does not appear to have been known by the *Ancrene Wisse*'s author, but both texts appear to share some features, although, in many ways, they are also quite different. The aim of this essay, therefore, is to introduce the barely known *Liber*, or *Manere of Good Lyvyng* in its unique Middle English version. It will examine questions of date, primary audience, authorship, contents and style, and more particularly, the *Liber*'s use of images.

## The *Liber*: Date

The *Liber* is a Latin devotional treatise written, like the *Ancrene Wisse*,[10] for a woman: a 'charissima . . . in Christo soror'/ 'wel beloved suster in Criste'.[11] As this text has not received much critical attention, and is only available in Migne's edition,[12] it is all the more difficult to date precisely, but it would seem that it was written in the second half of the twelfth century (or perhaps the very early thirteenth century). Of all the five Latin manuscripts of this text I have unearthed so far, the earliest is dated 1222, which gives a *terminus ante quem*.[13] It is undeniable that St Bernard had an influence on the *Liber*, probably mainly through his *Sermones super cantica canticorum*, which are generally thought to have been written between 1135 and 1153.[14] The existence of an Old French translation of the *Sermones*, dated approximately from the last quarter of the twelfth century, shows how quickly Bernard's text became well known.[15] Another important influence on the *Liber* is the *Expositio in regulam beati Augustini*, which was often attributed to

Hugh of St Victor, who died in 1141. Today, scholarly opinion no longer accepts this attribution; nonetheless, it is still believed that the *Expositio* dates from the first half of the twelfth century or mid-twelfth century.[16] Given the approximate dates of these two works, the *Liber* could hardly have been written before 1150. Internal evidence also suggests a date of composition within the second half of the twelfth century: the absence from the *Liber* of any of the usual series of seven (Seven Deadly Sins, Seven Virtues and so on) seems to confirm that this text antedates the Fourth Lateran Council of 1215.[17] It would appear, therefore, that the *Liber* was probably written after Aelred's *De institutione inclusarum* and before the *Ancrene Wisse*,[18] probably at some point between 1150 and 1222.

## The Recipient

It is not known who the female recipient of the *Liber* is, but textual evidence shows that she belongs to an order[19] and follows a Rule,[20] that she has never been married – she is frequently referred to as *virgo*[21] – and that she is still young when the *Liber* is sent to her.[22] One also learns that she comes from a wealthy and aristocratic milieu.[23] As far as her intellectual abilities are concerned, she is obviously *litterata*,[24] since the text is composed in Latin, but she is not another Eve of Wilton:[25] she is not told to read such works as St Augustine's *Confessionum libri tredecim* or Boethius' *De consolatione philosophiae*, and she is advised to 'venerare ... homines melioris scientiae, ac melioris vitae'.[26] Although the *Liber* is written in Latin and the *Ancrene Wisse* in the vernacular, the former does not demand a greater intellectual input from its reader.[27]

## Authorship

The *Manere of Good Lyvyng*, the Middle English version of the *Liber*, introduces the text thus: 'A devoute tretes of holy Saynt Bernard drawne out of Latyn into English callid the *Manere of Good Lyvyng*, which he sent unto his own suster: wherin is conteyned the Summe of every vertue necessary unto Cristis religion and holy conversacion.'[28] As this introduction intimates, the *Liber* is consistently attributed to St Bernard.[29] It is true that the abbot of Clairvaux had a sister, Humbelina, who experienced a spiritual conversion about 1122 and entered the monastery of Jully towards 1124. She later became prioress of Jully, where she died on 21 August 1141.[30] However, it is obvious on biographical grounds alone that St Bernard cannot be the *Liber*'s author.[31] It is common knowledge that Humbelina was married prior to her becoming her nun,[32] but the *Liber* makes it clear that its addressee is a virgin.[33] Hence the question: who wrote the *Liber*? The English Cistercian Thomas of Froidmont (or Thomas of Beverley)[34] has sometimes been put forward as a possible candidate, but this attribution has also been rejected.[35] To date, then, the *Liber* remains an anonymous work, but a new look at the text itself suggests that critics may not have been looking for its author in the right area.

It is possible on the evidence provided by the text to gain some knowledge about the author of the *Liber*. However, the man in question is hardly forthcoming about himself, for it is only in the last chapter of his work that he openly divulges some biographical information: 'Ego infelix peccavi in infantia, peccavi in pueritia, in adolescentia, in juventute; sed etiam, quod est gravius et periculosius, peccavi in senectute.'[36] He tells us only that he is an old man when he writes the *Liber*, but his frequent quotations from the Fathers of the Church[37] and his rhetorical style[38] suggest a 'highly trained cleric'.[39] The author's regular use of the first-person plural pronouns 'we' and 'us' intimates that, like his addressee, he is a member of a religious order.[40]

If the *Liber* author implies that he shares a religious vocation with the recipient, he does not disclose to which order he belongs, but on two occasions he alludes to the religious life thus: 'Specialia vota sunt, quando aliquis se *monachum* fieri, aut *canonicum*, aut *eremitam*, vel aliquid aliud promittit.'[41] And: 'Vere est mutatus habitu optimus religiosorum virorum, *videlicet monachorum, canonicorum, et santimonialium feminarum*, quando amplius componitur, ut placeat in conspectu populi, quam ut placeat in conspectu Dei.'[42] The presence of *canonicus* in these excerpts may not be a gratuitous repetition. Since the eleventh century saw the appearance of regular canons, monks and canons were often confused, but, as C. W. Bynum and G. Constable have shown, disputes and rivalries prove that they were also aware of their difference, a difference which the *Liber*'s author seems to acknowledge, since he distinguishes both categories twice.[43] As this differentiation would seem specially relevant to a member of a canonical order, the proposition that the *Liber*, like the *Ancrene Wisse*, may be the work of an Augustinian canon is worth pursuing.

Indeed, several other reasons may be adduced for claiming an

Augustinian origin for the *Liber*. It is striking, for example, that the text often mentions St Augustine but appears never to refer to St Benedict.[44] Furthermore, in the chapter where the author alludes to monks and canons for the second time, he also quotes directly from the Rule of St Augustine:

> Viri religiosi amplius debent gaudere in mensa pauperum fratrum, quam in mensa regum. Quare? Quia, *sicut ait Augustinus, melius est minus egere, quam plus habere*. Melius est pro Christo in monasterio paupertatem sustinere, quam in saeculo multas divitias habere.[45]

> *Melius est minus egere quam plus habere*. Melius est aliquid egestatis propter Dominum sustinere, quam superabundare.[46]

Another characteristic pointing towards an Augustinian authorship of the *Liber* is the extent to which it quotes the *Expositio in regulam beati Augustini* attributed to Hugh of St Victor, but without ever acknowledging its source. For example, chapter 47, entitled 'De murmuratione', begins thus:

> Hospitium cordis nostri per gratiam Dei sanctificatur, et per inhabitationem Spiritus sancti, quando intus est charitas, pax, bonitas, humilitas, concordia, mansuetudo et alia hujusmodi: hae sunt nostrae divitiae, scilicet boni mores, et virtutes. Sed si incipimus inter nos litigare, murmurare, contendere, statim ab his spiritualibus bonis vacui remanemus et nudi. Quare? Quia virtutes non possunt remanere cum vitiis. *Nam et modicum fermentum totam massam corrumpit.*[47]

This passage is taken from the *Expositio*'s eighth chapter 'De custodia rerum communium':

> Habitus cordis vestri sanctificatur per gratiam Dei; per inhabitationem Spiritus sancti, quando inest pax, charitas, bonitas, humilitas, patientia, concordia, mansuetudo, et alia hujus modi. Hae sunt nostrae interiores divitiae, scilicet boni mores et virtutes. Sed si incipimus inter nos contendere, murmurare et litigare, statim ab his spiritualibus bonis vacui remanemus. Virtutes enim cum vitiis remanere non possunt. *Nam fermentum modicum totam massam corrumpit* (I Cor. 5).[48]

Four more passages in this chapter of the *Liber* alone are taken from the *Expositio*[49] and further examples could be adduced, not to mention other Augustinian features such as the moderation which characterizes the whole of the *Liber*.[50] If one accepts the Augustinian origin of the *Liber*, this work and the *Ancrene Wisse* share a common origin and a similar audience.[51]

## The *Manere of Good Lyvyng*

Like the *Ancrene Wisse*, the *Liber* was translated into various European languages and remained in circulation well into the seventeenth century.[52] Although, in England, its appeal seems to have been limited, it was nonetheless translated at least once into Middle English, as the survival of this work in a single manuscript, under the title the *Manere of Good Lyvyng*, testifies. The manuscript in question is Oxford, Bodleian Library, MS Laud misc. 517.[53] The *Liber* was translated again into English and published in 1545, 1633 and 1886.[54]

On the whole, it seems that the *Manere of Good Lyvyng* translates the *Liber* quite closely. Some passages are abbreviated, but it is difficult to say whether this is due to the translator or to the Latin manuscript he translates.[55] One obvious addition, however, is the replacement of the chapter headings in the *Liber* by a brief argument in the *Manere of Good Lyvyng*. For example, chapter 7 in the *Liber* is simply entitled: 'De conversione'.[56] In the *Manere of Good Lyvyng* one reads instead: 'The vii exhortacon shewith what it ys to com to religion and of the disposicion of such þat entre religion and how they may shew charite to theyr naturall frendes.'[57] These arguments at the beginning of every chapter help the Middle English reader focus on what the translator feels to be its main points. Such additions are quite in the spirit of the *Liber*, which underlines in its chapter 'De lectione': 'valde nobis est necessaria lectio divina. Nam per lectionem discimus quid facere, quid cavere, quo tendere debeamus.'[58]

There is no clue to who the translator of the *Manere of Good Lyvyng* is, but the identity of the scribe is known: it is the Carthusian scribe William Darker (died at Sheen in 1513),[59] responsible for several other manuscripts.[60] Although there is no absolute certainty for whom William Darker copied MS Laud misc. 517, there is sufficient evidence to suggest that he did so for the Bridgittine house of Syon.[61] It is well known that William Darker copied at least one other manuscript for Elisabeth Gibbs, abbess of Syon Abbey.[62] It also seems that the *Liber* was one of St Bridget's favourite works: one Latin manuscript now in

Sweden bears the following inscription: 'Hunc librum qui intytulatur doctrina Bernardi ad sororem Beata mater nostra sancta Birgitta continuo in sinu suo ideo inter reliquias suas asseruandus est.'[63] If one accepts the *Liber*'s Augustinian origin, moreover, the latter would be of special interest to the monastery of Syon, since the Bridgittine Rule, the *Rule of St Saviour*, is a Bridgittine reading of the *Rule of St Augustine*.[64] A further possible clue is the systematic translation of gender-neutral expressions in the *Liber*, such as 'nemo', into 'man or woman' in the *Manere of Good Lyvyng*.[65] This would certainly be appropriate for a double foundation of monks and nuns.[66]

## Contents

As with the *Ancrene Wisse*, the *Liber* is a substantial treatise divided into seventy-three chapters of varying length. The text deals more or less equally with virtues (faith, hope, virginity, humility, etc.) vices (pride, envy, backbiting, etc.) and more external matters (the religious habit, possessions, singing, etc.).[67] When assessing the *Liber*'s contents, however, it is important to remember that the text is addressed to a member of a religious institution, a nun, who already follows a Rule and simply wishes for 'verba sanctae admonitionis'.[68] Contrary to Aelred's sister or to the *Ancrene Wisse*'s three addressees, the *Liber*'s sister has a Rule, and so does not require the same amount of guidance on external matters. This is not to say that these matters are never broached in the *Liber* but, when they are, their purpose is moral or spiritual, not primarily practical. Chapter 9, 'De habitu', for example, does not describe what kind of garments the nun is to wear, but what her mental attitude should be. It begins thus:

> Dominus noster Jesus Christus dicit in Evangelio: *Ecce qui mollibus vestiuntur in domibus regum sunt* (Matt. XI, 8). Mollia dicuntur vestimenta, quia mollem faciunt animum. Mollibus vestimentis delectatur regis curia: asperis vero et humilibus delectatur Christi Ecclesia. Talia debent esse vestimenta servorum et ancillarum Dei, in quibus nihil possit notari novitatis, nihil superfluitatis, nihil vanitatis, nihil quod pertineat ad superbiam, et ad vanam gloriam ... Soror charissima, ergo ornemus nosmetipsos spiritualibus ornamentis; scilicet charitate, humilitate, mansuetudine, obedientia et patientia. Haec sunt vestimenta quibus placere poterimus Jesu Christo coelesti sponso.[69]

The text clearly emphasizes that what the nun must strive for is her spiritual garments or, in other words, virtues.

In the version of the *Manere of Good Lyvyng* in MS Laud misc. 517, the shortest chapters occupy a couple of folios and the longest extend over ten folios.[70] Short chapters appear to be not much more than the basic contemplative point of view on a given topic,[71] but longer chapters often present interesting and persuasive developments.

## A Characteristic Chapter: 'De continentia'[72]

Chapter 22, 'De continentia', begins by the three states of life: marriage, widowhood and virginity, represented by the three numbers: thirty, sixty and a hundred.[73] As is traditional, the *Liber* favours virginity but, perhaps surprisingly, it also insists that physical incorruption in itself is insufficient and in some cases should be regarded as inferior to the two other states of marriage and widowhood:

> Chaste maryage ys good but the contynency of wydoes ys better and perfytte virgynyte ys best of all. Yit a meke widoue ys better than a proude virgyn. Better ys a widow mornyng for hyr synnes than a virgyn bostyng hyrself before men of hyr virginite. Better ys a wydow wepyng for hyr offencis and trespaces þan a virgyn exaltyng hyrself of hyr own meritis ... That virgyn þat dispyseth wydowes lyvyng chaste and servyng God, committeth pryde. Why? For better ys a meke synner than a prowde juste person. Therfor, reverent suster, dyspyse not þe women þat have forsake þe world, have had husbandis and bourn chyldren, for and ye dispyse them, ye shal be gretly to blame before God.[74]

The text later stresses that the sister must 'serve them [these widows] as a dowȝter'.[75] What is of particular interest in this extract is the unusual length to which the author goes to recognize the merits of marriage and widowhood. The strength of his position is also rhetorically reinforced by the triple repetition of 'better' and the crescendo: 'meke', 'mornyng for hyr synnes' and 'wepyng for hyr offencis and trespaces'.[76]

The chapter than turns to the question of children:

> My wel beloved suster in Cryst, saye not ye to yourself: oo I am as barayn as a drye stok, I am an unfrutefull tree bycause ye have no chyldren. For and yf ye love Cryst your spouse and drede hym as ye ouȝte, ye have vii chyldren. The fyrst chylde ys shamefastnes, [the] second pacience, the thyrd

sobernes, the iiiith temperance, the vth charite, the vith humylyte, the viith chastite. Loo, my reverent suster, by the grace of the Holy Goste ye have oute of an incorrupte wombe withoute payne brought furth to Cryst your spouse vii chyldren, so þat in yow may be veryfyed the sayeng of Scriptur: 'A baren woman hath borne vii chyldren', which my loved suster ye ouȝte to norysche, cherysche, and geve suk to, and to fede, comforte and chastyse. Norysch them with good maners, cherysche them in the bosom of fervent contemplacion, geve them the brestys of everelastyng swettnes, fede them with the love of hevenly gladnes, comforte them with the bred of lyfe, that ys with the worde of God, chastyse them with the scorge of the drede of God and cummaunde them þat they be not proude, nor lyght of conversacion, nor ynobedient, and þat they nevere goo from you, nor be oute of your presence.[77]

Again, the position exposed here is in no way new or controversial, for the notion of 'spiritual children' is an old one.[78] *Hali Meiðhad*, for instance, also tells its reader that the virgin should beget spiritual children: 'ȝef þe were leof streon, nim þe to him under hwam þu schalt i þi meiðhad temen dehtren ant sunen of gasteliche teames, þe neauer deie ne mahen ah schulen aa biuore þe pleien in heouene, þet beoð þe uertuz þet he streoneð in þe þurh his swete grace: as rihtwisnesse . . .'[79] What is more unusual in the *Liber*, however, is the way in which the author conveys his message. The tone of gentle encouragement which pervades this excerpt is markedly different from other prescriptive works and is quite typical of the text as a whole.[80] Kuczynski notes that 'for the most part [the *Liber*'s] theology is benign – his rhetoric soothes and encourages rather than chastises.'[81] This passage is also more personal in as much as the sister is directly addressed, the author choosing to use the second person rather than the more impersonal third person.[82] Again this holds true of the text in its entirety. Lastly, the text anchors its argument with a biblical quotation – 'A baren woman hath borne vii chyldren' – something that *Hali Meiðhad* could easily have done, but chooses not to. Instead, the latter compares the begetting of virtues to 'real' children who might be dying in infancy.[83] This particular use of biblical quotations rather than a reference to 'real' life is also a characteristic feature of the *Liber*.

'De continentia', then, ends in a personal devotional address which reminds the sister of the ultimate aim of her religious life:

> Ye knowe wele my loved suster þat vyrgyns have the principall place in heven and not unworthy, for they have utterly dispysed the world and therfor

they be hygh in heven to þe which he vouchsafe to bryng you in whos servyce he hath consecrated both your body and soule. Amen.[84]

Such an eschatological conclusion is a characteristic feature of most of the *Liber*'s seventy-three chapters, which regularly end in a similarly prayer-like fashion.

So far this essay has only examined questions of date, recipient, authorship and contents of the *Liber*; however, its style is also worthy of critical attention. Stylistically, this text shares many rhetorical devices with the *Ancrene Wisse*.[85] To mention but two such devices: both works use direct questions to intensify their instruction,[86] and both works rely heavily on various kinds of repetitions, of words, subjects or sounds.[87] It has been said that the *Ancrene Wisse*'s author 'is obviously heavily indebted to the mannered style of his biblical and patristic sources and he is also presumably under the influence of contemporary writers in Latin'.[88] The same claim could easily be maintained about the *Liber*. However, when one considers tropes and figures, the *Liber* and the *Ancrene Wisse* go their separate ways.

## A New Self in a New Place: the *Liber*'s Use of Images

The *Ancrene Wisse* has long been celebrated for its literary merits, most notably for its use of concrete and everyday images. The true anchoress, for example, is a silent one: 'nabbe ha nawt henne cunde. þe hen hwen ha haueð ileid; ne con bute cakelin.'[89] This preponderance of the concrete and the everyday has sometimes been explained in terms of its female audience. E. Robertson has remarked about the *Ancrene Wisse*: 'in the end, a man writing for women, and responding to his tradition's construction of them ... emphasize[s] the concrete, personal and contemporary, rather than the abstract and historical.'[90] Certainly the *Ancrene Wisse* is not a unique example, for other texts written for women also exhibit a decidedly concrete bent. The *Doctrina cordis* is another case in point.[91]

Whether or not one agrees with Robertson's view, this proposition is not tenable in relation to the *Liber*,[92] for such ordinary and everyday images are extremely rare in the latter.[93] This is not to suggest that the *Liber* favours a more abstract and philosophical approach; it is certainly full of images, but images of a different kind and, most importantly, images of a different origin. In its chapter about the grace of God, for instance, the *Liber* contends that only God is good:

> Homines vero sunt boni, et justi, et sancti, non per se, sed per gratiam Dei. Quod bene in Canticis canticorum sponsus Ecclesiae, scilicet Christus, designat, dicens: ego flos campi, et lilium convallium (Cantic. II, 1); quia odorem virtutis meae per universum mundum diffundo. Ego, inquit, sum flos campi, et lilium convallium: id est, Ego sum sanctitas, bonitas et justitia eorum qui cum humilitate in me confidunt: quia nullus eorum poterit esse sanctus, nec bonus sine me, sicut dixi in Evangelio, quia sine me nihil potestis facere (Joan. XV, 5). Ego sum flos campi, et lilium convallium. Sicut enim campus floribus adornatur et vernat, ita totus mundus fide Christi et notitia decoratur. Ego flos campi, et lilium convallium, quia illis hominibus amplius meam gratiam dono, qui non in sua bonitate, nec in suis meritis confidunt, se in me.[94]

This passage is typical of the many instances where images feature as part of the text. Such images are almost invariably taken from the Bible (often from the Song of Songs), and are generally accompanied by an allegorical interpretation. By functioning in this way, the *Liber* prevents its reader from connecting these images with the everyday world, no doubt sharing the *Cloud* author's concern that 'it nediþ greetly to haue moche warnes in vnderstonding of wordes þat ben spokyn to goostly entent, so þat þou conceyue hem not bodily, bot goostly, as þei ben mente.'[95] Even if the *Liber* resorts to images which ultimately refer to the everyday world (flowers in the above extract), this origin is transcended by grounding the images within a scriptural quotation: all links with the secular world are therefore severed.

Yet, this biblical use of images is not simply activated as an aid to achieve the required *contemptus mundi*, it also has a more positive function: to 'both replace and transfigure the world outside the cell'.[96] In the *Liber*, this process is at work implicitly throughout the text, but there is at least one interesting example where the reader is explicitly made to leave the physical world in order to enter this spiritual space:

> Nunc igitur audi quae dico, ausculta quae moneo. Melius est tibi in claustro sedere, quam plateas civitatis circuire: plus dilige in monasterio consistere, quam civitates videre. Melius est quiescere intra parietes monasterii, quam apparere in conspectu populi. Si te incluseris in claustro, amaberis a Christo. Quod bene in Canticis canticorum sponsus insinuat, cum sponsae loquitur, dicens: 'Hortus conclusus, soror mea, hortus conclusus, fons signatus

(Cantic. IV, 12)'. Unaquaeque sancta anima, hortus conclusus esse intelligitur, quia dum virtutes nutrit, flores gignit, virtutibus se nutrit, reficit: fructus quos germinat, eosdem custodit.[97]

The recipient is gently led out of the world and into the monastery, and once within she is guided out of her own physical self into the scriptural and allegorical garden of the Song of Songs.[98]

Replacing the secular world with its spiritual equivalent is all the more important given that the *Liber*'s recipient comes from an aristocratic milieu.[99] Great care, for instance, is given to replacing human relationships with spiritual ones. The text constantly refers to the nun's new family: she is repeatedly described as the author's sister, Christ's spouse and God's daughter.[100] If such a practice is not unique to the *Liber*, the frequency of these epithets is nonetheless higher than in similar texts.[101] The *Liber*'s addressee, therefore, appears to forge for herself a new and spiritual identity. This new self is perhaps most obvious when the roles of instructor and instructee are reversed and the 'brother/author' asks the sister:

> Sponsa Christi, etiam rogo, ut aliquid nobis de amore coelestis sponsi tui dicas. 'Fasciculus myrrhae dilectus meus mihi, inter ubera mea commorabitur (Cantic. I, 12).' Dic ergo charissima planius, ut ea quae dicis, intelligamus. 'Fasciculus myrrhae dilectus meus mihi, inter ubera mea commorabitur.' Locus cordis est inter ubera, hoc est, inter mammillas: ergo 'dilectus meus inter ubera mea commorabitur'; id est, memoria, dilectio, et amor Jesu Christi sponsi mei, semper erit inter mammillas meas, hoc est, in corde meo. Et sive in prosperis, sive in adversis semper ad memoriam reducam omnia bona quae mihi tribuit: quia dilexit me, et mortuus est pro me: atque ascendit ad coelos, et ut ad eum perveniam, quotidie vocat me dicens, 'Veni de Libano, sponsa, veni, coronaberis (Cantic. IV, 8)'.[102]

In this remarkable passage, the sister not only uses scriptural images herself, she has also achieved a transcendental metamorphosis: she *is* the Bride of Christ, for it is no longer possible to differentiate her voice from the voice of the Bride of the Song of Songs.[103]

## Conclusion

The *Liber* seems to have been written in the late twelfth or very early thirteenth century by a cleric who knew St Augustine's *Rule* and the *Expositio* once attributed to Hugh of St Victor quite well and who was also familiar with the work of St Bernard. At the moment, it is still impossible to say to what Augustinian family this anonymous writer might have belonged, nor is it possible to discover the identity of his recipient, beyond the bare fact that she must have been an aristocratic nun. The contents of the *Liber* are in no way controversial and offer an examination of the kinds of subjects that one expects from such a devotional work. These are also presented in the rhetorical style typical of clerical authorship. Nevertheless, if not original in its parts, the *Liber* is certainly unique as a whole: it is the product of a single and gentle mind who declares himself: 'sub mensa Patrum micas collegi, et si non ut debui, tamen ut potui, quas in hoc libro tuae sanctitati repraesento.'[104]

The twelfth and thirteenth centuries saw great numbers of women attracted to the religious life. If male institutions, such as the new religious orders, often regarded them with a certain suspicion and were reluctant to take charge of their spiritual and practical needs, nonetheless, some individual members were prepared to look after their spiritual sisters to the best of their abilities. Their singular efforts can still be traced today in the survival of the works that were written for a specifically female audience. Abelard's letters to Heloise, Aelred's *De institutione inclusarum* and the *Ancrene Wisse* are well-known instances of such works. Although much still remains unknown about the *Liber*, this text should find its place alongside the *De institutione* and the *Ancrene Wisse*, for it is a most interesting and valid witness to female religious life in the twelfth and thirteenth centuries.

## Appendix: Chapter Headings of the *Liber de modo bene vivendi ad sororem*[105]

*Praefatio.*
1. *De fide.*
2. *De spe.*
3. *De gratia Dei.*
4. *De timore Dei.*
5. *De charitate.*
6. *De primordiis conversorum.*
7. *De conversione.*
8. *De contemptu mundi.*
9. *De habitu.*
10. *De compunctione.*
11. *De tristitia.*
12. *De dilectione Dei.*
13. *De dilectione proximi.*
14. *De compassione.*
15. *De misericordia.*
16. *De exemplis sanctorum.*

17. *De contentione.*
18. *De disciplina.*
19. *De obedientia.*
20. *De perseverantia.*
21. *De virginitate.*
22. *De continentia.*
23. *De fornicatione.*
24. *De abstinentia.*
25. *De ebrietate.*
26. *De peccato.*
27. *De confessione peccatorum et poenitentia.*
28. *De communione.*
29. *De cogitatione.*
30. *De silentio.*
31. *De mendacio.*
32. *De perjurio.*
33. *De detractione.*
34. *De invidia.*
35. *De ira.*
36. *De odio.*
37. *De superbia.*
38. *De jactantia.*
39. *De humilitate.*
40. *De patientia.*
41. *De concordia.*
42. *De tolerantia.*
43. *De infirmitate.*
44. *De avaritia.*
45. *De cupiditate.*
46. *De paupertate.*
47. *De murmuratione.*
48. *De proprio.*
49. *De oratione.*
50. *De lectione.*
51. *De operatione.*
52. *De psalmis et hymnis.*
53. *De activa et contemplativa vita.*
54. *De curiositate.*
55. *De vigilantia.*
56. *De prudentia.*
57. *De fuga mulierum saecularium.*
58. *De cavendo virorum consortio.*
59. *De fugienda societate juvenum.*
60. *De vitando pravorum consortio.*
61. *De litteris vel munusculis clanculum on acceptandis.*
62. *De votis Deo reddendis.*
63. *De fine et scopo sui status semper considerando.*
64. *De studio placendi hominibus per pulchritudinem cavendo.*
65. *De risu immoderato fugiendo.*
66. *De non vagando foras.*
67. *De tentatione.*
68. *De somniis.*
69. *De brevitate vitae.*
70. *De morte.*
71. *De judicio.*
72. *Epilogus.*
73. *Sororis pro se intercessionem apud Deum rogat.*

## Notes

[1] B. S. James (tr.), *The Letters of St Bernard of Clairvaux* (Phoenix Mill, Gloucestershire, 1953; repr. 1998), letter 118, 180. 'Audi, me filia fidele audi consilium' (St Bernard of Clairvaux, *Epistolae*, ed. J. Leclercq and H. Rochais, 2 vols. (Rome, 1974–7), I, letter 115, 295).

[2] I would like to thank Dr Bella Millett for having read a draft of this chapter and for her many useful suggestions.

[3] J. T. Muckle, 'The Letter of Heloise on Religious Life and Abelard's First Reply', *Mediaeval Studies*, 17 (1955), 240–81 (242). 'All we handmaids of Christ, who are your daughters in Christ, come as suppliants to demand of your paternal interest . . . that you will prescribe some Rule for us and write it down, a Rule which shall be suitable for women, and also describe fully the manner and habit of our way of life, which we find was never done by the holy Fathers . . . At present the one Rule of St Benedict is professed in the Latin Church by women equally with men, although, as it was clearly written for men alone, it can only be fully obeyed by men, whether subordinates or superiors' (B. Radice (tr.), *The Letters of Abelard and Heloise* (London, 1974; repr. 1981), 160).

[4] The situation of religious women may have been particularly difficult in the twelfth and thirteenth centuries, but their difficulties were not restricted to this period. St Jerome, St Augustine and Caesarius of Arles had already written specifically for female religious, and the women question continued to arouse considerable attention in the fourteenth and fifteenth centuries. Richard Rolle and Walter Hilton in England, and Jean Gerson and Pierre of Luxembourg (fourteenth-century bishop and cardinal) on the Continent also address this issue.

[5] See S. Thompson, *Women Religious* (Oxford, 1991; repr. 1996), 94. The belatedness of the Cistercians' willingness to deal with religious women is clearly obvious when one considers that 1213 is also the year of the famous beguine Marie d'Oignies's death. See Jacques de Vitry, *The Life of Marie d'Oignies*, tr. M. H. King, 2nd edn (Toronto, 1989), 7. The women question, therefore, whether in relation to enclosed nuns, anchoresses or beguines, was an old problem by 1213.

[6] Aelred de Rievaulx, 'La vie de recluse', in C. Dumont (ed. and tr.), *La Vie de recluse, la prière pastorale*, SC 76 (Paris, 1961), 42–168 (42). 'For many years now, my sister, you have been asking me for a rule to guide you in the life you have embraced for the sake of Christ, to provide spiritual directives and formulate the basic practices of religious life.' Aelred of Rievaulx, 'Rule of Life for a Recluse', in M. P. Macpherson (tr.) and M. B. Pennington Knowles (ed.), *Treatises and Pastoral Prayer* (Kalamazoo, 1971; repr. 1995), 41–102 (43).

[7] *Liber de modo bene vivendi ad sororem*, PL 184. 1199–1306 (1199A),

henceforth abbreviated *Liber*. 'My wel beloved suster in Criste, ye have long desired þat I wold wryte som tretes of holy doctryne unto yowe' (The *Manere of Good Lyvyng*, Oxford, Bodleian Library, MS Laud misc. 517, fo. 1$^r$), henceforth abbreviated *Manere*. I am working on an edition of *Manere* to be published by Analecta Cartusiana.

[8] J. R. R. Tolkien (ed.), *The English Text of the Ancrene Riwle: Ancrene Wisse, edited from MS Corpus Christi College, Cambridge 402*, EETS OS 249 (London, 1962), 5/11–15. 'You, my dear sisters, have often and earnestly asked me for a rule. There are many kinds of rules, but I shall speak here of two out of all of them, because of your request, and with the help of God's grace.' M. B. Salu (tr.), *The Ancrene Riwle: The Corpus MS: Ancrene Wisse*, Exeter Medieval English Texts and Studies (London, 1955; repr. Exeter, 1990), 1.

[9] The *Ancrene Wisse*'s other manuscripts which preserve the prologue usually have a very similar, if not identical, quotation. The influence of the *De institutione inclusarum* on the *Ancrene Wisse* is well documented and will not be discussed here (see Aelred of Rievaulx, *De institutione inclusarum*, ed. J. Ayto and A. Barratt, EETS 287 (London, 1984), xxxviii–xliii).

[10] For the *Ancrene Wisse*'s audience, see B. Millett, '*Ancrene Wisse* and the Book of Hours', p. 21 in this volume.

[11] *Liber*, 1199A; *Manere*, fo. 1$^r$.

[12] M. P. Kuczynski, 'The Pseudo-Bernardine *Liber de modo bene vivendi ad sororem* and its Middle English Translation', in *Prophetic Song* (Philadelphia, 1995), 88–100, is the only critical study which devotes a few pages to the *Liber* and *Manere*.

[13] See J. Lopes de Toro et al., *Inventorio general de manuscritos de la biblioteca nacional*, 2 vols. (Madrid, 1956) II, MS 871, 480–481. The other manuscripts of the *Liber* that I have unearthed so far are Uppsala, University Library, MS C 240 (1300–50) and MS C 253 (1400–50); see M. Anderson-Schmidt and M. Hedlund, *Mittelalterliche Handschriften der Universitätsbibliothek Uppsala, Katalog über die C Sammlung*, 7 vols. (Uppsala, 1988–95), III, 150–1, 171–2; Padua, Bibl. Univ., MS 990 (1433) and Padua, Bibl. Univ., MS 2146 (fifteenth century); see J. Leclercq, 'Manuscrits cisterciens dans des bibliothèques d'Italie', *Analecta Sacri Ordinis Cisterciensis*, 10 (1954), 302–7 (305–6).

[14] See J. Leclercq, 'Les étapes de la rédaction', in *Recueil d'études sur Saint Bernard et ses écrits*, 5 vols. (Rome, 1962–92), I, 213–44.

[15] See S. Gregory (ed.), *La traduction en prose française du 12è siècle des Sermones in Cantica de Saint Bernard* (Amsterdam, 1994), xii.

[16] See D. Jones, *An Early Witness to the Nature of the Canonical Order in the Twelfth Century: A Study in the Life and Writings of Adam Scot, with Particular Reference to His Understanding of the Rule of St Augustine*, Analecta Cartusiana 151 (Salzburg, 1999), 7; see also C. W. Bynum, *Docere verbo et exemplo: An Aspect of Twelfth-Century Spirituality* (Missoula, 1979), 11.

[17] The Fourth Lateran Council put new emphasis on confession and penance

and thus initiated a plethora of devotional works in Latin and the vernacular which listed and examined the Seven Deadly Sins, the Seven Virtues, the Seven Sacraments, the Seven Works of Mercy, the Ten Commandments and other such series. There are no such lists in the *Liber*, nor is there much emphasis on confession and penance (the *Liber*'s chapter on confession incorporates an example of how the sister must confess, but does not do so in the more common way of acknowledging sins in each of these categories (see *Liber*, 1247D–1251C; *Manere*, fos. 81ᵛ–87ʳ)).

[18] The *De institutione inclusarum* is dated c. 1160–2 (see Macpherson and Knowles, *Treatises and Pastoral Prayer*, xi. For the *Ancrene Wisse*, see Millett, '*Ancrene Wisse* and the Book of Hours', p. 25–6.

[19] She is told: 'ut habitum Ordinis bonis ornes moribus' (*Liber*, 1216A), '[to] apparell the habyte of *your order* with good maners' (*Manere*, fo. 30ʳ); and later: 'non venisti ad claustrum, ut in vestimentis pretiosis resplendeas' (*Liber*, 1230C), 'ye came not to the *cloyster* to be gayly sen in preciouse clothyng' (*Manere*, fo. 53ᵛ) (my italics).

[20] The sister is advised: 'perfecte *preaceptis Regulae* adhaeseris' (*Liber*, 1297D), '[to] cleve parfitly to *your rewle*' (*Manere*, fo. 160ʳ) (my italics).

[21] She is addressed as 'honesta virgo' (*Liber*, 1203A, 1218B) or 'honestissima virgo' (*Liber* 1206C, 1208C–D), 'venerabilis virgo' (*Liber*, 1214B), 'virgo venerabilis' (*Liber*, 1215D) and so on.

[22] She is told: 'servias eis [honestis feminis], ut diligas eas quasi matres . . . [et] ideo debes eis servire quasi filia' (*Liber*, 1240B), '[to] serve [married women] and love them as moders . . . [and] to serve them as a dowȝter' (*Manere*, fo. 69ᵛ).

[23] In the chapter on pride, one reads: 'moneo te etiam . . . ut plus gaudeas de societate Angelorum et ancillarum Dei, quam de nobilitate generis tui. Rogo te . . . ut magis exsultes de societate pauperum virginum, quam de tuorum nobilitate parentum divitum' (*Liber*, 1259A), 'I counseyle youe . . . þat ye be more gladde of þe company of good aungellis and of the maydens of God, than of your noble byrth. I pray you to joye more of the company of poore virgins, than of the noblenes of your ryche frendis' (*Manere*, fo. 98ᵛ).

[24] For an account of nuns' familiarity with Latin, see D. N. Bell, *What Nuns Read* (Kalamazoo, 1995), 57–96.

[25] See B. Millett, 'Women in No Man's Land: English Recluses and the Development of Vernacular Literature in the Twelfth and Thirteenth Centuries', in C. M. Meale (ed.), *Women and Literature in Britain 1150–1500* (Cambridge, 1993), 86–103 (88). Her command of Latin is a further confirmation of her noble background.

[26] *Liber*, 1235A. 'Honour all that be better lerned and better in lyfe than ye be' (*Manere*, fos. 60ᵛ–61ʳ). Significantly, the *Liber*'s chapter on reading does not mention any work, and it strictly regards reading as a means to acquire good living: 'valde nobis est necessaria lectio divina. Nam per lectionem discimus quid facere, quid cavere, quo tendere debeamus . . . Per lectionem

sensus et intellectus augentur. Lectio nos ad orationem instruit et ad operationem, lectio nos informat ad activam et contemplativam vitam . . . lectio et oratio sunt arma quibus diabolus expugnatur; haec sunt instrumenta quibus aeterna beatitudo acquiritur' (*Liber*, 1272B–C). 'Very necessary ys to us godly redyng, for by redyng we lern what we ouȝt to doo: what to flye, whyther to goo . . . By redyng, knowlege and undurstandyng be increed. Redyng techyth us to praye and to werke. Redyng infourmeth to þe actyve and contemplatyve lyves . . . Redyng and prayer be wepyns that the devyl ys overecom with. Thes be instrumentis that heven ys com by' (*Manere*, fos. 120$^{r-v}$).

[27] The *Liber* is written in Latin, but does not use a specialized vocabulary, and the Latin is fairly simple. In addition to this, at least one of the Latin manuscripts of the text is written in a clear hand with relatively few abbreviations (see Uppsala, University Library, MS C 240, in Andersson-Schmidt and Hedlund, *Mittelalterliche Handschriften*, III, 150–1). I have not been able to examine any of the other manuscripts.

[28] *Manere*, fo. 1$^r$.

[29] This is still the case in printed versions of the text. The 1633 English translation has the following inscription before the Preface: 'A Rule of Good Life: Written by the Mellifluous Doctour S. Bernard (Monke and Abbot of the holie Order of S. Ben[net]) especially for Virgins and other Religious woemen . . .' St Bernard, *A Rule of Good Life 1633*, ed. D. M. Rogers, English Recusant Literature 79 (Menston, 1971), title page of the facsimile.

[30] See S. Thompson, 'The problem of the Cistercian Nuns in the Twelfth and Early Thirteenth Centuries', in D. Baker (ed.), *Medieval Women* (Oxford, 1978), 227–52 (229–30); see also Jean de la Croix Bouton, 'Saint Bernard et les Moniales', in Association Bourguignonne des Sociétés Savantes, *Mélanges Saint Bernard* (Dijon, 1953), 225–46 (228–30).

[31] St Bernard's seventeenth-century editor, Mabillon, already rejects the *Liber*'s attribution to St Bernard. See J. Mabillon, *Sancti Bernardi, Abbatis primi Clarae-vallensis opera omnia*, 2 vols. (Paris, 1690), II, cols. 815–16.

[32] Dimier mentions that the marriage took place in 1119. See R. P. M. A. Dimier, 'Saint Bernard et le recrutement de Clairvaux', *Revue Mabillon*, 42 (1952), 17–30, 56–78 (22).

[33] Migne simply repeats Mabillon's remark: 'Sequens Tractatus nec Bernardo convenit, nec ejus sorori Humbelinae, quae conjugata fuit in saeculo, antequam vitam monasticam profiteretur . . .' (*Liber*, 1199–1200).

[34] Thomas was born in Beverley (Yorkshire) around the middle of the twelfth century. Among his works, he wrote a *Vita* of Thomas Becket and he may have followed the latter into exile in France. He took the Cistercian habit in Froidmont after the archbishop's murder sometime in or after 1174.

[35] For the attribution to Thomas of Froidmont, see F. Cavallera, 'Bernard Saint', DS, I, 1454–1502 (1500); see, also, P. Glorieux, *Pour revaloriser Migne* (Lille, 1952), 74; Andersson-Schmidt and Hedlund, *Mittelalterliche*

*Handschriften*, III, 150–1, 171–2. For an argument against this attribution, see E. Mikkers, 'Een onuitgegeven brief van Thomas van Beverley, monnik van Froidmont', *Cîteaux in de Nederlanden*, 7 (1956), 245–63 (248); see also P. G. Schmidt, '*Peregrinatio periculosa*: Thomas von Froidmont über die Jerusalemfahrten seiner Schwester Margareta', in W. Maaz et al. (eds.), *Kontinuität und Wandel: Lateinische Poesie von Naevius bis Baudelaire* (Hildesheim, 1986), 461–71 (462–3); R. Sharpe, *A Handlist of the Latin Writers of Great Britain and Ireland before 1540* (Turnhout, 1997), 641–2.

[36] *Liber*, 1306A. 'I, ungracyous, offended in my chyldehode, I synned in my youthe, after I was of lawfull age and in my manhode, and þat ys more grevous and perylous, I have synned in myn age' (*Manere*, fo. 174$^r$).

[37] See chs. 7, 9, 18, 20, 21, 22 and so on. Although there is no obvious reason to doubt the authorship of these quotations, Migne only rarely provides references for them.

[38] For example, in his article 'The Rhetoric of *Ancrene Wisse*', T. P. Dolan mentions five methods of amplification used in the *Ancrene Wisse*; most if not all of them can also be found in the *Liber*. See T. P. Dolan, 'The Rhetoric of *Ancrene Wisse*', in H. Phillips (ed.), *Langland, the Mystics and the Medieval English Religious Tradition* (Cambridge, 1990), 203–13.

[39] E. J. Dobson, *The Origins of* Ancrene Wisse (Oxford, 1976), 6. The *Liber*'s author is also aware of the new twelfth-century interest in the rational faculty. In his discussion of faith he says: 'fides nequaquam vi extorquetur, sed exemplis atque *ratione* suadetur' (*Liber*, 1200A). '[Faith] is not hadd by compulsion, but perswadid by examples and *reson*' (*Manere*, fo. 2$^v$) (my italics).

[40] Latin writers often use a first-person plural pronoun even when they are referring only to themselves. This does not seem to be the case, however, in the *Liber*. In the first and the last chapters of the text, which are more personal, he prefers the first-person singular pronoun and, on other occasions, he also clearly indicates by his use of the plural pronoun that he refers to the recipient as well as himself. In ch. 3, for instance, he says: '*nolo* etiam te lateat, quod sine gratia Dei praeveniente, comitante, et cooperante, nihil boni *possumus* facere' (*Liber*, 1203A). '*I* wold ye shuld knowe *we* can doo no good thyng withoute þe grace of God preventyng *us*, beeng and perseveryng with *us*' (*Manere*, fo. 6$^r$) (my italics). Clerical status is not always at odds with monastical status. Regular canons sometimes see themselves as 'clerics'. See C. W. Bynum, 'The Spirituality of Regular Canons in the Twelfth Century: A New Approach', *Medievalia et Humanistica*, 4 (1973), 3–24 (17).

[41] *Liber*, 1292A. 'Speciall vowes be when a person promyseth to be *a monke, or channon, or heremyte* or eny such oþere' (*Manere*, fo. 151$^v$) (my italics).

[42] *Liber*, 1296D. 'Veryly the noble habite of religious persons ys chaunged as *of monkis, chanons, and religyous women* when it ys made more forto please in the sight of peple than in the sight of God' (*Manere*, fos. 158$^{r-v}$) (my

italics). There is yet another occurrence of *canonicus* in the text, but within a quotation: 'Soror in Christo dilecta mihi, audi sententiam beati Isidori: "Multi canonicorum, monachorum, sanctimonialium feminarum prae amore suorum parentum involvuntur terrenis curis . . ."' (*Liber*, 1211C–D). 'My loved suster in Cryst, here what holy Isider sayth: "Ther be many religious persons of chanons, monkys and religiouse wemen þat for þe love of theyr frendis be wrapped in worldly besynes . . ."' (*Manere*, fo. 22ᵛ).

[43] See G. Constable, *The Reformation of the Twelfth Century* (Cambridge, 1996), 44–87; see also, C. W. Bynum, 'The Spirituality of Regular Canons in the Twelfth Century', in *Jesus as Mother* (London, 1982; repr. 1984), 22–58.

[44] This absence of any mention of St Benedict is particularly striking in ch. 19 'De obedientia', since obedience is a fundamental concept for St Benedict. The *Liber*'s 'De obedientia' repeatedly insists on the nun's duty to obey her prelate, abbess or prioress but, contrary to what one may expect, it does not mention St Benedict. This is all the more strange seeing that St Bernard bases his own treatise, *De gradibus humilitatis et superbiae*, on Benedict's degrees of humility (see St Bernard, 'On the Steps of Humility and Pride', in G. R. Evans (tr.), *Bernard of Clairvaux: Selected Works* (New York, 1987), 99–143). St Bernard's treatise was extensively circulated and it is unlikely that this work was not known to the *Liber*'s author.

[45] *Liber*, 1297B (my italics). 'Religyous persons ouȝt to be more glad at the table of þeir pore brethern or sustern than at the kynges borde. Why? For, as Seynt Austen sayth: it ys better to lacke than to have to mych. Hit ys bettere to suffer poverte in religyon for Crystis sake than to have grete ryches in þe world' (*Manere*, fo. 159ʳ).

[46] *Expositio in regulam beati Augustini*, PL 176. 881–924 (896C–D), henceforth abbreviated *Expositio*. 'The glose seyth: it is better to suffer sum nede for Goddis sake than to have superhabundaunce of wordly pleasures' (Oxford, Bodleian Library, MS Bodley 255, fo. 15ᵛ), henceforth referred to as Bodley 255. This Middle English translation of the *Expositio in regulam beati Augustini* was made for the Dominican nuns of Barking (see Bell, *What Nuns Read*, 131–2). I am preparing an edition of this text for future publication.

[47] *Liber*, 1268C. 'The place of our hart by the grace of God and the presence of þe Holy Goste ys halowed and sanctifyed when ther ys withyn charyte, pees, goodnes, humylite, pacience, concorde, gentylnes with oþere such: these be our rycches, good maners and vertues. But when we begyn among us to brawle, to gruge, to stryve, anone we caste of thes spiritual vertues and remayne naked from all goodnes. Why? For vertues may not abyde with vyce. "A lytel sour dough or levyn corruptyth an hole bache"' (*Manere*, fos. 114ʳ⁻ᵛ).

[48] *Expositio*, 905D. 'The habite of our soule ys santyfyed by the grace of God, by the inhabitacion of the Holy Goste, whate tyme that in our hert is charyte,

peace, goddnesse, humylite, pacyence, concorde, mekenes and suche other. Thease be our inwarde riches, that is to say goode maners and vertues. But, if we begyn amonges ourselfe to make debate to grouge and stryve, anone we be voide and distitude from theas seid spirituall vertues. Vertues may not abyde with vices, for it is a commen sayeng: *Fermentum modicum totam massam perdit* (I Cor. 5), a litell sorowe dowghe saveryth all the batche' (Bodley 255, fo. 24ʳ).

⁴⁹ *Liber*, 1268D and *Expositio*, 906A (the *Liber* has here a quotation from St Gregory and the *Expositio* a similar quotation from the Scriptures); *Liber*, 1268D and *Expositio*, 911C; *Liber*, 1269A and *Expositio*, 911C; *Liber*, 1269B and *Expositio*, 911C.

⁵⁰ See below, 86–7.

⁵¹ For the *Ancrene Wisse*'s Augustinian, probably Dominican origin, see Millett, '*Ancrene Wisse* and the Book of Hours', 26–8. It has to be noted that a closer look also reveals substantial differences between the *Liber* and the *Ancrene Wisse*. First, in all likelihood, the *Liber* is produced earlier and on the Continent, the *Ancrene Wisse* in England. Secondly, the *Liber* is written in Latin and for an aristocratic audience, the *Ancrene Wisse* in the vernacular and for three gentlewomen. Thirdly, contrary to the *Ancrene Wisse*, the *Liber* does not purport to be a rule, but simply exhortations.

⁵² See L. Janauschek, *Xenia Bernardina, IV: Bibliographia Bernardina* (Vienna, 1891), 496.

⁵³ For *Manere*, see P. S. Jolliffe, *A Check-List of Middle English Prose Writings of Spiritual Guidance* (Toronto, 1974), H23, 101, O36, 143; see also V. M. Lagorio and M. G. Sargent, 'English Mystical Writings', in A. E. Hartung (ed.), *A Manual of the Writings in Middle English 1050–1500*, 9 vols. (New Haven, 1967–93), IX, no. 59, 3100–1 and no. 82, 3128–31.

⁵⁴ See A. W. Pollard and G. R. Redgrave (eds.), *A Short-Title Catalogue of Books Printed in England, Scotland, & Ireland*, rev. edn, 3 vols. (London, 1986, 1976, 1991), I, 80, no. 1908, 81, no. 1923; for the 1886 edition of the *Liber* in English, see J. Emmett et al. (eds.), *The British Library General Catalogue of Printed Books to 1975*, 360 vols. (London, 1979–87), XXVI, 462.

⁵⁵ A closer look at both Latin and Middle English manuscripts is needed to determine this question.

⁵⁶ *Liber*, 1210C.

⁵⁷ *Manere*, fo. 20ᵛ.

⁵⁸ *Liber*, 1273B. 'Very necessary ys to us godly redyng, for by redyng we lern what we ouȝt to doo, what to flye, whyther to go' (*Manere*, fos. 120ʳ⁻ᵛ).

⁵⁹ See B. Briggs, 'The Language of the Scribes of the First English Translation of the *Imitatio Christi*', *Leeds Studies in English*, New Series, 26 (1995), 79–111 (109–10, n. 43).

⁶⁰ See M. B. Parkes, *English Cursive Book Hands 1250–1500* (Oxford, 1969), 8, plate ii; see also A. I. Doyle, 'A Text Attributed to Ruusbroec Circulating

in England', in A. Anpe (ed.), *Dr. L. Reypens-Album*, Texttuitgauen van Ons Geestelijk 16 (Antwerp, 1964), 143–71 (160–1); Briggs, 'The Language of the Scribes', 93–6.

[61] For another text translated by a Carthusian of Sheen for a Syon sister, see Rebecca Selman's article in this volume, (p. 63). For an examination of Cistercian influence on the Bridgittines, see J. France, 'From Bernard to Bridget: Cistercian Contribution to a Unique Scandinavian Monastic Body', in J. R. Sommerfeldt (ed.), *Bernardus Magister* (Kalamazoo, 1992), 479–95.

[62] Glasgow, University Library, MS Hunter T. 6. 18, a Middle English version of the *Imitatio Christi* (see Briggs, 'The Language of the Scribes', 93).

[63] See Uppsala, University Library, MS C 240, Andersson-Schmidt and Hedlund, *Mittelalterliche Handschriften*, III, 150. This text was also later translated into Swedish (see Janauscheck, *Xenia Bernardina*, 445, no. 2423). There was at least one Latin copy of the *Liber* in the Syon Library. See M. Bateson (ed.), *Catalogue of the Library of Syon Monastery Isleworth* (Cambridge, 1898), M114, p.115. This Bridgittine copy of the *Liber* was kindly brought to my attention by Dr. V. Gillespie.

[64] For a brief assessment of the *Rule of St Augustine* and the *Rule of St Saviour*, see C. d'Evelyn, 'Instructions for Religious', in Hartung, *Manual*, II, 458–81, 650–9 (464–70, 656–7); see also, B. Morris, *St Birgitta of Sweden* (Woodbridge, 1999), 163–7; for an edition of the *Rule of St Saviour*, see J. Hogg (ed.), *The Rewyll of Seynt Sauioure*, Salzburger Studien zur Anglistik und Amerikanistik, 6 vols. (Salzburg, 1978–80), II–IV.

[65] For instance in the first chapter of the *Liber*, the sentence: '*nemo* potest venire ad aeternam beatitudinem nisi per fidem' (*Liber*, 1200A) is translated thus in *Manere*: 'No *man or woman* maye com to þe everlastyng blisse withoute fayth' (*Manere*, fo. 2ᵛ) (my italics).

[66] In this respect, it is interesting to note that the 1633 English translation, addressed to a Benedictine nun ('to the Venerable . . . sister, Dame Francis Gawen, of the holie Order of S. Benet,' p.a2), does not imitate the *Manere*. The same sentence translates: 'no *man* can attaine to eternall blisse, but by faith' (5) (my italics).

[67] For a list of the *Liber*'s chapters, see Appendix, 93. The *Liber* is sometimes bound with other shorter texts. In MS Laud misc. 517, for instance, *Manere* is followed by three small texts: the 'xii degrees of mekenes' (fos. 175ᵛ–181ʳ), 'Seynt Albert the Byschop seyth thes wordis' (fos. 181ʳ–182ʳ), and 'Of pacyens to be had in sekenes' (fos. 182ʳ–184ʳ). For an edition of the second, see Doyle, 'A text attributed to Ruusbroec', 153–71.

[68] *Liber*, 1199A, 'some tretes of holy doctryne' (*Manere*, fo. 1ʳ).

[69] *Liber* 1214C–D. 'Owre Lord Jhesu Cryste sayeth in þe gospell: "Suche as be clothed in easy and softe clothes, be in kyngys howsis". Clothes be called softe bycause they make the mynde softe and lyght. The kyngis courte deliteth in softe and fyne clothyng. The courte of Cryste delyteth in hard and cowrse clothyng. Suche ouȝte to be þe vestures of the servantis of God,

wheryn can be notyd nothyng of newelte, nothyng of vanyte, nothyng of superfluite, nothyng that perteyneth to pryde and vaynglorye ... Therfor, my loved suster, lete us aray ourself with spirituall ornamentis as charite, humylite, mekenes, obediens and paciens. Thes be þe vestures with þe which we maye please Jhesu Cryste þe celestyall spouse' (*Manere*, fos. 27ᵛ–28ʳ). The emphasis on a spiritual point of view is manifested from the very beginning of ch. 9, where the argument already points out: 'The ixth exhortacion sheweth how religiouse habite shuld not be precious nor curyous nor superfluous, and how the habite and good lyfe shuld agre togyther' (*Manere*, fo. 27ᵛ).

[70] See, respectively, ch. 30 'De silentio', *Manere*, 92ʳ–93ʳ and ch. 53 'De activa et contemplativa vita', *Manere*, fos. 126ᵛ–132ʳ.

[71] See, for example, chs. 30 to 37.

[72] In order to save space, this chapter deals only with *Manere*. The *Liber*'s original chapter does not present major differences from the *Manere*.

[73] This tripartite division of the three states goes back to St Paul in I Cor. 7, but it is commonly encountered in Middle English texts. For a brief critical assessment, see B. Millett (ed.), *Hali Meiðhad*, EETS 284 (London, 1982), xxxviii–xxxix.

[74] *Manere*, fos. 69ʳ⁻ᵛ. Interestingly, the proud virgin is also criticized in *Hali Meiðhad* but the argument does not mention widows and married women.

[75] *Manere*, fo. 69ᵛ.

[76] These rhetorical features are already present in the *Liber* (see *Liber*, 1239D). Such a positive assessment of marriage and widowhood is usually absent: *A Tretis of Maydenhod* cites the three states, but only to identify maidenhood as the best (see Cambridge, University Library, MS Ii 6. 39, fos. 71ᵛ–74ᵛ); *A Treatise for Maidens* similarly quotes the three states and again selects virginity as the best (see, London, British Library, MS Arundel 286, fos. 134ᵛ–148ʳ). The whole of *Hali Meiðhad* demonstrates that maidenhood is the best of the three states; Aelred extols virginity, but does not even mention marriage and widowhood; nor does the *Ancrene Wisse* appear to refer to either.

[77] *Manere*, fos. 70ʳ⁻ᵛ. *Manere* closely translates the *Liber* (see *Liber*, 1210B–D).

[78] See Millet (ed.), *Hali Meiðhad*, xli.

[79] Ibid., 20/15–19; for the whole argument, see ibid., 20/15–28.

[80] This is obvious when one compares this extract with *Hali Meiðhad*. The latter exhorts the virgin to beget virtues, as does the *Liber*, yet there are no comforting words in *Hali Meiðhad* telling the maiden not to see herself as a 'barayn drye stok'.

[81] Kuczynski, *Prophetic Song*, 88.

[82] This feature is already present in the *Liber* (see *Liber*, 1210B–D). There is a similar use of the second person in *Hali Meiðhad*, though not to the same extent. Further, the constant repetitions of 'my beloved sister' or the like continually remind the reader that the author addresses his message to her

[83] personally. This personal involvement of the addressee is reflected in the *Manere* where the chapters are referred to as 'exhortacions'.
[83] See Millett (ed.), *Hali Meiðhad*, 20.
[84] *Manere*, fo. 70ᵛ.
[85] As far as style is concerned, the *Liber* is most usefully compared to *Ancrene Wisse*, since both texts are of a similar length, whereas Aelred's *De institutione inclusarum* is much shorter. For a list and examination of rhetorical devices in the *Ancrene Wisse*, see Dolan, 'The Rhetoric of *Ancrene Wisse*', 203–13.
[86] For example: '(Interrogatio.) Dic mihi, quaeso, frater mi, quid est quod in sacra Scriptura legitur, quia nemo sanctus, nemo bonus, nemo justus, nisi solus Deus?' (*Liber*, 1203A). 'Peraventer ye wold aske me: Broþere, what ys it þat is radd in Scripture: *no man or woman ys holy, good and ryȝtwous, but oonly God*' (*Manere*, fo. 7ᵛ). ' "But, dear Master," someone may say, "is it then so excessively evil to peep out?" ' (Salu (tr.), *Ancrene Riwle*, 22).
[87] For repetitions in the *Ancrene Wisse*, see J. Grayson, *Structure and Imagery in Ancrene Wisse* (Hanover, NH, 1974), 57–79. Repetitions are an integral part of the *Liber* and can be seen at work throughout the quotations of the *Liber* cited in this chapter. But thematic repetitions are also important to the work as a whole: the theme of the foolish and wise virgins, the serpent and the dove, and, most of all, the portrayal of the reader as the Bride of Christ, are repeatedly referred to.
[88] Dolan, 'The Rhetoric of *Ancrene Wisse*', 213.
[89] Tolkien (ed.), *Ancrene Wisse*, 36, fo. 16a, lines 18–19. 'She should not have the characteristics of a hen, which when it has laid, can do nothing but cackle' (Salu (tr.), *Ancrene Riwle*, 29).
[90] E. Robertson, *Early English Devotional Prose and the Female Audience* (Knoxville, Tenn. 1990), 57.
[91] The following excerpt from a Middle English translation of the text clearly demonstrates the author's *penchant* for concrete details: 'Many þer ben, þe whiche done as a slow servaunt doth þat, whan sche schold swepe here house and put out þe filth, sche castiþ grene rusches above and hide þe filth. So done ypocrites whan þei schuld schew þe unclennes of here synnes þei hide it and telle þe fairnes and he castiþ above þe filth beute of gode werkis. Do þou not so, but first make alle clene þe flore of þi conscience fro alle maner filthes' (Oxford, Bodleian Library, MS Laud misc 330, fos. 3ʳ⁻ᵛ). For the Middle English translations of the *Doctrina cordis*, see Jolliffe, *A Check-List*, H1, 91 and O3, 134–5.
[92] When one considers that the *Ancrene Wisse*'s original addressees were three gentlewomen, but that the *Liber*'s recipient is an aristocratic nun, it may be that the social rank of a text's primary reader has as much to do with a particular choice of images as his or her gender. Neither is the use of everyday images exclusively reserved for texts aimed at women. J. France notes: 'both *Bernard and Bridget* make extensive use of images drawn from the

natural world around them' (France, 'From Bernard to Bridget', 481) (my italics).

[93] When the *Liber* does resort to concrete images, it usually stresses their rhetorical status quite clearly: '*exemplo* novellae arboris. . .' (*Liber*, 1200A), '*example* of a young tendre tree . . .' (*Manere*, fo. 2ᵛ); 'audi, . . . *congruentem similitudinem*. Saepe videmus per setam introduci linum . . .' (*Liber*, 1205D), 'here . . . a *convenient simylitude*. We se often þat by the brystell the cordenars threde ys drawen yn . . .' (*Manere*, fo. 12ʳ) (my italics).

[94] *Liber*, 1203 B–C. 'Other persons be good not by themself, but by God and his grace and, þerefor, God ys oonly good bycause he is of hymself good. The which shewith the spouse of þe chyrch, Cryste, seyeng in canticis: I am the floure of þe felde and þe lyly of þe valeyes, as ho seyth I am þe holynes, goodnes and veray justice of all them þat with mekenes truste in me. And as þe felde ys arayed with fresche flowres, so all þe worlde ys renewed with þe fayth and knowlege of Cryst. Also he sayth I am the flour of þe felde and lylye of the valeyes as ho sayth: I geve grete grace to thoos persons which putt noo confidens in their owne meritis but in me as þe gyver of all vertue and grace' (*Manere*, fos. 7ᵛ–8ʳ).

[95] P. Hodgson (ed.), *The Cloud of Unknowing*, Analecta Cartusiana 3 (Salzburg,1982), 52/38–40.

[96] N. Watson, 'The Methods and Objectives of Thirteenth-Century Anchoritic Devotion', in M. Glasscoe (ed.), *MMTE*, IV, 132–53 (141).

[97] *Liber*, 1297B–C. 'Now, therfor, here and merke what I saye and counsell. Hit ys bettere for you to sytte in your cloystere than to goo aboute the stretys of the cyte or town. Covette ye mor to abyde withyn your monasterye than to se citees and townes. Hyt ys better to abyde withyn the wallys of the monasterye than to be in þe siȝte of peple. And, if ye kepe yourself within þe monasterye ye shal be loved of Cryste, which he sheweth wele in Canticis canticorum sayeng: my suster, thou art as a close garden, as a close well. Every devoute soule ys called a closed garden, for when she noryscheth vertue, she bryngyth furth spirituall floures and refreschyth hyrself with vertue and the frutys þat she bryngeth furth, she kepyth' (*Manere*, fo. 159ᵛ).

[98] Notice the movement from an open space ('stretys of the cyte or town') into an enclosed one ('withyn your monasterye', 'withyn the wallys of þe monasterye'), and the transference from a bodily posture ('you sytte in your cloystere') to the fruition of her spirituality ('every devoute soule' . . . 'she bryngyth furth spirituall floures . . . frutys').

[99] The *Liber* itself emphasizes that nowadays 'viri Religiosi plus desiderant in palatio regis versari, quam intra claustrum monasterii commorari . . . [et] plus desirant audire superflua verba divitum quam praecepta Scripturarum . . . [et] plus laetantur in conviviis et locutionibus divitum, quam in paupertate et abstinentia religiosorum fratrum' (*Liber*, 1297A), 'religyous

persons covyt more to be conversaunte in the kyngis palace than to abyde withyn the cloystere or monasterye, and . . . they desyre more to here the superfluous talkyng of ryche men than the doctryne of scriptur, and . . . they [are] more glad at the festys of ryche men than in poverte and abstynence of religyous brethern' (*Manere*, fos. 158ᵛ–159ʳ).

[100] 'Charissima mihi in Christo soror', 'coelesti sponso', '. . . Dominum patrem tuum, qui te creavit quasi filiam' (*Liber* 1199A, 1199B, 1206B), 'my wel beloved suster in Criste', 'celestiall spouse', 'God your fader þat created you as his doughter' (*Manere*, fos. 1ʳ, 1ᵛ, 13ʳ). The author is addressed as the reader's brother: 'dic mihi . . . frater mi . . .' (*Liber*, 1203A), 'Peraventer ye wold aske me: "Broþere, what ys it . . . ?" (*Manere*, fo. 7ᵛ); the older nuns are regarded as her mothers and herself as their daughter: 'servias eis, ut diligas eas quasi matres . . . debes eis servire quasi filia' (*Liber*, 1240B), 'ye serve them and love them as moders . . . serve them as a dowȝter' (*Manere*, fo. 69ᵛ). Finally, the recipient is not without her own children: 'septem filios habes. Primus filius est verecundia . . .' (*Liber*, 1240B–C), 'ye have vii chyldren. The fyrst chylde ys shamefastnes . . .' *Manere*, fo. 70ʳ).

[101] Compare with the *Ancrene Wisse* and Aelred's *De institutione inclusarum*, where the recipients are less often addressed as 'sisters', for instance.

[102] *Liber* 1221C–D. 'Spouse of Cryst I pray the þat sumwhat þu wylt tell me of the love of thy celestyall spouse. My love, sayth she, lovyng to me abydeth betwene my brestis. Yit, lovyng spouse, speke more playner þat we may undirstand what thou sayest. The place of the hart ys between the brestys. My love abydeth betwen my brestys, þat is to saye the memorye, dileccion and the love of my spouse, Jhesu Cryst, shal be allweye betwen my brestys, þat is my hart, and wheþere I be in prosperite or in adversite I wyll contynually call to my remembraunce all the goodnes that he hath geven to me, for he hath loved me, he deyed for me and ascended to heven. And þat I shuld come to hym dayly he callyth me sayeng: "Com from Lybany, my spouse, com from Libany", that ys from the worlde, "come þou shalt be crowned"' (*Manere*, fos. 39ʳ⁻ᵛ).

[103] Such authority awarded the sister by a male writer is not unique, but is nonetheless quite rare. For another example, see the 'Sister Catherine treatise', attributed to Meister Eckhart, in B. McGinn et al. (trs.), *Meister Eckhart: Teacher and Preacher* (New York, 1986), Appendix, 347–87.

[104] *Liber*, 1199A ('I have . . . as y myght not as I ouȝte gadred togethyr som small lessons of religious conversacion oute of the writyngs of my forfathirs which in this litell boke I send unto youe, accordyng to your peticion' (*Manere*, fo. 1ᵛ).

[105] The chapter headings are taken from *PL* 184. 1199–1306.

# Part Three

*The Representation of Femininity in Anglo-Norman and Middle English Religious Poetry*

# 5
# A Fortress and a Shield: The Representation of the Virgin in the *Château d'amour* of Robert Grosseteste

## CHRISTIANIA WHITEHEAD

BAL memorably labelled Mary a 'sadistic' invention: a figure of imaginative perfection exercising enormous influence, whose perfection, centred upon bodily paradox, placed her in an impossible relationship to the rest of her gender. Mary encompassed an ideal, and that ideal was virginal maternity: a simultaneous affirmation of motherhood and devaluation of the body, which, necessarily beyond reach, was always going to relegate the historical female subject to a position of relative imperfection.[1] The historical female, caught between the choice of an unfruitful virginity or a fruitful sexuality, might look to Mary aspiringly, yet could never hope to repeat the supernatural paradox which she embodied. As a result, many woman religious writers of the Middle Ages, searching for bodies inside the faith with whom they could imaginatively empathize, turned their gaze away from Mary and focused instead upon the crucified Christ.[2] Their inventive reclamations of corporeality, well charted by Caroline Walker Bynum, lie outside the scope of this chapter. Instead, this essay will remain focused upon the image they implicitly rejected, an image fraught with difficulties for the contemporary feminist critic, the depiction of the metaphorical, marvellous Mary which was elaborated within a Latin clerical milieu from the early until the high Middle Ages.

Modern historians such as Graef and Warner have already provided a panoramic reading of the theological and cultural developments which mark the evolution of the Marian cult during the Middle Ages and beyond.[3] Other modern thinkers have emphasized the mythical and psychological connotations of Mary's medieval form.[4] This chapter complements the broader literature by singling out one very commonplace Marian metaphor in which the Virgin is envisaged as a protective fortress. It discusses this metaphor both diachronically and synchronically, utilizing it as a site where theological, sociological and psychological influences can be viewed in dynamic contention. Ultimately, it brings the conclusions of its investigation to bear upon the Bal verdict of 'sadism', and enquires whether or not this terminology can be sustained in the face of close analysis.

Mary is the doorway to eternal life, she is a temple of mercy for sinners, she is a strong tower, a fortification in which we may safely take refuge. Long before the thirteenth century many of these sentences had become formalized within liturgy as antiphons for Marian feasts or invocations within Marian litanies.[5] At what moment in the past were they born? At what point did they pass into common currency? As always, when dealing with phrases which have a long liturgical and homiletic history, it is hard to answer these questions with any certainty, and perhaps they are not always the best questions to ask. Nonetheless, by the eighth century, it seems clear that an architectonic depiction of Mary had already acquired some familiarity, since it is in around this period that a significant passage from Luke began to be included as one of the formal lections for the feast of the Assumption. The passage in question, located in the tenth chapter of Luke, describes the entry of Christ into the house of a woman named Martha in the village of Bethany.[6] This is, of course, that same Martha who was later to become a symbol for the active Christian life. From the festive context in which the passage was utilized, and from hints within the surviving sermons of the exegetes who expounded the lection, we can gather that the verse was read as an allegory of the Incarnation. It was taken to refer to the miraculous entry of Christ into the architectural stronghold of Mary's virginal body.[7] That reading was repeated and developed in later continental homilies upon the feast of the Assumption, and was finally popularized in England early in the twelfth century within the sermons of Ralph d'Escures, archbishop of Canterbury, and Aelred of Rievaulx.[8]

Up until the twelfth century, architecturalized reference to the Virgin seems to have been restricted to liturgical and homiletic utterances. However, from that period onwards, more imaginative, more *literary* patterns begin to appear in the assorted vernaculars. Faithful to the medieval principle that the best communication is anchored upon strong visual imagery, I would like to shape the analysis which follows by grounding it upon an unusually extended treatment of the metaphor which illustrates these new developments. That treatment occurs in the *Château d'amour*, a long Anglo-Norman poem, composed during the early thirteenth century by Bishop Robert Grosseteste.[9]

At this point it is necessary to make a small biographical excursus to supply the details regarding the poem's author and successive audiences. Robert Grosseteste lived between 1170 and 1253. Some might question whether he has been sufficiently highly estimated within the history of medieval intellectual thought, although he is, nonetheless, the subject of very good recent appreciation by Sir Richard Southern.[10] His origins, which were probably humble, remain obscure, and the earliest references we possess refer to his search for employment in the early 1200s in the household of William de Vere, bishop of Hereford, where he soon became active as a diocesan administrator. It used to be thought that Grosseteste spent some time studying in Paris. Recent historical research favours instead the idea that he underwent his schooling upon English soil.[11] Whatever the truth of that, he received his first benefice comparatively late, in 1225, and from then until 1235 was almost continuously associated with Oxford, administering, lecturing and contributing to the Franciscan education programme. Around 1231 he was appointed archdeacon of Leicester, forming a close friendship with Simon de Montfort, who had simultaneously been granted the earldom of Leicester. His sixteenth-century biographer, Richard of Bardney, also credits him with friendship and close access to the young King Henry III. In 1235 he was appointed bishop of Lincoln, a gigantic diocese, incorporating something like a fifth of the populace of England. In this capacity, he was remarkably active as an enforcer of ecclesiastical discipline and pastoral reformer, initiating the practice of episcopal visitation on an unprecedented scale, and eventually coming into conflict with the pope over the question of absentee appointments to English livings.

The poem we shall be examining, vernacular and popular in appeal, is not by any means representative of the general nature of Grosseteste's profuse scholarly output. On the contrary, his early writing was largely orientated toward matters of a strictly scientific and philosophical nature; mid-career, he occupied himself with various biblical commentaries and studies upon the Church Fathers, and in maturity, in the period following his appointment as bishop, a growing interest in the works of the Greek theologians became evident. He produced translations and commentaries upon philosophers and mystics such as

Aristotle and Pseudo-Dionysius, and declared himself to have been influenced by many others, including Basil the Great and Gregory of Nyssa.[12] However, despite the *Château*'s anomalous vernacular diction, the poem does stand as testament to important currents in Grosseteste's thinking. It exemplifies his pastoral sensibilities, and answers his concern that theological doctrine be made accessible to the widest possible audience.[13] Southern described the poem as the 'nearest that Grosseteste ever came to a *Summa theologiae*' and as 'the fullest expression of his pastoral theology for a popular audience'.[14]

The *Château d'amour* relates the chronology of salvation history from the beginning until the end of the world, conveying some of its theological ideas via interpolated allegorical interludes, such as the allegory of the King and the Thrall, and the allegory of the Four Daughters of God.[15] The lateral thrust of this historical chronology is modified within the poem by its organization around the epithets retrospectively applied to Christ in Isaiah 9:6: 'Wonderful Counsellor, Mighty God, Father Everlasting, Prince of Peace'. Hence, 'Wonderful' is taken to refer to the miraculousness of Christ's birth; 'Mighty God' is linked with the miracles which illustrate Christ's divinity; 'Father Everlasting' is connected to the era of the early Church; and 'Prince of Peace' is interpreted as the period of ultimate peace following on from the Last Judgement. This method of structuring material contains clues about the type of audience Grosseteste envisaged, for it suggests that the poem consciously adopted narrative and organizational ploys which would make it readily memorable to a large listening audience. The opening of the *Château* provides further information on this front:

> Tuz avum mester daie
> E tres tuz ne poent mie.
> Saver le langage en fin
> Debreu. de griu. ne de latin ...
> Ke chescun en son langage
> Le convisse sanz folage.
> Son deu. sa redempciun
> En romanz comenz ma reison.
> Por ceus ki ne sevent mie
> Ne lettrure ne clergie.[16]

The decision to speak in French rather than Latin, 'for those who have neither letters nor learning', implies a lay Anglo-Norman clientele. In addition, the initial address to the listeners: 'Oez seigneurs', and the broadly feudal and legal flavour of the allegorical interludes, all combine to suggest that the poem was designed to be sung or declaimed at sittings to an audience of knightly retainers in some manorial household.[17]

The poem enjoyed a healthy, continuous circulation from the time of its composition until the end of the Middle Ages, surviving in its Anglo-Norman form in at least sixteen manuscripts.[18] Portions from it were also translated into Middle English on four distinct occasions. Two of these translations, *The Castle of Love*[19] and the *Myrour of Lewed Men*,[20] include the allegory of the Virgin as a fortress with which we are concerned here. An examination of the ownership of manuscripts containing these translations, together with manuscripts containing the Anglo-Norman *Château*, reveals that, by the fourteenth and fifteenth centuries, the poem had moved into new and more devout reading circles. The Vernon and Simeon manuscripts containing *The Castle of Love* have been widely researched, and seem to have been compiled specifically with an audience of nuns or devout gentlewomen in mind.[21] The manuscript of the *Myrour of Lewed Men* has a Cistercian provenance,[22] and one of the manuscripts containing the Anglo-Norman version of the poem, Cambridge, Fitzwilliam Museum, MS McClean 123, includes inscriptions which reveal that the book was left to the nuns of Nuneaton Priory in the 1380s by their prioress, Margaret Sylemon. That the book was still in female hands in the fifteenth century is attested by a further inscription, the name Alicia Scheynton, in a fifteenth-century script. All these incidents combine to suggest the poem's use by devout female reading communities toward the close of the Middle Ages. Their *ruminatio* upon this text raises the question of their response to its one representation of exemplary womanhood: the castle of the Virgin, situated in the poem's heart.

In order to ponder this and other questions, it is necessary to detail the relevant episode of the poem. In the wake of a survey of Old Testament prophecies about the advent of Christ, the poem addresses the event of the Incarnation. But rather than reiterating the biblical narrative of stables and donkeys as the majority of cycle mysteries would have done at this moment, Grosseteste opts for a more doctrinally dictated approach. He depicts the Incarnation using a detailed, relatively self-contained allegory in which the Virgin's body is compared to the structure of an invincible fortress. In brief, after the Son has offered himself before the Father as a suitable ransom for mankind, He descends from the sky into a castle of love. This castle is situated upon the frontiers, well enclosed within deep ditches and founded upon hard, grey, polished rock. It has four turrets and three baileys, also seven barbicans, each with a door and a tower for those seeking help. The castle is painted in three colours: a foundation of green, a middle of blue, and an upper band of red. Inside, however, it is shining white. In the middle of the highest tower is a fountain which issues in four streams,[23] together with a throne of white ivory[24] approached by seven steps and overarched by a rainbow.[25] This physical outline is succeeded by an interpretation. The castle equates with the body of the Virgin; its positioning on the frontier represents her role as a shield against our enemies; the rock to which it is affixed is her heart which never softens toward evil. The colours of the castle also carry secondary significance: green symbolizes faith; blue, tenderness; and red, the fire of love. The four turrets equate with the four cardinal virtues; the three baileys which defend the keep are Mary's virginity, chastity and matrimony respectively; the barbicans comprise all seven of the virtues. The fountain within the highest tower flows with grace;[26] the ditches surrounding the castle are voluntary poverty by means of which the devil is overcome. God entered and left this castle through a closed gate. The poem then reverts briefly to the first person, at which point we discover that the narrator has included himself as a supplicant outside the castle walls, pleading to be let in and describing the intensity with which he is attacked by the world, the flesh and the devil.[27]

What light does this episode cast upon the Virgin? To work entirely from first principles for a moment, the description obviously underlines her moral invincibility and defensiveness at the expense of more tender possibilities. It paints her as a refuge for sinners and a potential medium of access to her Son. Finally, using abstract and monumental means, it exalts her as one in whom the virtues and grace exist in an ordered and congruous relation with one another. All these points will need exploring in considerably more detail, but it is perhaps most relevant to begin by examining exactly how the fortified representation of the Virgin fits into the evolution of her cult up to and beyond the thirteenth century. The fortified depiction, as mentioned above, implies that moral invincibility is a major factor in characterizing her perfection. It also associates her with the expression of power and feudal rule. The iconography of *Maria regina*, of which this characterization is a part, stems from a larger movement emphasizing Mary's earthly power, which was developed in Rome by the papacy in order to advance the hegemony of the Holy See.[28] Twelfth-century hymns addressing Mary as 'lady' or 'queen', such as the *Salve regina* and the *Ave regina caelorum,* bear testament to this new preoccupation. Cathedrals dedicated to Notre Dame and newly contrived images of the Coronation of the Virgin accentuate the trend. And the rising popularity of the Little Office of the Virgin, and the spread of the Cistercian order – an order looking toward the Virgin – serve as further examples which combine to bear witness to a gathering popular and monastic fascination with Mary in the course of the eleventh and twelfth centuries.[29]

Doctrinal developments also contributed to the majesty and status of the Virgin during this period. New liturgical feasts dedicated to her Conception and Presentation in the Temple,[30] and a flurry of writings arguing the case for Mary's Immaculate Conception and Bodily Assumption into heaven,[31] all fuelled the presentation of an image which threatened to lose touch with human nature and limitation altogether. Gilbert of Nogent is one devotional writer who was particularly explicit in attributing quasi-divine properties to Mary, but the idea is implicit in much other Marian theology of the twelfth century, and also permeates two rather specious treatises, *De laudibus sanctae Mariae* and *Mariale super missus est,* which enjoyed considerable popularity during the middle of the thirteenth century.[32] To draw upon the words of Hilda Graef, one of the most prolific Marian scholars of the late twentieth century, at this time Mary was presented increasingly as an 'all-but-independent power ruling the whole world by the side of her Son'.[33] She was repeatedly invoked as the mistress of the universe, a fountainhead of goodness and of salvation, and in some more extreme writings in her praise, which threatened to slant into heterodoxy, additionally revered for her omnipotence, her perfect knowledge of the future, her participation in the work of redemption and her plenitude of grace from which everything else derived. The Marian theology of the thirteenth century which developed within the mendicant orders tends to stand as a corrective to some of these more fanciful readings. Dominican thinkers such as Albert the Great and Thomas Aquinas opposed the doctrine of the Immaculate Conception and restricted Mary's participation in salvation to her example and her prayer. Their writings emphasize the infinite difference between Mary and her Son, and Aquinas takes pains to demonstrate that Mary's mediation of grace is wholly related to and dependent upon her proximity to Christ, the author of grace. The Franciscan mystic, St Bonaventure, makes some similarly cautious comments. In his second sermon he stresses man's need to fly to the mercy of Mary as to a port, but writes that, though men may turn to her for grace, nonetheless that fountain of grace derives from her dependence on Christ, who receives it in turn from the Father. On another occasion, writing upon Mary's power and authority, he describes her authority as 'the dominion of *praesidentia*, such as is accorded to the governor of a province, not an authority of majesty and omnipotence'.[34]

An alternative approach to Mary also began to become popular during this period. Great affective theologians such as Anselm and Bernard of Clairvaux extolled her as a *mater misericordiae*, foregrounding her 'feminine' qualities of tenderness, empathy and mercy, and writing fondly of the wonder of her maternal body.[35] However, it seems clear that in choosing to depict Mary as a fortress against danger, and in annulling the physicality of her maternal body, Grosseteste is aligning himself with the first of these two alternative depictions. The image in the *Château d'amour* carries clear connotations of power, queenliness and impassive refuge which correspond to Mary's western evolution as a *regina* and *dame*. Having won agreement on that, it is interesting to attempt to determine precisely where Grosseteste places himself in relation to the theological positions we have just been reviewing. Other writings within his corpus reveal that he placed enormous emphasis upon the Incarnation, seeing it not simply as a solution to the problem of original sin, but as a necessary conclusion to the work of Creation, an event so momentous in implication that it must have preceded Creation as part of God's original design.[36] This understanding accords well with his depiction of the Virgin as an invincible and enduring fortress, placed beyond the winds of temporal change: 'the Mother, prepared from the beginning'.[37] That said, what conclusions should be drawn from other elements in this architectural description? What interpretation is to be put upon her location on a frontier, implicitly between heaven and earth? How should we read the fountain of grace and throne of ivory which occupy the space within her?

It is hard to determine definitive theological positions from allegorical statements; however, I should like, tentatively, to place Grosseteste's exposition of Mary at a point midway between the extreme allegations of some twelfth-century exegetes and the more cautious sentiments of thirteenth-century mendicancy. Mary's positioning on a liminal frontier, presumably a reference to her simultaneous virginity and maternity as well as to her location between the material and the divine,[38] and her self-sufficiency in every virtue combine to suggest that Grosseteste may have numbered himself with thinkers such as Eadmer and Gilbert who attributed quasi-divine properties to the Virgin. Certainly, his pictorial rendition seems compatible with assent to the proposition of her Immaculate Conception, since her intact exterior and internal ordering of virtues imply an atemporal and pre-existent perfection as against a perfection founded entirely upon the mothering of Christ. Other ingredients in the description are perhaps harder to place theologically. But it is tempting, in the light of the episode's similarity to Bonaventure's comments, to wonder whether Grosseteste also envisaged Mary's spiritual power as that of the 'governor of a province'.[39] Notably, a vacant throne remains within the castle, implying readiness for and subordination to an authority higher than that of the edifice itself. The presence of this vacant throne and its proximity to the fountain of grace also helps to clarify the way in which Grosseteste viewed Mary's distribution of grace. It may imply, and again these conclusions are necessarily tentative, that the fountain derives its potency from the adjacent throne of Christ. This would move the episode more towards the thinking of the mendicants, a direction which, in larger terms, coincides with Grosseteste's general caution and regard for theological orthodoxy. It should also be noted at this point that the vacant throne and four streams of water issuing within the keep have para-scriptural origins which extend back to Hebraic legends regarding the Solomonic Temple.[40] That temple, with its vacant mercy seat, was reputed to be built upon a great rock situated at the oldest point of creation, beneath which the waters of the earth were confined and controlled, issuing forth as four rivers. Anselm's delineation of the Virgin as a temple of mercy takes on a new power in the light of Grosseteste's extended allegorical *ruminatio* upon this epithet.

We have commented upon the way in which the architectural representation of the Virgin acts as an appropriate response to advances in Marian doctrine which, promoting the concepts of the Immaculate Conception and the Bodily Assumption, increasingly detach her from human limitation, and from the flaws and changes associated with sin, sex, age and death. It remains to complete this inquiry by considering the manner in which allegorical architecture was commonly used, in order to determine whether this may cast extra light upon its meaning in relation to the Virgin. From the classical era onward, it is possible to plot a textual tradition, operative in both classical and Judaeo-Christian idioms, in which allegorical buildings were used to represent categorical properties or timeless entities such as Love, War, Nature,

Fame or the Church. The temples of Love in the writings of Claudian and Sidonius are cases in point. So, too, are the Houses of Mars and Sleep in Statius' *Thebaid*, the Houses of Fame and Nature in the *Anticlaudianus* of Alan of Lille, and the allegory of the tower as Church which occupies the third Vision and the ninth Similitude of the anonymous *Pastor of Hermas*.[41] In the light of this tradition of usage, I would suggest that the architectural representation of the Virgin, which increases both in frequency and in detail between the ninth century and the thirteenth, bears a strong relation to her theological movement from humanity to quasi-divinity, and acts as extra testimony to the way in which she was becoming increasingly perceived as the embodiment of certain timeless and categorical values, unchangeable through the ages.[42]

We noted, as part of our initial response to the *Château*'s blazon of the Virgin, Grosseteste's exploitation of her potential as a frame for ordering and organizing the virtues. This understanding of the Virgin as a figure representing the unity of the virtues materializes again in Grosseteste's sermon, *Tota pulchra est*,[43] and the two examples, taken in conjunction with Grosseteste's concern to edify the laity, suggest that her depiction as a visually memorable, thirteenth-century fortification may have had a mnemonic function. Mary Carruthers has written extensively on the way in which various visual structures, architecture prominent amongst them, were utilized in treatises and homilies of the twelfth and thirteenth centuries as *memorial frames* on which lists of moral essentials such as the cardinal virtues or the ten commandments could be hung for easy recall.[44] This practice derived from the belief, which grew more prevalent with the rediscovery of Aristotle, that it was the visual memory which was the most effective at retaining reams of material information. The use to which Hugh of St Victor puts the Noah's Ark in his three treatises on that subject,[45] and the allegorical cloister clothed with orderly spiritual meaning at the centre of Hugh of Folieto's *De claustro animae*, are just two examples of architecture utilized to this purpose within twelfth-century didactic literature.[46] It is interesting to contemplate exactly *how* the body is couched when it is brought into play with this mnemonic purpose in mind. For, in general, it seems true that when the body is being used as a metaphor either for religious or political purposes, all potential manifestations of disharmony or bodily incompletion are expelled from the text. On the contrary, in order to further the harmony and cohesion of the system being propounded, the body performs as a serene, bounded assemblage of smoothly interrelating parts, a confident totality, whose undisturbed contours make it a focus of aspiration and an object set apart from the more disorderly psyche of the reader.[47] Grosseteste's image of Mary functions as a textbook example of this ideological bodily completion. Pictured as an interdependent *schema* of converging walls and barbicans, her exemplary psyche is separated out into labelled parts whose smooth conjoining leaves little room for internal conflict or for turbulent subconscious activity. Instead, the emphasis upon structure and spatial relation conveys the belief that spiritual transformation to make oneself a suitable vessel for God is primarily a matter of ordering and sorting moral and mental activity into the correct set of relationships.

While Grosseteste's architectural depiction of the Virgin obviously meets the needs of his Incarnational theology, it is also important to realize that many features within the description are the result of a thirteenth-century cross-fertilization between devotional literature and French courtly romance. To liken Mary to a contemporary feudal stronghold, beautiful and delightful to behold, before whom the poet takes up a position of unrequited longing, is to picture her by reference to far-reaching new trends within French court culture. As part of these trends, at the court of Blanche of Castile, the twelfth-century troubadour lyric of illicit sexual desire for an aristocratic lady became diverted towards the affective adoration of a heavenly courtly *dame*, a heavenly queen. In other words, the Virgin became the revised recipient of a sublimated courtly passion expounded by French *clercs* and *chevaliers*.[48] This new trend, epitomized in various famous writings such as St Bernard's sermon series upon the Song of Songs, in which Mary was evoked as the courtly bride of Christ, and in St Anselm's great Marian prayers, amplified the papal stress upon the earthly power and authority of the Virgin. It also answered the Church's need to create an effective image of erotic chastity to use as a counter-challenge against the casual attitudes toward marriage promulgated by the Albigensian heresy and the creed of courtly adultery.

The deflection of courtly feeling onto the Virgin went a long way toward tempering the attitudes of misogyny and narcissism implicit in many troubadour lyrics. For, whereas the superlative woman of troubadour desire was often little more than a construction formed after the poet's own image, a 'mirror to vanity', the superlative values celebrated in Mary had the purpose of reducing the poet's ego, of forcing a public acknowledgement of his distance from a spiritual ideal.[49] That said, it remains the case that exaggerated self-effacement before an architecture of female power, whether secular or spiritual, never really moves beyond the realms of literary compliment, since, in the words of Jocelyn Wogan-Browne, however far these strongholds encode the sociopolitical function of female intercession, they are nonetheless unable to encode actual rule by women.[50] This is, itself, a helpful indicator of the way in which Grosseteste must have envisaged the nature of Mary's authority: picturing her as a fortress in a literary milieu where the architectualized female signifies intercessory rather than executive power serves as a timely corrective to the allegations of independent power which the allegory might otherwise arouse.

It is important to realize that the historical evolution of the Marian fortress and the history of the representation of *virginity* as a fortress are not one discourse. The two have overlapping but ultimately differentiated trajectories, out of which the architectural realization of virginity emerges as potentially the earlier. As long ago as the early third century Tertullian likened virginity to a citadel.[51] St Ambrose, writing around a century and a half later, created a metaphorical synthesis between virgin and soldier, between chastity and militarism, in his treatise *De virginibus*, driving together two alien temperaments as proof of the supernatural fusion of opposites that marked out the chosen of God.[52] From that period on, the fortified presentation of virginity was always a homiletic option, which, when the negative evaluation of sexual activity reached new ecclesial heights around 1200, became aired with increased frequency. The anonymous author of the important early Middle English treatise *Hali Meiðhad*, writes that: ' "Syon" wes sumhwile icleopet þe hehe tur of Ierusalem; ant "Syon" seið ase muchel on Englische ledene ase "heh sihðe". Ant bitacneð þis tur þe hehnesse of meiðhad, þe bihald as of heh alle widewen under hire ant weddede baðe.'[53] The fortified depiction of virginity by the Church during the early thirteenth century has an obvious relation to advances in Mariology during this period. It also corresponds to a heightened wish to seal and circumscribe the female form which is corroborated by other social and archaeological evidence of the time. Jocelyn Wogan-Browne writes of the emergence of new marriage patterns during the twelfth and thirteenth centuries showing an increased concern with the movement and control of women.[54] Equivalently, Roberta Gilchrist, investigating the gendering of space in castles and monasteries, concludes that the segregations and restrictions put upon high-status women were never more marked than in the late twelfth and early thirteenth centuries, when their quarters tended to be located at the top of towers in the heart of castle keeps in positions of pronounced architectural isolation.[55]

One of the most outstanding vernacular religious treatises of the first half of the thirteenth century, the *Ancrene Wisse*, a form of living for anchoresses, is particularly pertinent to this discussion, since it encompasses a continuously metaphorical train of thought upon virginity which shows close affinities to the approach adopted by Grosseteste in the *Château*. Time and time again within the treatise, the boundaries of the flesh which the recluse is exhorted to retain intact are fused with the stone boundaries of the cell in which she dwells. Time and time again, the chaste body is architecturalized as an enclosure of sealed or regulated entrances, which may correspond to the physical surround of the anchor house or be imaginatively aggrandized into the form of a contemporary baronial stronghold.[56] And frequently, that stronghold is placed in a siege situation, assaulted by the sensual munitions of the devil. The similarities in metaphorical vocabulary tempt one to enquire as to a possible relationship between the two genres. Is it possible that Grosseteste could have formulated his Marian castle out of ideas drawn from the contemporary literature of reclusion? Or, more daringly, is it conceivable that he might have envisaged his 'castle of love' *as* an anchoritic exemplum? In the light of such texts as the *Ancrene Wisse*, does the visual language by which Grosseteste encounters Mary suggest that he is seeking to foreground likenesses between her vocation of intact perfection and that of the thirteenth-century anchoress?

The answers to these questions must, of course, remain purely speculative. However, in addition to pondering them, it is also necessary to investigate the more general implications of envisioning virginity as a fortification. First, from a psychological angle, it is easy to see that the exercise heroicizes and activates the silent internal struggle to maintain chastity. For a nun or anchoress wrestling with sexual impulses, the imagination of the body as a citadel under siege was presumably a pleasurable project, compensating for social occlusion by rewriting restraint as an act of military endurance with public and national resonances. Moreover, while that imagination was clearly congruous with the background of some more aristocratic recluses, it is also easy to realize that it would pander to the desire for social betterment in others, re-expressing an austere and effacing existence as one which reflected the refinement and luxury of the courtly sphere. Second, the choice of allegory helps to give some indication of the degree of tension which surrounded issues of sexual surrender and denial in the first half of the thirteenth century. In mapping sexual resistance onto some of the most fraught pressure points of contemporary social confrontation, the ensiegement of walled towns and baronial strongholds, texts such as the *Ancrene Wisse* and Grosseteste's *Château* convey both the centrality and the acute trauma associated with maintaining virginity within the routine of thirteenth-century spirituality.

Bugge writes that, in the Middle Ages, the maintenance of sexual purity was deemed to confer sacramental immunity from the world of corruptive matter.[57] This immunity took its toll upon the articulation of the virginal body, effectively spiritualizing it out of material existence. Caroline Walker Bynum blends these ideas with extensive textual and medical historical research to note, from the clerical presentation of the bodies of medieval holy women and from their presentation of themselves, how frequently the sacralized female form was exhibited as closed and intact, at one remove from the world of physical flux.[58] This closure might manifest itself, as in the example of the *Ancrene Wisse*, by strictures upon the windows of the senses, but often the implication was much more straightforwardly literal: female sanctity would be repeatedly evoked by reference to the demise of the need to eat, excrete or menstruate. It is easy to see how the crenellated housing shell of the Virgin in Grosseteste's allegory harmonizes with such hagiographic material. Working in conscious contradiction to normative medical perceptions of fallen femininity as open, breachable and characterized by incompletion and excessive release of moisture,[59] the *Château* surrounds Mary with a wall of completion comprehending every necessary virtue, and modifies the female taint of liquidity by inscribing a fountain of grace which bursts forth modestly *within* her most circumscribed arena.[60] These miraculous assets, maintaining her totality, effectively countermand her breachable femininity and neutralize the dangerous inadequacy of her feminine gender as a vessel for God.

The neutralization, or even masculinization, of gender-signalling within Marian discourse is a topic which demands further discussion. We have just examined the way in which architectural metaphor is used to denote a bodily completion normally associated with the male physique. For keen-nosed Freudians, the fountain in the tower will also lend itself to a phallic interpretation; certainly it functions in this way in many medieval and Renaissance allegorical romances.[61] The choice of contemporary *castle* architecture also has gendered implications, since it succeeds in aligning Mary with a militaristic culture predominantly male in composition. This alignment helps legitimate the practice of militarism, and presumably reflects the new rapprochement between Church and military aristocracy, culminating in the religious warfare of the crusades. Nonetheless, in some ways it represents a diminution of the transsexual belligerence evident in the virtuous personifications of earlier Latin literature. Prudentius' *Psychomachia* is exemplary in this respect.[62] In his allegory of conflict between the vices and virtues, composed during the fourth century, the virtues are allegorized as terrible and effective battle-maidens, devising a variety of graphic demises for their vicious counterparts. From such beginnings, the twelfth- and thirteenth-century repositioning of the exemplary female as defensive architecture reads as a falling off. Militant female virtue reconvenes as defence, active combat upon the battlefield gives way to stasis and stonework in response to a contemporary concern with the enclosure and control of women religious which has already been addressed.[63]

The troping of the Virgin as a fortress is an exercise in masculinization. As I said earlier, this reordering of gender overtones may represent an ecclesiastical attempt to resolve the difficulties perceived in the selection of a woman as a bearer of Incarnate God. However, it is perhaps more satisfying to interpret the exercise as a literary demonstration of the *difference* between divine and natural modes of operation. The *supernaturalness* or 'other-naturalness' of divine practice is indicated by creating characters, obedient to the divine will, who perform in a way that actively contradicts the constraints associated with their natural gender. Thus, various female saints adopt the hagiographic guises of successful disputation, pedagogy, strength and public authority associated with male behaviour, whereas certain holy men, Christ being the supreme instance, acquire markedly female traits as a way of underlining the discrepancy between natural and divine practice.[64]

Virginity confers immunity from corruptive matter; it spiritualizes the body out of existence. Having discussed how the architectural metaphor interacts with advancing Marian doctrine and with the cult of sacramental virginity, it is now necessary to examine its effects upon the articulation of the female flesh. We looked above at the way in which Grosseteste's allegory succeeded in neutralizing or masculinizing conventional female incompletion. Yet, more important than this, one must also acknowledge how comprehensively the trope *erases* the literal presence of the body. The writing of Mary as a castle stands as a total annulment of her feminine physicality. It participates in a discourse of virginity which is, to use the words of Helen Solterer, 'completely detachable from the body'.[65] For the castle, as utilized in Marian homily, has no inherent nor even any analogous connection to the truth of the flesh. It works as a free-floating linguistic sign, unleashed from any intrinsic relation with its referent. Within the symbolic vocabularies of both courtly and religious ideologies it has been communally endorsed as a sign signifying virginity, yet it is a sign that reads blatantly, almost flagrantly, at the level of pure convention. Like the rose, another potent symbol for unplucked virginity within French courtly poetry, the castle completely eschews all contact with the female physique. Instead, it functions as a barricade: a sign which deflects and absorbs vision and which effectively *blocks out* contemplation of the sacred female flesh, especially in relation to the genitally orientated events of conception and pregnancy.

This erasure of bodily reality is not confined solely to the enactment of the architectural metaphor. In her chapter in this volume, Karin Boklund-Lagopoulou describes how the Virgin's body is displaced into a series of metaphorical epithets within the Middle English religious lyrics.[66] Here, as elsewhere, the recognition of female corporeality is carefully avoided. Instead, the Virgin is propelled between a long list of metaphorical presences – she is the star of the sea, a tower of refuge, the gate of heaven – which she is entitled to inhabit and exchange because her virginity and immaculate virtue have freed her from the gravitional ties of corruptible substance. In other words, moral perfection provides the licence by which one may float free of the corruptible flesh and hover at a level of continual linguistic metaphor. This has, of course, considerable consequences with regard to the evaluation of figurative discourse, but such discussions lie beyond the scope of this chapter. The Virgin's confinement in continual metaphor also lends itself to a couple of further explanations. First, her presentation as a fortress undoubtedly has the effect of deflecting our gaze from her female physique, a move which could conceivably be associated with clerical revulsion. However, this deflection can also be given a protective gloss. Namely, it works to protect the male recipients of Marian discourse, since it minimizes the likelihood of arousing unwanted desires in the course of contemplating the Virgin.[67] Female bodily erasure in the service of male sexual protection! Second, the erasure of corporeality in favour of the more unworldly embodiments of metaphor in some ways acts to increase Mary's transparency. While, on the one hand, the Virgin's embodiment as a castle blocks *out* a particular type of vision, preventing contemplation of her actual female form, on the other hand, her elevation to metaphor insubstantiates her, enabling readers to look *through* her to the Son to whom she indicates. Her confinement within the purely linguistic constructs of metaphor enables her transparency in favour of her Son. As Monica Brzezinski Potkay writes, the Virgin's most important characteristic in Marian lyrics is her invisibility, 'the way she disappears in front of our eyes'.[68]

It could be argued that the eradication of the flesh via the mechanism of allegory is not necessarily a gendered phenomenon, nor that, given a limited rhetorical menu of symbols, Grosseteste had other options of portrayal available to him. However, a short survey of allegorical antecedents, turning in particular to other works by Grosseteste, reveals that it was perfectly possible to anatomize the figurative castle into parts that corresponded with the physical bodily members.[69] In another treatise centred upon architecture, the Latin *Templum Dei*,[70] Grosseteste adopts an approach inherited from the Platonic *Timaeus* in which the foundations of a temple are likened to the human kidneys, its walls correlate with the breast, and the roof is paralleled with the head.[71] In the light of this, his decision to opt for a more archaic approach in the *Château d'amour*, and to give a figurative rendition of the Virgin confined to enumerating her spiritual and moral profile, serves as additional evidence of the presence of cultural taboos preventing over-close scrutiny of the bodily paradox of virginal maternity.

Finally, it seems appropriate to address the difficulties, or at least ambiguities, which surround the narrator's role within this allegorical episode. The narrator takes his stand outside the Marian fort as one hounded by worldly snares, petitioning for entry:

> Franche Pucele Reïne
> De refui forte fermine,
> A tei est ma alme venue
> Ki a ta porte huche e hue,
> Hue huche, e hue e crie
> Duce dame, aïe, aïe,
> Reine dame, ovrez, ovrez.
> Un peu puiser me lessez.[72]

On the face of it, this address is a wholly laudable intercession to the Virgin. Many pre-Conquest antiphons adopt a similarly emotional tone of personal entreaty,[73] and several twelfth-century prayers, including the influential trio composed by St Anselm, explicitly position the speaker before the Marian temple of mercy as a wounded soul in need of healing.[74] However, written in the early thirteenth century, the *Château* is unable to escape entirely from association with the secular romances to which it is also indebted. In such romances, as in associated courtly festivity,[75] the women who are the foci of troubadour desire are frequently figured as besieged fortresses whose defences serve to stimulate eroticism, but who are ultimately fated to be stormed and entered by their importunate suitors. Burdened with such a history, the recycling of this trope in a theological context means that pleas for entry from beyond the moat have the inadvertent effect of casting the poet-persona in the role of sexual supplicant, whose bids for access inevitably provoke the connotation of a demand for sexual favours. Not only does Grosseteste's allegory, as it stands, conspicuously fail to dispel the undesirable ambiguities awakened by these pleas; their existence also creates a further dilemma. Theologically, Mary's identity as a compassionate intercessor depends upon admitting supplicants into her care. However, whereas the courtly castle of the flesh is built to await violation, the religious castle of interrelated virtue is designed with an explicit eye to *difference*: a difference centred upon inviolability. In terms of this opposition and in the light of courtly tradition, any relaxation in defences inadvertently suggests the presence of moral compromise. This means that the poet's enterprise seems doomed to founder, since his pleas for entry, if met, can only succeed in compromising the moral efficacy of the desired refuge, rather than in fulfilling his spiritual requirements.

Bal labelled Mary a 'sadistic' invention. What sort of relevance does this have to the complicated metaphorical existences she enjoyed over the Middle Ages? The answer seems to me to pull in several directions. On the one hand, the numerous strands and influences which were assimilated to create her metaphorical body speak of a richness of appreciation, an enriching complexity of association, which enhanced the value of women in society. Mary's envisioning as a castle invested her with insignia of authority, with overtones of quasi-divinity, which elevated her gendered standing and made her a powerful locus of inspiration and invocation for women religious. On the other hand, the suspicion of quasi-divinity in her nature had the effect of diminishing her contact with an earthly 'sisterhood', and of making her assumption of regal and judicial roles largely irrelevant to the women who courted her. This, together with Mary's metaphorical tendency towards masculinization and bodily erasure, and her inhabitation of forms committed both to the suppression of female sexuality and the extension of female enclosure and control, depleted her efficacy as an object of aspiration for normal medieval women or, at least, located exemplary religious practice within behaviours which involved a diminution of biological female gender. Bal highlights several of these outcomes and underplays others in adopting the discourse of sadism. In order to modify the allegations of premeditated torment implicit in this discourse, I have attempted to outline some of the possible counter-readings which can be brought to Mary's allegorization as a fortress. I have also attempted to place these readings, for and against spiritual value, in relation to a historical continuum of metaphorical and doctrinal evolution. The selective investigation of this continuum historicizes interpretations of the mythic Mary which have in the past suffered from the prioritization of polemic over history. It also shows that the implication of premeditation in the construction of a metaphorical commonplace functions as an anachronism.

## Notes

[1] M. Bal, 'Sexuality, Sin and Sorrow: The Emergence of Female Character', in S. R. Suleiman (ed.), *The Female Body in Western Culture: Contemporary Perspectives* (Cambridge, Mass., 1986), 317–38.

[2] C. W. Bynum, *Fragmentation and Redemption: Essays on Gender and the Human Body in Medieval Religion* (New York, 1991), 130–1.

[3] H. Graef, *Mary: A History of Doctrine and Devotion*, 2 vols. (London and New York, 1963); M. Warner, *Alone of All her Sex: The Myth and Cult of the Virgin Mary* (London, 1976). See also J. Winston, 'The Face of the Virgin: Problems in the History of Representation and Devotion' (University of Columbia Ph.D. thesis, 1997); P. S. Gold, *The Lady and the Virgin: Image, Attitude and Experience in Twelfth-Century France* (Chicago, 1985).

[4] J. Kristeva, 'Stabat Mater', in *Histoires d'amour* (Paris, 1983); M. P. Carroll, *The Cult of the Virgin Mary: Psychological Origins* (Princeton, 1986).

[5] M. Clayton, *The Cult of the Virgin Mary in Anglo-Saxon England* (Cambridge, 1990), 71–3, 88, discusses the pre-Conquest office of Mary and her evocation as a door to eternal life in the New Minster Missal. Graef, *Mary*, 229–30, discusses *Alma Redemptoris Mater*, the Advent antiphon which hails Mary as Gate of Heaven and Star of the Sea.

[6] Luke 10:38–9.

[7] R. D. Cornelius, *The Figurative Castle: A Study of the Medieval Allegory of the Edifice* (Bryn Mawr, 1930), 37–47.

[8] Aelred of Rievaulx, 'Sermo 17: In Assumptione B. Mariae', in his *Sermones*, PL 195. 303–9.

[9] J. Murray (ed.), *Le Château d'amour de Robert Grosseteste* (Paris, 1918) (hereafter cited as *Château*, with page and line numbering). The only major secondary works upon this poem are M. Creek, 'The Sources and Influence of Robert Grosseteste's *Château d'amour*' (Yale University Ph.D. thesis, 1941), and K. Sajavaara, 'The Middle English Translations of Robert Grosseteste's *Château d'amour*', *Mémoires de la Société Néophilologique de Helsinki*, 32 (1967).

[10] R. W. Southern, *Robert Grosseteste: The Growth of an English Mind in Medieval Europe* (Oxford, 1986). The previous major retrospective upon Grosseteste was D. A. Callus (ed.), *Robert Grosseteste: Scholar and Bishop* (Oxford, 1955). The most recent volume-length study is G. Freiburgs (ed.), *Aspectus and Affectus: Essays and Editions in Grosseteste and Medieval Intellectual Life in Honour of R. C. Dales* (New York, 1993).

[11] Southern, *Robert Grosseteste*, 53–62.

[12] His writings are listed and classified in S. Harrison Thomson, *The Writings of Robert Grosseteste* (Cambridge, 1940).

[13] It is important to note here that Grosseteste wrote a second Anglo-Norman allegory, *Le Mariage de neuf filles du Diable*; also, that a further Latin treatise, *Templum Dei*, edited by J. Goering and F. A. C. Mantello (Toronto, 1984), has marked affinities with the *Château d'amour* in its organization around an allegorical architectural structure.

[14] Southern, *Robert Grosseteste*, 224–5.

[15] See H. Traver, *The Four Daughters of God: A Study of the Versions of this Allegory with Special Reference to those in Latin, French and English* (Bryn Mawr, 1907); T. Hunt, 'The Four Daughters of God: A Textual Contribution', *Archives d'histoire doctrinale et littéraire du Moyen Âge*, 48 (1981), 287–316.

[16] Grosseteste, *Château*, 89/15–18, 89/23–8. 'We all have need of aid, but assuredly we cannot all know the languages of Hebrew, Greek and Latin ... so that each one may know in his own tongue within himself without folly his God and his redemption, I begin my argument in French, for those who have neither letters nor learning.'

[17] Dominica Legge suggested more than thirty years ago that the poem could well have been designed for the entertainment and instruction of Simon de Montfort's sons who spent time in Grosseteste's household in 1252. M. D. Legge, *Anglo-Norman Literature and its Background* (Oxford, 1963), 222–4.

[18] Harrison Thomson, *Writings*, 152–4.

[19] Oxford, Bodleian Library, MS Eng. Poet. a. 1 (Vernon) (*c.* 1390); Oxford, Bodleian Library, MS Add. B. 107 (*c.* 1450); London, British Library, MS Add. 22283 (Simeon) (*c.* 1400); Sajavaara, 'Middle English Translations', 260–319.

[20] London, British Library, MS Egerton 927 (*c.* 1425); Sajavaara, 'Middle English Translations', 320–53.

[21] A. I. Doyle, *The Vernon MS: A Facsimile of Bodleian Library, Oxford. MS*

*Eng. Poet. a. 1* (Cambridge, 1987), 14–15, quoted in F. Riddy, 'Women Talking about the Things of God: A Late Medieval Sub-culture', in C. M. Meale (ed.), *Women and Literature in Britain 1150–1500* (Cambridge, 1993), 104–37 (106).

[22] London, British Library, MS Egerton 927 originates from the Cistercian abbey of Sawley in West Riding upon the river Ribble, and a prologue identifies its compiler as a 'munk of Sallay'.

[23] See Gen. 2:10–14.

[24] See 1 Kings 10:18–19.

[25] See Rev. 4:3.

[26] For the well of grace, see Is. 12:3, 55:1 and Jn. 4:14, 7:37.

[27] Grosseteste, *Château*, 104/567–111/818.

[28] Warner, *Alone of All her Sex*, 111.

[29] Ibid., 103–20; Clayton, *Cult of the Virgin*, 88–9; Graef, *Mary*, 210–64.

[30] Clayton, *Cult of the Virgin*, 82.

[31] Eadmer of Canterbury, c. 1060–1128, was the first to formulate the concept of the Immaculate Conception in his treatise, *De excellentia virginis Mariae*. St Anselm's treatise, *De conceptu virginali* (1099), is another important early work in this field. Honorius of Autun and Peter Abelard are two amongst many twelfth-century theologians who wrote in defence of Mary's Bodily Assumption. See Eadmer of Canterbury, *De excellentia virginis*, PL 159. 557–86; see also St Anselm, *De conceptuu virginali et originali peccato*, PL 158. 431–68.

[32] Graef, *Mary*, 266–73.

[33] Ibid., 221.

[34] Ibid., 283.

[35] R. Rambuss, 'Devotion and Defilement: The Blessed Virgin Mary and the Corporeal Hagiographies of Chaucer's *Prioress's Tale*', in L. H. Lefkovitz (ed.), *Textual Bodies: Changing Boundaries of Literary Representation* (New York, 1993), 75–99 (82).

[36] Southern, *Robert Grosseteste*, 221.

[37] Ibid., 227.

[38] Rambuss, 'Devotion and Defilement', 77, 79.

[39] Grosseteste was closely involved with the Franciscans at Oxford for many years although he never entered the order himself. Initially, he disapproved of their dependence upon begging, but he seems, gradually, to have moved some way towards their way of thinking, as attested by his own later relinquishment of many positions and revenues. See Southern, *Robert Grosseteste*, 74–5. The ditches of voluntary poverty which surround the Virgin's castle within the *Château d'amour* suggest that this depiction of the exemplary life has been influenced by the Franciscan ideal.

[40] See C. Whitehead, 'Castles of the Mind: An Interpretative History of Medieval Religious Architectural Allegory' (Oxford University D.Phil. thesis, 1995), 17–18.

[41] These and many other examples are pursued in more detail in Whitehead, 'Castles of the Mind', 5–68.
[42] For a stimulating discussion of the way in which chaste spirituality tends to be located in ahistorical bodies in the early thirteenth century, see J. Wogan-Browne, 'Chaste Bodies: Frames and Experiences', in S. Kay and M. Rubin (eds.), *Framing Medieval Bodies* (Manchester, 1994), 24–42 (24).
[43] J. McEnvoy, 'Grosseteste on the Soul's Care for the Body: A New Text and New Sources for the Idea', in Freibergs (ed.), *Aspectus and Affectus*, 37–56 (42–3).
[44] M. Carruthers, *The Book of Memory* (Cambridge, 1990); M. Carruthers, *The Craft of Thought: Meditation, Rhetoric, and the Making of Images, 400–1200* (Cambridge, 1998).
[45] Hugh of St Victor, *De arca Noë morali*, *De arca Noë mystica*, and *De vanitate mundi*, in *PL* 176. 618–838.
[46] See C. Whitehead, 'Making a Cloister of the Soul in Medieval Religious Treatises', *Medium Ævum*, 67.1 (1998), 1–29.
[47] See Kay and Rubin (eds.), *Framing Medieval Bodies*, 5; S. Delany, *Impolitic Bodies: Poetry, Saints and Society in Fifteenth-Century England: The Work of Osbern Bokenham* (Oxford, 1998), 27; M. Rubin, 'The Person in the Form: Medieval Challenges to Bodily "Order"', in Kay and Rubin (eds.), *Framing Medieval Bodies*, 100–22 (115).
[48] See P. S. Gold, *The Lady and the Virgin: Image, Attitude and Experience in Twelfth-Century France* (Chicago, 1985).
[49] R. M. Evitt and M. B. Potkay, *Minding the Body: Women and Literature in the Middle Ages, 800–1500* (London, 1997), 60.
[50] Wogan-Browne, 'Chaste Bodies', 34.
[51] Tertullian, *De Oratione et De Virginibus Velandis Libelli*, ed. G. F. Diercks, Stromata Patristica et Medievalia 4 (Antwerp, 1956).
[52] I am indebted to an unpublished paper, 'The Lamb and the Wolf: Militant Maidens and Men in Middle English Hagiography', presented by Paul Price at the Oxford Gender and Creativity Conference, January 1998, for some of the ideas included here.
[53] '"Zion" was once the name of the high tower in Jerusalem; and "Zion" corresponds to "high vision" in English. And this tower signifies the high state of virginity, which as if from a height sees all widows below it, and married women too.' B. Millett and J. Wogan-Browne (eds.), *Medieval English Prose for Women: Selections from the Katherine Group and Ancrene Wisse* (Oxford, 1990), 2–3.
[54] Wogan-Browne, 'Chaste Bodies', 31.
[55] R. Gilchrist, 'Medieval Bodies in the Material World: Gender, Stigma and the Body', in Kay and Rubin (eds.), *Framing Medieval Bodies*, 43–61 (50–8).
[56] M. Day (ed.), *The English Text of the Ancrene Riwle, edited from Cotton Nero A. xiv*, EETS OS 225 (London, 1952), 26–7, 192–3.

[57] J. Bugge, *Virginitas: An Essay in the History of a Medieval Ideal* (The Hague, 1975), 145.

[58] Bynum, *Fragmentation and Redemption*, 186–7.

[59] Elizabeth Robertson surveys Aristotelian, Galenic and Hippocratic medical views of the female in 'Medieval Medical Views of Women and Female Spirituality in the *Ancrene Wisse* and Julian of Norwich's *Showings*', in L. Lomperis and S. Stanbury (eds.), *Feminist Approaches to the Body in Medieval Literature* (Philadelphia, 1993), 142–67.

[60] The Virgin's body is conceived in a very similar manner in the Middle English religious lyrics. See the chapter on that subject within this volume by Karin Boklund-Lagopoulou.

[61] See Guillaume de Lorris and Jean de Meun, *Le Roman de la Rose*, ed. E. Langlois, 5 vols. (Paris, 1914–24), I, 51, lines 1511–37, and the episode of the Bower of Bliss in Edmund Spenser, *The Faerie Queene*, ed. T. P. Roche (Harmondsworth, 1978; repr. 1987), 376, Book 2, canto XII, stanzas 60–2.

[62] Prudentius, *Psychomachia*, in H. J. Thomson (ed. and tr.), *The Works of Prudentius*, 2 vols. (London, 1949), I, 274–343.

[63] Wogan-Browne, 'Chaste bodies', 31.

[64] Various medieval devotional writers, several of them female, associate the blood flowing from the wounds of the crucified Christ with the milk of lactation; see Bynum, *Fragmentation and Redemption*, 82, 96, 102; Robertson, 'Medieval Medical Views', 146. A further example: St Bernard of Clairvaux describes his abbatial relation to his monastic disciples using persistently maternal imagery.

[65] H. Solterer, 'At the Bottom of the Mirage, a Woman's Body: *Le Roman de la Rose* of Jean Renart', in Lomperis and Stanbury (eds.), *Feminist Approaches*, 213–33 (223–4).

[66] Boklund-Lagopoulou, '*Yate of heven*', 139.

[67] B. Semple, 'The Male Psyche and the Female Sacred Body in Marie de France and Christine de Pizan', in F. Jaouèn and B. Semple (eds.), *Corps mystique, corps sacré: Textual Transfigurations of the Body from the Middle Ages to the Seventeenth Century*, Yale French Studies 86 (New Haven, 1994), 164–86 (168).

[68] Potkay and Evitt, *Minding the Body*, 61.

[69] See Whitehead, 'Castles of the Mind', chs. 2.1, 2.3, 2.4.

[70] Robert Grosseteste, *Templum Dei*, ed. J. Goering and F. A. C. Mantello (Toronto, 1984).

[71] Ibid., 29, ch. 1.2.

[72] Grosseteste, *Château*, 111/789–96: 'Noble virgin queen, strong of refuge, fortification. My soul has come to you, [my soul] which is crying out and calling at your door. It cries, it calls out, and cries and shouts. Gentle lady, help, help. Queen lady, open up, open up. Let me draw a little [water].'

[73] Clayton, *The Cult of the Virgin Mary*, 71–3.

[74] Graef, *Mary*, 211–12.

[75] See R. S. Loomis, 'The Allegorical Siege in the Art of the Middle Ages', *American Journal of Archeology*, 2nd series, 23 (1919), 255–69.

# 6
# *Yate of Heven*: Conceptions of the Female Body in the Religious Lyrics

KARIN BOKLUND-LAGOPOULOU

RELIGIOUS lyrics in Middle English first appear in significant numbers shortly before the middle of the thirteenth century, in collections of homiletic or devotional material compiled by the friars (the Dominicans arrived in England in 1221, the Franciscans in 1224).[1] The Franciscans in particular seem to have been very active in the composition and circulation of vernacular religious lyrics, especially before the mid-fourteenth century.[2] Prominent among these poems are translations of Latin hymns and verses suitable for private devotion, such as lyrics on the Passion. Indeed, Rosemary Woolf has suggested that the great majority of Middle English religious lyrics 'served the purpose of a simple but organized form of meditation'.[3]

Although the religious lyrics seem to have reached a very wide public, there is evidence that women were prominent among the audience for these poems. Some lyrics, such as Friar Thomas de Hales's *Love Rune*,[4] were specifically addressed to women leading a cloistered life (it was written 'ad instanciam cuiusdam puelle deo dicate', the manuscript rubric explains). One, the *Ureisun of Vre Lefdi*,[5] is found in British Library, MS Cotton Nero A. xiv, together with the text of the *Ancrene Wisse* and the Wooing Group of prose meditations written for anchoresses. There are several religious lyrics in the Vernon manuscript,[6] which – as Christiania Whitehead points out in her chapter in this volume – appears to have been compiled for the use of a community of nuns. Both Franciscan and Dominican friars acted as spiritual directors to religious houses for women, and Patrick Diehl suggests that nuns were an important part of the audience for vernacular religious lyrics.⁷ But the friars were also confessors of devout laymen and women, and many religious houses seem to have had lively contacts with pious gentlewomen whose role as readers of devotional material, especially in the later Middle Ages, is well documented.⁸ There is thus good reason to believe that devout women, whether enclosed or living in the world, formed a significant part of the audience of Middle English religious lyrics.

This chapter investigates the textual constructions of the female body which the religious lyrics offer this audience. I shall argue that there is a semiotics of the body, and in particular of the female body, in the vernacular lyrics. Even when not addressed specifically to a female audience, these poems provide the woman reader with models for conceiving of her body which are quite different from the various models offered in secular poetry, but closely related to concepts of corporeality and womanhood in devotional prose texts for women.

Medieval devotional literature for women was written largely by men, and its views on the female body have often and justifiably been called misogynist. However, it is clear that this literature had a considerable appeal to women, who actively sought out and used devotional texts. While I do not wish to trivialize the message of inferiority and subordination which the devotional model of the female body implies, much recent scholarship has focused equally on the dynamic responses of medieval women to this material.⁹ I wish to argue here that the ways of writing the body in the religious lyric offered the meditating woman readings which, though certainly constraining, seem to have been imaginatively powerful conceptual tools as well.

At first approach, however, the religious lyrics do not appear to offer any conception of the female body at all. Explicitly, the lyrics are rarely concerned with women, and virtually never with women's bodies as such. This is brought out most strikingly if we compare for a moment the religious lyrics to some of their secular Middle English counterparts. Among the secular lyrics we have no difficulty in finding descriptions of female bodies. Courtly poems, for example, show intense awareness of the physical presence of the lady; in fact, the courtly lyric strikes us as almost obsessive in its erotic attention to the female body. The favourite rhetorical technique of the courtly lyric is a catalogue of the beauties of the lady's body, starting with her face and features and lovingly enumerating all her other physical parts. In the poem from the Harley lyrics known as 'The Fair Maid of Ribbesdale', for example,¹⁰ the reader follows the gaze of the poet as it travels the length of the body of the lady: her head is like the sunbeam, her eyes large and grey, her eyebrows bent and high, her nose seemly, the locks of her hair lovely and long, her chin choice and 'either cheke / Whit inogh and rode on, eke', her mouth merry, her lips lovely and red, her teeth 'white ase bon of whal', her arms long, her fingers fair, and 'Hire tittes aren anunder bis / As apples two of parays' ('Her breasts under fine linen are like two apples of Paradise'), as the poet invites the reader to see for himself ('youself ye mowen seo').

It is true that, as Gayle Margherita points out,[11] this obsessive attention to the lady's body is predicated upon her actual absence. The language of the poem, the catalogue of fragments of her body, is conjured up to substitute for the absent object of the poet's desire: 'Mighte ich hire have and holde / In world well were me.' Thus, in a sense, the very erotic focusing on the female body in the courtly lyric is a mechanism which disguises the absence of the body itself. Yet, however conventionally conceived, the courtly lady appears at least to be 'of blod and bon', as the Harley lyrics put it.

Against this conventionalized, fetishized set of body parts that glitter and shine like precious stones or sun and moon, the secular lyric can also draw on a misogynist satirical tradition, especially in the carols, where the female body appears as a grotesque parody, all flailing arms, scolding tongue, bottomless gullet and insatiable lust:[12]

> All that I may swynk or swet,
> My wyfe it wyll both drynk and ete;
> And I sey ovght, she wyl me bete;
>   Carfull ys my hart therfor.
>
> If I sey ovght of hyr but good,
> She loke on me as she war wod
> And wyll me clovght abovght the hod;
>   Carfull ys my hart therfor.
>
> If she wyll to the gud ale ryd,
> Me must trot all be hyr syd,
> And whan she drynk I must abyd;
>   Carfull ys my hart therfor.
>
> If I say, 'It shal be thus,'
> She sey, 'Thou lyyst, charll, iwovs!
> Wenest thou to ouercome me thus?'
>   Carfull ys my hart therfor.[13]

There are also a very few secular lyrics which suggest a conception of women in control of their own bodies and sexual desires. These are mainly fragments of women's dance songs that are quoted in sermons and collections of homiletic material.[14] Such songs, specifically identified in the manuscripts as performed by women singers and dancers, evince none of the scopophilic eroticism of the courtly lyrics, nor do they foreground the insatiable sexual appetite that the satirical tradition ascribes to women. They often show a female speaker choosing a lover, and they affirm her right to do so:

> Of my husband giu I noht.
> Another hauet my luue ybohit,
> For tuo gloues wyht ynoht.
> If Hic him luue, Y naue no woht.[15]

Just as often, however, the dance songs affirm the woman's right to *refuse* the company of men. The following verse was allegorized in a sermon preached on the occasion of the enclosure of an anchoress:[16]

> We shun makyn a ioly castel
> On a bank bysyden a brymme;
> Schal no man comyn theryn
> But yf he kun swymme,
> Or buth he haue a both of loue
> For to seylyn ynne.[17]

Fragmentary, conventionalized or misogynist as these conceptions in the secular lyrics are, however, they seem remarkably concrete when we compare them to the silence with which the religious lyrics surround the female body.

Not that the body in general is absent from devotional poetry. On the contrary, there is a well-defined tradition of *memento mori* verse in which the body appears in grimly realistic terms.[18] The lyrics on death conceive the body as the material prison of the soul. As such, it is both disgusting in its materiality and distressingly fragile. What Woolf calls 'the most popular of all Middle English death lyrics'[19] are lyrics which enumerate the Hippocratic Signs of Death, the signs by which a physician can tell that the patient is dying. When this list is taken over by the lyric to serve as a moral warning to the reader, the effect is to turn the physician's symptoms into a narrative of the gradual weakening of the bodily faculties, until the process of ageing seems to be literally the first step in the disintegration of the body in decomposition:

> Wanne mine eyhnen misten,
> and mine heren sissen,
> and mi nose koldet,
> and mi tunge ffoldet,
> and mi rude slaket,
> and mine lippes blaken,
> and mi muþ grennet,
> and mi spotel rennet,
> and min her riset,
> and min herte griset,
> and mine honden biuien,
> and mine ffet stiuien,
> al to late, al to late,
> wanne þe bere ys ate gate.[20]

The *memento mori* poems often provide their own catalogue of body parts, but unlike the courtly lyric they do not seem to be looking at the body from without. They seem rather to be experiencing it from *within*; in many ways the speaking subject of these poems appears to be *inhabiting* a body which, disconcertingly, is no longer functioning as expected. A similar conception of the body as temporary housing is found in another thirteenth-century poem:

> Wen þe turuf is þi tuur,
> & þi put is þi bour,
> Þi wel & þi wite þrote
> ssulen wormes to note.
> Wat helpit þe þenne
> al þe worilde wnne?[21]

This poem is usually read as a forceful statement of a set of Christian commonplaces about the smallness of the grave and the transitory nature of worldly goods.[22] The force comes partly from the manner in which the poem involves the reader in its process. It is addressed directly to a reading subject, and it implicates this subject in a transformation. The poem sets up a series of spaces: one set of interior spaces – tower, bower – which are above ground and meant for human habitation, and another set of exterior spaces – turf, pit – below ground and inhabited by another group of living, but decidedly non-human, creatures: the worms. The 'thou' of the poem, the reading 'I', is currently in possession of tower, bower, skin and white throat. I am about to be evicted, however, and not only from my living space but also from my *skin*, from the space of my own body. From *inhabitant* of the tower, I become *inhabited*; from *possessor* of 'al þe worilde wnne', I become the *possession* of another creature, who will now have the use of my skin and my body. This is deterritorialization with a vengeance: what used to be my body is simply a space of which I have the temporary use, and which will shortly be inhabited by someone else.

One semiotics of the body offered by the religious lyric, then, is that of the body as the material prison of the soul. In the lyrics on death, the body is seen as decaying flesh, as food for worms, as that which is submerged and dissolved in the material, filthy and corrupt. But the body which decays in the grave is a body to which gender is irrelevant. It is neither male nor female, merely disintegrating matter.

Related to the image of the body as decaying matter is a particular conception of the female body which we might well expect to find in lyrics written for enclosed women, namely the kind of misogynist view based on medieval theories of physiology and medicine which Elizabeth Robertson has identified in *Ancrene Wisse* and its related texts.[23] Robertson argues that female spirituality in the anchoritic tradition is predicated upon guarding against women's sexuality and sensuality. Woman is the daughter of Eve, whose unbridled appetites led to the Fall. Since all women inherit Eve's tendency to be ruled by the body, the religious life for women must concentrate on the need for control of the body: 'female sexuality leads to the downfall of mankind and ... a woman can achieve union with God only by recognizing that her body is responsible for that *poena damni.*'[24] The lyrics do not generally support such a reading. Sin may have been brought into the world by a woman, but the lyrics concern themselves very little with the supposedly greater disposition of women to sin or with their assumedly inescapable attachment to the body. With few exceptions (Friar Thomas's *Love Rune* is one) the religious lyrics do not much concern themselves with women at all.

Yet there is one woman who figures very largely in the religious lyrics, namely the Virgin Mary. From the earliest manuscripts, indeed already in the early Christian Latin lyrics, there are innumerable poems addressed to the Virgin. Is there no conception of the female body to be found in these? At first sight, one is tempted to answer in the negative. Although many of the poems to the Virgin make use of the language of courtly love, they never catalogue the beauties of Mary's body. Very occasionally, a poem may mention her eyes, which look on the believer with favour in a manner reminiscent of the courtly lady looking at her lover, as Douglas Gray has remarked.[25] But most poems to the Virgin appear to conceive of her physicality exclusively in terms of the breasts that nursed the Christ-child, the womb which bore him, the tears which she wept at the Crucifixion. Both Julia Kristeva and Marina Warner have written about this reduction to milk and tears as a dematerialization of Mary's body.[26]

Instead of cataloguing the beauties of the Virgin as the courtly lyric catalogues the features of the lady, the poems to Mary refer to her in multiple metaphors, derived from centuries of patristic biblical hermeneutics and usually mediated to the vernacular lyric by the Latin hymns (of which the vernacular lyrics are often translations or reworkings). An early fourteenth-century hymn to Mary, 'Marye mayde mylde and fre' (probably by the Augustinian canon William of Shoreham),[27] makes no mention of her body at all, but enumerates many of her traditional attributes in the form of a set of metaphors or *figurae*:

>Marye, mayde mylde and fre,
>Chambre of the trynyte . . .
>
>þou art quene of paradys,
>Of heuene, of erthe, of al þat hys . . .
>
>þou ert þe coluere of noe . . .
>
>þou art þe bosche of synay,
>þou art þe rytte sarray . . .
>
>þou ert þe slinge, þy sone þe ston,
>Þat dauy slange golye op-on;
>þou ert þe ȝerd al of aaron . . .
>
>þou ert þe temple salomon . . .
>
>þou ert þe gate so stronge so stel
>  Ac euere y-schet fram manne . . .

> Þou ert emaus, þe ryche castel
> Þar resteþ alle werye . . .
>
> Ine þe hys god by-come a chyld,
> Ine þe hys wreche by-come myld;
> Þat vnicorn þat was so wyld
>   Aleyd hys of a cheaste:
> Þou hast y-tamed and i-styld
>   Wyþ melke of þy breste.

Among the many different aspects of Mary which are rehearsed in this poem – she is the fairest of women, the promised bride, the spouse of the king, the champion who overcomes the fiend and mediates between God and man – there are repeated references to her flawless virginity, miraculously preserved even in childbirth: 'Þou bere þane kynge of blys / Wyþ-oute senne and sore.' She is the bush of Sinai that burned without being consumed, the rod of Aaron which flowered though dry, the chaste maid who tames the unicorn.

> Ase þe sonne takeþ hyre pas
> Wyþ-oute breche þorʒ-out that glas,
> Þy maydenhod onwemmed hyt was
> For bere of þyne chylde.

These rich and elaborate metaphors for the Virgin, which recur over and over again in hymns and devotional lyrics, thus convey a very specific conception of the female body: a conception emphasizing virginity. The poems never tire of stressing the virginity of Mary. 'Mayden moder milde', sing the Harley lyrics;[28] 'Be glad, of all maidens floure', bids a fifteenth-century poem;[29] 'I syng of a mayden that is makeles', proclaims the Sloane manuscript.[30]

The idea of virginity as an especially holy state has a long history in western culture. For the early centuries of Christian thought, this history has been elegantly chronicled by Peter Brown. Other scholars, among them John Bugge, Bella Millett,[31] Jocelyn Wogan-Browne, Elizabeth Robertson and Carolyn Walker Bynum, have written on the symbolic significance of virginity in the Middle Ages; it is also one of the focal points of Marina Warner's study of the development of Mariology.[32] There is little need to repeat here this discussion of virginity as such. Instead, I propose to examine how the religious lyrics explore and elaborate on the semiotics of virginity, and how they employ this concept to shape the experience of the female body for the pious women, enclosed or lay, who used the lyrics as part of their devotional exercises.

Marina Warner has argued that Mary, precisely because of her inimitable perfection, is too unique to offer a model for earthly women. However, ever since the Council of Nicaea in AD 325 stated that 'if therefore a girl wants to be called a virgin, she should resemble Mary',[33] literature addressed to religious women consistently advises imitation of Mary and special devotion to her. In England, St Aelred's twelfth-century *De institutione inclusarum*, written for his sister, a recluse, recommends Mary as a model for nuns and recluses. The *Ancrene Wisse* includes special daily devotions to the Virgin, and *Hali Meiðhad* specifies that the maiden is following in the steps of Our Lady.

Of the many things that the virginity of Mary can mean in the later Middle Ages, the lyrics focus on bodily intactness. The virgin body is the exact opposite of the corrupt, decaying body. The virgin body is clean, pure, without breach. 'Be glad, of virtues vessel clene', exhorts the fifteenth-century poem in Huntington MS 127. It is a closed, impenetrable space: 'Þou ert þe gate so stronge so stel / Ac euere y-schet fram manne.' It is the *hortus conclusus*, the enclosed garden of the Song of Songs, or a fortified castle: 'Þou ert emaus, þe riche castel / Þar resteþ alle werie.' This, as Christiania Whitehead points out elsewhere in this volume, is the metaphor elaborated in Robert Grosseteste's allegorical *Château d'amour*, where the castle of the virgin's body is at the same time her inviolate virginity, the fortress which defends sinners against the devil (and/or against the wrath of God), and a dwelling-place prepared for the incarnate Christ, 'Chambre of þe trynyte.'

Doctrinally, the virginity of Mary expresses her sinlessness, her purity of soul. But in the lyrics – and elsewhere in medieval religious literature – it seems at times to be the other way around: Mary is sinless because she maintains her bodily virginity, her intact and unpenetrated body. Because she is a virgin and thus physically pure, her body can become a conduit, a passage or gateway between heaven and earth, God and man, spirit and flesh. Christ descended from heaven into her body; but also, in a reverse movement, sinners can pass *through* Mary into heaven. 'And euer maden haldand state, / of hewen þow art þe sely yate', proclaims a fourteenth-century poem, 'wyndow of hewen mirth ... yate of hewen, ster of se';[34] or – in another poem from the same manuscript – 'Þou art in heuene an hole i-mad / Þorw which þe senful þorw-geþ glad; / Þou art þe kynges ȝate idȝht.'[35] Gate of heaven: this is what is at stake in the conception of the virgin body.

Virginity was, of course, an ideal for both men and women religious in the Middle Ages. But the concern to keep the body intact, to preserve one's maidenhead, was especially important for women. In the earliest Middle English texts destined for women religious, *Hali Meiðhad*, *Ancrene Wisse*, the Katherine Group saints' lives, we find applied to the female religious many of the same metaphors for the virgin body as in the Marian lyrics: it is a castle to be defended, a vessel of precious liquor, a bower to be kept locked.[36] The idea of the woman's virginity 'dictates the structure of the work', says Robertson of *Ancrene Wisse*.[37] Virginity is 'heovene cwen, ant worldes alesendnesse', ('queen of heaven and the world's redemption'), writes the author of *Hali Meiðhad*.[38] *Hali Meiðhad* also develops the idea of virginity as a tower, both in the sense of a closed, impenetrable space and in the sense of a passage between heaven and earth: 'The virgin, like a tower, is part of the earth, but reaches toward heaven. By maintaining herself in the heights of the tower, she can recreate a part of heaven on earth.'[39]

Friar Thomas de Hales's *Love Rune*, amongst the earliest lyrics specifically addressed to an audience of women religious, also argues that virginity places the maiden in special contact with heaven:

> He haveþ bi-tauht þe o tresur
>    þat is betere þan gold oþer pel,
> And bit þe luke þine bur,
>    & wilneþ þat þu hit wyte wel
> Wyþ þeoues, wiþ reueres, wiþ lechurs,
>    þu most beo waker and snel;
> Þu art swetture þane eny flur
>    hwile þu witest þene kastel.
>
> . . .
>
> Þis ilke ston þat ich þe nemne
>    Mayden-hod i-cleoped is;
> Hit is o derewurþe gemme,
>    of alle oþre he berþ þat pris,
> And bryngeþ þe wiþ-vte wemme
>    in-to þe blysse of paradis.
> Þe hwile þeu hyne witest vnder þine hemme,
>    þu ert swetture þan eny spis.[40]

The virgin body is the perfect human body, preserving on earth the state of Adam and Eve in Paradise.[41] As such, it is occasionally suggested that it might confer immunity from the physical corruption of death. Although the bodily assumption of Mary did not officially become doctrine until the twentieth century, Marina Warner cites early apocryphal texts on the death of the Virgin in which her body is taken up uncorrupted to heaven, precisely because she lived a life of absolute purity on earth.[42] The incorruptibility of the body after death is a frequent sign of holiness and, Bynum argues, 'a virtual requirement for female sanctity' after 1400.[43] The virgin body, the body which is closed to penetration from without, thus seems to be set in deliberate opposition to the corruptible body, the disintegrating corpse of the *memento mori* poems.

At issue in the religious lyrics' preoccupation with virginity, however, is not really the achievement of physical incorruptibility as such. Rather, it is the possibility of turning the body into an instrument, a space in which God can be manifested. William of Shoreham called Mary 'Chamber of the Trinity'. The virginal body imitates the body of Mary in that it becomes a point of communication between heaven and earth, flesh and spirit. This seems to be the sense of the assertion, repeated with such fervour by the texts, that virginity is the key to paradise. The body is as it were *emptied* of its sinful, corruptible substance and turned into a 'vessel clene' to receive God.

The virgin body of Mary was the original mortal vessel which received God in the Incarnation, and the Incarnation is frequently conceived in the lyrics as Christ taking flesh from Mary's body. 'When þou ȝeue hym my wede' is how Friar William Herebert expresses it:[44] Mary dresses Christ in clothing of human flesh. This image recurs often in medieval religious literature: in Middle English we find it, famously, both in Julian of Norwich's parable of the Lord and the Servant (who is Christ dressed in Adam's tunic), and in Langland's version of the Crucifixion (where Christ jousts dressed in Piers's armour, *humana natura*). Bynum points out that some medieval theories of reproduction held that the mother provides the material stuff of the child whereas the father provides the form; breast milk was considered a form of blood, so the nursing mother can be seen as actually feeding the child with her flesh.[45] Hence the emphasis on Mary's womb and breasts, the sites in her body where this 'enfleshing' occurs:

> Wel he wot he is þi sone
> *ventre quem portasti*;
> He wyl nout werne þe þi bone
> *paruum quem lactasti*.⁴⁶

The motherhood of Mary should not, I think, be seen as a purely sentimental motif in the lyrics. Certainly there are poems – such as the lullabies of Mary to the Christ-child – whose attractiveness derives largely from the idyllic portrayal of the relationship between a human mother and her baby. But in poems such as the macaronic lyric quoted above, the motherhood of Mary has to do with the sanctification of the body, the uniquely female body, the body which gives birth. William of Shoreham refers to the Incarnation quite concretely as 'þyne chyl-dynge', the act of childbirth.

In *Ancrene Wisse* the anchoress is urged to make her heart a nest or womb for Christ to enter.⁴⁷ Female saints have visions in which they touch or hold the Christ-child.⁴⁸ Implied in the frequent exhortations to religious women to imitate Mary is the notion of the devout believer as giving birth to Christ; in the *Book to a Mother*, the author (a priest writing instructions in good living for his widowed mother) argues that 'Þou maist conceyue þe same Crist and bere him not onlich nine monþes but wiþoute ende; and þat is bettur þan to bere him bodiliche as oure Ladi dide.'⁴⁹ While the lyrics generally do not conceive of the devout believer as giving birth to Christ, they frequently show Christ moving into the body of the believer in another sense. Christ is often depicted as a noble lover or husband who stands outside the 'heart' of the faithful and knocks on the door, asking for admittance,⁵⁰ as he does in a poem from the commonplace book of Friar John Grimestone:

> Vndo þi dore, my spuse dere,
> Allas! wy stond i loken out here?
>    fre am I þi make.
> Loke mi lokkes & ek myn heued
> & al my bodi with blod be-weued
>    For þi sake.
>
> Allas! Allas! heuel haue i sped,
> For senne iesu is fro me fled,
>    Mi trewe fere.
> With-outen my gate he stant alone,
> Sorfuliche he maket his mone
>    On his manere.

> Lord, for senne i sike sore,
> Forȝef & i ne wil no more,
> With al my mith senne i forsake,
> & opne myn herte þe inne to take.
> For þin herte is clouen oure loue to kecchen
> Þi loue is chosen vs alle to fecchen;
> Min herte it þerlede ȝef i wer kende,
> Þi suete loue to hauen in mende.
> Perce myn herte with þi louengge,
> Þat in þe i haue my duellingge. Amen[51]

The imagery of Christ as lover is, of course, very highly developed in medieval mysticism.[52] It also occurs in devotional literature, including the *Ancrene Wisse*. This poem is a rather understated version, yet here also the imagery is present: Christ is the *mate* of the believer, who is his *spouse*; she *opens* her heart to *take him in*, in the sense of providing a house for him like a good wife, but also in the sense of *being penetrated* by him – 'perce myn herte with þi louengge'.

The mystical tradition of Christ the bridegroom and lover apparently appealed especially to women mystics, for whom it had official theological sanction in the frequent descriptions of the nun as the bride of Christ. But the position of the (feminine) spouse of Christ is cultivated by male mystics as well. One of the originators of this mystical discourse is St Bernard, and the author of the Middle English poem above, Friar John Grimestone, wrote several other lyrics of this type. In its fully developed form, the moment of penetration is a moment of ecstasy, as in Bernini's famous statue of St Theresa of Avila.

The imagery of Christ as lover can lead to fantasies of being married to God. Margery Kempe, who had her own struggles with the ideal of virginity,[53] recounts her wedding to God the Father while on pilgrimage to Rome, in the church of the Holy Apostles before Christ and the Holy Ghost and a congregation consisting of the Virgin, the twelve apostles, St Katherine and St Margaret and many other saints, virgins and angels. It can also lead in the direction of being carried away – ravished, raped, possessed. John Grimestone's poem hints at this in the couplet which describes the heart of Christ as cleft to *catch* our love, to *fetch* us all. But once Christ has moved in, there really is no room left for anyone else, including the original inhabitant. As St Paul puts it, 'With Christ I am nailed to the cross, yet I live now not I, but Christ in me' (Gal. 2:20). The identification ideally is complete; the mystic finds his or her identity in being taken over by God.

Having Christ move into you and moving yourself into Christ often seem to be equivalent forms of identification. The installation of Christ in the heart of the believer is casually reversed in the last line of Grimestone's poem: 'Þat in þe i haue my duellingge.' The journey of the believer into the body of Christ entails a rather different set of metaphors, however. Grimestone has another poem in which he elaborates on this reverse journey:

> Gold & al þis werdis wyn
> Is nouth but cristis rode;
> I wolde ben clad in cristis skyn,
> Þat ran so longe on blode,
> & gon t'is herte & taken myn In –
> Þer is a fulsum fode,
> Þan ȝef i litel of kith or kyn,
> For þer is alle gode. Amen.[54]

In addition to moving into Christ's heart and taking up residence, the poet here also wants to dress in Christ's skin. Julian of Norwich returns to this imagery repeatedly: Christ is 'oure clothing, that for love wrappeth vs and wyndeth vs, halseth vs and all becloseth vs, hangeth about vs for tender love'.[55] In her tenth revelation Christ guides her into his own body through the wound in his side, 'and ther he shewyd a feyer and delectable place, and large jnow for alle mankynde that shalle be savyd and rest in pees and in loue'.[56]

The images of Christ dressed in man's flesh, Christ the lover-knight doing battle for his beloved, the soul, and Christ's body as dwelling-place for the believer are combined in remarkable fashion in the poem 'In the vaile of restles mynd', an extended address by the crucified Christ to the soul with the recurring refrain *Quia amore langueo*.[57]

The poem opens with the poet searching (in the interior space of the 'vaile of restles mynd') for a 'treulofe' and finding it in the person of a wounded man sitting on a hill under a tree, 'A semely man / to be a kyng'. He has been grievously wounded in battle because of his love for 'my sistur, mannys soule . . . / My faire love and my spouse bryght'. She provided his clothing, his bleeding flesh:

> loke vnto myn handys, man!
>   thes gloues were geuen me / whan I hyr sowght;
> they be nat white / but rede and wan,
>   embrodred with blode / my spouse them bowght;

> they wyll not of / I lefe them nowght,
>   I wowe hyr / with them / where euer she goo.
> thes handes full frendly for hyr fowght,
>   *Quia amore langueo.*

The knight has prepared a room for his spouse inside the wound in his side:

> In my syde / I haf made hyr nest,
>   loke in me / how wyde a wounde is here!
> this is hyr chambre / here shall she rest,
>   that she and I may slepe in fere.
> here may she wasshe / if any filth were;
>   here is socour for all hyr woo;
> cum if she will / she shall haf chere,
>   *Quia amore langueo.*

But when the spouse, the believer, enters the body of Christ and rests in the chamber prepared for her, a final metamorphosis takes place. The spouse becomes a child nesting in its mother's womb, nursed with the milk of her breast:

> My spouse is in chambre, hald ʒowre pease!
>   make no noyse / but lat hyr slepe;
> my babe shall sofre noo disease,
>   I may not here my dere childe wepe,
> for with my pappe I shall hyr kepe;
>   no wondyr / thowgh I tend hyr to,
> thys hoole in my side had neuer ben so depe,
>   but *Quia amore langueo.*

Moving into the body of Christ is moving back into the imaginary maternal body as the point of ultimate return, the source of birth and of life. It is, thus, surely no accident that Julian of Norwich, who writes of wrapping Christ around us like a blanket, of travelling into Christ's heart through the wound in his side, should also have elaborated famously on the concept of the motherhood of Christ.

Christ is often seen as a mother in mystical discourse.[58] The wound in his side is paralleled both in literature and in iconography to a breast, and the blood that flows from it is the milk with which he nourishes the faithful in the Eucharist. Bynum gives examples of images in which the crucified Christ is shown giving birth to the Church through the wound in his side, which thus functions as an opening into a womb.[59] Since the body, being matter, is in the Middle Ages often felt to be 'female' as compared to the 'male' intellect, the fact that Christ was incarnated – had a material human body – leads to a way of thinking in which Christ is seen as symbolically female, and, since his love for humankind is unconditional, it is seen as 'maternal'. As Julian of Norwich puts it:

> The moders servyce is nerest, rediest and surest ... This office ne myght nor could nevyr none done to the full but he alone. We wytt that alle oure moders bere vs to payne and to dyeng ... But oure very moder Jhesu, he alone beryth vs to joye and to endless levyng ... The moder may geue her chylde sucke hyr mylke, but oure precyous moder Jhesu, he may fede vs wyth hym selfe ... The moder may ley hyr chylde tenderly to hyr brest, but oure tender mother Jhesu, he may homely lede vs in to his blessyd brest by his swet opyn syde ...[60]

But the comfortable and familiar image of the mother caring for her child which we find in Julian is in a certain sense misleading precisely in its familiarity. For Julian's voyage into the heart of Christ takes place in the course of an extended meditation on Christ's *crucified* body, with an excruciating fixation on details of blood flowing in thick drops, thorns pulling at the skin, the body blackening and drying in dehydration and death. At one point Julian is so distressed by her own vision that she is tempted to turn her eyes away and look up to heaven instead, which would provide a more pleasant and reassuring, and theologically apparently equivalent, version of the Godhead. But she resists the temptation, answering, 'Nay, I may nott, for thou art my hevyn.'[61] The bliss of return to the maternal body is to be found only through identification with the tortured and torn body of the crucifixion; the standard road to Christ's heart is through the wound in his side, the mother's milk with which he suckles the believer is his blood.[62] The condition for this vision of a kind of pre-natal union with the mother, then, involves an explicit recognition of the mortality and materiality of, and identification with, the suffering body of Christ. Since the desire for identification with, and rebirth through, the suffering body of Christ is overwhelmingly the most common topic of Middle English religious lyrics and devotional prose, our reading would thus lead us to conclude that the female body is not as absent from medieval religious literature as it would seem at first sight, but that it is, as it were, disguised – in a body which is sexually male, but symbolically often female.

The body as decay and corruption, the open, bleeding body in the torments of birth/crucifixion or the closed, virginal body of the Chosen Vessel – which is, then, the conception of the female body in the religious lyrics? To attempt an answer, I would like to mention briefly one more aspect of the medieval conception of the body of Christ. The Ebstorf map, an early thirteenth-century map of the world from Kloster Ebstorf in Germany,[63] depicts the entire earth as Christ's body: the circle of the earth is shown with Christ's head, hands and feet at top, sides and bottom. Through the Incarnation, Christ has taken up into himself all of the material universe, and through the Resurrection – of the body, as the Creed emphasizes – he has sanctified it. In the most archaic Christian practices, death is treated as a sort of temporary storage of the body while waiting for the resurrection of the Last Judgment: hence the stacking of the dead neatly on the shelves of the catacombs, the emphasis on keeping the dead body intact either in undisturbed burial or by collecting and storing the bones.[64] The dead are referred to as 'sleeping'. What exactly becomes of the soul in this theology is less clear: it is said to be enjoying a 'foretaste' of the condition in which it will find itself permanently after the Last Judgement. But it is the body which will be resurrected; Bynum cites several examples of theologians who argue that the soul 'yearns' for its body and that the human being will not be perfect and complete without the reunion of soul and body.[65] The bodies of exceptionally holy men and women are in a sense never quite dead.[66] The relics of saints' bodies continue to possess the same power to work miracles as the saint himself or herself did when alive, and are treated in many respects as if they were alive (greeted, revered, given presents in the form of candles and votive offerings, carried in procession, etc.).

In the light of the above evidence for a view of the material body as sanctified, I would speculate that there might, paradoxically, ultimately be less distance than we think between Christ's maternal body, which provides bliss and nourishment to the believer, and the body of Mother Earth in which the dead body of the believer is placed in order to dissolve and disintegrate. In both cases, it is perhaps ultimately a matter of being absorbed and consumed, of dissolving as an individual.[67] The mystic seeks to be united with Christ as lover or bride, travelling into Christ's body or accepting Christ into her or his heart. The goal seems to be precisely the dissolution of the individual self until it is nothing but a conduit for the mystical revelation itself. But to become a conduit, a pure vessel in which God can be revealed or through which humankind can be saved, was, as we saw, the purpose of the virginal body, the hole into heaven, the Chamber of the Trinity. The image of Christ moving into the virginal body of the believer can thus be found inside, as it were, the image of the believer journeying into the body of Christ.

Ultimately, then, I would like to argue that the body in the religious lyrics, which seems at first to be virtually without gender, may in fact be seen as in a certain sense generically female. The ideal of virginity, while applicable to both men and women, was felt to be of particular urgency for women. The most perfect expression of that ideal, the Virgin Mother of God, was emphatically a woman. Christ addresses the believer as a man addressing a woman, enters the heart of the believer as a husband comes to his spouse or a lover to his mistress. Christ takes human flesh from a woman; his flesh is to some degree itself 'female', and his love is maternal. The crucified Christ gives birth through his wounds. The believer is absorbed into Christ, and the body into which she or he enters is a maternal body: the believer rests in Christ's heart like a child in its mother's womb. The dissolution of the self and its absorption into the maternal body – of Christ or Mother Earth – whether in mystical ecstasy or in death is a necessary precondition for its rebirth, in a resurrection in which, as the Middle Ages saw it, the body will retain its gendered nature, male or female, through all eternity.

## Notes

[1] The fundamental critical studies on the Middle English religious lyrics are those by R. Woolf, *The English Religious Lyric in the Middle Ages* (Oxford, 1968) and D. Gray, *Themes and Images in the Medieval English Religious Lyric* (London and Boston, 1972). The standard editions are C. Brown, *English Lyrics of the Thirteenth Century* (Oxford, 1932*)*, *Religious Lyrics of the Fourteenth Century* (Oxford, 1924), and *Religious Lyrics of the Fifteenth Century* (Oxford, 1939). I have used these editions if not otherwise stated.

[2] On the role of the Franciscans, see D. L. Jeffrey, *The Early English Lyric and Franciscan Spirituality* (Lincoln, 1975), esp. 203–14. Woolf, *English Religious Lyric*, 373–6, discusses the nature and provenance of the manuscripts of religious lyrics and also notes the prominence of the Franciscans.

[3] Woolf, *English Religious Lyric,* 13.

[4] Brown, *English Lyrics of the Thirteenth Century*, no. 43.

[5] Ibid., no. 3.

[6] Oxford, Bodleian Library, MS Eng. Poet. a.1.

[7] P. S. Diehl, *The Medieval European Religious Lyric: An Ars Poetica* (Los Angeles and London, 1985), 48–56 (52).

[8] On the friars as confessors to the nobility, see Gray, *Themes and Images*, 22; on the relationships between religious houses and devout laywomen, see esp. F. Riddy, ' "Women Talking about the Things of God": A Late Medieval Sub-culture', in C. M. Meale (ed.), *Women and Literature in Britain 1150–1500* (Cambridge, 1996), 104–27; see also Gray, *Themes and Images*, 19–26. The essay by B. Millett, 'Women in No Man's Land: English Recluses and the Development of Vernacular Literature in the Twelfth and Thirteenth Centuries' (also in Meale (ed.), *Women and Literature*, 86–103), as well as her contribution to the present volume, points out the role of anchoresses as an intermediary audience for vernacular material which eventually also circulated among the laity.

[9] I am thinking particularly of C. W. Bynum, *Holy Feast and Holy Fast: The Religious Significance of Food to Medieval Women* (Los Angeles and London, 1987), and of J. Wogan-Browne's nuanced approach to *Ancrene Wisse* in 'Chaste Bodies: Frames and Experiences', in S. Kay and M. Rubin (eds.), *Framing Medieval Bodies* (Manchester and New York, 1994), 24–42. Note also P. Brown's sensitive treatment of the ideal of virginity in late classical antiquity in *The Body and Society: Men, Women and Sexual Renunciation in Early Christianity* (New York, 1988); his study focuses on an earlier age, but one whose legacy was fundamental in determining later medieval attitudes.

[10] G. L. Brook (ed.), *The Harley Lyrics*, 4th edn (Manchester, 1968), no. 7, 37–9.

[11] G. Margherita, *The Romance of Origins: Language and Sexual Difference in Middle English Literature* (Philadelphia, 1994), 63–70.

[12] Laurie Finke has argued that the opposition between the ideal body of the courtly tradition and the body of the satirical literature in many ways reproduces Mikhail Bakhtin's distinction between the 'classical' and the 'grotesque' body; L. A. Finke, 'Mystical Bodies and the Dialogics of Vision', in U. Wiethaus (ed.), *Maps of Flesh and Light: The Religious Experience of Medieval Women Mystics* (Syracuse, NY, 1993), esp. 36–40.

[13] Edited in R. L. Greene, *The Early English Carols*, 2nd edn (Oxford, 1977), no. 406 (Oxford, Bodleian Library, MS Eng. Poet. e. 1 (29734), *c*. 1480).

[14] Many are printed by S. Wenzel in ch. 7 of his *Preachers, Poets, and the Early English Lyric* (Princeton, 1986), 209–42.

[15] Ibid., 216.

[16] See Christiania Whitehead's discussion in this volume of the castle as a metaphor for the virgin body.

[17] Wenzel, *Preachers, Poets, and the Early English Lyric*, 228.

[18] The lyrics on death are extensively discussed by both Woolf, *English Religious Lyric*, 67–113, 309–55, and Gray, *Themes and Images*, 176–83, 190–7.

[19] Woolf, *English Religious Lyric*, 78.

[20] Brown, *English Lyrics of the Thirteenth Century*, no. 71 (Cambridge, Trinity College, MS 43, thirteenth century).
[21] Ibid., no. 30 (Cambridge, Trinity College, MS 323, second half thirteenth century).
[22] See Gray, *Themes and Images*, 195–6.
[23] E. Robertson, *Early English Devotional Prose and the Female Audience* (Knoxville, Tenn., 1990), 44–76; see also Wogan-Browne, 'Chaste Bodies: Frames and Experiences'.
[24] Robertson, *Early English Devotional Prose*, 46.
[25] As in the poem 'Leuedie, ic þonke þe', in Brown, *English Lyrics of the Thirteenth Century*, no. 27 (Cambridge, Trinity College, MS 323); see Gray, *Themes and Images*, 91–2.
[26] See J. Kristeva, 'Stabat Mater', in T. Moi (ed.), *The Kristeva Reader* (New York, 1986), 160–86; M. Warner, *Alone of All her Sex* (London, 1976), 192–223.
[27] Brown, *English Lyrics of the Fourteenth Century*, no. 32 (British Library, MS Additional 17376, early fourteenth century).
[28] Ibid., no 87.
[29] Brown, *Religious Lyrics of the Fifteenth Century*, no. 34 (California, Huntington Library, MS HM 127, fifteenth century).
[30] Brown, *Religious Lyrics of the Fifteenth Century*, no. 81 (British Library, MS Sloane 2593, fifteenth century).
[31] B. Millett (ed.), *Hali Meiðhad*, EETS OS 284 (London, 1982).
[32] Much of this literature has already been touched upon by Christiania Whitehead in her essay in this volume on the representation of the Virgin Mary as an allegorical fortress.
[33] Quoted in Warner, *Alone of All her Sex*, 68.
[34] Brown, *Religious Lyrics of the Fourteenth Century*, no. 41 (Oxford, Merton College, MS 248, fourteenth century).
[35] Ibid., no. 38.
[36] There is an important literature on these texts to which I am greatly indebted. Several studies have already been cited. See especially the studies by Millett, Robertson and Wogan-Browne; see also the introductions to two anthologies: B. Millett and J. Wogan-Browne (eds.), *Medieval English Prose for Women* (Oxford, 1990), and A. Savage and N. Watson (eds.), *Anchoritic Spirituality* (New York, 1991).
[37] Robertson, *Early English Devotional Prose*, 59.
[38] Millett (ed.), *Hali Meiðhad*, 5.
[39] Robertson, *Early English Devotional Prose*, 81.
[40] Brown, *English Lyrics of the Thirteenth Century*, no. 43/145–68 (Oxford, Jesus College, MS 29, mid-thirteenth century).
[41] Brown, *The Body and Society*, 444–7.
[42] Warner, *Alone of All her Sex*, 81–102.

⁴³ C. W. Bynum, *Fragmentation and Redemption: Essays on Gender and the Human Body in Medieval Religion* (New York, 1992), 187.
⁴⁴ Brown, *Religious Lyrics of the Fourteenth Century*, no. 16 (British Library, MS Additional 46919, early fourteenth century (William Herebert died in 1333)).
⁴⁵ Bynum, *Holy Feast*, 260–72.
⁴⁶ Brown, *English Lyrics of the Thirteenth Century*, no. 17b (British Library, MS Egerton 613, late thirteenth century).
⁴⁷ Robertson, *Early English Devotional Prose*, 58.
⁴⁸ See E. A. Matter, 'Interior Maps of an Eternal External', in Wiethaus (ed.), *Maps of Flesh and Light*, 68–9.
⁴⁹ A. J. McCarthy (ed.), *Book to a Mother: An Edition with Commentary*, Studies in the English Mystics 1, Elizabethan and Renaissance Studies 92 (Salzburg, 1981), 44; see also N. B. Warren, 'Pregnancy and Productivity: The Imagery of Female Monasticism within and beyond the Cloister Walls', *Journal of Medieval and Early Modern Studies*, 28 (1998), 535–43.
⁵⁰ This aspect of the lyrics has been especially researched by R. Woolf, 'The Theme of Christ the Lover-Knight in Medieval English Literature', *Review of English Studies*, 13 (1962), 1–16, and *English Religious Lyric*, 32–66, 183–238.
⁵¹ Brown, *Religious Lyrics of the Fourteenth Century*, no. 68 (National Library of Scotland, Advocates MS 18.7.21, second half fourteenth century; Brown dates the MS to 1372).
⁵² Christ as the divine Bridegroom, the Lover of the soul, is a recurring theme within the discourse of male and female medieval mystics. A sample of women's mystical writings and suggestions for further reading can be found in E. A. Petroff (ed.), *Medieval Women's Visionary Literature* (Oxford, 1986). On the mystical tradition in England, see also the *MMTE* volumes edited by Marion Glasscoe.
⁵³ Margery Kempe's efforts to construct a place for herself within the late medieval model for devout feminine behaviour are discussed in the chapters by Naoë Kukita Yoshikawa and Samuel Fanous in this volume.
⁵⁴ Brown, *Religious Lyrics of the Fourteenth Century*, no. 71.
⁵⁵ E. Colledge and J. Walsh (eds.), *A Book of Showings to the Anchoress Julian of Norwich* (Toronto, 1978), Part II, ch. 5, 299.
⁵⁶ Ibid., Part II, ch. 24, 394–5.
⁵⁷ F. J. Furnivall (ed.), *Political, Religious and Love Poems from Lambeth MS. 306 and other sources*, EETS OS 15 (London, 1866; repr. 1962), 180–9 (Cambridge, University Library, MS Hh.4.12, latter half fifteenth century). For commentary, see Woolf, *English Religious Lyric*, 187–91; see also Gray, *Themes and Images*, 143–5.
⁵⁸ Sarah Beckwith has pointed out the systematic elaboration of maternal imagery with regard to Christ in the vernacular devotional text *The Prickynge of Love*; for example: '& him that I eer fonde in his modres

wombe I fele now how he voucheth-saf to bere my soule as his child withinne his blessid sides', quoted in S. Beckwith, *Christ's Body: Identity, Culture and Society in Late Medieval Writings* (London and New York, 1993), 58.

[59] Bynum, *Fragmentation and Redemption*, esp. 79–117, 151–79.
[60] Colledge and Walsh (eds.), *A Book of Showings*, 595–9.
[61] Ibid., 371.
[62] '... In late medieval crucifixion piety it is the borders and boundaries of Christ's body ... that become the objects of obsessive interest and attention ... For affective piety is obsessed with belonging, with the fantasy of fusion and the bitter reality of separation, and so with the entrances to Christ's body. For "the wounds are clearly an entrance", as it says in the *Meditations on the Life of Christ*' (Beckwith, *Christ's Body*, 42).
[63] Reproduced in P. D. A. Harvey, *Medieval Maps* (London, 1991), figs. 21, 28.
[64] The Orthodox Church even today will not permit cremation of the dead.
[65] 'The thirteenth and fourteenth centuries saw ... much discussion of the resurrection of the body ... [I]n several papal and conciliar pronouncements Christians were required to hold that damned as well as saved rise bodily, nevermore to suffer corruption ...' (Bynum, *Fragmentation and Redemption*, 224). This would of course imply that the resurrected body remains gendered throughout eternity. In her discussion of the body/soul relationship Bynum cites, amongst other sources, Thomas Aquinas's *Quaestiones disputata de potentia Dei absoluta* and the bull *Benedictus Deus* issued in 1336 by Pope Benedict XII (Bynum, *Fragmentation and Redemption*, 222–38).
[66] P. Brown, *The Cult of the Saints* (Chicago, 1981) is a fascinating study of the early history of this phenomenon.
[67] Beckwith argues that Franciscan affective piety 'introduces a complex language of identification whereby through the medium of Christ's body, identities are restored, transformed, revived, absorbed and submerged'; see *Christ's Body*, 52.

Part Four

*Veneration, Performance and Delusion in*
The Book of Margery Kempe

# 7
# Measuring the Pilgrim's Progress: Internal Emphases in *The Book of Margery Kempe*[1]

SAMUEL FANOUS

OF all its deficiencies, structural disorganization is one of the most frequently cited but least discussed characteristics of *The Book of Margery Kempe*.[2] While Professor Meech's Chronological Table represents the earliest and most direct attempt to remedy this deficiency (by imposing a linear progression upon the narrative), much subsequent Margery criticism can be seen, in one sense, as an indirect attempt to order this desultory text.[3] Yet the imposition of external structures on *The Book* can deflect attention from its own internal subtext, unwittingly concealing emphatic structures beneath the text's literal surface. Moreover, it can obscure authorial links with external traditions. If *The Book* is to be dismissed as infelicitous to chronological concerns and a sense of time or place, it seems self-evident that its use of temporality and geography must be taken seriously: references should be collated and evaluated with one another; notable exceptions should be scrutinized. Collectively, these citations, together with the exceptions, should then be compared with an external standard to determine how the treatment of time and place differs in a related genre, with special consideration given to relevant topoi and convention. While this chapter is concerned primarily with the unique evidence of *The Book*'s use of time and place, it will address briefly its broad approach to temporality and geography in attempting to gauge its attitude to convention. Although patently not a saint's life, *The Book* is nevertheless in many ways most closely related to the hagiographic genre. In the absence of a contemporary genre to accommodate Margery's unique œuvre, it may be illuminating to examine criteria surrounding the deployment of time and place allusions in hagiography and to weigh *The Book*'s use of these against these hagiographic conventions.

Having rejected Alan of Lynn's offer to pen her spiritual memoirs, Margery found her literary progeny at the mercy of a singularly ill-trained putative writer, in all likelihood her own son, whose good will and enthusiasm were severely undermined not only by his editorial inexperience but, far more seriously, by a crippling incapacity to write 'neiþyr good Englysch ne Dewch' (5). As in so many enterprises, initial errors of judgement and omission acquired structural proportions and it is unlikely that this 'euel wretyn' text (4), unfaithful to elementary orthographic principles, was any more felicitous to authorial convention. Consequently, the second amanuensis's reticence to fulfil his promise to rewrite the book was as much predicated by a knowledge of the Herculean task he faced in deciphering, reorganizing and resetting the salvaged narrative shreds of this 'so vnresonably wretyn' work as by the gossip about Margery's religious eccentricity circulating among the Lynn bourgeoisie, an axiom underscored by the requirement of a miracle to unlock the redactive process.[4] Miracles notwithstanding, certain limitations proved insuperable and the indifference to chronological continuity extant in his inherited manuscript proved too great an obstacle for the second amanuensis to overcome fully. Making a virtue of necessity, he prefaced his work with a forewarning, simultaneously defining the parameters of his editorial strategy:

> Thys boke is not wretyn in ordyr, euery thyng aftyr oþer as it wer don, but lych as þe mater cam to þe creatur in mend whan it schuld be wretyn, for it was so long er it was wretyn þat sche had for-getyn þe tyme & þe ordyr whan thyngys befellyn. (5)

With no shortage of evidence to corroborate this admission, readers have tended to accept *ad verbum* this apology, rightly ascribing the text's perceived temporal disunity to the multiple-redaction problem described in the Proem, a view buttressed by the work's overall lack of structural cohesion.[5] But this apparent inattention to chronology and place belies a high degree of selectivity, perhaps nowhere more evident than in the contrast between Margery's continental and domestic travels.

The Holy Land narrative is crammed full of interesting data regarding her far-flung pilgrimages, the very aspect of her story which appeals to modern readers. Indeed, part of *The Book*'s growing appeal lies in the accessibility of the sections treating the foreign travels, which in fact are not unrelated to some forms of contemporary travel writing. Foreign names are recorded with precision: 'Seryce, Pruce, Wilsnak, Venyce, Boleyn de Grace, Mownt Syon, Iherusalem' – if not quite with confidence.[6] Experiences are retold in bright, vivid detail, with considerable attention to facts, everyday concerns, topography and, to a limited extent, ethnography. The narrative is marked by a genuine concern to convey candidly the essence of the pilgrimage experience in a remarkably objective light, as is evidenced by the amanuensis's refusal to cannibalize contemporary guidebooks to the Holy Land. This objectivity is perhaps the result of two independent but related phenomena. The itinerary of this momentous journey and its attendant circumstantial details were likely to have been fixed permanently in Margery's memory as she lived through the experience, facilitating near-complete and accurate recall at the editorial stage some twenty years later.[7] Moreover, the subtext on these journeys, that God loves, protects and honours his faithful servant Margery whom the world despises and only the righteous recognize (like the Jerusalem Grey Friars (73)), requires virtually no special treatment or manipulation. Yet this apparent objectivity sits ill at ease with the comparative silence as regards her Compostela experience, throwing into sharp relief the effervescence of detail from her Rome and Jerusalem pilgrimages.[8] How shall we possibly account for the glaring duality in the supply of details on these two journeys without calling her Compostela pilgrimage into question?

Equally conspicuous is the absence of substantial mention of Walsingham. Considering its proximity to Lynn, the distances Margery was accustomed to travelling and the shrine's huge international popularity, it would be surprising if she had only once visited it.[9] The network of roads leading to the shrine, the pilgrim ways, passed directly through Lynn where a special chapel was reserved for pilgrims. It was also the main stop-over point for continental pilgrims to the shrine who came from the Low Countries down the Wash. The famous octagonal red-brick tower in Lynn, the Red Mount Chapel, contained the image of Our Lady of the Red Mount, most likely a reproduction of the one in the Holy House of Nazareth.[10] Yet, despite Walsingham's significance to the Lynn community, her sole recorded visit there, undertaken at the age of sixty and then only as an afterthought, receives parenthetical treatment. A famous preacher's sermon in 'a lityl village a lityl owt of hir wey' was far more to her immediate concerns than the beaten path to Walsingham (227). Margery's stay in York and its environs is described in five long chapters (chs. 50–4), though this was at least her second visit to York. A previous visit, probably in the summer of 1413, became a footnote to events on the return journey.[11] Likewise, Margery's visits to Bridlington, twice mentioned, attract the sparsest comment (chs. 11 and 53).[12] While her itinerary is presented as divinely ordained and, as such, beyond her control, Margery nevertheless attached higher value to certain journeys and it is these which are singled out for narrative inclusion.[13] Thus the domestic travels are circumscribed by a high degree of selectivity which focus by design on a discrete set of events and circumstances. Paradoxically, this selectivity is obscured by the overall structural dislocation and the informality of the internal links or logical progressions: moving from town to town through 'diuers placys of relygyon', these travels are joined not by a rationale for selectivity but by the briefest tags, 'þen sche went on to . . .', creating a synthesis which becomes organic by its very consistency.

Not only are these domestic journeys (subsequent to her return from Rome) selective, but they conceal almost as much as they reveal. They begin immediately and abruptly on her return to England and continue apace until her return to Lynn. Occupying more than 15 per cent of the manuscript (fos. 54$^r$–66$^v$), they are taken up almost exclusively with a series of hostile confrontations (linked by the briefest clauses) with implacable, obdurate, towering temporal and ecclesiastical authorities in whose favour the odds are heavily thrown. The places (Canterbury, Lincoln, Leicester, York, London and Bristol) and individuals she visits (Arundel, Repingdon, Alnwick, Bowet and Pevrell) were all distinguished for their anti-heretical activity. Though not formal proceedings, these trials, however casual, were occasions for forms of genuine testing where Margery was detained, victimized, threatened, reviled and unjustly treated. The suffering she endured in these places is remarked on at considerable length and is compared implicitly and explicitly with Christ's suffering. Collectively, these encounters constitute perhaps the most carefully constructed section in *The Book*, whose theme is Margery's trials, but whose true subtext is nothing less than 'The Passion of Margery Kempe'.[14] Here again, the picture that emerges from these two sharply contrasting attitudes to geography is one of high selectivity. The section narrating her trials demonstrates a selectivity of place for apparently strategic purposes which is radically at odds with the picture of objective presentation on the Jerusalem pilgrimage and of random disclosure created by the text's chronological disunity and its overall lack of structural cohesion.

Even more revealing are the fifty-five temporal references. These fall into two main categories: specific references to days or dates, such as 'Wednysday in Whitson-weke', 'iij days be-forn Lammes Day', and the commoner references to periods of time given in days, years or seasons, 'ij ʒer', 'iij wekys er', etc. This latter category accounts for just over thirty of the total time references, which act as rough chronological girders underpinning the historical integrity of the narrative. Even the more significant examples serve by design to provide a narrative framework rather than a running chronology: 'The fyrst ij ʒer whan þis creatur was þus drawyn to owyr Lord, sche had gret qwiete of spyryt as for ony temptacyons', 'þan sche had iij ʒer of gret labowr wyth temptacyons' (13, 12). More frequently, they are cursory, making only gestures to temporality: 'þis creatur whych many ʒerys had gon wyl & euyr ben vnstable' (1–2). Usually, they are cited without reference to other events, rendering their value relative only to related experiences: 'in þe secunde ʒer of hir temptacyons . . .' (14). Sometimes they are downright vague: 'Whan þis creatur was xx ʒer of age or sumdele mor' (6). Far more common are the completely vague temporal references which, paradoxically, describe some of the most significant events, such as her journeys: 'Whan tyme cam þat þis creatur xuld vysiten þo holy placys' (60). She travels from England to Jerusalem and on to Venice, Assisi and finally to Rome without supplying a single date regarding her movements. Likewise, the date of her departure to Santiago is given simply as 'And aftyrward, whan tyme cam þat sche wolde gon to Seynt Iamys' (105). Other significant events in her life and the life of the local community are treated with equal indifference to dates. For example, the date of the Lynn fire which threatened to burn down the great church of St Margaret's and which she is credited with miraculously extinguishing, is given only as 'on a tyme' (162). The fall of John Kempe, engendering his precipitous decline in health, is temporally qualified by the almost mythical formula, 'it happyd on a tyme' (179). The overall effect of this temporal vagueness is to lift the narrative out of its historical context into a world where time is subordinate to action. When, by contrast, dates appear they make an increased claim on attention by their very scarcity. Of the thirty vague time references described above, eighteen cite specific days or dates, and of these eleven give the date (usually by saint's day), and only two provide the unusual double reference of the weekday and date. Only two references cite the day and the year: the composition dates of Books I and II (6, 221), though these are little more than authorial convention and clearly the work of the second scribe. Finally, several chapters begin by citing the day and a precise location, and it is these which demonstrate the most interesting uses of specificity in *The Book*.

The first date supplied (after the date of Book I's composition) is that of Margery's proposition by a friend and fellow parishioner (14ff.). This took place one evening as Margery was about to make her way to church, when a man she knew and loved well made known his desire to make love to her. They separated and proceeded into church, Margery revolving the matter over in her mind during the liturgy. When afterwards she finally agreed to submit to his desire, the man played coy, feigning pretences. This event, the amanuensis carefully notes, took place on 'Seynt Margaretys Evyn be-for euynsong'. Considering that more than half of the time references in *The Book* are of an extremely casual nature, it is surprising that the author has not introduced the narrative with a vague temporal indicator, such as 'on a tyme, be-fore euyensong', or 'on a day' or 'it happenyd on a tyme', as he does so frequently elsewhere, to draw as little attention as possible to Margery's shameful behaviour on this occasion. Not only is the day cited but attention is drawn specifically to the place, just a few lines later: 'for her cherch was of Seynt Margaret' (14–15), forcing the reader to apprehend the full weight of the correlation and its significance in relation to Margery's behaviour. We are to understand that the action takes place on St Margaret's Eve in St Margaret's Church. This unusual alignment of temporal and geographic specificity and the precise concurrence of space and time under the banner of St Margaret reveal serried ranks of meaning behind the text's literal surface. St Margaret's Day in this episode is no mere calendar reference but has a supra-literal, civic significance: it is the high point in the local community's corporate identity, for not only was St Margaret's Day one of the *festa ferianda,* when the laity would have been expected to fast on the eve of the feast and desist from most forms of manual labour the following day, it was also Lynn's patronal festival.[15] It has a moral dimension as well: the church she and her imminent lover are about to enter is not merely the parish church of the story's protagonist but one established to honour St Margaret. On this day, on which the universal Church honoured the virgin martyr of Antioch, Margery succumbs to the carnival atmosphere of the summer festivities in Lynn and consents to adultery. Moreover, Lynn's parish church was also dedicated to all the virgins.[16] Thus Margery commemorates the day on which the local community honours the host of celestial virgins by a most flagrant exhibition of sexual inconstancy. This is no bride of Christ but a *Carmina burana* character, abandoning herself to the carnal pleasures associated with the worst excesses of medieval revelry.

The glaring contradiction between the moral and religious significance of the occasion and Margery's conduct cannot be read outside the totality of her experience. *The Book of Margery Kempe* opens, we recall, with the story of her mental instability, which has been diagnosed as postpartum depression.[17] After she was delivered of her firstborn, Margery called for the priest because she 'dyspered of hyr lyfe'; when she did experience a breakdown, she imagined herself 'damnyd . . . in Helle' (6–8). Now, on realizing her moral failure on St Margaret's Eve in chapter 4, 'þan fel sche half in dyspeyr. Sche thowt sche wold a ben in Helle' (16). Both mental and moral failure engender despair and a terrible fear of infernal damnation, expressed in almost identical language. Just as Margery's mental instability immediately after childbirth in chapter 1 throws into greater relief her healing miracle of the woman suffering from a similar condition towards the end of *The Book* (ch. 75), this incident marks the height of sexual inconstancy, sharply contrasted by her mystical marriage and her induction into the company of celestial virgins in chapter 35. To embrace Christ, both physically and metaphorically, Margery must be seen to turn away from something. Consummation cannot be achieved without testing and testing must be preceded by rejection. To see Margery rejecting the world, we must first see what that world has to offer her. We must see its desirability to her, or what the revised Prayer-Book calls 'the glamour of evil', and her desirability to it. Only then can 'pompe & pryde' be rejected. In her moral failure Margery's glorious future as the *sponsa Christi* is foreshadowed, for the temporal and spatial references localizing the action contain a polarity of behaviour which not only contrast the ideal with the imperfect but have a deeper resonance. It is in the imperfection of the temporal and the local that the achievement of Margery's promised universality originates, for Christ promises Margery the same grace enjoyed by St Margaret and all the virgin saints (52). As a healer Margery begins in infirmity; as the spouse of Christ, in infidelity; and as a putative saint, in abject moral failure. The reasons behind this inversion are not far to see.

As Caesarius of Heisterbach and the host of medieval *exemplum* writers knew, narrative had to engage the reader's imagination, no matter how dry the spiritual lesson. The story of a protagonist penitent over mere housewifery was unlikely to make exciting reading. Like a hagiographer, Margery had to choose between casting herself in the mould of a prodigy or penitent. Autobiographical narrative was hardly the place for the former. Having rejected the *puer senex* motif, she now had to have something to show for her penitence and, with typical gusto, she chooses the sin most associated with medieval woman, presenting herself as a type of the Magdalen.[18] This is not to suggest that the affair on St Margaret's Eve did not take place or that it was invented for hagiographic expediency. Rather, its inclusion in *The Book* (against a background of high selectivity) and its careful presentation as the genesis of Margery's conversion in the mode of St Mary Magdalen is calculated to trigger certain associations. Recalling that the dedication of Lynn's church was not just to St Margaret and all the virgins but also encompassed St Mary Magdalen, we realize the excellent propriety of this story to the place and time associated with St Margaret. Thus, we must be extremely careful in accepting verbatim Margery's self-presentation as the penitent. Elements of her experience resemble the Magdalen's life precisely because she has adopted a Magdalenesque pose.[19]

Such extremes were literary necessities since the moral distance travelled by a penitent could be crucial to the success of his or her *vita*.[20] That this was not solely a hagiographic device is proven by Lydgate's protracted commentary on his boyhood excesses. His exaggerated catalogue of youthful vice, a recognizably hagiographical device employed in an autobiographical context, casts him into a type of the penitent and highlights his moral progress.[21] Moreover, his stealing of apples and, more importantly, his inclusion of this detail in his poem, strongly associates his actions with St Augustine, who singled out his boyhood sin of stealing pears for special treatment in his autobiography.[22] Lydgate aligns his text to the venerable tradition of Augustinian spiritual autobiography, simultaneously revealing his intentions and providing an insight into his thoughts and intentions.[23] The French abbot Guibert of Nogent adopted the same technique in his own autobiography, where he detailed his own childhood vice in highly conscious imitation of St Augustine's *Confessions*, though the circumstances of their lives bore little in common. Guibert's parallels went much further, encompassing the alignment of his mother to St Monica, to whom she bore very little relation.[24] We should not doubt that Margery found genuine solace in the model of the Magdalen, whose elevation from a fallen state of sexual activity to a kind of spiritual perfection provided a source of enormous hope. Nor, however, should we think that this sincerity was at odds with a structuring of the text to emphasize precisely this point. Indeed, it is the ritualization of penitence which reveals the true import of this event to Margery's story.

The next significant time and space reference, and the second chapter in *The Book* to begin with temporal and geographic specificity, is chapter 11, which narrates one of the most frequently cited passages in *The Book*. Whereas most chapters begin with the vague 'On a tyme', 'Anoþer tyme', or 'On a day long befor þis tyme', this chapter begins with a flourish of specificity: 'It befel up-on a Fryday on Mydsomyr Evyn in rygth hot wedyr, as þis creatur was komyng fro-ȝorkeward' when Margery appealed to her husband for his consent to her proposal regarding their chaste marriage. Refusing her offer initially, since the only collateral she advances is her prayers for his salvation and eternal reward, he suggests a compromise: her desired chastity for the payment of his debts, the abandonment of her Friday fast, and their continued sharing of the marriage bed. Margery consults Christ over these terms 'wyth gret habundawns of teerys' and is advised to accept, since her fasting had not been ordained, as she had thought, for the mortification of her flesh but, rather unexpectedly, for the fulfilment of her desired chastity. Margery accepts (except for the mutual bed) and is freed from the marriage debt. The saturation of this extraordinary narrative with dialogue consisting of short, sharp exchanges, its psychological processes, its limited but powerful character development, and its small deft touches, such as the bottle of beer and the cake carried in the breast, all create a highly episodic quality. It is this seductively vivid realism which draws the reader into apprehending the story on a historical level. Yet for all its apparent spontaneity, the narrative teems with convention and symbolic significance.

While the dominance of the chastity issue throughout *The Book* undoubtedly reflects the persuasiveness of the Church's teaching on the primacy of virginity and the high esteem attached to a life of sexual abstinence, the acquisition of the chastity agreement is a fundamental prerequisite to Margery's mystical marriage and hence to her deeply desired vocation as the contemplative *sponsa Christi*. Her wish to exchange comparatively late in life the identity of an honourable burgher's daughter and wife for what she regarded as a superior calling was fraught with complications. In her self-assessment against the ideal of virginity characteristic of the bride of Christ, Margery was painfully conscious of her inadequacy.[25] As a putative saint measuring herself against the catalogue of saints of her own gender, she was also aware that the single most defining feature of female sanctity was sexual status. Men might be classified by their religious or clerical position or membership of an order but women saints were usually virgins or widows. The reminders of virginal superiority were everywhere displayed for admiration and emulation.[26] Contemplative precedents like Mechtild of Hackeborn reinforced the supremacy of the virginal ideal in uncompromising terms.[27] Catechetic texts which discussed the estates of chastity also drove home the message 'þat þis is þe fairest estaate þat is in erþe'.[28] Preachers like Chaucer's Parson commended chastity while underscoring the irreversibility of the loss of virginity.[29] The various liturgical feasts in honour of the holy virgins presented in highly evocative terms the desirability of the state of virginity.[30] Moreover, the service of consecration for virgins, which in a large urban church like St Margaret's would have been performed many times in the course of a year, must also have reinforced to Margery the high estate of virginity.[31] Small wonder that she exclaims in a deeply heartfelt lament the loss of her virginity: 'me thynkyth I wolde I had ben slayn whan I was takyn from þe funt-ston' (50), implicitly aligning herself with the innocents of Rev. 14:4 and, by extension, all the celestial virgins. Of course, a mother or penitent wife may have found an archetype in the Magdalen, as we have just seen Margery herself did, yet the road to her sanctity was undeniably more arduous by the blemish of sexuality. The examples of the *mulieres sanctae* like Elizabeth of Hungary, Dorothy of Montau and Bridget of Sweden made possible the aspiration of devout married woman to mystical marriage, though only if celibacy was adopted.[32] This was the *sine qua non* of the *sponsa Christi* – a prerequisite of which Margery was acutely cognizant. Consequently, such a momentous occasion, when she actually took possession of her chastity, was unlikely to have been consigned to memory, recalled and retold without a sense of struggle reflecting the value of her acquired prized pearl. Indeed, even if the narrative did not demand an amplification of the conflict, the highly practical circumstances surrounding the actual terms of the bargain necessitated dramatic treatment. For while Margery Kempe's reply to her husband's famous question ('For-soþe I had leuar se ȝow be slayn þan we schulde turne a-ȝen to owyr vnclennesse') demonstrates the depth of her feeling for chastity, it has nothing to do with the actual bargain at all, which was almost exclusively a financial arrangement with a promise to desist from fasting tagged onto it. To subordinate this incident to the level of a footnote to the legacy she received on her father's death several months earlier which made possible her payment of John Kempe's debts and therefore the agreement itself, would have been grossly unsatisfactory. The crude mercantilism of the burghers, whose precepts Margery and John knew and instinctively responded to, was unsuited to the application of high spiritual matters.[33] Divine petitions, prayer, weeping, testing and, perhaps above all, an inevitable sense of encounter and conflict were far more suited to the occasion. The necessity of a sense of conflict can be gauged by the remarkably hagiographic dimension of the story. The sense of drama and struggle created by the primary elements, such as the journey on the open road, the sudden introduction of the threat of beheading, the unsheathed sword, the heroine's pivotal life-giving or -denying response, all give this story the appearance of a vignette straight out of a Bokenham *vita virginis*, transforming this eminently practical arrangement into an archetypal hagiographic narrative. Again, this is not to deny the incident out of hand or to suggest that the narrative elements have been invented for the sake of a good story. Rather, it is to suggest that its treatment reflects authorial priorities and its fundamental import in the drama of Margery's salvation. Accordingly, it is decorated with a supra-literal ornament. As in hagiography, amplification often serves as a guide to signification.

The next notable time–space reference occurs in chapter 35, more than half of which is taken up with Margery's 'gostly' and 'bodily comfortys'. The discourse on 'comfortys' is occasioned by Margery's meditations, which she had practised long before her pilgrimages. Concentrating her thoughts on the gospel events, she entered into the drama of the Passion in the style of meditation advocated by the Pseudo-Bonaventurian *Meditationes*, imagining herself a participant in the joys and sorrows of the Holy Family, where she identified especially with 'þe manhood of Crist'.[34] It was this capacity to empathize with the sufferings of the Crucified which was singled out as exemplary when God the Father proposed to her on behalf of the Godhead. Marking the apogee of her contemplative career, this chapter begins with a precise temporal and geographic locator: 'As þis creatur was in þe Cherch [of St Lateran] at Rome on Seynt Laterynes Day' (ch. 35). Previously separated from the dancing celestial virgins, Margery now entertains them as guests and witnesses at her wedding feast, receiving their best wishes for the happiness of the newly wed couple. The fulfilment of Christ's promise to take her by the hand and lead her in the celestial dance of virgins (ch. 22) is here foreshadowed by his taking her hand in matrimony in the company of the virgins. Margery's contemplative career, as we have seen, hinges on her status as the *sponsa Christi*, which in turn rests on her arduously won chastity. From her perspective, the acquisition of her chastity and her mystical marriage are perhaps the two single most important events in her life because they underpin all other achievements. Accordingly the passages narrating these two events are given unusually precise spatial and temporal definition.

Only one other chapter opens with a specific temporal–spatial citation, chapter 5: 'Than on a Fryday beforn Crystmes Day, as þis creatur, knelyng in a chapel of Seynt Iohn wythinne a cherch of Seynt Margarete in N.' The contents of the chapter are extremely significant in determining the shape of Margery's life and career. It is the first time in *The Book* that she is addressed directly by Christ. Yet this speech is remarkable for its comprehensiveness. Significantly, it contains first and foremost the all-important call narrative in which Margery is commanded to lead a separated life. Christ offers a very practical kind of summary lay Rule which covers rubrics for prayer, eucharistic reception, spiritual supervision, diet and dress. He ordains the nature of her vocation, assigning her contemplative exercises; he foretells her trials and celestial rewards. He promises lifelong contrition; foreshadows her mystical marriage; calls himself by the name she inscribes in her wedding ring; promises her sufficient grace to answer all clerks; and, last but by no means least, invokes the first reference to a repeated promise of universal fame. The contents of this speech form a touchstone throughout Margery's life and are subsequently recalled, invoked, applied and modified repeatedly.

Surely, it is no coincidence that the three chapters (5, 11 and 35) detailing events of the greatest significance to her identity open with temporal and geographic specificity, while more than fifty chapters describing lesser events begin with vague, oblique time references.[35] On the contrary, we might say that the majority of chapters are careful not to open with date or place citations precisely to draw attention to the indicative use of the opening time–place references. Considered cumulatively, these chapters act as monuments of significance in the landscape of Margery's spirituality. Beginning in the abject failure of her adulterous consent, Margery repents and is called to a contemplative vocation. She achieves her prized chastity which itself facilitates her mystical marriage. Her consent to adultery, agreement to chastity, and mystical marriage mark the turning-point of the will away from sexual instability towards the desire for chastity, its acquisition, the longing for nuptial intimacy, and the spiritual consummation of her contemplative passions. By applying temporal and geographic specificity to these three chapters and the affair on St Margaret's Eve, attention is drawn to these passages in a way that it is not with the rest of the narrative passages in *The Book*. How does this highly selective use of time and place against a background of chronological disunity compare with hagiographic convention?

Chronological disunity can by no means be regarded as a trope germane to saints' lives. On the contrary, strict though uncodified guidelines governed the process of *vita*-writing, and the competent hagiographer was acutely conscious of the need to follow conventions of genre. Texts like the *Vita Martini*, *Vita Benedicti* and *Vita Gregori* crystallized and transmitted to generations of subsequent hagiographers patterns of style and presentation to be read, imitated and copied. So strong was the need to conform to generic convention that texts inconstant to the accepted mode of hagiographic presentation were likely to be rewritten.[36] The prevailing attitude to chronology (and geography) that emerges from these and other seminal texts is nowhere defined by contemporary sources but is easily characterized. Generally, hagiography gives the appearance of being unconcerned with the idea of time or place. A sense of geography is loosely evoked; some place-names are provided, though usually only to satisfy the demands of narration and add an element of probability. The action may move through several towns or cities but seldom engages with the local ethnography. Foreign locations witness to the saint's universality and add an element of the exotic. The various locations are not joined by strong internal links. On the whole, hagiography seems uninterested in details of place, an attitude which points to the text's otherworldly landscape, which is the true locale of all sanctity. Time, too, is weakly characterized. Few references are provided, such as the saint's age at various junctures or the day of the week, again to satisfy the demands of narration and create a sense of continuity. Cameos from the saint's life which constitute the whole are generally not linked by a chronological unity. The historical sweep is useful only insofar as it yields up the events of outstanding significance or demonstrates the in-breaking of the divine in the path of the saint. Historicity is subordinate to ethics. Temporality is a human concern and is therefore replaced by a sense of divine timing that is not linear but typological, emphasizing the symbolic nature of the life. In general, the saint's life stands outside time and place, in an ideal, abstract setting of the virtues. So consistent is this approach as to be regarded fundamentally characteristic of hagiographic discourse.[37] On this impressionistic canvas of temporal and geographic vagueness, the competent hagiographer coloured details of time and place indicatively. By deploying a minimum of specificity, the hagiographer highlighted the significant features of the life or drew attention to seminal or transcendent events by marking them with indicators of temporality or geography. This indicative use of specificity is the hallmark of capable hagiographers evident in the better-constructed lives.[38]

This, in fact, is precisely what Margery's amanuensis does. Bound by the limitations of his text, he was incapable of overcoming some of its imperfections, most obviously its disregard for basic linear progression. While he managed to group some experiences thematically, others remained, defying chronological presentation. Conscious of the similarity between the chronological disunity of his text and the convention of temporal and geographic vagueness of saints' lives, the amanuensis made a virtue of necessity, using temporal and geographic specificity to highlight significant themes and events in Margery's life, beginning with Margery's affair on St Margaret's Eve. Like the most competent hagiographers, he did so sparingly, recognizing that the limited use of time and place references makes an increased demand on the reader's attention by its very scarcity. Even in his apology for the remaining chronological infelicities, he was actually following hagiographic precedent, for Bonaventure's life of St Francis opens with a similar statement.[39]

Through the mere citation of a highly charged temporal and spatial reference, Margery's amanuensis draws attention to the penitential topos used by Lydgate, Guibert of Nogent and others. Paradoxically, critics who have argued against a hagiographic reading of *The Book* on the grounds that it contains material of an 'embarrassingly personal nature' often cite this incident of her consent to adultery, failing not only to recognize the symbolic value its authors attach to it, but its place in the progression of Margery's sanctity and its resonance of seminal, hagiographical antitheses.[40] Next, the amanuensis casts the acquisition of chastity in the tradition of hagiography by presenting Margery as the weaker, embattled woman who must struggle against hegemonious male figures to acquire the freedom to choose her own sexual status. This was true not only for the virgin martyrs, who were tortured as much if not more for their refusal to bend their bodies to the desires of their kings, prefects and torturers as for their refusal to worship pagan idols, but also for Margery's married contemporaries like Dorothy of Montau and Jane Marie of Maille, who suffered various forms of physical punishments from their husbands for their insistence on maintaining their various lifestyles.[41]

Of course, to ascribe this level of authorial engineering to the amanuensis is not to deny Margery's engagement in the writing or redactive process. These experiences were no less significant to her because of their editorial treatment. On the contrary, her keen apprehension of contemporary spirituality and the inspiration she drew from the life of the contemplative precedents she admired combined to mark out these events as significant milestones in the progress of her spiritual pilgrimage. It is her perception of the significance of these events that underlines their authorial treatment. This thorough grasp of contemporary spirituality and, more significantly, of the fundamental issue surrounding self-representation in a literary context is perhaps nowhere more evident than in the selectivity at work in describing her foreign pilgrimages and domestic journeys. Indeed, the amanuensis's deployment of hagiographic techniques can be seen as an extension of the selectivity exercise, a process which occurred over many years in the crucible of Margery's memory and imagination.

Ultimately, author and scribe were not working at cross-purposes and what the amanuensis observed as notable was likely to have been apprehended by Margery as deeply relevant and indeed providential many years prior to the authorial stage. Having mentally exercised editorial selectivity over the range of her experiences, Margery conveyed her stories to her first and second amanuenses. Working beside Margery, the second amanuensis brought to bear upon the enterprise his considerable knowledge of hagiographic convention. While his use of specificity for emphatic purposes hardly does away with the need for his apology regarding 'þe tyme & þe ordyr whan thyngys befellyn', it belies his assertion that the stories flowed from his pen as vividly recalled from Margery's retentive memory, 'lych as þe mater cam to þe creatur in mend when it schuld be wretyn'. For, while Margery's voice rings clearly from the text, it is evident that the narrative has been shaped in a highly sophisticated way by a clerical mind familiar with and competent in hagiographic modes of discourse.

## Notes

[1] Developing out of my University of Oxford D.Phil. thesis, 'Biblical and Hagiographical *Imitatio* in the *Book of Margery Kempe*' (1997), this chapter is an attempt to explore further the authorial processes behind the construction of *The Book*.

[2] All references and quotations (followed by page number in parentheses) are from S. B. Meech and H. E. Allen (eds.), *The Book of Margery Kempe*, EETS OS 212 (Oxford, 1940; repr. 1961) (hereafter cited as *The Book*).

[3] See *The Book*, xlviii–li.

[4] 'Than was þer so euel spekyng of þis creatur & of hir wepyng þat þe prest ... voyded & deferryd þe wrytyng of þis boke wel on-to iiij ȝer' (4). On the miracle and the redactive process, see R. Ellis, 'Margery Kempe's Scribe and the Miraculous Books', in H. Phillips (ed.), *Langland, the Mystics and the Medieval English Religious Tradition: Essays Presented in Honour of S. S. Hussey* (Cambridge, 1990), 161–76. In the light of his contribution, it seems self-evident that *The Book* is as much 'authored' by Margery as by the amanuensis. See J. Hirsh, 'Author and Scribe in *The Book of Margery Kempe*', *Medium Ævum*, 44 (1975), 145–50. For the opposite view, see the essays in S. J. McEntire (ed.), *Margery Kempe: A Book of Essays* (London, 1992). A more radical view is conjectured by L. Staley in *Margery Kempe's Dissenting Fictions* (University Park, Pa., 1994); and 'The Trope of the Scribe and the Question of Literary Authority in the Works of Julian of Norwich and Margery Kempe', *Speculum*, 66 (1991), 820–38.

[5] E.g. 'Ferthermore her folwyth a rygth notabyl matere ... & it is wretyn her for conuenyens' (58). Cf. the editorial comments at the close of ch. 16.

[6] 'Yf þe namys of þe placys be not ryth wretyn, late no man meruelyn, for sche stodyid mor a-bowte contemplacyon þan þe namys of þe placys, & he þat wrot hem had neuyr seyn hem' (233).

[7] The centrality of images to cognition underpinned the medieval idea of the mind as a storehouse of images. See M. J. Carruthers, *The Book of Memory: A Study of Memory in Medieval Culture* (Cambridge, 1990), 51–4, 58–9, 192–3; E. R. Harvey, *The Inward Wits: Psychological Theory in the Middle Ages and the Renaissance*, Warburg Institute Surveys 6 (London, 1975); A. Minnis, 'Affection and Imagination in *The Cloud of Unknowing* and Hilton's *Scale of Perfection*', *Traditio*, 39 (1983), 323–66; idem, 'Langland's Theory of Ymaginatif and Late-Medieval Theories of Imagination', *Comparative Criticism*, 3 (1981), 71–103; and M. W. Bundy, *The Theory of Imagination in Classical and Medieval Thought*, University of Illinois Studies in Language and Literature 12.2–3 (Urbana, Ill., 1927); F. A. Yates, *The Art of Memory* (London, 1966), 32–49.

[8] A very large number of organized activities awaited pilgrims in Compostela; see H. and M.-H. Davies, *Holy Days and Holidays: The Medieval Pilgrim-*

*age to Compostela* (Lewisburg, Pa., 1982). On the Rome pilgrimage, see D. J. Bird, *Pilgrimage to Rome in the Middle Ages: Continuity and Change*, Studies in the History of Medieval Religions (Cambridge, 1998).

[9] J. C. Dickinson, *The Shrine of Our Lady of Walsingham* (Cambridge, 1956).

[10] V. and E. Turner, *Image and Pilgrimage in Christian Culture: Anthropological Perspectives* (New York, 1978), 175–87; F. Blomefield and C. Parkin, *An Essay towards a Topographical History of the County of Norfolk*, 11 vols. (1805–10), VIII, 513–14, 524; H. J. Hillen, *History of the Borough of King's Lynn*, 2 vols. (Norwich, 1907), I, 208–14.

[11] Later in York she visits an anchoress 'wheche had louyd hir wel er sche went to Ierusalem' (119), indicating that perhaps she had been to York on more than one occasion previously.

[12] That Margery had a confessor in Bridlington is interesting in its own right, but given her choice of Sleytham as confessor, a priest who performed the same office for the recently canonized St John, and H. E. Allen's suggestion that Bridlington was a saint-making centre in Margery's day, her visits there acquire added interest (*The Book*, 315–16 n. 128/34).

[13] For example, she is 'meuyd in hir sowle to go vysyten certeyn places for gostly helth' (22).

[14] I have argued this point more fully in my 'Biblical and Hagiographical *Imitatio*', chs. 5–7.

[15] C. R. Cheney, 'Rules for Observance of Feast-Days in Medieval England', *Bulletin of the Institute of Historical Research*, 34 (1961), 117–47 (esp. 128–9, 139).

[16] On the popularity of the cult of the virgin martyrs in late medieval England, see E. Duffy, 'Holy Maydens, Holy Wyfes: The Cult of Women Saints in Fifteenth- and Sixteenth-Century England', in W. J. Shields and D. Wood (eds.), *Women in the Church*, Studies in Church History 27 (Oxford, 1990), 175–96; idem, *The Stripping of the Altars: Traditional Religion in England c. 1400–c. 1580* (New Haven, 1992); and T. J. Heffernan, *Sacred Biography: Saints and Their Biographers in the Middle Ages* (Oxford, 1988).

[17] C. Atkinson, *Mystic and Pilgrim: The Book and the World of Margery Kempe* (Ithaca, 1983), 209.

[18] See the very fine paper by S. Eberly: 'Margery Kempe, St Mary Magdalene, and Patterns of Contemplation', *Downside Review*, 107 (1989), 209–23 (214–15).

[19] A very revealing case of *imitatio Magdalenae* will be found in Isabella of Warwick's funerary instructions in F. J. Furnivall (ed.), *The Fifty Earliest English Wills . . . 1387–1439*, EETS OS 78 (London, 1882), 116–19 (116), on which see G. M. Gibson, *The Theater of Devotion: East Anglian Drama and Society in the Late Middle Ages* (Chicago, 1989), 11–12. For the post-Reformation vogue for portraits of noblewomen as the Magdalen, see S. Haskins, *Mary Magdalen: Myth and Metaphor* (London, 1993).

[20] See A. Vauchez, *La Sainteté en occident aux derniers siècles du moyen*

âge, d'après les procès de canonisation et les documents hagiographiques, Bibliothèque des études françaises d'Athènes et de Rome 241 (Rome, 1981), 593–5; Vauchez stresses the importance attached to conversion in the canonization processes. On the stylization of presentation in saints' lives, see C. F. Altman, 'Two Types of Opposition and the Structure of Latin Saints' Lives', in *Medieval Hagiography and Romance, Medievalia et Humanistica*, NS, 6 (Cambridge, 1975), 1–12; and Heffernan, *Sacred Biography*. For an example contemporary with Margery, see J. Alford, 'Biblical *Imitatio* in the Writings of Richard Rolle', *English Literary History*, 40 (1973), 1–23; idem, 'The Biblical Identity of Richard Rolle', *Mystics Quarterly*, 11 (1976), 21–5; and idem,'The Scriptural Self', in S. B. Levy (ed.), *The Bible in the Middle Ages: Its Influence on Literature and Art* (Binghamton, NY, 1992), 1–21.

[21] 'Testament of Lydgate', in H. N. MacCracken (ed.), *The Minor Poems of John Lydgate*, 2 vols., EETS ES 107, OS 192 (1911, 1934), I, no. 68/395–408, 607–739.

[22] St Augustine, *Confessions*, ed. J. J. O'Donnell, 3 vols. (Oxford, 1992), I, 18–22, Book 2, chs. 4–8. In discussing Augustine's extensive treatment of the theft, O'Donnell highlights the calculated imitation inherent in Augustine's presentation of the act of Adam and Eve's taking of the fruit.

[23] 'Testament of Lydgate', I, no. 68/638.

[24] Guibert of Nogent, *De vita sua sive monodiarum suarum libri tres*, PL 156. 837–962; see also J. F. Benton (ed. and tr.), *Self and Society in Medieval France*, Medieval Academy Reprints for Teaching 15 (Toronto, 1984; repr. 1991). On the literary legacy of the *Confessiones*, see P. Courcelle, *Les Confessions de saint Augustin dans la tradition littéraire: Antécédents et postérité* (Paris, 1963), 201–327.

[25] '"A, Lord, maydenys dawnsyn now meryly in Heuyn. Xal not I don so? For be-cawse I am no mayden, lak of maydenhed is to me now gret sorwe"' (50). While *Ancrene Riwle* (M. Day (ed.), *The English Text of the* Ancrene Riwle, EETS OS 225 (London, 1952) likens the state of virginity to a glass vessel which if broken through sexual intercourse can be mended through confession and penance, the irreversibility of virginity was emphasized in more extreme texts like *Hali Meiðhad* (B. Millett (ed.), *Hali Meiðhad*, EETS OS 284 (Oxford, 1982)). On sexuality and sanctity, see D. Weinstein and R. M. Bell, *Saints and Society: The Two Worlds of Western Christendom, 1000–1700* (London, 1982), 73–99; and M. Glasser, 'Marriage and Medieval Hagiography', *Studies in Medieval and Renaissance History*, NS, 4 (1981), 3–34. On virginity, see J. Bugge, *Virginitas: An Essay in the History of a Medieval Ideal* (The Hague, 1976); C. Atkinson, '"Precious Balsam in a Fragile Glass": The Ideology of Virginity in the Later Middle Ages', *Journal of Family History*, 8 (1983), 131–43; and M. W. Bloomfield, 'Piers Plowman and the Three Grades of Chastity', *Anglia*, 76 (1958), 227–53.

[26] See, for example, a representation of the Three Estates of Virginity, Continence and Marriage from an early thirteenth-century stained glass in the north aisle of the choir of Canterbury Cathedral reproduced in H. Read, *English Stained Glass* (London, 1926), 47.

[27] 'Virgines pro omnibus Sanctis in tribus honoravi. Primum est quod eas pro omni diligo creatura . . . Secundum est quod eas super omnes ditavi . . . Tertium est quod eas super omnes glorificavi' (Mechtild of Hackeborn, *Liber Specialis Gratiae*, in L. Paquelin (ed.), *Revelationes Gertrudianae ac Mechtildianae cura solemnensium*, 2 vols. (Paris, 1875–7), II, 36) ('I have honoured virgins above all other saints in three ways. First, that I love them more than any other creature . . . Second, that I have enriched them more than any other saints . . . Third, that I have glorified them above all other saints'); see T. A. Halligan (ed.), *The Book of Gostlye Grace*, Studies and Texts 46 (Toronto, 1979), 133.

[28] W. N. Francis (ed.), *The Book of Vices and Virtues*, EETS OS 217 (Oxford, 1942), 252.

[29] 'Namoore may maydenhede be restoored than an arm that is smyten fro the body may retourne agayn to wexe. She may have mercy . . . but nevere shal it be that she nas corrupt' (L. D. Benson (ed.), *The Riverside Chaucer* (Boston, 1987), *CT*, X, 870–1; cf. 921ff.).

[30] F. H. Dickinson (ed.), *Missale ad usum insignis et praeclare ecclesia Sarum* (Burntisland, 1861–83), 726*.

[31] On this point, I am indebted to Dr Santha Bhattacharji.

[32] See S. Dickman, 'Margery Kempe and the English Devotional Tradition', in M. Glasscoe (ed.), *MMTE* I, 156–72; idem, 'Margery Kempe and the Continental Tradition of the Pious Woman', in M. Glasscoe (ed.), *MMTE* 3, 150–68; A. Barratt, 'Margery Kempe and the King's Daughter of Hungary', in McEntire (ed.), *Margery Kempe*, 189–201; U. Stargardt, 'The Beguines of Belgium, the Dominican Nuns of Germany, and Margery Kempe', in T. J. Heffernan (ed.), *The Popular Literature of Medieval England*, Tennessee Studies in Literature 28 (Knoxville, Tenn., 1985), 277–313. Perhaps the finest recent study of Margery's spirituality is S. Bhattacharji, *God is an Earthquake: The Spirituality of Margery Kempe* (London, 1997). On chastity, see D. Elliott, *Spiritual Marriage: Sexual Abstinence in Medieval Wedlock* (Princeton, 1993), ch. 5, and the examples in R. Kieckhefer, *Unquiet Souls: Fourteenth-Century Saints and their Religious Milieu* (Chicago, 1984). More generally, see B. Bolton, 'Mulieres Sanctae', in D. Baker (ed.), *Sanctity and Secularity: The Church and the World*, Studies in Church History 10 (Oxford, 1973), 77–95; M. Goodich, 'The Contours of Female Piety in Later Medieval Hagiography', *Church History*, 50 (1981), 21–32; and R. Voaden, *Prophets Abroad: The Reception of Continental Holy Women in Late-Medieval England* (Cambridge, 1996). For a more radical view, see C. W. Bynum, *Holy Feast and Holy Fast: The Religious Significance of Food to Women* (Berkeley, 1987); and idem, *Fragmentation*

*and Redemption: Essays on Gender and the Human Body in Medieval Religion* (New York, 1991).

[33] Meech conjectures this incident took place in 1413 (269, n. 23/9). On the date of John Brunham's death, see *The Book*, 361, Appendix III, II, no. 11.

[34] Surveys of this tradition include M. G. Sargent, 'Bonaventure English: A Survey of the Middle English Prose Translations of Early Franciscan Literature', in *Spätmittelalterliche geistliche Literatur in der Nationalsprache*, Analecta Cartusiana 106.2 (Salzburg, 1984), 145–76; and E. Salter, *Nicholas Love's Myrrour of the Blessed Lyf of Jesu Christ*, Analecta Cartusiana 10 (Salzburg, 1974), 55–178. See also E. Cousins, 'Francis of Assisi and Christian Mysticism', in S. T. Katz (ed.), *Mysticism and Religious Traditions* (Oxford, 1983), 163–90; and 'The Humanity and the Passion of Christ', in J. Raitt (ed.), *Christian Spirituality 2: High Middle Ages and Reformation* (London, 1987), 375–91.

[35] Chs. 45, 62, 69, 73 and 82 open with citations of liturgical time and/or place, though note that these references are indicative of liturgical events of narrative significance. In these cases, the lack of date references would seriously affect our comprehension of the devotional significance of the narrative, as it would not in chs. 5, 11 and 35.

[36] It was for this reason that Bede rewrote the *Life of St Cuthbert*: to eliminate characteristic details and amplify the element of the traditional; see B. Colgrave (ed. and tr.), *Two Lives of Saint Cuthbert: A Life by an Anonymous Monk of Lindisfarne and Bede's Prose Life* (Cambridge, 1940). See C. G. Loomis, 'The Miracle Traditions of the Venerable Bede', *Speculum*, 21 (1946), 404–18.

[37] R. Boyer, 'An Attempt to Define the Typology of Medieval Hagiography', in H. Bekker-Nielsen, P. Foote, J. H. Jörgensen et al. (eds.), *Hagiography and Medieval Literature: A Symposium* (Odense, 1981), 27–36.

[38] C. W. Jones, *Saints' Lives and Chronicles in Early England* (Ithaca, 1947), 73–9; Heffernan, *Sacred Biography*, 97.

[39] St Bonaventure, *Legenda Maior S. Francis*, Analecta Franciscana 10 (1926–41), 555–652. For an English translation, see Bonaventure, *The Soul's Journey into God. The Tree of Life. The Life of St. Francis*, tr. E. Cousins, The Classics of Western Spirituality (New York, 1978), 177–327.

[40] See, for example, E. P. Armstrong, ' "Understanding by Feeling" in Margery Kempe's *Book*', in McEntire (ed.), *Margery Kempe*, 17–35 (esp. 20). Armstrong admits reminiscences with hagiography but concludes *The Book* has little in common with the genre.

[41] Kieckhefer, *Unquiet Souls*, 24, 54–5.

# 8

# Veneration of Virgin Martyrs in Margery Kempe's Meditation: Influence of the Sarum Liturgy and Hagiography

## NAOË KUKITA YOSHIKAWA

THE veneration of saints is one of the most distinctive aspects of late medieval piety.[1] The Church's liturgy, devotional literature and the images of the saints were all designed to help believers attain closeness to saints who had attained the pinnacle of faith and now resided with God. The saint was invoked by those who called upon him or her for the purposes of intercession. The cult of saints also functioned to invert the normative relationship between the spiritual and the material. For the spiritual power of the saints came to be manifested in their material remains which were widely disseminated during the late Middle Ages, inspiring Christians with the desire to collect the physical remains as talismans.[2]

Margery Kempe was deeply immersed in a religious culture in which the veneration of saints was central.[3] Like other devout believers she desired to attain the requisite closeness to the saints, but, rather than attempting to accomplish this through proximity to saints' relics, she practised meditation upon the love of God using the help of the saints. Although she continued to go on pilgrimages and to join her community in the supplication and celebration of holy figures, nonetheless her approach is less material and pragmatic than most. In her devotion to the saints she pursued a highly personal kind of piety enacted through direct spiritual communication.

Margery's mode of meditation is indebted to the Church's liturgy, closely aligned with the iconographic tradition of the time, so that the references to saints in her meditation seem to be rooted in the Sarum liturgy and in popular hagiography. The saints who appear in her meditation are drawn from both the biblical and post-biblical periods; most of them have a feast day in the Sarum *Proprium sanctorum*, and their lives occur in such popular hagiographies and homilies as Jacobus de Voragine's *Legenda aurea* and Mirk's *Festial*. That she often mentions the saints in a group seems to reflect the style of liturgy in which saints are celebrated not only individually, as in the Proper of Saints, but also in a group according to the virtue they represent, as in the Common of Virgin Martyrs.

Importantly, through the experience of venerating a saint, the devout are able to experience what modern theorists define 'as a state of liminality'.[4] In liturgical ceremonies, the worshipper is separated from normal everyday life and enabled to participate with others in a communal and transcendental ritual through which he or she may be enriched and changed.[5] Such a state of liminality can be effected through the experience of Christian pilgrimage; however, it is also accessible to congregations as they experience the liturgical rites which commemorate a saint's feast day.

This context of liturgically induced liminality and subsequent spiritual transformation provides a key to Margery's account of her meditative understanding. Her participation in liturgical celebration acts as a release or separation from the mundane structure of her daily society, enabling her to enter a new, deeper level of existence where she can experience a state of liminality. This powerful experience has a transformative effect upon her inner self. Nurturing a unique mode of veneration expressed through affective imagination and imitation, it sharpens her spiritual perception, making her susceptible to the spiritual message conveyed in the liturgy. Ultimately, it enables her to establish privileged relationships with saints, relationships in which, taking the role of intimate confidants, they inform Margery about the secret knowledge of God.

It is this aspect of liturgical experience which enables us to see the liturgy as a dynamic channel for Margery, moving her in the direction of revelation. The revelatory experience that grows out of this liturgically induced liminality is deeply embedded in her meditation on the saints. She receives spiritual lessons from the saints during what she labels as 'dalyawns' with them. She confides her meditation to the vicar of St Stephen's: '[Sumty]me Seynt Petyr, sumtyme Seynt Powyl, symtym Seynt / Kateryn, er what seynt in Heuyn sche had deuocyon to aperyd to hir sowle & tawt hir how sche xuld louyn owyr Lord & how sche xuld plesyn hym' (39).[6] A similar vision is reported by her in chapter 87, where she suggests that such privileged communication with saints had been continuing for more than twenty-five years.[7]

Furthermore, there are several distinctive traits noticeable in her reference to the saints: all seem to have been intentionally chosen by Margery to elaborate some fundamental issue in her own religious life. These saints can be roughly divided into three categories which seem to have held particular significance for Margery: the category of virgin martyr and *sponsa Christi* represented by Mary Magdalen, Katherine of Alexandria, Margaret of Antioch and Barbara; the repentant sinner who went through spiritual conversion, such as Mary Magdalen, Mary of Egypt, Peter and Paul; and those who pursued an evangelistic calling, such as Mary Magdalen, Peter and Paul.

This chapter will focus on St Katherine with brief references to St Margaret, St Barbara and Mary Magdalen, and consider how these saints articulate the significance of their identities as *sponsa Christi* in the context of Margery's pursuit of heavenly union with God.[8] The fervent veneration of virgin martyrs in the late Middle Ages is closely related to the issue of virginity and chastity; and the appearance of the virgin saints in Margery's meditation – its frequency and context – demonstrates the extent to which Margery strove to bring her own life in line with these models of *sponsa Christi*. Margery was keenly aware that virginity was a principal path to holiness from which she was technically excluded. The conflict between sexual experience and chastity repeatedly tormented Margery's aspiration for holiness until she was assured of her spiritual security in heaven by Christ himself.

I will initially consider the situation of the laity's devotional practice and literacy in order to establish how Margery knew the liturgy. I will then reconstruct various saints' lives, referring to the *Legenda aurea* as a model text, and exploring the dissemination of their hagiography in medieval England. I will lastly examine the official liturgy in the Sarum Missal and Breviary in order to argue that Margery's meditation was nurtured within a cultural milieu in which liturgical experience shaped the spiritual paradigm of her veneration of the saints, and that her meditation was inspired particularly by the bride mysticism stressed in the liturgy.

An examination of the peculiar situation of the laity's devotional practice in the late Middle Ages is potentially problematic. Although it remains debatable whether the laity in the fifteenth century could read prayers in Latin, the literary texts and visual arts accommodated in the liturgy supposedly served as aids to devotion. In medieval manuscript culture, liturgical books were assimilated into an oral milieu in which manuscripts were commonly read aloud even when the reader was alone.[9] Recent studies on the evolution of reading habits in the late Middle Ages attempt to categorize reading ability into two types: phonetic literacy, defined by the ability to decode texts syllable by syllable and pronounce them orally, and comprehension literacy, defined as the ability to decode a written text silently, word by word, and understand it fully in the very act of gazing upon it.[10] Research into literacy in late medieval France shows that, by the fifteenth century, reading a Latin prayer aloud or reciting a written text from memory was a pious act that could be performed by many monks and laymen who were insufficiently literate in Latin to be able to translate devotional prose or verse into the vernacular.[11] It is also arguable that a lifetime's immersion in the Church's liturgy and sacraments gave to an enthusiastic worshipper such as Margery a practical education in Latin, enabling her to understand what the liturgy conveyed, although the exact extent of her knowledge is not easy to speculate.

Furthermore, by the fourteenth and fifteenth centuries, a large number of laymen and clerics who only possessed phonetic literacy in Latin had acquired comprehension literacy in the vernacular. That the vernacular Hours of the Virgin, or Primers, were so increasingly popular among the laity as to be often carried to churches, attests to the spread of comprehension literacy in the vernacular. The bilingual structure of Books of Hours in which rubrics are written not in Latin but in the vernacular also suggests that this genre of books for the laity developed in a milieu in which these two levels of reading ability existed side by side.[12] Margery mentions that she carried a book to the church for prayers: 'Sche knelyd up-on hir kneys, heldyng down hir hed and hir boke in hir hand, prayng owyr Lord Crist Ihesu for grace and for mercy' (21).[13] At the same time it was possible for the unlettered who sought a private devotional experience to substitute the reading of books with meditation upon the pictures contained in them. Jean Gerson was amongst the writers who advocated such a practice. Illustrations placed beside text provided parallels to, and representations of, theological concepts.[14] In this respect, the scenes from the lives of saints illustrated in Books of Hours are designed to inspire the devout to acts of piety and devotion. This evidence helps to give us some idea about the nature of Margery's knowledge of the liturgy.

The virgin martyrs enjoyed fervent veneration for the entirety of the late Middle Ages, and suffrages addressed to them are included in almost all Books of Hours. St Katherine, St Margaret and St Barbara all share an identity as early Roman virgin martyrs, and they also assume mystical identities as Brides of Christ. All three have vivid and spectacular legends where emphasis is placed on the sufferings and tortures endured to preserve virginity at crises of sexual bribery and threat.[15]

The cult of St Katherine allegedly began in the ninth century at Mount Sinai, to which her body was supposed to have been transported by angels. The legend of this saint defines Katherine as a noble girl, persecuted for Christianity, who despised marriage with the emperor because she had been made into a 'bride of Christ' through mystical marriage. Katherine was also known for her brilliant eloquence and disputed successfully with fifty philosophers who tried to refute her teaching of Christianity. The martyrdom of Katherine is marked by the physical torture of being bound between four wheels, rimmed with spikes; however, the machine was broken by a great burst of flame from Heaven. She was then beheaded, and the legend goes that milk instead of blood flowed from her severed head.[16]

The cult built on this legend strongly appealed to the popular imagination throughout the Middle Ages.[17] There are many Middle English versions of the St Katherine legend and a large variety of Latin texts available to serve as models for them. The earliest vernacular text belongs to the Katherine Group,[18] and her life is also recounted in long-line verse in the *South English Legendary,* which was composed before 1285, using Jacobus's *Legenda aurea* as a part of its source.[19]

*The Life of St Katharine of Alexandria* written in verse by John Capgrave, a prior of the Austin Friary at Lynn in Norfolk, around 1438–45 attests to the popularity and special devotion towards this virgin martyr in East Anglia.[20] Among fifteenth-century metrical legends, Osbern Bokenham's *Lyvys of Seyntys* or *Legendys of Hooly Wummen*, written in Suffolk about 1443–7, celebrates in verse the lives of Katherine, Margaret and eleven other virgin martyrs who frequently appear on the rood screens of East Anglia. As the source of these English versions of the legend, the influence of the *Legenda aurea* is considerable. Jacobus used the Latin text written by Ainard and known as the Vulgate version of the Katherine legend as the main source for his version (*c.* 1270), summarizing and condensing it to make it suitable to the tastes of laymen.[21] Eliminating most of the lengthy theological discussions which exist in the Latin, Jacobus emphasizes Katherine's identity as the bride of Christ. Her intercession is to be valued because she is a bride of Christ, a successful advocate of Christianity, a protectress of the dying. Jacobus elaborates upon how she exhorted her followers:

> With words of encouragement the virgin strengthened their resolution in the face of martyrdom and diligently instructed them in the faith; and when they were troubled because they would die without being baptized, she told them: 'Have no fear, the shedding of your blood will be counted for you as baptism and crown!' ... 'I have given myself as his bride to Christ ... Neither blandishments nor torture will draw me away from his love!'[22]

He continues, saying that at the place of execution she prayed to Jesus: ' "I beg of you that anyone who honors the memory of my passion, or who invokes me at the moment of death or in any need, may receive the benefit of your kindness." A voice was heard saying to her: "Come, my beloved, my spouse ... I promise the help from heaven for which you have prayed." '[23]

Although the *Legenda aurea* does not mention the episode of the mystical marriage of Katherine to Christ, it occurs in vernacular versions of the legend. The late Middle English prose legend includes the episodes of conversion and her marriage to Christ as we find them in Capgrave's *Life*.[24] All accounts of these episodes differ slightly, but all include the following details: after the conversion, when Katherine was praying in her chamber, Christ, the King of Glory, came to her in fine array with a great company of saints and angels and placed a ring on her finger in token of her marriage to him, promising perpetual comfort and strength.[25]

Margery's meditation on her mystical marriage to the Godhead in Rome seems to have been indebted to this episode from St Katherine's legend. She recounts the incident:

> þe Fadyr toke hir be þe hand in hir sowle be-for þe Sone & þe Holy Gost & þe Modyr of Ihesu and alle þe xij apostelys & Seynt Kateryn & Seynt Margarete & many oþer seyntys & holy virgynes wyth gret multitude of awngelys, seying to hir sowle, 'I take þe, Margery, for my weddyd wyfe, for fayrar, for fowelar, for richar, for powerar ...' (87)

The mystical marriage takes place according to the Order of Matrimony in the Sarum Missal. But Margery also emphasizes that it is performed in a mystical pageantry attended by a great company of saints and angels. Margery's inclusion of St Katherine as an attendant at the ceremony underlines that she was well aware of the same incident in Katherine's legendary life. An Old French version of this theme, for example, is revealing in that it narrates Katherine's celestial wedding ceremony with an emphasis upon a special relationship enjoyed only by Katherine.[26] By emulating Katherine's status as a privileged bride of Christ, Margery imagines her own mystical marriage as an event which enables her admittance to Christ's inner circle.

The other important virgin martyr present with Katherine is St Margaret. Although Margaret never existed as a historical person, she nonetheless enjoyed immense popularity during the later Middle Ages.[27] The *Legenda aurea*, for example, extols her power over temptation and her preaching, and recounts how her chastity was tested: 'Again the devil, still trying to deceive Margaret, changed himself to look like a man ... But she grabbed him by the head, pushed him to the ground, planted her right foot on his head, and said: "Lie still at last, proud demon, under the foot of a woman!" '[28]

In England the name of St Margaret first appears in English litanies of the seventh century. By the early thirteenth century, her veneration seems to have reached its culmination through the inclusion of her day by the Council of Oxford of 1222 in amongst the great feast days of the year.[29] Her life appeared in vernacular literature before the close of the thirteenth century for, together with the life of Katherine, it was judged to exemplify the Church's ideal of chastity and to glorify the virginal lifestyle with its sublimation of earthly desire toward the joy of mystic communion with Christ.[30]

Chastity is the crucial issue for virgin saints who desire union with their Divine Lover in the ineffable sweetness of his presence. Significantly, Margery succumbs embarrassingly to a sexual temptation on St Margaret's Eve, the day celebrating the saint who victoriously overcame the devil's temptations :

> a man whech sche louyd wel seyd on-to hir on Seynt Margaretys Evyn be-for euynsong þat for any-thyng he wold ly be hir & haue hys lust of hys body ... And he dede it for to preue hir what sche wold do, but sche wend þat he had ment ful ernest as þat tyme and seyd but lytyl þerto ... sche went to þe man befor-seyd þat he xuld haue hys lust, as sche wend þat he had desyred, but he made swech symulacyon þat sche cowd not knowe hys entent ... At þe last thorw inoportunyte of temptacyon & lakkyng of dyscrecyon sche was ouyrcomyn, & consentyd in hir mend. (14–15)

Margery's experience parallels Margaret's in that both were faced with a temptation of the devil which threatened their chastity: 'Þe Deuyl put in hir mende þat God had forsakyn hir, and ellys xuld sche not so ben temptyd. She leuyd þe Deuelys suasyons & gan to consentyn for be-cause sche cowde thynkyn no good thowt' (15). Margaret's legend does not imply that she was tempted by her own sexual desire; rather, her determined resistance contrasts sharply with the sin of lechery which Margery had painfully to overcome. Margery's memory of this temptation as occurring on St Margaret's Eve illustrates both her vulnerability to the devil's temptation and her aspiration towards the model of chastity provided by Margaret. Moreover, her mortifying experience eventually ushers in an experience of conversion which takes place during the Advent season: a conversion marking the beginning of her spiritual pursuit for a contemplative vocation as a laywoman.[31]

St Barbara is often found with St Katherine and St Margaret on late medieval English screens and paintings. Her legendary life also follows a recurrent narrative pattern – it is a tale of a holy and beautiful Christian maiden who refuses the blandishments and threats of a pagan ruler, and who maintains her chastity and status as a bride of Christ to the point of preferring physical suffering and a martyr's death.[32]

The Mass of St Barbara in the Sarum Missal attests to the popularity and devotion shown towards this saint. The liturgy emphasizes her mystical identity as the bride of Christ by including readings taken from passages in Isaiah 61 and 62: 'I will greatly rejoice in the Lord, and my soul shall be joyful in my God: for he hath clothed me with the garments of salvation: and with the robe of justice he hath covered me, as a bridegroom decked with a crown, and as a bride adorned with her jewels' (*Missal* II, 234).[33]

The martyrdoms of Katherine, Margaret and Barbara seem to have exerted a considerable influence upon Margery's meditation. Although she is not specific, nonetheless her own wish for martyrdom is in line with the accounts of the three saints. Margery records: 'Sche ymagyned in hir-self what deth sche mygth deyn for Crystys sake. Hyr þow[t] sche wold a be slayn for Goddys lofe ... þat was to be bowndyn hyr hed & hir fet to a stokke & hir hed to be smet of wyth a scharp ex for Goddys lofe' (29–30).

The violence of Margery's image is affected both by details contained in the written accounts of the virgin martyrs and by visual depictions. The violent image of being tied at her head and feet to a stake and of having her head struck off by an axe seems to be modelled upon details from the three virgins' martyrdoms which can be found both in their written texts and also in the visual iconography that occurs in Books of Hours. Katherine's determined voice at the moment of martyrdom is vividly conveyed in the *Legenda aurea*: '[S]he rose from her prayer and said to the headsman: "Brother, take your sword and strike me!" He did so and took off her head with a single stroke.'[34] Late medieval emphasis on the bizarre yet miraculous episodes of the virgin martyrs thus colours Margery's meditation upon her own martyrdom.

More importantly, Margery imbibes spiritual lessons from the saints. She is inspired particularly by the liturgical stress upon female saints as brides of Christ, a status which empowered them and gave them the eloquence to function as effective instruments of God. In this respect, it is Katherine who seems to play the most crucial role in Margery's moral and spiritual development. Of the three, it is Katherine who is most frequently recalled by Margery and who is commemorated with an elaborate liturgy upon her feast day. Feasts of major importance have elaborate services typified by a large number of proper texts and proper chants, and by solemn ceremonial. Katherine's life is fully recounted in the Office of her feast, and the nine long readings are interspersed by antiphons, responsories and hymns: a textual elaboration which suggests the importance and popularity of the devotion to this particular virgin martyr.[35] The Sarum liturgy emphasizes Katherine's identity as a bride of Christ, and it elaborates the theme of bride mysticism in order to stimulate the worshipper's imagination.

The qualities of inspired wisdom, eloquence and integrity, and heroic martyrdom, exhibited by Katherine and celebrated in the Sarum liturgy, seem to have been a source of inspiration and consolation for Margery, who incurred the hostility of neighbours and ecclesiastical authorities as the result of her spiritual life. At Leicester, she was forced to go through an inquisition by the mayor. In response to his questions, she eloquently explained her family background. However, this triggered a vicious condemnation. The mayor replied: 'Seynt Kateryn telde what kynred sche cam of & ȝet ar ȝe not lyche, for þu art a fals strumpet, a fals loller, & a fals deceyuer of þe pepyl, & þerfor I xal haue þe in preson' (111–12).[36] This seemingly minor episode provides us with a glimpse into how keenly Margery was aware of episodes from Katherine's life, and how strongly she identified herself with Katherine.

This identification can be further traced within the Sarum liturgy. *Lectio iiii* from Katherine's Proper in the Breviary praises her for the love and courage which she showed during her martyrdom: 'Christus me sibi sponsam adoptavit: ego me Christo sponsam indissociabili foedere coaptavi. Ille gloria mea, Ille amor meus, Ille dulcedo et dilectio mea. Ab ejus amore non rerum blandimenta, non exquisita tormenta ab ejus confessione poterunt revocare.'[37]

At her heresy trial, Margery stands firm on the matter of her belief in and love of God, just as Katherine did in the face of instruments of torture:

> Þer men callyd hir loller ... crying to þe pepil, 'Brennyth þis fals heretyk.' ... Þan she seyd to hem, 'I suffir not so mech sorwe as I wolde do for owr Lordys lofe, for I suffir but schrewyd wordys, & owr merciful Lord Crist Ihesu, worshepyd be hys name, suffyrd hard strokys, bittyr scorgyngys, & schamful deth at þe last for me and for al mankynde.' (129–30)

A further example enhances our sense of the intense affinity which Margery felt with Katherine. Just as God visited Katherine in the prison through heavenly light, Christ appears to Margery, arrested in Beverley, and consoles her with the promise of salvation. The responsory and the following antiphon from Katherine's Proper in the Breviary run:

> Virgo flagellatur crucianda fame religatur: carcere clausa manet lux caelica fusa refulget. Fragrat odor dulcis, cantant caeli agmina laudes. (Responsorium)
> Cum coetu virgineo adveniens Salvator, Sponsus sponsam pie visitat, consolatur et roborat, constans esto filia, tecum ego sum, nil paveas.[38]

In the same way, Margery reports that Christ visits her in her vision, thanks her, consoles her and assures her of the salvation of her soul:

> 'Dowtyr, it is mor plesyng vn-to me þat þu suffyr despitys & scornys, schamys & repreuys, wrongys & disesys ... fere þe nowt what any man can seyn on-to þe, but in myn goodnes & in thy sorwys þat þu hast suffryd þerin hast þu gret cawse to joyn, for whan þu comyst hom in-to Heuyn, þan xal euery sorwe turnyn þe to joye.' (131)

The similarity between Katherine and Margery is also found in their common determination to observe the commandments of God. Margery reports several times that she chided her own countrymen for swearing oaths: 'sche informyd in þe lawys of God as wel as sche cowde – & scharply sche spak a-geyns hem for þei sworyn gret othys & brokyn þe comawndment of owr Lord God'(101). The order of service for the

Mass celebrating the virgin martyrs emphasizes the commandments of the Lord and praises those who walk in the law of the Lord. It is of interest that the offices said at the Masses for Katherine and Margaret begin: 'The ungodly laid wait to me to destroy me; but I will consider thy testimonies, O Lord. I see that all things come to an end: but thy commandment is exceeding broad' (Ps. 118:95–6), and continue: 'Blessed are they that are undefiled in the way: and walk in the law of the Lord' (Ps. 118:1) (*Missal* II, 414, 582). Furthermore, the communion of Margaret contains the verse: 'Therefore hold I straight all thy commandments: and all false ways I utterly abhor' (Ps. 118:128) (*Missal* II, 415), while the office said in the Mass celebrating Barbara begins: 'I will speak of thy testimonies also, even before kings . . . my delight shall be in thy commandments: which I have loved' (Ps. 118:46, 47) (*Missal* II, 234).

Indeed, Psalm 118 is frequently quoted in the Sarum Missal for the virgin martyrs. This psalm invokes the commandments of God in order to elucidate his holy will for us. It is necessary to note here that the love and observance of the law of God encouraged by the psalm are taken to signify love for God. Hence, the virgins' fidelity to the commandments is an indispensable prerequisite to their claims to be blessed martyrs and brides of Christ. Margery sought an equivalently impregnable fidelity and obedience to the law of God throughout the entirety of her life.[39] Arguably, the service for virgin martyrs performed in her parish church gave an impetus to her emulation of their virtues. Despite struggles, Margery strives to walk in the law of the Lord as a bride of Christ, faithfully keeping the commandments, giving charity and proclaiming the love of God.

Furthermore, the liturgy for Katherine, Margaret and Mary Magdalen provides an important context of bride mysticism with which to address Margery's meditation in chapter 22. She envisages her own deathbed:

'A, Lord, maydenys dawnsyn now meryly in Heuyn. Xal not I don so? For be-cawse I am no mayden, lak of maydenhed is to me now gret sorwe . . .' 'A, dowtyr, how oftyn-tymes haue I teld þe þat thy synnes arn forʒoue þe & þat we ben onyd to-gedyr wyth-owtyn ende? . . . I behote þe þu schalt haue a synguler grace in Hevyn, dowtyr, & I be-hest þe <þat I shal> come to þin ende at þi deyng wyth my blyssed Modyr & myn holy awngelys & twelve apostelys, Seynt Kateryne, Seynt Margarete, Seynt Mary Mawdelyn, & many oþer seyntys pat ben in Hevyn . . . I haue preuyd þe be many tribulacyons . . . & many grevows sekenes in so mech þat þu hast ben a-noy[n]ted for deed, & al thorw my grace hast þu skapyd. Þerfor drede þe nowt, dowtyr, for wyth myn owyn handys, whech wer nayled, to þe Crosse, I xal take þi sowle fro þi bodd wyth gret myrthe & melodye, wyth swet smellys & good odowrys, & offyr it to my Fadyr in Heuyn, þer þu xalt se hym face to face, wonyng wyth hym wythowtyn ende.' (50–1)

The fundamental issue in this meditation is that of sexual purity. As her meditation demonstrates, Margery has been obsessed by the fear of damnation caused by her lack of virginity which appears an essential prerequisite of her spiritual quest to be the perfect bride of Christ.

Against this background, the liturgy for the virgin saints gives a glimpse into the rationale underlying the virgin martyrs' appearance within her deathbed meditation. The gospel reading for St Katherine's day in the Sarum Missal is taken from Matthew 13:44–52, and it elucidates the central issues surrounding Margery's salvation:

> The kingdom of heaven is like unto a treasure hidden in a field . . . Again the kingdom of heaven is like to a merchant seeking goodly pearls. Who when he had found one pearl of great price, went his way, and sold all that he had, and bought it . . . So shall it be at the end of the world. The angels shall go out, and shall separate the wicked from among the just. (*Missal* II, 584)

The same passage is read at the masses for Barbara, Margaret, Agnes, Agatha and Lucy, who are all celebrated virgin martyrs. It is also found in the Common of Virgin and Martyr in the Missal. Margery might have felt some affinity with a parable that was told using a mercantile vocabulary. But, more important than this, the passage in question has a bearing upon her painful anxiety, for its core lies in its reference to the end of the world when 'the angels shall go out, and shall separate the wicked from the just' (Matt. 13:49). Both Margery's ongoing fear of the Last Judgement and her anxious hope of salvation are heightened by this gospel message reiterated within the Church's liturgy.

Katherine and Margaret appear in Margery's meditation as perfect virgins who are entitled to be grouped amongst the just because of their status as maidens. But the presence of Mary Magdalen, who shares sexual sins with Margery but is pardoned as the result of her conversion, is yet more illuminating. It is no wonder that Margery identified herself with Mary Magdalen, for the Magdalen represents the shame and sorrow over sinfulness from which Margery suffered.[40] So, the presence of Katherine, Margaret and Mary Magdalen, all of whom are significant for sexual purity, though in different ways, serves to stress Margery's own anxiety about the subject and, simultaneously, to provide a means of relief from that anxiety.

The Common Memorials of St Katherine, St Margaret and St Mary Magdalen in the Sarum Missal suggest how ordinary devout women might relate to these saints when they attend the service. The Collect relates the virginal holiness of these female saints:

> God, who hast granted to thy most holy virgins Katherine and Margaret, the palm of martyrdom, and to Mary Magdalen pardon of her sins; mercifully grant unto us that, through the intervention of their merits and prayers we may be found worthy to be decorated with the grace of chastity, and to be absolved from the bonds of our sins. (*Missal* II, 136)

The Secret has: '... let the holy virgins Katherine and Margaret obtain for us purity of mind and the blessed Mary Magdalen a saving penitence' (*Missal* II, 137). Katherine and Margaret are praised for their virginal purity; however, the prayers emphasize spiritual purity rather than physical virginity. Furthermore, Mary Magdalen is also included in the company of these virgin saints and remembered for the pardon she gained through the love of God.

Thus, Margery's vision is supported by this promise of salvation. Although she is not a virgin, the possibility of becoming bride of Christ nonetheless remains open to her. Christ assures her that her lack of virginity does not hinder his love for her: 'I lofe þe as wel as any mayden in þe world ... I loue þe wyth all myn hert & I may not forberyn þi lofe' (49). Furthermore, Christ promises the salvation of her soul and declares:

> for-as-mech as þu art a mayden in þi sowle, I xal take þe be þe on hand in Hevyn & my Modyr be þe oþer hand, & so xalt þu dawnsyn in Hevyn wyth oþer holy maydens & virgynes, for I may clepyn þe dere a-bowte & myn owyn derworthy derlyng. I xal sey to þe, myn owyn blyssed spowse. (52–3)[41]

Margery's vision of her deathbed may also have been influenced by iconography of the Assumption of the Virgin Mary. The Mass celebrating the Assumption makes only a brief mention of the fact that Christ comes himself with his angels to welcome the Virgin, the fair spouse of God;[42] however, the popular account of the Assumption in the *Legenda aurea* has a much closer relationship with the details of Margery's vision. Jacobus narrates that when the apostles were brought together at her deathbed, Jesus came with companies of angels and choirs of virgins and that Mary's soul went forth from her body and flew into the arms of her Son.[43] Traditional visual iconography of the Assumption correlates with Jacobus's vision: it depicts the apostles attending Mary's deathbed and Christ spreading forth his hands to receive her spotless soul, accompanied by various celestial hosts.[44]

Margery's vision, however, is intriguing in that it includes two post-biblical virgin saints – Katherine and Margaret – who could never have appeared in the Assumption of the Virgin. Yet the Office of St Katherine helps illuminate Margery's account. The Office is centered upon Katherine's mystical identity as bride. Katherine's feast day begins with a suffrage to Katherine, the bride of Christ:

> Ave virginum gemma Katherina, ave sponsa Regis regum gloriosa, ave viva Christi hostia, tua venerantibus patrocinia implorata non deneges suffragia. (Super Psalmos Antiphona)
>
> Jam Christo juncta Sponso que tuo sociata. (Versicle)[45]

The Office celebrates Katherine for her chastity, brilliant wisdom and charismatic power to convert the pagan. Her heroic martyrdom is elaborated through the sequence of readings, and the devout supplicate her intercession through their pious remembrance of the virgin martyr's passion. Nevertheless, it seems that the efficacy of her intercession derives most prominently from her identity as the bride of Christ.[46]

Furthermore, through a mystical interpretation of the relationship between God and his beloved in his chamber, the antiphon at Lauds elucidates the perfect efficacy of Katherine's prayer to her Lover/God: 'Vox de caelis insonuuit, veni dilecta mea veni, iontra thalamum Sponsi tui quod postulas impetrasti, pro quibus oras salu erit (Ant).'[47]

Katherine's mystical identity as the bride of Christ is the source of her intercessory power, it also leads her into ecstatic union with God in heaven. The Sarum liturgy elaborates on this profound aspect of bride mysticism: both the *Oratio* from Katherine's Proper in the Breviary and the Collect said in the Mass for Katherine use the same text: 'Omnipotens sempiterne Deus, qui corpus gloriosae virginis et martyris tuae Katherinae in montem Synai ab angelis deferri jussisti: concede, quaesumus, ejus obtentu nos ad arcem virtutum provehi, ubi visionis tuae claritatem mereamur intueri. Per Dominum nostrum' (Oratio).[48]

This event, after Katherine's death, when her body was carried by angels to Mount Sinai is widely known as a result of the liturgy. The suffrage of St Katherine in the 'de Brailes Hours', for example, depicts this scene among other dramatic events from her life.[49] The beatific vision of God in his glory – the ultimate goal of mystical experience – is thus evoked in the Sarum liturgy in order to encourage the devout to emulate St Katherine and to cultivate the virtues she exemplifies as a way of attaining full union with God after death. Thus, by emulating the holiness and virtues manifested in Katherine's life, Margery pursues a contemplative *unitas* with the Divine which will ultimately be actualized at the glorious end of her bridal pilgrimage.

I have explored the significance and centrality of the virgin martyrs in Margery's meditation. Her mode of venerating the saints not only illuminates her trust in the efficacy of their intercession; it also illustrates her tendency to envisage them as living models. Margery's meditation draws on both the Church's liturgy and hagiography as building blocks in the process of assembling a unique understanding of, and relationship with, the saints. In producing her autobiographical account, she and her amanuensis knowingly make use of hagiographic conventions;[50] however, I would like to emphasize that it is not just the texts of the saints' lives but, more particularly, the liturgical celebration of them, which play an especially central role in the dynamic of Margery's aspiration to contemplation and spiritual identity as a bride of Christ.

Margery's liturgical experience enriches her spiritual interior by enabling her to experience a state of liminality; it thus exercises an influence upon the way in which her meditations become revelatory for her. At the same time, it is the revelatory nature of Margery's meditations which leads her to embrace the theological teaching and to emulate the exemplary virtues which are represented within the liturgy. The liturgy thus plays an essentially dynamic role in the development of Margery's meditative understanding: Margery aspires to attain beatific salvation by emulating the saints, inspired by the bride mysticism which is emphasized in the liturgy.[51]

## Notes

[1] For the medieval mentality of venerating saints, see R. Kieckhefer, *Unquiet Souls: Fourteenth-Century Saints and Their Religious Milieu* (Chicago and London, 1984); for a historical viewpoint on the saints, see A. Vauchez, *La Sainteté en occident aux derniers siècles du Moyen Age d'après les procès*

*de canonisation et les documents hagiographiques* (Rome, 1981); for a socio-historical viewpoint, see D. Weinstein and R. M. Bell, *Saints and Society: The Two Worlds of Western Christendom 1000–1700* (Chicago, 1982). See also R. Blumenfeld-Kosinski and T. Szell (eds.), *Images of Sainthood in Medieval Europe* (Ithaca and London, 1991).

[2] On material remains and the cult of relics, see C. W. Bynum, *The Resurrection of the Body in Western Christianity, 200–1338* (New York, 1995).

[3] See C. W. Atkinson, *Mystic and Pilgrim: The Book of and the World of Margery Kempe* (Ithaca and London, 1983), esp. ch. 6; E. Duffy, *The Stripping of the Altars: Traditional Religion in England 1400–1580* (New Haven and London, 1992), esp. ch. 5.

[4] V. and E. Turner, *Image and Pilgrimage in Christian Culture* (New York, 1978), 1–39.

[5] C. Davidson (ed.), *The Saint Play in Medieval Europe* (Kalamazoo, 1986), 2–3.

[6] All references to *The Book of Margery Kempe,* with page number in parentheses following quotations, are to the following edition: S. B. Meech and H. E. Allen (eds.), *The Book of Margery Kempe*, EETS 212 (Oxford, 1940; repr. 1961) (hereafter cited as *The Book*).

[7] See *The Book*, 214–25.

[8] For recent research on Margery, see the following chapters in this volume: S. Fanous, 'Measuring the Pilgrim's Progress: Internal Emphases in *The Book of Margery Kempe*'; D. Renevey, 'Margery's Performing Body: The Translation of Late Medieval Discursive Religious Practices'; and R. Lawes, 'Psychological Disorder and the Autobiographical Impulse in Thomas Hoccleve, Margery Kempe and Julian of Norwich'.

[9] See W. J. Ong, 'Orality, Literacy, and Medieval Textualization', *New Literary History: A Journal of Theory and Interpretation*, 16 (1984), 1–12.

[10] See P. Saenger, 'Books of Hours and the Reading Habits of the Late Middle Ages', *Scrittura et civiltà*, 9 (1985), 239–69 (240–1).

[11] Ibid., 241.

[12] Ibid., 241.

[13] See C. M. Meale, ' "... alle the bokes that I haue of latyn, englisch, and frensch": Laywomen and their Books in Late Medieval England', in C. M. Meale (ed.), *Women and Literature in Britain 1150–1500* (Cambridge, 1993), 128–58 (133).

[14] See Saenger, 'Books of Hours', 259.

[15] J. Wogan-Browne explores the female writers of Anglo-Norman saints' lives and argues that those referring to virgin martyrs offer exemplary narratives in which the saint's best demonstration of sanctity is shown through her preference for death over dishonour; see ' "Clerc u lai, muïne u dame": Women and Anglo-Norman Hagiography in the Twelfth and Thirteenth Centuries', in Meale, *Women and Literature*, 61–85. Wogan-Browne also mentions that the narrative biographies of the virgin martyrs show that they die

a tormented death through a passion of loyalty to their bridegroom, Christ; see 'Chaste Bodies: Frames and Experiences', in S. Kay and M. Rubin (eds.), *Framing Medieval Bodies* (Manchester, 1994), 24–42.

[16] See D. H. Farmer, *The Oxford Dictionary of Saints* (Oxford, 1987), 77–8; G. Ferguson, *Signs and Symbols in Christian Art* (London, 1961), 110–11.

[17] For the history of its transmission, see S. Nevanlinna and I. Taavitsainen (eds.), *St Katherine of Alexandria: The Late Middle English Prose Legend in Southwell Minster MS 7* (Cambridge, 1993), 3–4. For the history of documents about the cult of Katherine, see pp.3–10.

[18] See S. T. R. O. d'Ardenne (ed.), *The Katherine Group edited from MS. Bodley 34* (Paris, 1977), and S. R. T. O. d'Ardenne and E. J. Dobson (eds.), *Seinte Katerine: Re-Edited from MS Bodley 34 and the other Manuscripts*, EETS SS 7 (London, 1981). On the lives of St Katherine and St Margaret in the AB texts, see E. Robertson, *Early English Devotional Prose and the Female Audience* (Knoxville, Tenn., 1990), esp. ch. 6, 94–125.

[19] C. d'Evelyn and A. J. Mill (eds.), *The South English Legendary*, 2 vols., EETS OS 235 and 236 (London, 1956; repr. 1967), II, 533–43.

[20] See C. Horstmann (ed.), *The Life of St Katharine of Alexandria by John Capgrave*, EETS OS 100 (London, 1893; repr. 1973), xxiii.

[21] See Nevanlinna and Taavitsainen, *St Katherine*, 9.

[22] Jacobus de Voragine, *The Golden Legend: Readings on the Saints*, tr. W. G. Ryan, 2 vols. (Princeton, 1993), II, 337.

[23] Jacobus, *Golden Legend*, II, 339.

[24] See, for example, the text in Southwell Minster, MS 7, fo. 182$^v$/520–31, in Nevanlinna and Taavitsainen, *St Katherine*, 82, and 'Christ weds St Katherine', in Horstmann (ed.), *Life of St Katharine*, 247.

[25] See Nevanlinna and Taavitsainen, *St Katherine*, 12–13.

[26] See W. McBain, 'St Catherine's Mystic Marriage: The Genesis of a Hagiographic *Cycle De Sainte-Catherine*', *Romance Languages Annual*, 2 (1990), 135–40 (137–9).

[27] See Farmer, *Oxford Dictionary*, 281–2; and Ferguson, *Signs and Symbols*, 131.

[28] Jacobus, *Golden Legend*, I, 369. In Christian iconography, the immaculate Virgin treads the serpent underfoot: the implication is that Mary conquers the serpent which misleads humanity through its temptations.

[29] For the history of the cult of St Margaret, see F. M. Mack (ed.), *Seinte Marherete: þe Meiden and Martyr*, EETS OS 193 (London, 1934; repr. 1958), x–xii.

[30] See Mack, *Seinte Marherete*, xii.

[31] See *The Book*, ch 5. Samuel Fanous, in his essay in this volume, has pointed out an unusual alignment of temporal and geographic specificity and argues that the abject moral failure on St Margaret's Eve paradoxically foreshadows Margery's future as the bride of Christ as she makes spiritual progress.

[32] For the life of Barbara, see Ferguson, *Signs and Symbols*, 107.

[33] *The Sarum Missal in English*, tr. F. E. Warren, 2 vols. (London, 1911–13). Henceforth abbreviated as *Missal* I and II. All citations to the *Missal* are from this translation and will be followed by the page number in parentheses.

[34] Jacobus, *Golden Legend*, I, 370.

[35] See A. Hughes, *Medieval Manuscripts for Mass and Office: A Guide to their Organization and Terminology* (Toronto, 1982), 237.

[36] Margery would have had no difficulty in associating 'fals strumpet' with Mary Magdalen and Mary of Egypt and identifying her suffering with theirs.

[37] F. Procter and C. Wordsworth (eds.), *Breviarium ad usum insignis ecclesiae Sarisburiensis*, 3 vols. (Cambridge, 1879–86; repr. Farnborough, 1970), III, 1108. Hereafter *Breviarium*. Unless otherwise stated, all translations from *Breviarium* are my own. 'Christ adopted me as his bride. By an unbreakable contract with Christ, I associated myself to be his bride. He is my glory, He is my love, He is my sweetness and my beloved. Neither the charms of objects nor refined torments will be able to prevent me from venerating him for his love.'

[38] *Breviarium* III, 1112–13. 'The virgin is scourged, bound by torturing hunger: she is kept shut in prison, broad heavenly light shines out. A sweet smell is emitted, the celestial companies sing praises (Responsory).

With virginal union, the Savior comes, the Bridegroom visits his bride piously. He consoles and strengthens her: "Be firm in your faith, I am with you, do not fear." (Antiphon).'

[39] See, for example, *The Book*, ch. 63.

[40] Fanous also argues that the genesis of Margery's conversion lies in the model offered by Mary Magdalen. See his chapter in this volume.

[41] As the bride of Christ, Margery could be privileged to become a perfect intercessor before God, thus fulfilling her spiritual ambition; see *The Book*, ch. 22/10–14.

[42] *Missal*, II, 467.

[43] Jacobus, *Golden Legend*, II, 77–97. The assumption or dormition of the Virgin seems to have originated in a belief contained in apocryphal literature from the fourth century onwards which had a profound influence on Christian theology and practice in East and West. For the various accounts of this theme, see J. K. Elliott (ed.), *The Apocryphal New Testament* (Oxford, 1993), 691–723. The first feast of the Assumption was instituted after the Council of Ephesus in 431 and it was accepted at Rome shortly after 650. For details of its origin and transmission, see 'Marian Feasts', in *New Catholic Encyclopaedia* (New York, 1967), IX, 211. Clayton argues that the feast of Assumption is one of the Roman feasts established in Anglo-Saxon England from the second half of the eighth century onwards; see M. Clayton, *The Cult of the Virgin Mary in Anglo-Saxon England* (Cambridge, 1990), 30–51. The Catholic dogma of the Assumption of the Virgin was not defined until 1950 when the Papal Bull *Munificentissimus Deus* was proclaimed; see

H. Denzinger and A. Schonmetzer (eds.), *Enchiridion symbolorum: definitionum et declarationum de rebus fidei et morum*, 2nd edn (Freiburg, 1965), 3900 (2331 for the old edition); see *Missal*, II, 462–74, for the liturgy celebrating the Assumption.

44 See, for example, the Assumption and the Feast of the Assumption of the Virgin in the Carmelite Missal, British Library, MS Loan 82, fo. 132$^v$. The Assumption of the Virgin in this Carmelite Missal is reproduced in M. Rickert (ed.), *The Reconstructed Carmelite Missal: An English Manuscript of the late XIVth Century in the British Museum (Additional 29704–5, 44892)* (London, 1952).

45 *Breviarium*, III, 1102. 'Hail, Katherine, virgins' jewel; hail, glorious bride of the King of Kings; hail, Christ's living sacrificial victim. Please do not deny the suffrage to those who venerate your patronage. (Antiphon) [Katherine], you are already united to Christ and married to your bridegroom (versicle).'

46 See the antiphon and responsory in *Breviarium*, III, 1104–5.

47 *Breviarium*, III, 1117. 'A voice from heaven resounds: "Come my lover, come into the nuptial chamber of your Bridegroom; what you request has [already] been granted to you. Those for whom you pray will be saved!"'

48 *Breviarium*, III, 1103. The translation is taken from *Missal* II, 582. 'Almighty everlasting God, who commanded that the body of your glorious virgin and martyr Katherine should be borne by angels to Mount Sinai; grant, we beseech you, that by her aid we may be led to the citadel of virtues, where we may be found worthy to gaze on the splendour of your vision. For our Lord (Collect).'

49 See C. Donovan, *The de Brailes Hours: Shaping the Book of Hours in Thirteenth-Century Oxford* (London, 1991), 63.

50 See S. B. Fanous, 'Biblical and Hagiographical *Imitatio* in The Book of Margery Kempe' (University of Oxford D.Phil. thesis, 1997).

51 This essay was researched and written before the doctoral thesis of Samuel Fanous was available for consultation. Both Fanous's work and this chapter argue that virgin martyrs are spiritual models to whom Margery aspires, and that the accounts of their lives bear a resemblance to the life of Margery. Fanous concentrates on hagiography and the parallels between the lives of the Virgin Martyrs and Margery's experience which are embedded in her text. He argues that they point to her own ambitions for sainthood and illuminate both her desire for public recognition and the second amanuensis's willingness to make *The Book* a saint's life. This chapter, however, emphasizes the centrality of the liturgical celebration of the saints in the dynamic of Margery's spiritual progress as a bride of Christ.

# 9
# Margery's Performing Body: The Translation of Late Medieval Discursive Religious Practices

### DENIS RENEVEY

IN her description of the death of an old Sioux woman, Margaret Many Wounds, Susan Power in her short story 'Moonwalk' reports through the eyes of Harley, her grandson, a particularly momentous event. For a little while, neglected by his mother and aunt, Harley sits in front of the television screen watching the astronauts walking on the moon. To his great surprise, he suddenly finds his grandmother taking part in this historic moment. Her performance, a dance modelled on Sioux powwow steps, takes on new meaning as it becomes a part of one of the greatest historical moments of the second half of this century:

> Harley was no longer lonely or invisible on the chair. He saw his grandmother's figure emerging on the screen, dancing toward him from the far horizon behind the astronauts. He recognized her weaving dance as Sioux powwow steps, but her beautiful blue-beaded dress was unfamiliar to him.
> He said to himself, *Grandma is young*. But then she smiled at him, and the smile was old. Her hair was black and her hair was white. Her progress was steady, and she didn't bounce like the men in space suits. He waited for Armstrong and Aldrin to see her, but they must have seen only the ground. Finally she came upon them, and Harley caught his breath because Margaret danced through Neil Armstrong. The astronaut never ceased digging at the ground, leaving footprints like heavy tank treads, but his oxygen system quivered a little as she passed.
> Margaret Many Wounds was dancing on the moon. *Look at the crooked tracks I make like a snake*, she thought. At first it seemed it would take her a long time to make the circuit. *Am I dancing or flying?* she wondered when instead she completed it very quickly. Names came to her, though she had never learned them.[1]

This arresting story captures one of the central issues which will be addressed by this chapter, using a work very remote from the writings by Power on the Sioux tribes. *The Book of Margery Kempe* offers a number of scenes in which Margery Kempe, author and main protagonist of this autobiography, inscribes her life into a history, sacred history, and into a particular story based upon the incidents of the Passion.[2] *The Book of Margery Kempe* is, in part, an account of this literary inscription. In the same way that the television screen provides Harley with a new window into his own inner world, the book invites us to become witness to a rare moment where Margery's body, relieved of spatio-temporal constraints, manages, through visionary experience and meditation, to reconstruct and interact with the characters of sacred history.[3] It is my intention to consider this performance as a multi-layered act of translation, conceiving of the latter as a hermeneutic process.[4] What layers of translation are to be detected in the bodily performance of Margery? First, the figuring of her body within a new dimension necessitates moving it from one dimension through into another (*translatio* as transference). Secondly, this act of encoding is enabled by Margery's own personal translation of the late medieval discursive practices which prevailed among hermits, anchorites and devout lay people throughout Europe.[5] Thirdly, the several stages which saw the writing of *The Book of Margery Kempe*, without which this account of Margery's performance would have been lost, can also be considered as stages in a translation act. These stages are described by Margery's second scribe in a Prologue in which he traces the process by which Margery's performative act was transformed into an illegible text written in a gibberish of German and English, ultimately to be replaced by a new rendering of the first text into the version which has been preserved for us by the Carthusians of Mount Grace.

The hermeneutic process involved in the making of *The Book of Margery Kempe* is extraordinarily complex and escapes the limitations imposed by this essay.[6] As a consequence, only the first two modes of translation enumerated above will be attended to here. Without wishing to undervalue the complex encoding of the performative act as textual material, I would nevertheless like to concentrate here upon Margery's role as a performer rather than a writer.[7] The degree of Margery's authorial involvement during her dictation of her experiences to her amanuenses is difficult to measure. However, considering the material importance of the book within medieval culture, it is necessary to pay attention to the second amanuensis's account of *The Book*'s evolution, even if an initial failure to decipher the text devalues the significance of the first attempt at textual recording. Despite the desire to credit the second attempt with miraculous and hagiographic qualities, it seems nonetheless that it was Margery's authorial involvement, rather than the presence of the initial text, which finally enabled the successful, though painful, translation of events experienced more than twenty years before onto manuscript parchment: 'Þe preste, trustyng in hire prayers, be-gan to redyn þis booke, & it was mych mor esy, as hym þowt, þan it was be-forn tym. & so he red it ouyr be-forn þis creatur ery word, sche sum-tym helpyng where ony difficulte was' (5).

For a period of over twenty years Margery offered her body as her ading material. If she initially refused to have her story written down the Carmelite Alan of Lynn, a Doctor of Divinity of Cambridge, ause 'sche was warnyd in hyr spyrit þat sche xuld not wryte so e'(6), it was also partly because, at that time, her body stood as the chment on which God actively encoded his signs.

have shown elsewhere how Margery's own gesticulations, sobbing, ping and wailing translate sacred history. Her body belongs to the nos and obeys the same divine laws as those governing the forces ature. God says to her '& ryth so I far wyth þe, dowtyr, whan it h me to spekyn in þi sowle' (183).[8] She is part of the *liber naturae*. ever reads her astutely will be able to uncover a divine message.[9]

e is, however, another peculiar manifestation of this performance *e Book*. Margery's vocal and bodily signs often result from her ction through dreams and visions with the characters and events red history. Her involvement with the Passion narrative is a good in point. With regard to this particular issue, it is my contention Margery's devotional practices, especially in their high-powered rmative dimensions, were informed by a well-established tradi- rooted in English anchoritic practices, but also manifested in late val devotions.[10] In other words, it is possible to gain important insights into the peculiar performance of Margery Kempe by ating it in the light of the Anselmian tradition which influenced nth-century anchoritic culture.

## Anselm and the Anchoritic Tradition

nselmian spiritual tradition, with its severe outlook on the soul's ss, fashions to a great extent the spirituality pertaining to the anchoritic tradition. The penitent soul contemplates its sins and expiates its faults by meditating on its worthlessness in comparison to the beauty and glory of the maker. The deity's grandest act of generosity, the Incarnation, is an important element in this penitential voyage. The soul contemplates the sufferings of this glorious God made man and measures its own debased state and relative comfort against the pain and tortures inflicted on such a Lord. Wearing a hair-shirt, beating oneself, kneeling and kissing the ground, digging one's own grave in one's cell, all those activities partake in a process which serves to mark the inner landscape of the contemplatives with the stamp of sinfulness. Some of those painful physical activities serve as devices for re-enacting the Passion incidents in an attempt to feel something of the pain endured by Jesus on the cross.[11]

*Ancrene Wisse*, the Middle English thirteenth-century rule for anchoresses, abounds with evidence of performative activity. The paraliturgical passages of *Ancrene Wisse* require elaborate performances from the three anchoresses for whom this rule was originally written.[12] In the intimacy of their cells, they are asked to participate in penitential performative acts as a part of their daily religious activities.[13] The enclosure in a cell, and the vocal and bodily utterances, are all conventions used to signify their inner sinful nature and their desire to acknowledge God's generous act. The precise information which regulates their performance in the cell serves to make the majority of their gestures spiritually significant.[14] In other words, it is generally the case that anchoresses participate in a performance demonstrative of their sinful nature, with God as the sole witness.[15]

Beyond the physicality of their ascetic practices – which find an echo in Margery's vocal and bodily manifestations – anchoresses express their relationship with God by meditating almost exclusively on the events of the Passion. From the very beginning of the anchoritic life, death is an ongoing theme. The ceremony of enclosure uses part of the *Officium mortuorum* as a way of representing the important tenets and values of the anchoritic life.[16] Life in the cell is a form of death, a personal re-enactment of the Passion of Christ. Again, the relative comfort experienced by the anchoresses in their cells is often contrasted first, with Christ's uncomfortable birth, and then with other event experienced during his life.[17] In the texts of the Wooing Group, which possibly address the anchoresses mentioned in *Ancrene Wisse*, the Passion incidents play a central part.[18] To take one example, in *þ Wohunge of ure Lauerd*, the narrator's invitation to his audience t engage affectively with the Passion material opens up many new possibilities for devotional performance.[19] Such a tone encourages specifically creative participation on the part of the audience. Nonetheless, in order to circumscribe a horizon of performance beyond which the creative imagination should not trespass, the narrator remains Anselmian in tone. He moderates the possible achievements of his audience, and is eager to stress the limitations created by their sinful nature. Thus anchoritic writings influenced by the Anselmian tradition prevent too close an identification with the crucified Christ or his mother.[20] There is no destination upon the affective journey which the reader is invited to follow. Instead, a transference or translation of this affective input takes place – if the events of the Passion cannot be lived internally, they must be lived externally through ritualized anchoritic practices.[21] Such visionary elements serve to give meaning to the earthly life of anchoresses who have accepted their own death to the world at the time of the ceremony of enclosure.

Paradoxically, it is by its affective incompletion that the narration of the Passion incidents in such writings serves best to stimulate and justify the anchoritic life. Absence of closure allows for transference and justification within one's own life. *A Talkyng of the Love of God*, a fourteenth-century compilation of some of the texts of the Wooing Group, provides interesting evidence showing how the compiler/author negotiates with the Passion incidents when deletion of the anchoritic framework has taken place.[22] Without going into too many details, it is possible to detect a desire to refashion the Passion incidents so as to allow fuller, more complete affective identification with Jesus and, ultimately, at the moment of his death, with Mary. Lacking the performative guidelines used by anchoresses within the closed space of the anchorhold, which allow for the Passion performance to be transposed, the audience of *A Talkyng of the Love of God* needs to stay longer and more firmly in the realm of the visionary to ensure that its meditation is effective.[23] This fourteenth-century compilation of some of the Wooing Group pieces is forced to signpost its affective strategies, having lost many of the tools provided by the anchoritic culture from which those pieces first emerged.

Equally, Julian of Norwich's account of her own understanding and perception of some of the Passion incidents provides additional evidence for a contextually loose apprehension of those events.[24] Julian's three wishes demonstrate an eagerness to empathize with the sufferings of Jesus, and the vision she receives triggers one of the most subtle visionary accounts in medieval literature. However, Julian deals with the Passion incidents in a very idiosyncratic way. Her creative and imaginative input contribute toward the production of a text which entirely surpasses those considered thus far. Her contribution attests to the ever-increasing hermeneutic scope offered to those outside the monastic and anchoritic milieux who have an interest in the contemplative life. However, it is significant to note that she later embarked upon the anchoritic life – a way modelled as closely as possible on the life of Christ and his mother who, in *Ancrene Wisse*, is regarded as the model for all anchoresses[25] – in order to make meaning out of her vision.[26]

We know that the anchoritic life required the support of the entire community and that most spheres of society were in contact with anchoresses, whether in the capacity of patrons, spiritual guides, confessors, maids, or simply as fellow parishioners.[27] The reading by the laity of the Offices to the Virgin and the Office of the Dead in Books of Hours in church or in private chapels is an indicator of religious practices which closely imitated those of solitaries.[28] It should therefore be of no surprise to us to see Margery Kempe, a woman of the world, go to the anchoress Julian of Norwich to seek approval with regard to her own peculiar performance.

## Love's *Myrrour*

Although it would be possible at this stage of my analysis to explicate Margery's performing body as a peculiar translation of anchoritic contemplative practices, I would like to turn to another religious text in order to broaden the scope of my approach. Nicholas Love's *The Myrrour of the Blessed Lyf of Jesu Christi*, a translation of the Latin *Meditationes vitae Christi*, invites people of simple understanding to use the book to assist their meditations.[29] Love offers an imaginative account of the life of Christ for those who have difficulty in meditating on spiritual invisible things. He insists on the imaginative quality of his piece, defending his move away from Scripture with the following remark: 'Wherfore we mowen to stiryng of deuotion ymagine & þenk diuerse wordes & dedes of him & oþer, þat we fynde not writen, so þat it be not aȝeyns þe byleue, as seynt Gregory & oþer doctours seyn, þat holi writte may be expownet & vnderstande in diuerse maneres, & to diuerse purposes, so þat it be not aȝeyns þe byleue or gude maneres' (*Mirror* 10/43–11/4). Love defines his commentary upon the life of Jesus, specifically designed for 'lewed men and wommen', as part of an old hermeneutic practice established by the Doctors of the Church.[30] The writing of meditations upon the life of Christ, as suggested by Love, is therefore a part of the commentary tradition. Such meditations participate in the edification of the Christian soul according to the words of St Paul in his letter to the Romans (Rom. 15:4). As Love informs his reader, imagination plays an important role in this hermeneutic process. Neither is that role limited to the writing process. Rather, Love exhorts his readers to engage affectively with his material in order to become active in filling the affective gaps left blank by his text and the gospel accounts. The account of the Nativity is introduced in the following manner: 'And so ymagine we & set we oure mynde & our þouht as we were present in þe place where þis was done at Betheleem! beholdyng how þees þre kynges comen with gret multitude & a wirchipful company of lordes & oþer seruantes, & so by token of þe Sterre firste ledyng & after restyng vp on þat place, þat the child Jesus was inne!' (*Mirror* 43/28–33). The reader has to perform as though, with Love, he were a participant in those momentous events. Love's guiding presence remains strong in the text and prevents any devious use of the imagination on the part of the 'lewed' reader. Elsewhere, when writing on the sufferings of Christ, Love insists on stressing how completely the person of Jesus experienced the suffering inflicted upon his body. Such strategies disallow a passive reading of his text and invite further affective identification with the events described:

> At þe bigynnyng þou þat desireste to haue sorouful compassion þorh feruent inwarde affection of þe peynful passion of Jesu; þou most in þi mynde depart in manere for þe tyme þe miht of þe godhede fro þe kyndely infirmite of þe manhede þouh it so be in soþenes þat þe godhede was neuer departede fro þe manhede. For þere beþ many so blynde gostly by vnresonable ymaginacion of þe miht of þe godhede in Jesu, þat þei trowe not þat any þinge miht be peynful or sorouful to hym as to a noþer comune man þat haþ onely þe kynde of man. *(Mirror* 161/3–12)

In accordance with the declaration of intention made in the prologue, the manhood of Jesus receives careful attention. It is no coincidence that such a comment appears before the meditations describing the Passion incidents. Anchoritic writings also focus consistently upon the humanity of Jesus, selecting from the abstract, Neoplatonic repertoire of twelfth-century monastic spirituality, only those passages and words which describe Jesus in affective, sensuous and human terms.[31] Unlike the Wooing Group texts, the wide readership addressed by Love disables him from creating the conditions of reading, encompassing a playful and didactic movement in and out of sacred history, which are so characteristic of anchoritic texts. The game which the anchoress was allowed to perform of affectively correlating her reading material with her living conditions is no longer possible. Instead, Love firmly locates his reader as an attentive but passive witness to the Passion: 'Wherefore if þou þat redist or herest þis boke, haste herebefore bisily taken hede to þoo þinges þat hauen be writen & spoken of þe blessede life of oure lorde Jesu criste in to þis tyme; miche more now þou shalt gedire alle þi mynde & alle þe strengh of þi soule to þoo þinges þat folowen of his blessede passion' (*Mirror* 162/33–8). The vivid description offered by Love succeeds in creating a strong affective response on the part of his reader. It is also possible that some of the injunctions scattered within the text may trigger an improvised meditation on the Passion incidents on the part of its most creative readers. Love therefore advocates a kind of performance, but within certain limits, and in accordance with specific intentions:[32] 'Oo lord god in what state was þat tyme his modere soule, when she sawh him so peynfully faile, wepe & dye? Soþely I trowe þat for þe multitude of anguishes she was alle out of hir self & vnfelable made as half dede, & þat now mich more; þan what tyme she mette with him, beringe þe crosse as it is seide' (*Mirror* 180/34–9). Love provides a popular hermeneutics in the form of an imaginative re-enactment of the life of Christ, which the audience is invited to perform inwardly.[33] But, as with the example quoted above, Love provides the interpretative solutions to the questions raised by the arresting, emotionally moving scenes within his textual landscape. His creation is a textual one, offering limited access to closely controlled, performative activity.[34]

## Margery's Performance

Margery Kempe was probably familiar with Love's text or its Latin source.[35] We are at least certain that she was familiar with the tradition of meditation on the events of Christ's life through Rolle's *Meditations on the Passion* and the *Stimulus amoris* which were read to her. The essay offered by Selman attests further to a flourishing affective tradition where the imitation of biblical characters appears to have been a recurring performative activity. It is against the backdrop of anchoritic material and the pervasive tradition of meditation on the events of Christ's life that I want to offer my own reading of Margery's performance.[36] As Bella Millett clearly points out in her chapter in this volume, the *Ancrene Wisse*, and anchoritic culture in general, have had a far greater impact on lay devotional practices than has previously been acknowledged. I argue that it is possible to make sense of Margery's eclectic, original and performative spirituality by viewing it as an offshoot of this tradition.

Kempe's merit consists in the way in which she has been able to accommodate elements from anchoritic and affective traditions into an idiosyncratic translation which incorporates her own body as an important performative element within sacred history.[37] To make such a manifestation credible, Margery must first undergo several rites of passage entailing ever closer degrees of identification with Jesus, until a point is reached when he provides her with the following information:[38] 'For, whan þow gost to chyrch, I go wyth þe; whan þu syttest at þi mete, I sytte wyth þe; whan þow gost to þi bed, I go wyth þe; &, whan þu gost owt of towne, I go wyth þe' (31).

Margery's conversations with Christ, based on existing models, create an intimacy between her and Christ which is unequalled in other English vernacular writings.[39] Christ participates in her daily activities with the same degree of intensity with which we see him perform sacred history. Margery and Christ enter a multifaceted and exclusive relationship: 'Þerfor I preue þat þow art a very dowtyr to me & a modyr also, a syster, a wyfe, and a spowse, wytnessyng þe Gospel wher owyr Lord seyth to hys dyscyples, "He þat doth þe wyl of my Fadyr in Heuyn he is bothyn modyr, broþir, & syster un-to me"' (31).

Margery's slow, but unrelenting entry into the framework designated by the Gospel texts initially takes place via powerful assertions in which she depicts herself as an appropriate counterpart to the disciples, and a character capable of appearing and performing in amongst the great dramatic heroes of the New Testament. This process of representation makes use of all the possible affective identifications which Margery can find between her life and that of Christ. Death figures importantly in Margery's life and helps to reinforce her presence in the accounts of Jesus' own death. Her affective engagement corresponds to the solicitations found in anchoritic texts which ponder the events of

the death of Christ. In the anchoritic tradition the audience often
attempts to empathize with the feelings of the closest witnesses to the
crucifixion. Margery's performance effectively echoes that of an
anchoritic audience, although in her case it is triggered by her active
participation in the liturgical celebrations of the lay community: 'On
þe Holy Thursday, as þe sayd creatur went processyon wyth oþer pepil,
sche saw in hir sowle owr Lady, Saynt Mary Mawdelyn, & þe xij
apostelys. And þan sche be-held wyth hir gostly eye how owr Lady
toke hir leue of hir blysful Sone, Crist Ihesu, how he kyssed hir & alle
hys apostelys & also hys trewe louer, Mary Mawdelyn' (174). Margery's participation in the Gospel events takes place while she is walking
in a procession with her fellow Christians. In other words, the neatly
regulated bodily performance which took place within the secrecy of
the *reclusorium* or the monastic cell is dramatically and loosely translated by Margery before a large public.[40] Her translation of those events
is enacted before a disapproving public unable to read her rendition of
discursive religious practices. The description of the parting of Jesus
from Mary, the disciples and Mary Magdalene continues in the following manner: 'Whan sche beheld þis sygth in hir sowle, sche fel down
in þe feld a-mong þe pepil. Sche cryid, sche roryd, sche wept as þow
sche xulde a brostyn þer-with. Sche myth not mesuryn hir-self ne
rewlyn hir-selfe, but cryid & roryd þat many man on hir wonderyd.
But sche toke non heed what ony man seyd ne dede, for hir mende was
ocupyid in owr Lord' (174). Selman shows in her essay how, in the
*Speculum devotorum*, a Syon nun is invited to identify with Mary. In
many respects, the kind of identification suggested by the *Speculum*
author bears a resemblance to what Margery offers in her book. However, the difference lies in the double performance which is offered by
Margery, one part consisting of her own translation of anchoritic practices and private meditations in public, the other consisting in a performance regulated by the liturgical events of the Christian calendar.
Margery proves unable to perform either of these translations wholly
satisfactorily, and it is the tensions and frictions which result from this
double act which become the hallmark of her peculiar mysticism.
During her confrontations with her audience, Margery has constantly
to provide a justification for her behaviour. Her performing body needs
an accompanying gloss in the form of an oral commentary.

Concern for death allows Margery to inscribe herself even more penetratingly into sacred history. Her empathy with the feelings of the
Virgin Mary lead her to behave in her visions in exactly the same

manner as she does when in the presence of her fellow parishioners. Her peculiar behaviour before the apostles makes them respond according to the same paradigms which regulate her real audience's reactions:

> Anoþer tyme þe seyd creatur beheld how owr Lady was, hir thowt, in deying & alle þe apostelys knelyng be-forn hir & askyng grace. Þan sche cryid & wept sor. Þe apostelys comawndyd hir to cesyn & be stille. The creatur answeryd to þe apostelys, 'Wolde ȝe I xulde see þe Modyr of God deyin & I xulde not wepyn? It may not be, for I am so ful of sorwe þat I may not wythstonde it. I must nedys cryin & wepyn.' And þan sche seyd in hir sowle to owr Lady, 'A, blyssyd Lady, prey for me to ȝowr Sone þat I may come to ȝow & no lengar be terijd fro ȝow, for, Lady, þis is al to gret a sorwe for to be boþe at ȝowr Sonys dethe & at ȝowr deth & not deyin wyth ȝow but leuyn stille a-lone & no comfort han wyth me.' (175)

Her bodily performance is marked as a divine message whose signs require the interpretation which is provided by Margery for the apostles. The support provided by Margery's own commentary reinforces the divine nature of her affective and physical output.[41] Her personal concern with death allows for her intimate involvement in some of the events contingent upon the death of Christ. At the same time, these events take her back to meditations about her own death, which she is able to predict: 'The sayd creatur on a day, heryng hir Messe & reuoluyng in hir mende þe tyme of hir deth, sor syghyng & sorwyng for it was so long delayd, seyd on þis maner, "Alasse, Lord, how long xal I thus wepyn & mornyn for thy lofe & for desyr of thy presens?"' (176).

This constant movement back and forth from Margery's own daily preoccupations into the events of sacred history echoes the iterations of the anonymous authors who invited anchoresses to measure their own life alongside that of Christ. Margery's project recovers many of the anchoritic themes and textual structures which exercised an appeal for a vast lay audience. Nonetheless, the conditions within which they are restored are drastically removed from their original settings.

The re-enactment of the Passion incidents by Margery is provocatively challenging. In Love's *Mirrour*, the audience remains passively observant as they engage affectively with the events which are described. Margery, instead, creates a very important role for herself as a character. The performance which follows is carefully planned and Margery Kempe, in a bold attempt to snatch away the leading female role from the Virgin, enacts the substitution of roles almost imperceptibly:

> Whan þe sayd creatur beheld þis gloriows syght in hir sowle & saw how he blissyd hys Modyr & hys Modyr hym, & þan hys blissyd Modyr myth not spekyn o word mor to hym but fel down to þe grownde, & so þei partyd a-sundyr, hys Modyr lying stille as sche had ben ded, þan þe sayd creatur thowt sche toke owr Lord Ihesu Crist be þe clothys & fel down at hys feet, preyng hym to blissyn hir, & therwyth sche cryid ful lowde & wept rith sor, seying in hir mende, 'A, Lord, wher schal I become?' ... Than answeryd owr Lord to hir, 'Be stille, dowtyr, & rest wyth my Modyr her & comfort þe in hir, for sche þat is myn owyn Modyr must suffyr þis sorwe.' (188–9)

The visual quality of Margery's affective re-enactments enables the construction of a powerful stage act. As a character, Margery's movement in and out of sacred history creates a sense of fluidity and evanescence which is unmatched in any other mystical account. This double performance blends the two different stages on which she has inscribed her acts, so that the reader loses track of spatio-temporal dimensions. How is the reader to interpret Margery's prostration before the feet of Jesus in the passage above? Is she performing only in her mind here, or is her body responding to her visualizations? It seems that the most powerful visualizations trigger vivid vocal and bodily performances:

> And þan hir thowt þe Iewys spokyn a-geyn boystowsly to owr Lady & put hir a-way fro hir Sone. Þan þe forseyd creatur thowt þat sche cryid owt of þe Iewys & seyd, 'Ʒe cursyd Iewys, why sle Ʒe my Lord Ihesu Crist? Sle me raþar & late hym gon.' And þan sche wept & cryid passyngly sor þat myche of þe pepil in þe chirche wondryd on hir body. (192)

Although her first responses carefully blur the barriers between those two dimensions by leaving the location of her vocal performance undetermined ('thowt þat sche cryid'), eventually we can precisely locate her performance, assisted by the responses of her unsympathetic public. Margery's re-enactment of the Passion generates the most vociferous and unusual performances. Although they are a far cry from the measured responses of the anchoresses for whom the Wooing Group was written, they nevertheless stand as an extension of this tradition, affectively inflated by a woman with a creative imagination and an uncontrollable body. Margery's difficulties reside in her inability to provide a coherent bodily translation of these discursive practices. Her public generally fails to read her body properly. The divine message which it attempts to convey is lost on the ordinary Christian who witnesses to her performance:

> þan þe sayd creatur, desiryng to a-bydyn stille be þe graue of owr Lord, mornyd, wept, & sorwyd wyth lowde crying for tendyrnes & compassyon þat sche had of owr Lordys deth & many a lamentabyl desyr þat God put in hir mende for þe tyme. Wherfor þe pepil wondryd vp-on hir, hauyng gret merueyl what hir eylyd, for þei knewe ful litil þe cawse. Hir thowt sche wolde neuyr a partyd þens but desiryd to a deyd þer & ben berijd wyth owr Lord. (194)

Margery's body is her initial book. However, its reading proves problematic to the general public who fail to perceive the divine message encoded within.[42] Despite Margery's initial beliefs, the conditions for reading her body prove largely unsuccessful, since she remains unable to provide a commentary with which to accompany this particular text. Her performance of the Passion would make sense if her audience were to receive information relating to her own involvement in those events. Appropriate reading conditions would imply the audience's presence alongside her upon both stages, following her backwards and forwards in a way which helps them to make sense of her external physical manifestations.

Two examples should suffice to demonstrate how Margery's prolific imagination pushes hermeneutic practices to their very limits. Devotional objects trigger her visions in the most powerful way. Margery invents a new grammar for the translation of devotional practices. We have seen how she attempts to steal the main feminine role from the Virgin Mary. At one point she declares 'Lady, I wil sorwe for ȝow, for ȝowr sorwe is my sorwe' (193). It therefore comes as no surprise to realize that this new syntax achieves articulation through appropriating many of the feelings which were attributed to the Virgin Mary in late medieval culture. Our Lady chapels, which were very much in vogue towards the end of the fourteenth century, are twice used as the sites for some of Margery's most idiosyncratic visions:[43]

> An-oþer tyme, þe seyd creatur beyng in a chapel of owr Lady sor wepyng in þe mynde of owr Lordys Passyon & swech oþer gracys and goodnes as owr Lord ministryd to hir mynde, & sodeynly, sche wist not how sone, sche was in a maner of slep. & a-non in þe sygth of hir sowle sche sey owr Lord standyng rygth up ouyr hir so ner þat hir thowt sche toke hys toos in hir hand & felt them, & to hir felyng it weryn as it had ben very flesch & bon. (208)

The sheer physicality of such a vision proves puzzling, until we accept that everything is happening inside the mind of Margery. However, it is more than plausible that this vision, activated inside a location specifically designed to celebrate events connected with the humanity of Jesus, feeds upon the wall paintings, sculptures and other artefacts which serve this purpose. Margery's translations rely upon some of the practices found within the anchoritic tradition; however, they are also often simultaneously triggered by the instruments which support late medieval lay devotions. It is not impossible that the vision of the Lord standing over her is an inner transposition of a sculpture at which Margery would have been gazing before she fell into her slumber.[44] The significance of Margery's devotions as material for her visions becomes apparent further on, in an episode in which, once again, an Our Lady chapel is named as the chosen location:

> An-oþer tyme, as þis creatur was in an hows of þe Frer Prechowrys wythinne a chapel of owr Lady, stondyng in hir preyerys, hir ey-ledys went a lityl to-gedyr wyth a maner of slep, & sodeynly sche sey, hir thowt, owr Lady in þe fayrest sygth þat euyr sche say, holdyng a fayr white kerche in hir hand & seying to hir, 'Dowtyr, wilt þu se my Sone?' & a-non forthwyth sche say owr Lady han hyr blissyd Sone in hir hand & swathyd hym ful lytely in þe white kerche þat sche myth wel be-holdyn how sche dede. (209)

Obviously, this vision does not feed upon some incident found inside the Gospels; rather, it proceeds from the observation of some kind of devotional object which Margery was able to infuse with new creative energy. Margery's mysticism was thus heavily reliant upon devotional practices which were current during her lifetime, and she made particular use of various devotional objects in order to create new layers of meaning for them. This contribution toward the creation of a new grammar rendered her peculiar performance meaningful to those who were able to recognize in it the utmost extension of long-established devotional and meditative practices.

## Conclusion

This essay has focused on a sequence of visions which take place in the last chapters of Book 1, shortly after her conversion, and before her long pilgrimage to Jerusalem. They are set within a liturgical context and consist for the most part in re-enactments of the events of the

Passion within a liturgical frame. The scribe's final words ending this sequence sound like a kind of retraction: 'And neuyr-þe-lesse þe fyr of loue encresyd in hir, & hir vnderstandyng was mor illumynyd & hir deuocyon mor feruent þan it was be-for whyl sche had hir meditacyon & hir contemplacyon only in hys manhod . . .' (209).

Margery's performing body is unable to convey the more ineffable aspects of her mysticism. Her book, which stands as a translation of her performative practices, does not deviate from its primary function, nor does it illuminate its readers about other aspects of Margery's spirituality. Our modern preoccupation with the various degrees of the mystical life, and our demand for rational categorization in a field which remains evasive, load the dice unfavourably against the account offered to us by Margery. If her performance remains puzzling to most of us, nevertheless it stands as an outstanding attempt at translation which combines several distinct traditions into a very idiosyncratic product. It was when interacting with her fellow citizens that Margery's body performed at its best, and the book would fail to do justice to this activity if its gaze remained purely directed toward the more ineffable aspects of her spirituality. For there, at this level, like Margaret Many Wounds, Margery's cosmic performance would come to a halt: 'She set off, no longer dancing, walking briskly toward the council fire, five steps beyond the edge of the universe.'[45]

## Notes

[1] S. Power, 'Moonwalk', in *The Grass Dancer* (London, 1995), 113–14.

[2] All references to *The Book of Margery Kempe*, with page number in parentheses following quotes, are to the following edition: S. B. Meech and H. E. Allen (eds.), *The Book of Margery Kempe*, EETS OS 212 (Oxford, 1940; repr. 1961).

[3] For a study which also addresses some issues presented in this chapter, see S. Beckwith, *Christ's Body: Identity, Culture and Society in Late Medieval Writings* (London and New York, 1993), esp. 78–111. Kay and Rubin offer a detailed survey of some of the most significant ideological currents, such as social history, psychoanalysis and post-structuralism, which have contributed to our understanding of bodies as cultural constructs; see S. Kay and M. Rubin (eds.), *Framing Medieval Bodies* (Manchester, 1994), 1–9.

[4] See R. Copeland, *Rhetoric, Hermeneutics, and Translation in the Middle Ages: Academic Traditions and Vernacular Texts*, Cambridge Studies in Medieval Literature 11 (Cambridge, 1991).

[5] For a general but groundbreaking study of female religious practices, with special reference to food, see C. W. Bynum, *Holy Feast and Holy Fast: The Religious Significance of Food to Medieval Women* (Berkeley, 1987).

[6] For a general account of medieval hermeneutic practices, see A. J. Minnis, *Medieval Theory of Authorship: Scholastic Literary Attitudes in the Later Middle Ages* (Aldershot, 1988).

[7] The idea for this essay emerged and developed from another paper given at a conference on performance organized by the Swiss Association of University Teachers of English (SAUTE); see my 'Mystical Texts or Mystical Bodies? Peculiar Modes of Performance in Late Medieval England', in P. Halter (ed.), *Performance*, Swiss Papers in English Language and Literature 11 (Tübingen, 1999), 89–104.

[8] For further evidence of this form of translation, see my 'Mystical Texts'.

[9] Michael Camille provides visual evidence for the use of the image of the human body to represent the cosmos. Moreover, his final example demonstrates how Opicinus, *scriptor* at the Avignon papal court in the first half of the fourteenth century, inscribes his body as the central part of a cosmic map which must be read allegorically. Although the thought processes of Opicinus do not find their equivalent in Margery, both frame their own bodies as part of a system of signs which abounds with spiritual meaning. See M. Camille, 'The Image and the Self: Unwriting Late Medieval Bodies', in Kay and Rubin (eds.), *Framing Medieval Bodies*, 62–99.

[10] I am also well aware of the importance of the influence of continental women upon Margery. See the pioneering work of H. E. Allen in her commentary to the edition of *The Book*. For further research on continental mysticism and its impact on the English tradition, see R. Voaden (ed.), *Prophets Abroad: The Reception of Continental Holy Women in Late-Medieval England* (Cambridge, 1996), esp. J. Dillon, 'Holy Women and their Confessors or Confessors and their Holy Women? Margery Kempe and Continental Tradition', 115–40. The study of religious performance in the *vitae* of thirteenth-century beguines by Simons provides additional evidence supporting the claim that Margery translates specialized (anchoritic) religious practices as an officially unregulated bodily performance; see W. Simons, 'Reading a Saint's Body: Rapture and Bodily Movement in the *Vitae* of Thirteenth-Century Beguines', in Kay and Rubin (eds.), *Framing Medieval Bodies*, 10–23.

[11] See for instance *The Prayers and Meditations of St. Anselm: With the Proslogion*, ed. B. Ward (Harmondsworth, 1988).

[12] For a study of anchoritic practices and culture, see E. Robertson, *Early English Devotional Prose and the Female Audience* (Knoxville, Tenn., 1990), esp. ch. 2: 'An Anchorhold of her Own: The Anchoress in Thirteenth-Century England', 13–31.

[13] Part 1 of *Ancrene Wisse*, sometimes called Devotions, is filled with information about bodily performance: see J. R. R. Tolkien (ed.), *The English Text of*

the *Ancrene Riwle: Ancrene Wisse: edited from MS Corpus Christi College Cambridge 402*, EETS OS 249 (London, 1962), 5–29; for a modern English version, see A. Savage and N. Watson (eds.), *Anchoritic Spirituality: Ancrene Wisse and Associated Works*, The Classics of Western Spirituality (New York, 1991), 53–66. For brief but useful information on the mass as ritual drama, see R. Beadle, '"Devoute ymaginacioun" and the Dramatic Sense in Love's *Mirror* and the N-Town Plays', in O. Shoichi, R. Beadle and M. S. Sargent (eds.), *Nicholas Love at Waseda: Proceedings of the International Conference 20–22 July 1995* (Cambridge, 1997), 1–17 (13–14).

[14] Here is a brief enumeration of the first 'stage directions' offered by the author: 'When you first get up, cross yourself and say . . .'; '. . . bowing forward on your knees on the bed . . .'; 'When you are fully dressed, sprinkle yourself with holy water . . .'; '. . . and prostrate yourself toward there with these salutations . . .'; 'After this, fall to your knees before the crucifix . . .'; 'And with these words beat your breast . . .'; see Savage and Watson, *Anchoritic Spirituality*, 53–4. For further information on Part 1, see Bella Millett's essay within this volume, with its appendix.

[15] See, for example, W. M. Thompson (ed.), *Þe Wohunge of ure Lauerd*, EETS OS 241 (Oxford, 1958), 36–7.

[16] See Revd Dr Henderson (ed.), *Missale ad usum insignis ecclesiae Eboracensis*, vol. 2, SS 60 (1874), 273–86.

[17] See the numerous references made to the increasing poverty of Jesus in *Þe Wohunge of ure Lauerd*, 28–9.

[18] For a close analysis of the spiritual practices found in the texts which make up the Wooing Group, see my piece, 'Enclosed Desires: A Study of the Wooing Group', in W. F. Pollard and R. Boenig (eds.), *Mysticism and Spirituality in Medieval England* (Cambridge, 1997), 39–62; for a study of *Þe Wohunge* using French feminist theory, see S. M. Chewning, 'Mysticism and the Anchoritic Community: "A Time . . . of Veiled Infinity"', in D. Watt (ed.), *Medieval Women in their Communities* (Cardiff, 1997), 116–37.

[19] For instance, the translation of the Crucifixion into a chivalric performance by the author of *Ancrene Wisse* may provide new meaning to the devotions performed by the anchoresses who need to respond to their lover-knight using a charade which takes into account the parameters regulating the (fictional) relationship of the lover-knight with the *domina*. See *Ancrene Wisse*, 199–200; Savage and Watson, *Anchoritic Spirituality*, 191–2.

[20] See, for instance, the last sixteen lines of 'Þis is on wel swuþe god ureisun of God almihti', in *Þe Wohunge of ure Lauerd*, 9; see also, Savage and Watson, *Anchoritic Spirituality*, 324.

[21] The enclosure image is perceptively explored by Wogan-Browne in the context of anchoritic culture, where she notes that the anchoress's physical and spiritual existence in *Ancrene Wisse* is mediated as a series of enclosures;

see J. Wogan-Browne, 'Chaste Bodies: Frames and Experiences', in Kay and Rubin (eds.), *Framing Medieval Bodies*, 24–42.

[22] For a modern edition of this text, see S. Westra (ed.), *A Talking of the Love of God* (The Hague, 1950).

[23] For a study of this text which looks at the hermeneutic practices of the compiler, see my piece, 'The Choices of the Compiler: Vernacular Hermeneutics in *A Talkyng of the Love of God*', in R. Ellis, R. Tixier and B. Weitemeier (eds.), *The Medieval Translator* 6 (Turnhout, 1998), 232–53.

[24] The two modern editions of Julian's text, based on different manuscripts, are: M. Glasscoe (ed.), *Julian of Norwich: A Revelation of Love* (Exeter, 1993), and E. College and J. Walsh (eds.), *A Book of Showings to the Anchoress Julian of Norwich* (Toronto, 1978). References to Julian's text are to the former-mentioned edition, hereafter cited as *A Revelation*.

[25] Mary is first invoked as the model for all women in view of the few utterances (four) which she is known to have expressed during her life. Elsewhere in the *Ancrene Wisse*, she is associated with the solitary woman enclosed between four walls and she thus becomes a historic model for female anchoritism; see *Ancrene Wisse*, 41–2, 84; Savage and Watson, *Anchoritic Spirituality*, 76–7, 108.

[26] It is worthwhile comparing the kind of engagement Julian wishes to have with the Passion with some of the thirteenth-century anchoritic texts and with the extravagant performance of Margery Kempe. In the passage below, Julian expresses the same desire to become a participant in sacred history: 'Methought I would have beene that time with Mary Magdalen and with other that were Crists lovers, and therefore I desired a bodily sight wherein I might have more knowledge of the bodily peynes of our saviour, and of the compassion of our lady and of all his trew lovers that seene that time his peynes, for I would be one of them and suffer with him' (*A Revelation*, 3).

[27] On patronage and anchoritic culture, see A. K. Warren, *Anchorites and their Patrons in Medieval England* (Berkeley, 1985).

[28] For a perceptive view on the Book of Hours and anchoritic devotions, see Bella Millett's chapter in this volume.

[29] See M. G. Sargent (ed.), *Nicholas Love's Mirror of the Blessed Life of Jesus Christ: A Critical Edition Based on Cambridge University Library Additional MSS 6578 and 6686*, Garland Medieval Texts 18 (New York, 1992). References to this volume are by page and line numbers.

[30] However, as Meale shows, Love's *Mirror* caters for the needs of all echelons within secular and religious society: see C. M. Meale, ' "oft siþes with grete deuotion I þought what I miȝt do pleysyng to god": The Early Ownership and Readership of Love's *Mirror*, with Special Reference to its Female Audience', in Shoichi, Beadle and Sargent (eds.), *Nicholas Love at Waseda*, 19–46; for the early dissemination of this text among noblewomen, gentlewomen and nuns, see esp. 34.

[31] See G. Constable, *Three Studies in Medieval Religious and Social Thought* (Cambridge, 1998), 143–217.

[32] Beadle argues that such dramatic life is unusual in medieval English prose; see Beadle, ' "Devoute ymaginacioun" ', 7.

[33] It is not unlikely that Love may have used Rolle as one of his models with regard to text performance; see my 'Mystical Texts or Mystical Bodies', 91–5.

[34] The reason for limiting participation via the 'deuoute ymaginacioun' in the creation of a narrative may stem from the wish not to shock the Wycliffite sensibilities which claimed the self-sufficiency of Scripture; see Beadle, ' "Devoute ymaginacioun" ', 8–9.

[35] See B. Windeatt (ed.), *The Book of Margery Kempe* (London, 1988), 17; 44 out of a total of 113 extant manuscripts of the *Meditationes* survive in English libraries, and most are of English provenance; see Sargent, *Nicholas Love's Mirror*, xix. Meale provides a good summary of the critical discussion on this matter, without, however, offering new evidence for Margery's knowledge of that text; see Meale, ' "oft siþes" ', 45 (n. 86).

[36] On Nicholas Love and Mount Grace, see Sargent, *Nicholas Love's Mirror*, xxi–xxix.

[37] For an argument which corroborates this one, with a focus on Margery's tears, see D. B. Mahoney, 'Margery Kempe's Tears and the Power over Language', in S. J. McEntire (ed.), *Margery Kempe: A Book of Essays* (New York and London, 1992), 37–50.

[38] The privileging of female experience in the *Mirror* could have encouraged Margery Kempe's easy identification and empathy with Jesus and the Virgin; see Meale, ' "oft siþes" ', 40.

[39] See S. Bhattacharji, *God is an Earthquake: The Spirituality of Margery Kempe* (London, 1997), 99–114.

[40] For a detailed account of Margery's complex interaction with the community, see J. Wilson, 'Communities and Dissent: The Secular and Ecclesiastical Communities of Margery's Book', in Watt (ed.), *Medieval Women in their Communities*, 155–85.

[41] For an early clerical example where the narrator's individual body is inscribed with spiritual meaning, see the account on Opicinus in Camille, 'The Image and the Self', 87–95.

[42] The pardoner's body in Chaucer's *Canterbury Tales* and its reading by his fellow pilgrims help illuminate the medieval cosmic and systemic understanding of the world. If the Pardoner's rhetoric fails ultimately, it is because his body speaks in a language contradicting the rhetorical utterances which he produces; see R. Copeland, 'The Pardoner's Body and the Disciplining of Rhetoric', in Kay and Rubin (eds.), *Framing Medieval Bodies*, 138–59.

[43] For a study of textual representations of the Virgin which were aimed to contribute to the decoration of Thoresby's Lady Chapel at York Minster, see V. Gillespie, 'Medieval Hypertext: Image and Text from York Minster', in

P. R. Robinson and R. Zim (eds.), *Of the Making of Books* (Aldershot, 1997), 206–29.

[44] The statement by Camille that 'the image, not the Word, mediated most powerfully between God and the believer in late medieval spirituality' finds confirmation in the extravagant visions of Margery Kempe which are mentioned in this paper; see Camille, 'The Image and the Self', 74.

[45] Power, *The Grass Dancer*, 114.

# 10
# Psychological Disorder and the Autobiographical Impulse in Julian of Norwich, Margery Kempe and Thomas Hoccleve

RICHARD LAWES

AERS, in a recent essay, questions the current tendency, in certain influential works by early modernists, to view the Middle Ages as 'a static homogeneous collective in which there simply could not be any self-conscious concern with individual identity or subjectivity because these simply could not exist in that society. Much less could there be any problematization of individual identity.' Aers counters this view vigorously, pointing out the ways in which the medieval period has been constructed by early modernists as 'a homogeneous and mythical field which is defined in terms of scholars' needs for a figure against which "Renaissance" concerns with inwardness and the fashioning of identities can be defined as new'.[1]

Autobiographical writing, perhaps the most direct sort of literary evidence of self-reflective subjectivity, is certainly thinner on the ground in the medieval period, yet it does exist. Autobiography is, of course, a modern word, and very few medieval texts would correspond to the general modern understanding of the genre as a coherent narrative rendering of one's whole life story. However, despite this, the term 'autobiographical' may still be meaningful in medieval studies if, as Abbott suggests, it is used to refer 'less to the text's precise genre than to certain of its qualities'.[2]

Any list of the most 'autobiographical' of English medieval texts would be likely to include *The Book of Margery Kempe*, the *Revelations* of Julian of Norwich and several of Thomas Hoccleve's poems.

What is immediately striking about these three authors is that the presence of psychological disorder has been suggested as an important ingredient in the work of each. Medcalf, in 'Inner and Outer', an essay on medieval psychology, refers to a study of mental illness among medieval subjects as 'an important byway into medieval minds'.[3] In what follows, examination of texts by Julian of Norwich, Thomas Hoccleve and Margery Kempe in the light of the psychiatry of the 1990s will ask what scrutinizing the 'byways' of medieval autobiography from such a perspective might contribute to the understanding of medieval subjectivity. At first sight, these texts may appear too disparate to be juxtaposed. Julian and Margery Kempe are 'mystics' whose concerns are spiritual and theological, and an expanding volume of scholarship has stressed the importance of their gender in any discussion of their subjectivity. Hoccleve is a male poet, who, despite sharing the same overall framework of medieval Catholic belief, has a much more secular agenda. Yet, viewed from the perspective of psychobiological illness, such a juxtaposition may suggest avenues for interpreting the autobiographical impulses which are common to all three.

The passages in Hoccleve which have most often been read as autobiographical are found in *La Male regle* (1406), the Prologue to the *Regement of Princes* (1412), the *Complaint* (1422) and the *Dialogue with a Friend* (1422). Diagnostic scrutiny of possible mental illness in Hoccleve involves accepting, at the outset, two premises which have caused great contention among scholars, namely that Hoccleve does write in a directly autobiographical manner about his own experiences, and that his discussions of psychophysical symptoms in these passages are not simply conventional. Those, notably Doob, who challenge the reading of these passages as autobiography point to what they believe to be clear conventionality in their descriptions of psychological disorder.[4] In response, Burrow, giving perhaps the most convincing defence of autobiographical readings of Hoccleve, makes two key points which are echoed by a number of other scholars. Firstly, there is some firm external corroborating evidence, reported by Brown, that Hoccleve was unable to come in person to the Exchequer between 1414 and 1417, which would be quite consistent with his poems' references to mental illness. Secondly, Burrow makes the crucial point that convention in medieval literature need not be incompatible with realism and reporting of actual events, whether external events or the internal events of thought and emotion. The two may coexist in the same work.[5]

Although the theoretical issues this particular debate raises could be discussed much further, the intention here is to accept Burrow's arguments, and his belief that these passages can validly be read as, on one level, directly autobiographical, as a point of departure. The question which can then be addressed is: what can a directly psycho-diagnostic approach to the material yield? In fact, there have been very few previous attempts to answer this question in terms of twentieth-century psychiatry. Doob, whilst strongly questioning the presence of autobiography at all in Hoccleve's work, makes the grudging suggestion that 'If Hoccleve did go mad, I am inclined to think that his insanity was a short but intense fit of depression.'[6]

The psychiatrist Ryle, asked by Medcalf for his opinion, offered a brief report concluding that Hoccleve suffered from a 'bi-polar manic-depressive illness', which in more recent diagnostic classification would be termed bipolar affective disorder. Unfortunately, Ryle does not go into very much detail about the grounds for this opinion, nor quote from any of the primary texts.[7] Harper dwells on Hoccleve's profound sensitivity to his friends' perceptions, and suggests that 'Thomas's public shaking and sweating are suggestive of what we might now call a panic disorder'.[8] Claridge, Pryor and Watkins make the most thorough attempt so far at a diagnosis which refers to specific details in Hoccleve's work. They disagree with Ryle's opinion, concluding that Hoccleve was never manic, but did show evidence of a severe unipolar depressive disorder.[9]

Hoccleve's *Complaint* is perhaps the best starting-point for diagnostic scrutiny. Although it is not chronologically the first of the relevant works, it gives the most detail about his main episode of mental illness, and also about his subsequent mental state and the reactions of his friends and acquaintances. The episode of overt illness ended five years before he wrote the *Complaint*: 'whiche at alle halwemesse / Was five yeere, neither more nor lesse'.[10]

This episode is described as a 'wilde infirmite' which 'oute of my silfe caste and threwe' (20/42). Although severe depressive disorders can involve agitation, the word 'wilde' is much more suggestive of a mania, in which the affect is generally inappropriately elevated and expansive, with such features as uncontrollable laughter, irrepressible optimism and gaiety, and sometimes extreme irritability and rage. Recklessness, in sexual behaviour or overspending, for example, is common in mania. Hoccleve's report that it 'oute of my silfe caste and threwe' evokes that profound and violent disruption of the sense of self which is a central feature of psychotic illnesses. That something was seriously wrong seems to have been obvious to Hoccleve's friends, who saw the problem as one of illness:

> How it with me stood was in every mannes mouthe,
> And that ful sore my frendis affright.
> They for myn helthe pilgrimages hight. (20/45–7)

The poem goes on to yield finer detail about symptoms. There is memory loss: 'the substaunce of my memorie / Wente to pleie, as for a certein space . . .' (20/50–1).

Memory loss is a general feature of severe affective disorders, and may be found in depression or in mania. It means that Hoccleve must rely on the reports of his friends about his mental state and behaviour. These say he appeared 'as a wilde steer, / And so my looke aboute I gan to throwe' (22/120–1). Their comments, 'Ful bukkish is his brayn, wel may I trowe' and 'no sadnesse is in his hed', suggest that he was failing to make sense. This would certainly be consistent with formal thought disorder, or with delusional thought content, features often found in psychoses. Although severe depression may also involve delusional beliefs, these are almost always of a depressive nature, for instance that one's innards are rotting. Disruption of the thought processes themselves, expressed as 'talking nonsense', which seems to be implied by 'no sadnesse is in his hed' is not a feature of depression, but is often found in mania.[11]

The next stanza gives some vivid impressions of restless movement, inability to keep still or concentrate:

> For here and there forthe stirte I as a roo:
> Noon abood, noon areest, but al brainseke.
> Another spake and of me seide also,
> My feet weren ay wavynge to and fro
> Whanne that I stonde shulde and with men talke,
> And that myn yen soughten every haulke. (23/127–32)

Burrow suggests that this refers to what his friends are looking for in his present behaviour, but I favour the opinion of those who take it to be his friends' account of his earlier illness. In any case, his friends would be likely to look out for the same symptoms they earlier observed. Though agitation and inability to concentrate on a conversation may be present in severe depression, severe anxiety or panic disorder, this passage evokes the sort of constant movement typical of mania.[12]

In keeping with Hoccleve's descriptions of his illness as 'the wilde infirmite' (20/40) and 'that wildenesse' (22/107) is his reference to his friends' opinion of him as 'A rietous persone ... and forsake' (21/67). This would fit much better with the reckless and wild behaviour found in mania than with the restricted social behaviour and melancholy withdrawal characteristic of depression. A number of other expressions in the poem suggest wildness rather than melancholy. For instance, Hoccleve's friends are reported to speak of his 'syknesse savage' (21/86). Hoccleve compares his mental state in his illness, when 'my witte were a pilgrim / And wente fer from home ...' (26/232–3), to that of a drunken man, and refers to 'the grevouos venim / That had enfectid and wildid my brain' (26/234–5).

The illness was of sudden onset, was widely known among his friends and immediately recognized as illness. This fits far better with the spectacular wildness of a manic episode than the quieter, more insidious onset of depression. It is of interest to note some of the diagnostic criteria currently used in British psychiatry to diagnose a manic episode:

> A Manic Episode is defined by a distinct period during which there is an abnormally and persistently elevated, expansive, or irritable mood. The mood disturbance must be accompanied by at least three additional symptoms from a list that includes inflated self-esteem or grandiosity, decreased need for sleep, pressure of speech, flight of ideas, distractibility, increased involvement in goal-directed activity, psychomotor agitation, and excessive involvement in pleasurable activities which have a high potential for painful consequences ... the mood ... is recognized as excessive by those who know the person well ... Mood may shift rapidly to anger or depression. Depressive symptoms may last moments, hours, or, more rarely, days. Not uncommonly, the depressive symptoms and manic symptoms occur simultaneously.[13]

I believe, then, that Claridge et al. are mistaken to dismiss mania as an explanation for this first episode.

However, as they rightly point out, there are many depressive features in the *Complaint*'s account. Hoccleve describes his reaction to his friends' discussing him:

> For why, as I had lost my tunges keie
> Kepte I me cloos, and trussid in my weie,
> Droupinge and hevy and al wo bistaad.
> Smal cause hadde I, me thoughte, to be glad. (23/144–7)

At this point, clearly, he was low in mood. Far from the increased talking or 'pressure of speech' characteristic of mania, he spoke less, and kept his thoughts to himself. Could the initial episode then have been simply depressive, as Claridge et al. suggest? Not necessarily. The DSM diagnostic criteria make it clear that a period of low mood and other depressive symptoms often follow on from, or even coexist with, a manic episode. More importantly, these lines seem to refer to a later period near the time of writing, when Hoccleve is distressed by his friends' constant fears about him relapsing. Clarification of the poem's internal chronology is important for diagnosis.

Most manic episodes are followed later, perhaps years later, by depression, and the prologue to the *Complaint* sets a thoroughly depressive tone at the outset:

> Aftir that hervest inned had hise sheves,
> And that the broun sesoun of mihelmesse
> Was come and gan the trees robbe of her leves
> That grene hed ben and in lusty freisshenesse,
> And hem into colour of yelownesse
> Had died and doun throwen undir foote,
> That chaunge sanke into myn herte roote. (19/1–7)

In serious depression, the sufferer's actual perception of the natural world may change, so as to resonate with his gloomy and distorted inner world.[14] The poem continues with a depressive train of cogitations about the unstableness of the world, leading to the conclusion that: 'Deeth undir foote shal him thriste adoun; / That is every wightes conclusioun . . .' (19/13–14).

Though the darkening, 'ende of Novembre' setting may be a useful literary convention, as Burrow suggests, to contrast with Chaucer's April opening to *The Canterbury Tales*, it is also the case that there is a firm scientific connection between the waning of daylight and the onset of depressive disorders.[15] Seasonal affective disorder, or SADS, which has been increasingly well publicized in recent years, is one manifestation of this, but it is also well established that seasonal change may precipitate episodes of bipolar affective disorder, for example, the regular appearance of depression between the end of October and the end of November.[16] Literary convention does not exclude a true report of the author's psychology. The interplay between realism and convention is much more complex than a simple 'either–or' dichotomy, and this is as true in medieval literature as in that of later periods. The onset of winter was, of course, imbued with rich symbolic meaning for medieval people. This is in no sense incompatible with the suggestion that Hoccleve, if predisposed to depression, may have suffered lowering of mood, for biological reasons, as the autumn light faded. The result would be an interplay of the symbolic and the psycho-physiological. Just as discussion of psycho-physical realism in Margery Kempe or Julian of Norwich cannot ignore the complex contexts of medieval Catholic spirituality, Hoccleve is, of course, an artist creating poetry within contexts of artistic convention. But cultural contexts and conventions are always involved in mediating accounts of psychiatric symptoms, and even of physical symptoms, in all ages and societies, whether the accounts are oral or written. Any attempt at understanding through diagnosis must engage with a realism which is always mediated through culture and edited, filtered and structured in many ways, some highly sophisticated, whilst often leaving underlying, biologically driven patterns recognizable.

Hoccleve's lines suggest a number of other symptoms of depression. He has insomnia associated with anxious ruminations:

> Sighynge sore as I in my bed lay
> For this and othir thoughtis wiche many a day
> Byforne I tooke, sleep cam noon in myn ye,
> So vexid me the thoughtful maladie. (19/18–21)

He also mentions anhedonia, loss of enjoyment of life: '. . . my spirite / To lyve no lust had ne no delite' (19/27–8). There are several references to low mood, for instance: 'The greef aboute myn herte so sore swal / And bolned evere to and to so sore' (19/29–30), and 'Vexacioun of spirit and turment / Lacke I right noon. I have of hem plente' (29/323–4).

Anxiety is usually a feature in depressive disorder, and Hoccleve clearly has strong autonomic anxiety symptoms, verging on panic, in the presence of others:

> And for the verry shamee and feer I qwook.
> Though myn herte hadde be dippid in the brook,
> It weet and moist was ynow of my swoot,
> Wiche was nowe frosty colde, nowe firy hoot. (23/151–4)

His vivid description of repeatedly checking his face in the mirror to make sure he looks sane enough also gives the impression of anxiety, expressed in rather obsessional self-consciousness. Thoughts of death are pervasive in the poem, and at one point he seems almost passively suicidal:

> Hie tyme is me to crepe into my grave.
> To lyve joilelees, what do I here? (27/261–2)
>
> Sithen othir thing than woo may I noon gripe,
> Unto my sepulcre am I nowe ripe. (27/265–6)

Though space precludes it here, interesting comparisons might be made between Hoccleve's interrogation of his negative, depressive cognitions, written as a dialogue with a personified 'Resoun', and the modern technique of Cognitive Therapy, perhaps the most effective current psychotherapeutic treatment for depression, which operates by challenging negative thoughts in just the same rational way.[17]

Moving from the *Complaint* to other autobiographical passages in Hoccleve, one finds more evidence of depressive symptoms. In *La Male regle* (1406), he declares: 'now my body empty is, and bare / Of joie, and ful of seekly hevynesse . . .' (47/15–16). He makes some firm connections between his misbehaviour and his low mood: 'Excesse of mete and drynke is glotonye; / Glotonye awakith malencolie . . .' (56/300–1). The Prologue to the *Regement of Princes* (1412) starts with a vivid description of anxious rumination and insomnia due to 'thought'.

> Besyly in my mynde I gan revolve
> The welthe unseure of every creature, (73/15–16)
>
> And of the brotylnesse of hyr nature
> My tremlyng hert so grete gastenesse hadde
> That my spirites were of my lyfe sadde. (73/18–20)

Three stanzas are given over entirely to describing the symptoms of anxiety and depression, in terms which fit very well with modern diagnostic manuals. The inability to concentrate on conversation so often found in depression is vividly pictured:

> Whan to the thoughtful whyght is tolde a tale,
> He heryth hit as though he thennis were.
> Hys hevy thoughtys hym so pluke and hale
> Hider and thider, and hym greve and dere,
> That hys eres avayle hym not a pere.
> He understandythe nothyng what men say,
> So ben hys wyttes forgone hem to play. (76/99–105)

His 'troubly dremes, drempte al in wakyng' (76/109) could also suggest anxious preoccupation, and the reference to 'frosty swote and fyry hote fervence' (76/108) may again suggest physical symptoms of anxiety. Hoccleve may have been particularly sensitive to his bodily as well as psychological symptoms, as evidenced by his analysis, later in the same poem, of the ailments to which writers are prone:

> Stomak ys oon, whom stoppyng, oute of drede,
> Annoyeth sore; and to oure bakkys nede
> Mot yt be grevous; an the thrydde, oure yen
> Uppon the wyte mochell sorowe dryen. (87/1019–22)

As with the *Complaint*, the *Regement* finds him in a passively suicidal frame of mind: '... aftyr dethe ful oftyn han I gapyd' (76/112). The *Dialogue with a Friend* (1422), a sequel to the *Complaint*, is less suggestive of psychiatric symptoms, though his discussion of ageing and inevitable death has a strongly depressive flavour:

> Of age am I fifty wintir and three.
> Ripenesse of deeth faste uppon me now hastith.
>
> More am I hevy nowe uppon a day
> Than I sometime was in daies five.
> ... The hony from the hive
> Of my spirit withdrawith wonder blyve.
> Whanne al is doon, this worldis swetnesse
> At ende turneth into bitternesse. (37/246–59)

Hoccleve's poems do, then, suggest a level of realistic description of psychological suffering and diagnosable disorder. They suggest several depressive episodes, with one episode of probable mania: 'The essential feature of Bipolar I Disorder is a clinical course that is characterized by the occurrence of one or more Manic Episodes . . . Often individuals have also had one or more Major Depressive Episodes.'[18] On this realistic level, a close examination of the texts thus supports Ryle's original diagnostic suggestion of what he terms 'Manic Depression'. This form of depression is now thought to originate mainly in biochemical disturbances in the brain, strongly linked to genetic factors, and so to be much more 'biological' than environmental in its causation.[19]

The degree to which a disorder's causation is 'biological' may appear too remote from literary studies to be of interest to a medievalist, but it is directly relevant when discussing possible evidence of psychopathology in a medieval text. This is because the objection which usually arises is that it may not be appropriate to apply the most modern medical science to the literature of a different culture and a different age. This question of applying modern medical psychiatry to subjects in a remote historical period is analogous to the question of applying modern medical psychiatry to present-day subjects in so-called Third World cultures. It is, in fact, essentially the same question.

Within psychiatry, increasing attention is being given to research into cultural differences in the manifestation of psychiatric disorder. Some disorders, or at least their patterns of expression, do seem to be linked to certain cultures. Most sufferers of anorexia nervosa, for instance, are from western countries, and some eastern cultures seem to produce their own patterns of expression of anxiety, depression or psychosomatic disturbances, such as Latah, Amok and Koro. But recent research suggests that those disorders whose manifestation is most stable across cultures are those whose aetiology can most firmly be linked to biological factors in brain function. Hoccleve's bipolar affective disorder would certainly come into this category. Mania in rural India expresses itself in much the same way as mania in New York.[20] It is because such disorders can be explained to such a large extent in terms of genetics and of neurotransmitter imbalance rather than cultural factors, and because human neurobiology is stable across such massive expanses of time, that it is valid to apply to medieval subjects diagnostic schemata derived from the increasingly large body of modern psychobiological knowledge.

It is also important to be aware of the nature of medieval medical paradigms. In a recent study of Julian's *Revelations* in relation to medieval gynaecological writing, Barratt makes the observation that 'the scientific and medical context of medieval texts is often neglected ... if we do continue to ignore them, we run the risk of inadvertently falling into ... essentialism.'[21] In fact, the modern psychobiological approach aligns quite well with the equally biological, organicist medieval Galenism, in which the soul, though immortal and immaterial, was held to express itself through the physical brain. Psychological disorder could be traced to imbalance of the four humours. The governing faculties were to be found physically located in the cerebral ventricles. Therefore a variety of physical treatments could be used, such as opium, hellebore, mandrake and other herbs, massages, bleeding and sometimes surgery. The idea of mental disorder as illness was widely accepted, and old theories about the dominance of demonological approaches and general cruelty towards the insane among medieval subjects have been overturned by more recent research on original records.[22]

In the light of these correspondences, it is interesting to re-examine Doob's contention that medieval descriptions such as Bartholomaeus Anglicus's list of diagnostic criteria for 'frenesye' in *De proprietatibus rerum* are derived from the Bible, rather than from direct observation:

> the symptoms of literary madmen, which are astonishingly consistent throughout history, seem to be based primarily on accounts of biblical madmen ... Perhaps this is one instance when literature influences perception: if literary tradition clearly defines certain standard symptoms of insanity, then a man will assume that anyone exhibiting those symptoms is mad ... .[23]

Medcalf also maintains that Bartholomaeus's description is conventional. Yet in a number of respects it matches very closely the DSM IV diagnostic criteria for mania quoted earlier, which are based on decades of scientifically rigorous research. The characteristic sleeplessness, agitation and emotional lability would be recognized by any modern psychiatrist: 'with woodnes and contynual wakinge, mevynge and castinge aboute the iyen, ragynge, stretchinge, and casinge of hondes ... Alwey he wole arise of his bedde; now he singeth, now he laugheth, now he wepith ... .'[24]

Knowing that Hoccleve suffered from a specific disorder, whose characteristics are well understood and repeated in most sufferers, allows deeper understanding of his experience. Hoccleve encapsulates one aspect of it in a telling phrase:

> Witnesse uppon the wilde infirmitie
> Wiche that I hadde, as many a man wel knewe,
> And wiche me oute of my silfe caste and threwe. (20/40–2)

Personified, the illness violently wrenches his inner self to the point where it is actually divided. A fundamental fracture opens up between Hoccleve and his 'silfe'. This massive disturbance of identity and sense of self is a feature characteristic of psychoses such as mania. With the subsequent process of reconstitution of the self in the recovery phase, it is likely to leave the person not only less self-confident but also more aware of the motions of his own inwardness. The language of a divided self is somewhat echoed later in the same poem:

> Not have I wist hou in my skyn to tourne,
> But nowe my silfe to my silfe have ensurid
> For no such wonderinge aftir this to mourne. (28/303–5)

A direct link between introspection and the impulse to write autobiography concerned with the inner world seems intuitively likely, and a perplexing disruption of the self due to a serious mental illness such as Hoccleve's may generate or accentuate such introspection by its very nature. But in Hoccleve there is little or no evidence of those other, religiously conditioned ways in which medieval subjects fostered inwardness. Aers, in the essay quoted above, points to various religious ways in which medieval people were encouraged to be introspective and self-analytical, particularly in the universal discipline of confession, which priests, monks, nuns and others consecrated to God practised to a special degree. In one study of the early development of autobiographical forms, Zimmermann raises the possibility of connections between the Catholic sacrament of confession and the development of the autobiographical impulse.[25]

Another aspect of the Catholic fostering of inwardness is the ancient idea that self-knowledge and the knowledge of God are inseparable. Abbott highlights the importance of this idea in Julian of Norwich, who states that 'we may never come to full knowyng of God til we know first clerely our owne soule'.[26] It is among the intensely spiritual, the 'mystics' of medieval society, that one could expect a deeper cultivation of inwardness, a focus which might seek autobiographical expression. Self-knowledge involves knowledge of the body and sensitivity to its changes, and modern scholarship on the spirituality of the medieval female mystics puts great stress on sensitivity to the bodily in their writings.[27] Physical, biological dimensions of self-awareness and spirituality are of great importance both in *The Book of Margery Kempe* and in Julian's *Revelations*, and it is at the level of physical, or psychophysical, illness that the texts of both these women generate the greatest sense of precise, realistic autobiographical detail. It is this detail which invites psychobiological discussion.

The history of scholarship on Margery Kempe's *Book* shows repeated attempts to apply psychiatric or medical theory to the text, though mostly to generate psychodynamic formulations, and the opinion that she was 'hysterical' is common. However, the fact that the concept of hysteria is considered both outdated and confusing in much current psychiatric practice must be addressed, and elsewhere I have maintained that careful attention to *The Book* supports neither the nearest modern diagnostic equivalent to hysteria, namely histrionic personality disorder, nor the recent suggestion that Margery was intermittently psychotic, or in lay terms 'mad', for much of her life.[28] Yet psychological disturbance is still strongly suggested by some aspects of *The Book*'s account.

Most obviously, it is suggested by the episode at the start of *The Book*, in which 'þis creature went owt of hir mende' at the age of twenty after the birth of her first child. This has a number of features strongly suggesting a depressive psychosis of the puerperium.[29] In the pregnancy, she was 'labowrd wyth grett accessys', probably physical sickness, known to be a risk factor for post-natal depression. Soon after the birth she 'dyspered of hyr lyfe', and showed a preoccupation with her sinfulness, often a feature of depressive illnesses regardless of religious belief. *The Book* may well be right in suggesting that not being able to confess some past sin was the psychological stressor which precipitated her going 'owt of hir mende'.

Her report of 'deuelys opyn her mowthys al inflammyd wyth brennyng lowys of fyr as thei shuld a swalwyd hyr in' suggests something seen in external space, a visual hallucination congruent with her depressed mood and thought content. She also hears the devils, who 'cryed up-pon hir wyth greet thretyngs', again in external space, not inwardly, suggesting an auditory hallucination. She also injures herself, and 'wold a fordon hir-self many a tym'. All this is consistent with a severe depressive psychosis of the puerperium, the most common postnatal psychosis, and we are told that Kempe's resolved within eight months, roughly the time course which modern medicine would expect.

That this first episode involves psychotic mental illness is as widely accepted by modern commentators as it was by Kempe and her contemporaries. But what of psychological disorder in the rest of *The Book*? Can such features as Margery's exaggerated emotionality and tendency to 'wepyn and sobbyn ful hedowslych', or those experiences of seeing, smelling and hearing things, which so often suggest visual, auditory or olfactory hallucinations, be explained in terms of any modern diagnostic schemata? If these things are to be explained, on one level, in terms of psychiatric disorder, then I would suggest that temporal lobe epilepsy is a much more likely diagnosis than any form of recurrent psychotic 'madness'.

Temporal lobe, or psychomotor, epilepsy is a form of epilepsy affecting emotions and sensory perceptions, but not causing epileptic fits in the usual sense of loss of consciousness or shaking. Hallucinatory sensations of smell are a characteristic feature.[30] One passage may connect such a sensation with another feature of the condition, 'déjà-vu', a strong sense of having already experienced a situation, which in turn may cause a feeling of being able to predict the future:

> Than, as sche went on a tyme in þe White Frerys cherch at Lynne up and down, sche felt a wondyr swet sauour & a heuenly þat hir thowt sche myth a leued þerby wythowtyn mete or drynke ȝyf it wolde a contynwyd. & in þat tyme owr lord seyd unto hir, 'dowtyr, be þis swet smel þu mayst wel know þat ther schal in schort tyme be a newe prior in Lynne . . .' (171)

When Margery hears unusual sounds, the text is careful in its description. Often, Christ converses with her inwardly, in her 'gostly undirstonding'. When St John the Evangelist appears to hear her confession, 'he seyd "Dominus" verily in hir sowle þat sche saw him & herd hym in hire gostly undirstondyng as sche xuld a do an-oþer prest be hir bodily wittys' (81). *The Book* makes a clear distinction between such episodes and others in which the sound is heard externally, with the 'bodily' ears: 'Sum-tyme sche herd wyth hir bodily erys sweche sowndys & melodies þat sche myth not wel heryn what a man seyd to hir in þat tyme les he spoke þe lowder' (87–8). This is much more consistent with an auditory hallucination. Rushing sounds, likened to a bellows in her right ear are mentioned. What may well be simple visual hallucinations also occur, as in the following passage:

> Sche sey wyth hir bodily eyne many white thyngys flying al a-bowte hir on

every syde as thykke in a maner as motys in the sunne ... Sche sey hem many dyvers tymes & in many dyvers placys, boþe in chirche & in hir chawmbre, at hir mete & in hir praerys, in felde & in towne, bothyn goyng & syttyng. And many tymes sche was a-ferde what þei myth be, for sche sey hem as wel on nytys in dyrkenes as on day-lygth. (88)

This last point, of the constant visibility of these things even at night, suggests an endogenous psychological or neurological aetiology. The incident in chapter 20 in which the sacrament at mass 'shok & flekyrd to & fro as a dowe flekeryth wyth hir wengys' may represent a similarly hallucinatory experience.

There are further correspondences between *The Book*'s account and temporal lobe epilepsy. For instance, temporal lobe epilepsy is associated with a higher than average interest in religion and reporting of mystical experiences, as well as emotional lability.[31] That a first episode of post-natal depressive psychosis should be followed by further episodes of temporal lobe epilepsy is in keeping with the fact that psychotic episodes are more common in temporal lobe epilepsy sufferers, and may be precipitated by it.[32]

The issue of temporal lobe epilepsy has also been raised, in very plausible ways, in relation to Teresa of Avila, Ignatius of Loyola and Paul of Tarsus. The assertion of the authors of these studies is that the possible presence of temporal lobe epilepsy, or of any neuro-psychiatric disorder, does not 'explain' all dimensions of religious experience, nor exclude coexisting mystical experiences unrelated to any pathology. It simply allows us to discuss the text in the light of what is known about these conditions, their time course and symptoms, and the subjective experiences they are likely to generate. It helps us to explore in more depth the idea that, as Pepler asserts of Julian of Norwich, illness 'played some part in the experience'.[33]

The construction of autobiographical accounts involves arrangement of memories of a previous self, structured and filtered after reflection. It is relevant to consider what effects mental illness might be expected to have on this process. Like Hoccleve, Kempe seems to have suffered only one episode of psychosis. For both, this one-off experience would have involved the loss of connection with reality and profound disturbance of identity and sense of self which are central features of psychotic illnesses. As with Hoccleve's later depressions, Kempe subsequently had episodes of a psychological disorder which was not psychotic. Whilst these later episodes may have reactivated anxieties about psychological disturbance and again threatened the sense of self, they would not have overturned processes of reflection or attempts to understand the experience to the extent that recurrent psychoses would. For both Hoccleve and Kempe, the result would be, to use Aers's phrase, 'puzzled selves' rather than selves too damaged by chronic mental illness to reflect on their inner world.

At one level, psychological illness causes disjunction between the individual and the community, seen in the reactions of Hoccleve's friends, ever distrustful of his sanity. Harper rightly notes and explores Hoccleve's acute awareness of a difference between his inner world and the deliberately cultivated 'sane' face he shows to the outer social world.[34] But severe mental illness and strange or perplexing experiences also fracture the subject's inner world. Hoccleve's anxious visits to the mirror may be as much to allay his own fears about the return of mental illness as to compose a face of sanity for others' benefit. For him, a dual process, involving explanation and justification to others and also to oneself, of reintegration with the outer culture and reintegration of the inner self, seems to be involved.

Justification of opinions and actions, and processes of self-understanding and discernment of experiences are also central in *The Book of Margery Kempe*. In her case, both aspects may be illuminated with some reference to the discourse of *discretio spirituum*. Throughout, *The Book* remains very aware of the need to justify Kempe's insights, experience and behaviour to Church authorities ready to scrutinize her. In this respect, *The Book*'s engagement with the tradition of *discretio* has been explored by several authors, particularly Voaden, who concludes that Margery Kempe often fails to meet the Church's expectations of holy women, for instance by refusing always to accept the advice of her confessors and other Church authorities.[35]

But there is also an internal dimension to *discretio*, in which the individual examines and assesses the quality and meaning of her own experiences. This 'autodiagnostic' *discretio* in Kempe has received less attention. The disruption of identity involved in a psychotic illness such as Kempe's post-natal episode, the lasting loss of self-confidence in its wake, the dread of the illness's return, and ongoing puzzling experiences generated by, quite possibly, temporal lobe epilepsy, might be expected to produce self-questioning. Is this reflected in the text? There are certainly many points at which Kempe appears very self-confident about the meaning of her experiences, and more than ready to defend them before powerful Church authorities. But there are also signs in

*The Book* of a process of self-scrutiny: 'Sum-tyme sche was in gret heuynes for hir felyngys, whan sche knew not how þei schulde ben vndirstondyn many days to-gedyr, for drede þat sche had of decetys & illusyons' (219). *The Book* stresses her awareness of the pitfalls of trusting inward experiences: 'for reuelacyons be hard sum-tyme to undirstondyn. & sumtyme þo þat men wenyn wer reulacyonis it arn decetys & illusions, & þerfor it is not expedient to ȝeuen redily credens to euery steryng but sadly abyden & preuyn yf þei be sent of God . . .' (219–20). In her 'Prayers of the creature', which she is said to have recited daily, she repudiates the Devil, and also 'al þat euer I haue don, seyd, er thowt, aftyr þe cownsel of þe Deuyl, wenyng it had be þe cownsel of God & inspiracyon of þe Holy Gost' (248).

Julian of Norwich, who also had striking religious experiences in the context of serious illness, might be expected to understand the need for careful discernment, as well as the need for confidence in those insights discerned to be genuine. Discussing Julian's advice to Margery, Bhattacharji makes the important observation that it 'is perhaps a response to what strikes many readers as the most obvious self-advertising aspect of Margery's behaviour: her constant retelling of her experiences, and of her whole life, to any person of spiritual authority who crosses her path . . .'[36]

Uncertainty about the nature of perplexing experiences, perhaps uncertainty of one's identity, may generate a strong autobiographical impulse, and a need to recount one's story, to persuade others of its value, explore it, make sense of it and psychologically 'digest' it. Such processes are, of course, involved in many modern forms of psychotherapy, and may be reflected in the dialogue form which recurs in Hoccleve's poetry. The cathartic aspect of telling the story of troubling experiences is strongly expressed at the end of the Prologue to his *Complaint*:

> The greef aboute myn herte so sore swal
> And bolned evere to and to so sore
> That nedis oute I muste ther withal.
> I thoughte I nolde kepe it cloos no more,
> Ne lete it in me for to eelde and hore.
> And, for to preve I cam of a womman,
> I braste oute on the morwe and thus bigan. (19–20/29–35)

Burrow feels that Hoccleve probably wrote his autobiographical passages in a quest for payment owed by his employer.[37] This is possible, but it is as plausible that the autobiographical element in Hoccleve is driven by factors directly related to his mental illness itself. Like Margery Kempe, Hoccleve seeks to situate his intense and puzzling experiences within the Catholic Christian traditions which define not only medieval society and culture, the 'outer' world to which behaviour and experience must be justified, but also his inner world, identity and sense of self. He tries to interpret his experiences to others and to himself in the light of his religious beliefs, and the widespread understanding that illness is linked with sin. This, as Doob rightly asserts, he accepts without question.[38] Illness happens as 'goddis strook', may well be the fruit of sin and has a purgative effect: 'Such suffraunce is of mannes gilte clensinge' (29/349). But unlike Margery Kempe and Julian, he draws no deep mystical insights from his experiences, nor does he feel called by them to a deeper spiritual life.

For Julian of Norwich, as for Margery Kempe, the experience of illness is a stimulus which feeds the religious imagination and the life of faith. The richness and complexity of Julian of Norwich's *Revelations* invite many levels of explanation and interpretation, and recent studies from feminist and psychoanalytical as well as theological perspectives have responded to this richness. But what of that level of understanding, arguably more mundane yet equally valid, which involves analysing bodily, psychobiological processes? The importance of Julian's illness itself as a concrete event remembered in an autobiographical way has been highlighted by a recent study by Abbott, who interprets the whole structure of Julian's text in the light of key moments of autobiographical realism.[39] Though there have been fewer psycho-diagnostic studies of Julian of Norwich's *Revelations* than of Margery Kempe's *Book*, suggestions have been made, though, as with Margery Kempe, more from psychodynamic than from psychobiological perspectives.

Pepler feels that Julian was 'apparently delirious' and diagnoses 'an acute neurosis, induced perhaps by an over-enthusiastic life of penance and solitude'.[40] Knowles, writing at a time when the concept of hysteria was still in vogue, is very dismissive of the diagnostic enterprise altogether: 'She describes some of her symptoms very vividly, but it is useless to enquire what the illness was, or indeed whether it was organic or infective or, in part at least, hysteric.'[41] Despite his curious despair about diagnosis, Knowles is quite correct about the vivid relation of symptoms, which are concentrated at the beginning and the end of the *Revelations*. Julian's illness descriptions have, at times, a quality of great clinical precision. The accounts in the long and short texts are very similar, the short text offering a little more detail at some points, and the long text at others.

At the age of thirty, in May 1373, Julian experienced a short 'bodelye syeknes' lasting a week or so, and it is clear from the descriptions that many of her symptoms were unambiguously 'bodily'. On the fourth day of the sickness, those around her send for the priest, implying expectation of death. After another three days of sickness, Julian and her attendants all again expect her imminent death. The short text continues:

> Thus I enurede tille daye, and by than was my bodye dede fra the myddys downwarde, as to my felynge. Than was I styrrede to be sette vppe ryghttes, lenande with clothes to my heede, for to have the mare fredome of my herte to be atte goddes wille, and thynkynge on hym whilys my lyfe walde laste; and thay that were with me sente for the personn, my curette, to be at myne endynge. He come, and a childe with hym, and brought a crosse; and be thanne I hadde sette myn eyenn and myght nou3t speke.[42]

The cloths applied to Julian's head are a very strong indication of high fever, and her urge to sit upright suggests breathlessness. She continues to gaze upon the crucifix:

> Aftyr this my syght by ganne to fayle, and it was alle dyrke abowte me in the chaumbyr, and myrke as it hadde bene nyght, save in the ymage of the crosse there helde a common lyght, and I wyste nevere howe. Alle that was besyde the crosse was huglye to me, as 3yf it hadde bene mykylle occupyede with fendys.
> 
> Aftyr this the overe partye of my bodye beganne to dye, as to my felynge. Myne handdys felle downe on aythere syde, and also for vnpowere my heede astylde downe oon syde. The maste payne that I felyd was shortnes of wynde and faylynge of lyfe. Than wende I sothelye to hafe bene atte the poynte of dede.[43]

Again, breathlessness, 'shortnes of wynde', is prominent. By far the most thorough and systematic psychobiological study of Julian's illness to date is that done in 1984 by McIlwain, who considers several possible medical diagnoses, most of them very rare, including diphtheria, Guillain-Barre syndrome, tick paralysis and botulism, eventually coming down in favour of the last.[44] The main features of the illness which he seeks to explain are high fever, breathlessness and a sense of muscle weakness. Julian's description could be interpreted to mean that this weakness ascended from her feet to her arms and possibly the muscles supporting her head. Analysis of each of McIlwain's diagnostic suggestions in detail would take considerably more space than is available here, but some basic observations need to be made.

Firstly, he makes the very important point that Julian's illness is indeed 'bodily', and that no other mental illness need be invoked to explain psychological features of her account in terms of altered brain function. There is no evidence in either version of the text that Julian had any hallucinatory experience after this episode of sickness, so functional psychoses such as schizophrenia or affective psychoses, which generally recur at intervals throughout a sufferer's life, are very unlikely. Nor is there any external evidence, for instance in Margery Kempe's account of their meeting, that Julian was reputed to be mentally unstable, and there is certainly no evidence in the text of thought disorder in Julian as authorial, 'remembering' self. Whatever psychological disorder may have been present in her sickness, it was clearly directly related to a temporary, 'one-off', organic, 'bodily' disturbance of brain function.[45]

Secondly, though McIlwain's suggestion of botulism neatly accounts for paralysis as well as fever, because it is a form of food poisoning, it is, by his own admission, usually responsible for multiple cases, yet Julian mentions no other victim. It is also extremely rare by modern standards, though this does not rule it out. Julian's account may indicate a genuinely neurological paralysis, but it is also quite possible that her extreme muscle weakness is no more than a general effect of a very serious, debilitating febrile illness, in which case more common causes of fever and breathlessness, such as pneumonia, must be considered more likely.

As the account progresses, in her fever Julian appears to enter a 'twilight' state of consciousness, and in this state she begins to experience her revelations, at the same time losing her awareness of pain. As in *The Book of Margery Kempe*, careful phenomenological distinction is made between different modes of perception: 'All this was shewid by thre: that is to sey, be bodily sight and by word formyd in my understanding and be gostly sight.'[46] Whereas she says of her vision of the Mother of God: 'I saw hir ghostly in bodily likeness', she insists that when she looks at the crucifix and sees Christ bleeding and suffering, it is a 'bodyly sight', and so more suggestive of a hallucination.[47]

## PSYCHOLOGICAL DISORDER AND AUTOBIOGRAPHY 237

The first fifteen visions are interspersed with some physical discomfort, until eventually, in chapter 66 of the long text, Julian becomes fully aware of pain again. She is able to speak to a 'religious person', telling him she 'had ravid today'. There then follows a vivid experience of the devil in visual, tactile and olfactory modalities, which the long text describes as follows:

> and than I gan to slepyn. And in the slepe, at the begynnyng, methowte the fend set him in my throte, puttand forth a visage ful nere my face like a yong man; and it was longe and wonder lene; I saw never none such. The color was rede like the tilestone whan it is new brent, with blak spots therin like blak steknes, fouler than the tilestone. His here was rode as rust, evisid aforn, wyth syde lokks hongyng on the thounys. He grinnid on me with a shrewd semelant, shewing white teeth; and so mekil methowte it the more oggley. Body ne hands had he none shaply, but with his pawes he held me in the throte and would have stranglid me ... This oggley shewing was made slepyng ... The persons that wer with me beheld me and wet my temples, and my herte began to comforten. And anon a lyte smoke came in the dore with a grete hete and a foule stinke. I said: 'Benedicte domine! Is it al on fire that is here!'[48]

If Julian's recollection of sleep is correct, then this is not a hallucination but a dream, the kind of vivid nightmare common in states of high temperature, or possibly that form of half-waking hallucination known as 'hypnagogic' or 'hypnopompic'.[49] The wetting of her temples confirms ongoing fever, and her report of heat and fire is consonant with this. The sensation of choking may be related to whatever was causing the breathlessness, probably a respiratory infection, possibly involving her throat, and the 'foule stinke' is very likely to have a correlate in her own infected mucus or the general smell of the sickroom. There are also suggestive comparisons to be made between the dryness due to dehydration which fever brings, indicated in Julian's report of being 'as baren and as drye as I never had comfort but litil',[50] and the dryness and desiccation so striking in her descriptions of Christ's passion:

> This was a swemful chonge to sene this depe deyeng, and also the nose clange and dryed, to my sigte, and the swete body was brown and blak, al turnyd oute of faire lifely colowr of hymselfe onto drye deyeng ... it was a dry, harre wynde and wond colde ... Blodeleshede and peyne dryden within and blowyng of wynde and cold comyng fro withouten ... And these ... dryden the fleshe of Criste ...[51]

These correlations between the biological level of Julian's 'bodily illness' and the conventions of affective piety informing such physical descriptions of the passion, far from creating reductionist explanations, allow resonances which enrich meaning. An approach on multiple levels is similarly called for by Margery Kempe's account of rushing sounds in her right ear:

> a maner of sownde as it had ben a payr of belwys blowyng in hir ere. Sche, beyng a-bashed þerof, was warnyd in hir sowle no fer to have, for it was the sownd of the Holy Gost. & þan owyr Lord turnyd þat sownde in-to þe voys of a dowe, & sithyn he turnyd it into þe voys of a litel bryd whech is callyd a red brest þat sang ful merily oftyn-tymes in hir ryght ere. (90)

Interpretation of this passage could not exclude awareness that such sounds are highly suggestive of auditory hallucinations explicable in terms of organic brain disease. But the medieval convention of the Holy Spirit as a dove speaking into the ears of saints, and the tradition of Rollean mystical sounds and melodies are no less relevant, just as Julian's devil must be related to the artistic conventions of medieval diabology.[52] To exclude the theological, the artistic or the biological levels of interpretation is to exclude intriguing dimensions of ambiguity in the text and to truncate the fullness of its meaning. This is not only because, as McIlwain rightly states, the content of dreams or hallucinations of organic origin usually reflects the subject's waking preoccupations.[53] These texts are not, any more than any other autobiography, or even than any verbally delivered modern psychiatric case history, unmediated realistic description. They are complex and many-layered products of remembering and interpretation.

Generating broad theories about the medieval autobiographical impulse based on such a small number of texts could rightly be seen as a questionable enterprise. Nevertheless, juxtaposing them stimulates suggestions about some aspects of the medieval expression of subjectivity. The most striking features of these accounts of mental illness, and, in Julian and Kempe also of the 'mystical', are the intensity of the experiences, the sheer 'unusualness' of them, and the way in which they cause perplexity and self-questioning in the subject.

Disjunctions occur between an individual's inner experience and the cultural expectations of the outer world. In Kempe's case, this involves expectations of appropriate behaviour in a woman aspiring to holiness; in Hoccleve's, it involves his friends' expectations of sane behaviour.

Despite Julian's avowed orthodoxy, it may be argued, and has been argued, that some disjunction exists between the insights which flow from her revelations and certain emphases in Church teaching, leading her 'to balance orthodoxy with heterodoxy as she discovers within her own experiences a mode of spiritual exercise'.[54]

Further disjunctions within the inner world of the individual emerge in these texts, and can be related to the disruption caused by psychobiological disorder: in Hoccleve's case mania, in Kempe's post-natal psychosis and temporal lobe disease, and in Julian's the psychological effects of physical illness. Deep psychological trauma of any kind may create crises of identity and intense self-scrutiny. The loss of a child, for instance, is held by many psychiatrists to be among the most devastating of all life events, and this might help us interpret that current of 'autobiographical' realism which many find underlying the many-layered richness of *Pearl*.[55] But it could be argued that psychological disturbances of more biological origin are even more perplexing to the subject, more challenging to self-identity because more 'endogenous', and harder to explain in terms of external events in the subject's life.

Interpreting medieval 'autobiography' involves engagement with texts on many levels, and such is the complex interplay of convention and realism in these writings that attempts to pin down all their meaning to the 'bodiliness' of medical diagnoses must be at best simplistic and at worst grotesque. Nevertheless, because the effects of biological brain diseases are so stable across time and culture, when they present themselves in texts such as these, they can offer the modern reader an important window into the 'otherness' of medieval subjectivity. More than this, the hypothesis which emerges is that the medieval impulse to record life events and subjective experience on a realistic level is, in these texts, related to the intensity and strangeness of the experience itself and the strength of its challenge to the coherence of the individual's inner world. These texts not only give ample evidence that splits between outer realities and inner forms of being, problematizations of individual identity, and 'puzzled selves', were entirely possible in pre-modern England. They also suggest that psychological disorder, at least that of 'bodily' origin, may have been a stimulus to autobiographicality itself.

## Notes

[1] D. Aers, 'A Whisper in the Ear of Early Modernists; or, Reflections on Literary Critics Writing the "History of the Subject"', in D. Aers (ed.), *Culture and History 1350–1600: Essays on English Communities, Identities and Writing* (London, 1992), 177–202 (187, 192).

[2] C. Abbott, *Julian of Norwich: Autobiography and Theology* (Woodbridge, 1999), 5.

[3] S. Medcalf, 'Inner and Outer', in S. Medcalf (ed.), *The Context of English Literature: The Later Middle Ages* (London, 1981), 108–71 (171).

[4] See P. B. R. Doob, *Nebuchadnezzar's Children: Conventions of Madness in Middle English Literature* (London, 1974), ch. 5, 208–31.

[5] J. A. Burrow, 'Autobiographical Poetry in the Middle Ages: The Case of Thomas Hoccleve', *Proceedings of the British Academy*, 68 (1982), 389–412.

[6] See Doob, *Nebuchadnezzar's Children*, 226.

[7] See Medcalf, 'Inner and Outer', 129–30.

[8] S. Harper, ' "By cowntynaunce it is not wist": Thomas Hoccleve's *Complaint* and the Spectacularity of Madness in the Middle Ages', *History of Psychiatry*, 7 (1997), 387–94 (esp. 390).

[9] G. Claridge, R. Pryor and G. Watkins, *Sounds from the Bell Jar: Ten Psychotic Authors* (London, 1990), ch. 3, 49–70.

[10] B. O'Donoghue, *Thomas Hoccleve: Selected Poems* (Manchester, 1982), 20/55–6. All references to Hoccleve's poetry are to this volume, with page and line numbers given in parentheses following quotes.

[11] See R. E. Kendell and A. K. Zealley, *Companion to Psychiatric Studies*, 5th edn (Edinburgh, 1993), 427–9.

[12] See Kendell and Zeally, *Companion to Psychiatric Studies*, 427–8.

[13] American Psychiatric Association, *Diagnostic and Statistical Manual of Mental Disorders*, 4th edn (Washington, 1994), 328–30.

[14] This is described in A. Sims, *Symptoms in the Mind* ( London, 1988), 64.

[15] See J. A. Burrow, 'Hoccleve's Series: Experience and Books', in R. F. Yeager (ed.), *Fifteenth Century Studies: Recent Essays* (Hamden, Conn., 1984), 259–73 (261).

[16] See American Psychiatric Association, *Diagnostic and Statistical Manual*, 389.

[17] For general discussion of these techniques in Cognitive Therapy, see K. Hawton, P. M. Salkovskis, J. Kirk and D. M. Clark, *Cognitive Behaviour Therapy for Psychiatric Problems: A Practical Guide* (Oxford, 1989).

[18] American Psychiatric Association, *Diagnostic and Statistical Manual*, 350–1.

[19] For discussion of the genetic studies, see M. Weller and M. Eysenck (eds.), *The Scientific Basis of Psychiatry*, 2nd edn (London, 1992), 273–7.

20 For a very general overview of these issues, see M. Roth and J. Kroll, *The Reality of Mental Illness* (Cambridge, 1986), 40–4; see also Weller and Eysenck (eds.), *The Scientific Basis*, ch. 27, 469–90. The latest (4th) edition of the *Diagnostic and Statistical Manual* of the American Psychiatric Association now has a whole section on culture-specific disorders, 843–9.

21 See A. Barratt, ' "In the Lowest Part of our Need": Julian and Medieval Gynaecological Writing', in S. McEntire (ed.), *Julian of Norwich: A Book of Essays* (London, 1998), 239–56 (255).

22 See, for instance, the helpful and thorough discussion of these issues in A. G. De Pablo, 'The Medicine of the Soul: The Origin and Development of Thought on the Soul, Diseases of the Soul and their Treatment, in Medieval and Renaissance Medicine', *History of Psychiatry*, 5 (1994), 483–516. See also R. Neugebauer, 'Treatment of the Mentally Ill in Medieval and Early Modern England: A Reappraisal', *Journal of the History of the Behavioural Sciences*, 14 (1978), 158–69, and J. Kroll and B. Bachrach, 'Sin and Mental Illness in the Middle Ages', *Psychological Medicine*, 14 (1984), 507–14.

23 Doob, *Nebuchadnezzar's Children*, 31.

24 M. C. Seymour et al. (eds.) *On the Properties of Things: John Trevisa's Translation of Bartholomaeus Anglicus De proprietatibus rerum: A critical Text* (Oxford, 1975), 349. The description of 'frenesye' is on 348–9.

25 See T. C. Price Zimmermann, 'Confession and Autobiography in the Early Renaissance', in A. Molho and J. A. Tedeschi (eds.), *Renaissance Studies in Honor of Hans Baron* (Florence, 1971), 121–40.

26 For a discussion on this topic, see Abbott, *Julian of Norwich*, 10.

27 For a discussion of the performative dimension of 'bodiliness' in Margery Kempe, and of her body as religious text, see Denis Renevey's study, 'Margery's Performing Body: The Translation of Late Medieval Discursive Religious Practices', in this volume.

28 The suggestion of intermittent 'madness' has been made in P. R. Freeman, C. R. Bogarad and D. E. Sholomskas, 'Margery Kempe, a New Theory: The Inadequacy of Hysteria and Postpartum Psychosis as Diagnostic Categories', *History of Psychiatry*, 1 (1990), 168–90. Farley, a psychiatric nurse, makes an excellent case for the validity of psychiatry as a critical tool in approaching *The Book*, and offers a very helpful critique of arguments against this in M. H. Farley, 'Her Own Creature: Religion, Feminist Criticism and the Functional Eccentricity of Margery Kempe', *Exemplaria*, 11.1 (1999), 1–21. However, I take issue with her suggestion that the primary psychiatric explanation for Kempe's behaviour and experiences is Hystrionic Personality Disorder, roughly equivalent to 'Hysteria'. As she admits herself (p.7), this diagnosis is by no means a perfect description of Margery Kempe. I address these particular issues in detail in R. Lawes, 'The Madness of Margery Kempe', in M. Glasscoe (ed.), *MMTE VI*, 147–67.

29 The portion of ch. 1 describing this episode is in S. B. Meech and H. E. Allen (eds.), *The Book of Margery Kempe*, EETS 212 (Oxford, 1940; repr.

1961), 6–9. Hereafter given as *The Book*. All quotations are from this edition, and page number is given in parentheses following each quotation.

[30] Helpful summaries of the features of this condition may be found in M. B. Barton, 'Saint Teresa of Avila: Did she have Epilepsy?', *The Catholic Historical Review*, 68 (1982), 581–98 (583), and in W. A. Lishman, *Organic Psychiatry: The Psychological Consequences of Cerebral Disorder*, 2nd edn (Oxford, 1987), 218–20.

[31] Considerable research has been conducted into the correlation between 'religiosity' and religious experience and temporal lobe activity. See, for instance, the classic paper by S. G. Waxman and N. Geschwind, 'The Inerictal Behavior Syndrome of Temporal Lobe Epilepsy', *Archives of General Psychiatry*, 32.12 (1975), 1580–6; see also M. A. Persinger, 'Religious and Mystical Experience as Artifacts of Temporal Lobe Function: A General Hypothesis', *Perceptual and Motor Skills*, 57 (1983), 1255–62, which reviews the key research evidence and also constructs the author's own, still controversial 'overall hypothesis'.

[32] For a psycho-neurological study of Margery Kempe reaching different conclusions to my own, see N. Stork, 'Did Margery Kempe Suffer from Tourette's Syndrome?' *Medieval Studies*, 59 (1997), 261–300. Whilst this paper, like that of Freeman, Bogarad and Sholomskas, offers a helpful critique of the term 'hysteria' and contributes to the questioning of the overwhelming Freudian hegemony in psycholiterary studies, and whilst the suggestion of Tourette's Syndrome is intriguing, the essence of this disorder is explosive vocal or motor 'tics'. In my opinion the phenomenology exhibited by Margery Kempe is too rich and complex, (including, for instance, probable auditory, visual and olfactory hallucinations), for Tourette's to account for it. Nor need one link the 'picking' of the skin Margery shows in her post-natal illness with Tourette's (see Stork, 289), as such behaviour is common in affective psychoses.

[33] See Barton, 'Saint Teresa of Avila'; W. W. Meissner, *Ignatius of Loyola: The Psychology of a Saint* (New Haven, 1992); D. Landsborough, 'St. Paul and Temporal Lobe Epilepsy', *Journal of Neurology, Neurosurgery and Psychiatry*, 50 (1987), 659–64; C. Pepler, *The English Religious Heritage* (London, 1958), 312.

[34] I am indebted to the analysis of 'inner and outer' in Harper, ' "By cowntynaunce it is not wist" ', 338–9.

[35] R. Voaden, *God's Words, Women's Voices: The Discernment of Spirits in the Writings of Late-Medieval Women Visionaries* (York, 1999).

[36] S. Bhattacharji, *God is an Earthquake: The Spirituality of Margery Kempe* (London, 1997), 32.

[37] See Burrow, 'Autobiographical Poetry', 407–12.

[38] See Doob, *Nebuchadnezzar's Children*, 212.

[39] See Abbott, *Julian of Norwich*, 1–46.

[40] Pepler, *The English Religious Heritage*, 309, 312.

[41] D. Knowles, *The English Mystical Tradition* (London, 1961), 121–2.
[42] E. Colledge and J. Walsh (eds.), *A Book of Showings to the Anchoress Julian of Norwich* (Toronto, 1978), 208.
[43] Ibid., 208.
[44] See J. T. McIlwain, 'The "bodelye sykenes" of Julian of Norwich', *Journal of Medieval History*, 10.3 (1984), 167–79. Guillain-Barre syndrome is a long-recognized progressive neurological paralysis occurring after infections. It is often very serious, leaving the patient temporarily paralysed and sometimes unable to breathe. McIlwain describes it in detail.
[45] See McIlwain's discussion of these issues in ' "bodelye syknes" ', 171.
[46] M. Glasscoe (ed.), *Julian Norwich: A Revelation of Love* (Exeter, 1976), 14.
[47] Ibid., 6, 10.
[48] Ibid., 108–9.
[49] These are hallucinations occurring whilst going to sleep or on waking respectively, and are usually not pathological. See Sims, *Symptoms in the Mind*, 77.
[50] Glasscoe, *Julian of Norwich*, 108.
[51] Ibid., 24.
[52] For a discussion focused on Julian's diabology, see D. F. Tinsley, 'Julian's Diabology', in McEntire (ed.), *Julian of Norwich*, 209–37.
[53] See McIlwain, ' "Bodelye sykenes" ', 172.
[54] See S. J. McEntire, 'The Likeness of God and the Restoration of Humanity in Julian of Norwich's *Showings*', in McEntire (ed.), *Julian of Norwich*, 3–34 (30).
[55] For attempts to rate life-event severity, see, for example, T. Holmes and R. H. Rahe, 'The Social Adjustment Rating Scale', *Journal of Psychosomatic Research*, 11 (1967), 213–18.

# Bibliography

## Manuscripts

Beeleigh Abbey, Maldon, Essex, MS Foyle.
California, Huntington Library, MS HM 127.
Cambridge, Trinity College, MS 43.
Cambridge, Trinity College, MS 323.
Cambridge, University Library, MS Hh. 4. 12.
Cambridge, University Library, MS Ii. 6. 39.
Glasgow, University Library, MS Hunter T. 6. 18.
London, British Library, MS Additional 17376.
London, British Library, MS Additional 22283 (Simeon).
London, British Library, MS Additional 37790 (Amherst).
London, British Library, MS Additional 46919.
London, British Library, MS Arundel 286.
London, British Library, MS Egerton 613.
London, British Library, MS Egerton 927.
London, British Library, MS Harley 2253.
London, British Library, MS Sloane 2593.
Madrid, Biblioteca Nacional, MS 871.
National Library of Scotland, Advocates MS 18.7.21.
Oxford, Bodleian Library, MS Additional B. 107.
Oxford, Bodleian Library, MS Eng. Poet. a. 1 (Vernon).
Oxford, Bodleian Library, MS Douce 365.
Oxford, Bodleian Library, MS Laud misc. 330.
Oxford, Bodleian Library, MS Laud misc. 517.
Oxford, Bodleian Library, MS Bodley 255.
Oxford, Merton College, MS 248.
Oxford, Jesus College, MS 29.
Padua, Bibl. Univ., MS 990.
Padua, Bibl. Univ., MS 2146.
Uppsala, University Library, MS C 240.
Uppsala, University Library, MS C 253.

## Primary Texts

Abelard and Heloise, 'The Letter of Heloise on Religious Life and Abelard's First Reply', ed. J. T. Muckle, *Mediaeval Studies*, 17 (1955), 240–81.

——, *The Letters of Abelard and Heloise*, tr. B. Radice (London, 1974; repr. 1981).

Aelred de Rievaulx, *De institutione inclusarum*, in A. Hoste and C. H. Talbot (eds.), *Aelredi Rievallensis: Opera omnia*, CCCM 1 (Turnhout, 1971), 635–82.

——, *De institutione inclusarum*, ed. J. Ayto and A. Barratt, EETS 287 (London, 1984).

——, *Sermones*, PL 195 209–361.

——, *La vie de recluse, la prière pastorale*, ed. and tr. C. Dumont, SC 76 (Paris, 1961), 42–168.

——, *Treatises and Pastoral Prayer*, tr. and ed. M. P. Macpherson and M. B. Pennington Knowles (Kalamazoo, 1971), 41–102.

*The English Text of the Ancrene Riwle, edited from Cotton Nero A. XIV*, ed. M. Day, EETS OS 225 (London, 1952).

*The English Text of the Ancrene Riwle: Ancrene Wisse, edited from MS Corpus Christi College, Cambridge 402*, ed. J. R. R. Tolkien, EETS OS 249 (London, 1962).

*The French Text of the Ancrene Riwle, edited from British Museum MS. Cotton Vitellius F. vii*, ed. J. A. Herbert, EETS OS 219 (London, 1944).

*The Ancrene Riwle: The Corpus MS: Ancrene Wisse*, tr. M. B. Salu, Exeter Medieval English Texts and Studies (London, 1955; repr. Exeter, 1990).

*Ancrene Wisse: Guide for Anchoresses*, tr. H. White (London, 1993).

Anselm, St, *The Prayers and Meditations of St. Anselm: With the Proslogion*, ed. and tr. B. Ward (Harmondsworth, 1988).

Augustine, St, *Confessions*, ed. J. J. O'Donnell, 3 vols. (Oxford, 1992).

Benedict, St, *Regula cum commentariis*, PL 66. 215–932.

——, *The Rule of Saint Benedict*, tr. J. Mc Cann, rev. edn (London, 1976; repr. 1989).

Bernard of Clairvaux, 57, *Opera omnia*, ed. J. Mabillon, 2 vols. (Paris, 1690).

——, *The Letters of St Bernard of Clairvaux*, tr. B. S. James (Phoenix Mill, Gloucestershire, 1953; repr. 1998).

——, *Bernard of Clairvaux: Selected Works*, tr. G. R. Evans (New York, 1987).

——, *La traduction en prose française du 12ème siècle des* Sermones in Cantica *de saint Bernard*, ed. S. Gregory (Amsterdam, 1994).

Bokenham, O., *Legendys of Hooly Wummen by Osbern Bokenham*, ed. M. S. Serjeantson, EETS OS 206 (London, 1938).

Bonaventure, St, *Legenda Maior S. Francis*, Analecta Franciscana 10 (1926–41), 555–652.

——, *The Soul's Journey into God. The Tree of Life. The Life of St. Francis*, tr. E. Cousins, The Classics of Western Spirituality (New York, 1978).
*The Book of Vices and Virtues*, ed. W. N. Francis, EETS OS 217 (London, 1942).
*The Book to a Mother: An Edition with Commentary*, ed. A. J. McCarthy, Studies in the English Mystics 1, Elizabethan and Renaissance Studies 92 (Salzburg, 1981).
*Breviarium ad usum insignis ecclesiae Sarisburiensis*, ed. F. Procter and C. Wordsworth, 3 vols. (Cambridge, 1879–86; repr. Farnborough, 1970).
Bridget of Sweden, St, *The Liber Celestis of St. Bridget of Sweden: The Middle English Version in British Library MS Claudius Bi, together with a Life of the Saint from the Same Manuscript*, ed. R. Ellis, EETS OS 291 (Oxford, 1987).
Brown, C. (ed.), *Religious Lyrics of the Fourteenth Century* (Oxford, 1924).
—— (ed.), *English Lyrics of the Thirteenth Century* (Oxford, 1932).
—— (ed.), *Religious Lyrics of the Fifteenth Century* (Oxford, 1939).
Capgrave, J., *John Capgrave: The Life of St. Katharine of Alexandria*, ed. C. Horstmann, EETS OS 100 (London, 1893; repr. 1973).
Casagrande, C. (ed.), *Prediche alle donne del secolo xiii*, Nuova Corona 9 (Milan, 1978).
Catherine of Siena, St, *The Orcherd of Syon*, ed. P. Hodgson and G. M. Liegey, EETS OS 258 (London, 1966).
*The Chastising of God's Children and the Treatise of Perfection of the Sons of God*, ed. J. Bazire and E. Colledge (Oxford, 1957).
Chaucer, G., *The Riverside Chaucer*, ed. L. D. Benson et al. (Boston, 1987).
*The Cloud of Unknowing*, ed. P. Hodgson, Analecta Cartusiana 3 (Salzburg, 1982).
Colgrave, B. (ed. and tr.), *Two Lives of Saint Cuthbert: A Life by an Anonymous Monk of Lindisfarne and Bede's Prose Life* (Cambridge, 1940).
*The Desert of Religion*, in A. Mc Govern-Mouron (ed.), 'The *Desert of Religion* and its Theological Background', 2 vols. (University of Oxford D.Phil. thesis, 1996).
*Enchiridion symbolorum: Definitionum et declarationum de rebus fidei et morum*, ed. H. Denzinger and A. Schonmetzer (Freiburg, 1965).
*Expositio in regulam beati Augustini*, PL 176. 881–924.
Furnivall, F. J. (ed.), *Political, Religious and Love Poems from Lambeth MS. 306 and other sources*, EETS OS 15 (London, 1866; repr. 1962).
—— (ed.), *The Fifty Earliest English Wills 1387–1439*, EETS OS 78 (London, 1882; repr. 1964).
Greene, R. L. (ed.), *The Early English Carols*, 2nd edn (Oxford, 1977).
Grosseteste, R., *Le Château d'Amour de Robert Grosseteste*, ed. J. Murray (Paris, 1918).
——, *Templum Dei*, ed. J. Goering and F. A. C. Mantello (Toronto, 1984).

Guibert of Nogent, *De vita sua sive monodiarum suarum libri tres*, PL 156. 837–962.
*Hali Meiðhad*, ed. B. Millett, EETS OS 284 (London, 1982).
*The Harley Lyrics*, ed. G. L. Brook (Manchester, 1968).
Hoccleve, T., *Thomas Hoccleve: Selected Poems*, ed. B. O'Donoghue (Manchester, 1982).
Hoornaert, R. (ed.), 'La plus ancienne règle du Béguinage de Bruges', *Annales de la Société d'Émulation de Bruges*, 72 (1929), 1–79.
Hugh of St Victor, *De arca Noë morali*, *De arca Noë mystica*, and *De vanitate mundi*, PL 176. 618–838.
Humbert of Romans, *De eruditione praedicatorum*: see Casagrande, C. (ed.).
Jacobus de Voragine, *The Golden Legend: Readings on the Saints*, tr. W. G. Ryan, 2 vols. (Princeton, 1993).
Jacques de Vitry, *The Historia Occidentalis of Jacques de Vitry: A Critical Edition*, ed. J. F. Hinnebusch, Spicilegium Friburgense 17 (Fribourg, 1972).
——, *The Life of Marie d'Oignies*, tr. M. H. King, 2nd edn (Toronto, 1989).
Johannis de Caulibus, *Meditaciones vite Christi: olim S. Bonauenturo attributae*, ed. M. Sallings-Taney, CCCM 153 (Turnhout, 1997).
Julian of Norwich, *A Book of Showings to the Anchoress Julian of Norwich*, ed. E. Colledge and J. Walsh (Toronto, 1978).
——, *Julian of Norwich's Revelations of Divine Love: The Shorter Version*, ed. F. Beer (Heidelberg, 1978).
——, *A Revelation of Love*, ed. M. Glasscoe, 3rd rev. edn, Exeter Medieval English Texts and Studies (Exeter, 1993).
*The Katherine Group edited from MS. Bodley 34*, ed. S. T. R. O. d'Ardenne (Paris, 1977).
Kempe, M., *The Book of Margery Kempe*, ed. S. B. Meech and H. E. Allen, EETS OS 212 (London, 1940; repr. 1993).
——, *The Book of Margery Kempe*, ed. B. Windeatt (London, 1988).
*King Horn, Floris and Blauncheflur, The Assumption of our Lady*, ed. J. R. Lumby, rev. G. H. Mc Knight, EETS OS 14 (London, 1866; repr. 1962).
Langland, W., *The Vision of Piers Plowman*, ed. A. V. C. Schmidt (London, 1987).
Lefèvre, Pl. F. (ed.), *Les statuts de Prémontré, réformés sur les ordres de Grégoire IX et d'Innocent IV au xiii$^e$ siècle*, Bibliothèque de la Revue d'Histoire Ecclésiastique 23 (Louvain, 1946).
—— and W. M. Grauwen (eds.), *Les statuts de Prémontré au milieu du xii$^e$ siècle*, Bibliotheca Analectorum Praemonstratensium 12 (Averbode, 1978).
Le Grand, L. (ed.), *Statuts d'Hôtels-Dieu et de léproseries: Recueil de textes du xii$^e$ au xiv$^e$ siècle* (Paris, 1901).
*Liber de modo bene vivendi ad sororem*, PL 184. 1199–1306.
*Liber ordinis sancti Victoris Parisiensis*, ed. L. Jocqué and L. Milis, CCCM 61 (Turnhout, 1984).
Love, N., *Nicholas Love's Mirror of the Blessed Life of Jesus Christ: A Critical*

*Edition Based on Cambridge University Library Additional MSS 6578 and 6686*, ed. M. Sargent, Garland Medieval Texts 18 (New York, 1992).

Luria, M. and R. L. Hoffman (eds.), *Middle English Lyrics* (New York and London, 1974).

Lydgate, J., *The Minor Poems of John Lydgate*, ed. H. N. MacCracken, 2 vols., EETS ES 107 and OS 192 (London, 1911 and 1934).

Mechtild of Hackeborn, *Liber specialis gratiae*, in L. Paquelin (ed.), *Revelationes Gertrudianae ac Mechtildianae cura Solemnensium*, 2 vols. (Paris, 1875–7), II.

——, *The Booke of Gostlye Grace of Mechtild of Hackeborn*, ed. T. A. Halligan, Studies and Texts, Pontifical Institute of Mediaeval Studies 46 (Toronto, 1979).

Meersseman, G. G. (ed.), *Dossier de l'ordre de la Pénitence au xiii$^e$ siècle*, Spicilegium Friburgense 7 (Fribourg, 1961).

Millett, B. and J. Wogan-Browne (eds.), *Medieval English Prose for Women: Selections from the Katherine Group and Ancrene Wisse* (Oxford, 1990).

*Mirk's Festial: A Collection of Homilies*, ed. T. Erbe, EETS ES 96 (London, 1905).

*Missale ad usum insignis ecclesiae Eboracensis*, ed. Revd Dr Henderson, SS 60 (1874).

*Missale ad usum insignis et praeclare ecclesiae Sarum*, ed. F. H. Dickinson (Burntisland, 1861–83; repr. Helsinki, 1972–84).

*The Myroure of Our Lady*, ed. J. H. Blunt, EETS ES 19 (London, 1873).

Peter of Celle, 'The School of the Cloister', in *Selected Works*, tr. H. Feiss, Cistercian Studies Series 100 (Kalamazoo, 1987), 63–130.

Petroff, E. A. (ed.), *Medieval Women's Visionary Literature* (Oxford, 1986).

Porete, M., *Marguerita Porete. Le Mirouer des simples ames. Margaretae Porete. Speculum simplicium animarum*, ed. P. Verdeyen and R. Guarnieri, CCCM 69 (Turnhout, 1986).

——, '*Þe Mirrour of Simple Soules*: An Edition and Commentary', ed. M. Doiron (Fordham University Ph.D. thesis, 1964).

——, *Marguerite Porete: The Mirror of Simple Souls*, ed. E. Babinsky (New York, 1993).

Power, S., *The Grass Dancer* (London, 1995).

Prudentius, *Psychomachia*, in H. J. Thomson (ed. and tr.), *The Works of Prudentius* (London, 1949).

Pseudo-Eckhart, 'Sister Catherine Treatise', in B. Mc Ginn, F. Tobin and E. Borgstadt (trs.), *Meister Eckhart: Teacher and Preacher* (New York, 1986), 347–87.

Raine, J. (ed.), *Testamenta Eboracensia: A Selection of Wills from the Registry at York*, SS 45 (Durham, 1865).

*The Rewyll of Seynt Sauioure*, ed. J. Hogg, Salzburger Studien zur Anglistik und Amerikanistik, 6 vols. (Salzburg, 1978–80), II–IV.

Rolle, R., *The Fire of Love and The Mending of Life or the Rule of Living:*

*Translated from the Latin of Richard Rolle by Richard Misyn*, ed. R. Harvey, EETS OS 106 (London, 1896; repr. 1973).
*Le Roman d'Eneas*, ed. A. Petit (Paris, 1997).
*A Rule of Good Life 1633*, ed. D. M. Rogers, English Recusant Literature 79 (Menston, 1971).
Ruusbroec, J., *Jan van Ruusbroec. Opera omnia*, ed. G. de Baere, CCCM 110 (Turnhout, 1991).
*The Sarum Missal in English*, ed. F. E. Warren (London, 1911–13).
Savage, A. and N. Watson (trs.), *Anchoritic Spirituality: Ancrene Wisse and Associated Works*, The Classics of Western Spirituality (New York, 1991).
*St Katherine of Alexandria: The Late Middle English Prose Legend in Southwell Minster MS 7*, ed. S. Nevanlinna and I. Taavitsainen (Cambridge, 1993).
*Seinte Katerine: Re-edited from MS Bodley 34 and the other Manuscripts*, ed. S. R. T. O. d'Ardenne and E. J. Dobson, EETS SS 7 (London, 1981).
*Seinte Marharete: Þe Meiden ant Martyr*, ed. F. Mack, EETS OS 193 (London, 1934; repr. 1958).
*The South English Legendary*, ed. C. d'Evelyn and A. J. Mill, 2 vols., EETS 235 and 236 (London, 1957; repr. 1967).
*The Speculum Devotorum of an Anonymous Carthusian of Sheen, Edited from the Manuscripts Cambridge University Library Gg. I. 6 and Foyle, with an Introduction and a Glossary*, ed. J. Hogg, 2 vols., Analecta Cartusiana 12–13 (Salzburg, 1973–4).
——, 'An Edition of *Speculum Devotorum*, a Fifteenth-Century English Meditation on the Life and Passion of Jesus Christ, with an Introduction and Notes', ed. B. Wilsher, 2 vols. (University of London MA thesis, 1956).
*Summa virtutum de remediis anime*, ed. S. Wenzel (Athens, Ga., 1984).
Suso, H., *Heinrich Seuses Horologium Sapientiae: Erste kritische Ausgabe unter Benützung der Vorarbeiten von Dominikus Planzer OP*, ed. P. Künzle, Spicilegium Friburgense: Texte zur Geschichte des kirchlichen Lebens 23 (Freiburg, 1977).
*A Talking of the Love of God*, ed. S. Westra (The Hague, 1950).
Tertullian, *De oratione et de virginibus velandis libelli*, ed. G. F. Diercks, Stromata Patristica et Medievalia 4 (Antwerp, 1956).
Thomas of Froidmont, 'Een onuitgegeven brief van Thomas van Beverley, monnik van Froidmont', ed. E. Mikkers, *Cîteaux in de Nederlanden*, 7 (1956), 245–63.
Thomas, A. H. (ed.), *De oudste constituties van de Dominicanen: Voorgeschiedenis, tekst, bronnen, ontstaan en ontwikkeling (1215–1237)*, Bibliothèque de la Revue d'Histoire Ecclésiastique 42 (Louvain, 1965).
*The Use of Sarum*, ed. W. H. Frere, 2 vols. (Cambridge, 1898, 1901).
William of Nassington, *Speculum vitae*, ed. J. W. Smeltz (Ann Arbor, Mich., 1977).
*Þe Wohunge of ure Lauerd*, ed. W. M. Thompson, EETS OS 241 (Oxford, 1958).

# Secondary texts

Abbott, C., *Julian of Norwich: Autobiography and Theology* (Cambridge, 1999).

Ackerman, R. W., 'The Liturgical Day in *Ancrene Riwle*', *Speculum*, 53 (1978), 734–44.

Aers, D. (ed.), *Culture and History 1350–1600: Essays on English Communities, Identities and Writing* (London, 1992).

Alexander, J. J. G. and M. Gibson (eds.), *Medieval Learning and Literature: Essays presented to R. W. Hunt* (Oxford, 1976).

Alford, J., 'The Biblical Identity of Richard Rolle', *Mystics Quarterly*, 11 (1976), 21–5.

——, 'Biblical *Imitatio* in the Writings of Richard Rolle', *English Literary History*, 40 (1973), 1–23.

Altman, C. F., 'Two Types of Opposition and the Structure of Latin Saints' Lives', *Medieval Hagiography and Romance, Medievalia et Humanistica*, NS, 6 (Cambridge, 1975), 1–11.

American Psychiatric Association, *Diagnostic and Statistical Manual of Mental Disorders*, 3rd rev. edn (Washington, 1987).

Anderson-Schmidt, M. and M. Hedlund, *Mittelalterliche Handschriften der Universitätsbibliothek Uppsala, Katalog über die C Sammlung*, 7 vols. (Uppsala, 1988–95).

Ange, A. (ed.), *Dr. L. Reypens-Album*, Texttuitgauen van Ons Geestelijk 16 (Antwerp, 1964).

Atkinson, C., ' "Precious Balsam in a Fragile Glass": The Ideology of Virginity in the Later Middle Ages', *Journal of Family History*, 8 (1983), 131–43.

——, *Mystic and Pilgrim: The Book and the World of Margery Kempe* (Ithaca, 1983).

Baily, T., *The Procession of Sarum and the Western Church*, Pontifical Institute of Medieval Studies 21 (Toronto, 1971).

Baker, D. (ed.), *Medieval Women* (Oxford, 1978).

—— (ed.), *Sanctity and Secularity: The Church and the World*, Studies in Church History 10 (Oxford, 1973).

Bartlett, A. Clark, T. H. Bestul, J. Goebel and W. F. Pollard (eds.), *Vox Mystica: Essays on Medieval Mysticism in Honor of Professor Valerie M. Lagorio* (Cambridge, 1995).

Barton, M. B., 'Saint Teresa of Avila: Did she have Epilepsy?', *The Catholic Historical Review*, 68 (1982), 581–98.

Bateson, M. (ed.), *Catalogue of the Library of Syon Monastery Isleworth* (Cambridge, 1898).

Beckwith, S., *Christ's Body: Identity, Culture and Society in Late Medieval Writings* (London and New York, 1993).

Bekker-Nielsen, H., et al. (eds.), *Hagiography and Medieval Literature: A Symposium* (Odense, 1981).

Bell, D. N., *What Nuns Read* (Kalamazoo, 1995).
Bhattacharji, S., *God is an Earthquake: The Spirituality of Margery Kempe* (London, 1997).
Bird, D. J., *Pilgrimage to Rome in the Middle Ages: Continuity and Change*, Studies in the History of Medieval Religions (Cambridge, 1998).
Blamires, A., *The Case for Women in Medieval Culture* (Oxford, 1998).
Blomefield, F. and C. Parkin, *An Essay towards a Topographical History of the County of Norfolk*, 11 vols. (Norwich, 1805–10).
Bloomfield, M. W., 'Piers Plowman and the Three Grades of Chastity', *Anglia*, 76 (1958), 227–53.
Blumenfeld-Kosinski, R. and T. Szell (eds.), *Images of Sainthood in Medieval Europe* (Ithaca and London, 1991).
Bouton, J. de La Croix, 'Saint Bernard et les moniales', in Association Bourguignonne des Sociétés Savantes, *Mélanges Saint Bernard* (Dijon, 1953), 225–46.
Briggs, B., 'The Language of the Scribes of the First English Translation of the *Imitatio Christi*', *Leeds Studies in English*, NS, 26 (1995), 79–111.
British Museum, Department of Manuscripts, *Catalogue of Additions to the Manuscripts in the British Museum in the years MDCCCCVI–MDCCCCX* (London, 1912).
Brown, P., *The Cult of the Saints: Its Rise and Function in Latin Christianity* (Chicago, 1981).
——, *The Body and Society: Men, Women, and Sexual Renunciation in Early Christianity* (New York, 1988).
Bugge, J., *Virginitas: An Essay in the History of a Medieval Ideal* (The Hague, 1975).
Bundy, M. W., *The Theory of Imagination in Classical and Medieval Thought*, University of Illinois Studies in Language and Literature 12 (Urbana, Ill., 1927).
Burrow, J. A., 'Autobiographical Poetry in the Middle Ages: The Case of Thomas Hoccleve', *Proceedings of the British Academy*, 68 (1982), 389–412.
Burton, J., *Monastic and Religious Orders in Britain 1000–1300* (Cambridge, 1994).
Bynum, C. W., 'The Spirituality of Regular Canons in the Twelfth Century: A New Approach', *Medievalia et Humanistica*, 4 (1973), 3–24.
——, *Docere verbo et exemplo: An Aspect of the Twelfth-Century Spirituality* (Missoula, Mont., 1979).
——, *Jesus as Mother* (London, 1982; repr. 1984).
——, *Holy Feast and Holy Fast: The Religious Significance of Food to Medieval Women* (Berkeley, 1987).
——, *Fragmentation and Redemption: Essays on Gender and the Human Body in Medieval Religion* (New York, 1991).

——, *The Resurrection of the Body in Western Christianity, 200–1338* (New York, 1995).
Carroll, M. P., *The Cult of the Virgin Mary: Psychological Origins* (Princeton, 1986).
Carruthers, M., *The Book of Memory: A Study of Memory in Medieval Culture* (Cambridge, 1990).
——, *The Craft of Thought: Meditation, Rhetoric, and the Making of Images, 400–1200* (Cambridge, 1998).
Chartier, R. (ed.), *The Culture of Print: Power and the Uses of Print in Early Modern Europe*, tr. L. G. Cochrane (Cambridge, 1989).
Cheney, C. R., 'Rules for Observance of Feast-Days in Medieval England', *Bulletin of the Institute of Historical Research*, 34 (1961), 117–47.
Claridge, C., R. Pryor and G. Watkins, *Sounds from the Bell Jar: Ten Psychotic Authors* (London, 1990).
Clayton, M., *The Cult of the Virgin Mary in Anglo-Saxon England* (Cambridge, 1990).
Colledge, E., 'The *Treatise of Perfection of the Sons of God*: A Fifteenth-Century English Ruysbroeck translation', *English Studies*, 33 (1952), 49–66.
Constable, G., *The Reformation of the Twelfth Century* (Cambridge, 1996).
——, *Three Studies in Medieval Religious and Social Thought* (Cambridge, 1998).
Cooper, J. G., 'Latin Elements of the "Ancrene Riwle"' (Birmingham University Ph.D. thesis, 1956).
Copeland, R., *Rhetoric, Hermeneutics, and Translation in the Middle Ages*, Cambridge Studies in Medieval Literature (Cambridge, 1991).
Cornelius, R. D., *The Figurative Castle: A Study of the Medieval Allegory of the Edifice* (Bryn Mawr, 1930).
Courcelle, P., *Les Confessions de saint Augustin dans la tradition littéraire: Antécédents et postérité* (Paris, 1963).
Creek, M., 'The Sources and Influence of Robert Grosseteste's *Château d' Amour*' (Yale University Ph.D. thesis, 1941).
Dahood, R., 'Design in Part 1 of *Ancrene Riwle*', *Medium Ævum*, 56 (1987), 1–11.
Daiches, D., and A. K. Thorlby (eds.), *Literature and Western Civilization in the Medieval Period* (London, 1973).
Davidson, C. (ed.), *The Saint Play in Medieval Europe* (Kalamazoo, 1986).
Davies, H. and M.-H. Davies, *Holy Days and Holidays: The Medieval Pilgrimage to Compostela* (Lewisburg, Pa., 1982).
De Pablo, A G., 'The Medicine of the Soul: The Origin and Development of Thought on the Soul, Diseases of the Soul and their Treatment, in Medieval and Renaissance Medicine', *History of Psychiatry*, 5 (1994), 483–516.
Delany, S., *Impolitic Bodies. Poetry, Saints and Society in Fifteenth-Century England: The Work of Osbern Bokenham* (Oxford, 1998).
Dickinson, J. C., *The Shrine of Our Lady of Walsingham* (Cambridge, 1956).

Diehl, P. S., *The Medieval European Religious Lyric: An Ars Poetica* (Berkeley and London, 1985).
Dimier, R. P. M. A., 'Saint Bernard et le recrutement de Clairvaux', *Revue Mabillon*, 42 (1952), 17–30, 56–78.
Dobson, E. J., *The Origins of* Ancrene Wisse (Oxford, 1976).
Donovan, C., *The de Brailes Hours: Shaping the Book of Hours in Thirteenth-Century Oxford* (London, 1991).
Doob, P. B. R., *Nebuchadnezzar's Children: Conventions of Madness in Middle English Literature* (London, 1974).
Dor, J. (ed.), *A Wyf Ther Was* (Liège, 1992).
Doyle, A. I., 'A Survey of the Origins and Circulation of Theological Writings in English in the 14th, 15th, and Early 16th Centuries with Special Consideration of the Part of the Clergy Therein', 2 vols. (University of Cambridge Ph.D. thesis, 1954).
——, 'Carthusian Participation in the Movement of Works of Richard Rolle between England and Other Parts of Europe in the 14th and 15th centuries', Analecta Cartusiana 55.2 (1981), 109–20.
——, *The Vernon MS: A Facsimile of Bodleian Library, Oxford. MS Eng. Poet. a. 1* (Cambridge, 1987).
Duffy, E., *The Stripping of the Altars: Traditional Religion in England 1400–1580* (New Haven and London, 1992).
Eberly, S., 'Margery Kempe, St Mary Magdalene, and Patterns of Contemplation', *Downside Review*, 107 (1989), 209–23.
Eliott, J. K., *The Apocryphal New Testament* (Oxford, 1993).
Elkins, S., *Holy Women of Twelfth-Century England* (London, 1988).
Elliott, D., *Spiritual Marriage: Sexual Abstinence in Medieval Wedlock* (Princeton, 1993).
Ellis, R. and R. Evans (eds.), *The Medieval Translator* 4 (Exeter, 1994).
——, R. Tixier and B. Weitemeier (eds.), *The Medieval Translator* 6 (Turnhout, 1998).
Elm, K., 'Die Stellung der Frau in Ordenswesen, Semireligiosentum und Häresie zur Zeit der heiligen Elisabeth', in *Sankt Elisabeth, Fürstin, Dienerin, Heilige* (Sigmaringen, 1981), 7–28.
Emmet, J. et al. (eds.), *The British Library General Catalogue of Printed Books to 1975*, 360 vols. (London, 1979–87).
Engel, J. Jr. and T. A. Pedley (eds.), *Epilepsy: A Comprehensive Textbook*, 2 vols. (New York, 1998).
Evans, R. and L. Johnson (eds.), *Feminist Readings in Middle English Literature: The Wife of Bath and All her Sect* (London and New York, 1994).
Evitt, R. M. and M. B. Potkay, *Minding the Body: Women and Literature in the Middle Ages, 800–1500* (London, 1997).
Fanous, S. B., 'Biblical and Hagiographical *Imitatio* in the *Book of Margery Kempe*' (University of Oxford D.Phil. thesis, 1997).
Farmer, D. H., *The Oxford Dictionary of Saints* (Oxford, 1987).

Ferguson, G., *Signs and Symbols in Christian* Art (London, 1961).
Forey, A., *The Military Orders from the Twelfth to the Early Fourteenth Centuries*, New Studies in Medieval History (London, 1992).
Freeman, P. R., C. R. Bogarad and D. E. Shomskas, 'Margery Kempe, a New Theory: The Inadequacy of Hysteria and Postpartum Psychosis as Diagnostic Categories', *History of Psychiatry*, 1 (1990), 169–90.
Freibergs, G. (ed.), *Aspectus and Affectus: Essays and Editions in Grosseteste and Medieval Intellectual Life in Honour of R. C. Dales* (New York, 1993).
Gallyon, M., *Margery Kempe of Lynn and Medieval England* (Norwich, 1995).
Georgianna, L., *The Solitary Self: Individuality in the* Ancrene Wisse (Cambridge, Mass. and London, 1981).
Gibson, G. M., *The Theater of Devotion: East Anglian Drama and Society in the Late Middle Ages* (Chicago, 1989).
Gillespie, V., '*Lukynge in haly bukes*: Lectio in some Late Medieval Spiritual Miscellanies', Analecta Cartusiana 106.2 (1984), 1–27.
Glasscoe, M. (ed.), *MMTE*, see List of Abbreviations.
——, *English Medieval Mystics: Games of Faith* (London and New York, 1993).
Glasser, M., 'Marriage and Medieval Hagiography', *Studies in Medieval and Renaissance History*, NS, 4 (1981), 3–34.
Glorieux, P., *Pour revaloriser Migne* (Lille, 1952).
Gold, P. S., *The Lady and the Virgin: Image, Attitude and Experience in Twelfth-Century France* (Chicago, 1985).
Goodich, M., 'The Contours of Female Piety in Later Medieval Hagiography', *Church History*, 50 (1981), 21–32.
Graef, H., *Mary: A History of Doctrine and Devotion*, 2 vols. (London and New York, 1963).
Gray, D., *Themes and Images in the Medieval English Religious Lyric* (London and Boston, 1972).
Grayson, J., *Structure and Imagery in* Ancrene Wisse (Hanover, NH, 1974).
Grundmann, H., 'Litteratus-illitteratus: Der Wandel einer Bildungsnorm vom Altertum zum Mittelalter', *Archiv für Kulturgeschichte*, 40 (1958), 1–65.
Guarnieri, R., 'Lo *Specchio delle anime semplici* e Margharita Poirette', *L'Osservatore Romano*, 141, 16 June 1946, 3.
Halter, P. (ed.), *Performance*, Swiss Papers in English Language and Literature 11 (Tübingen, 1999).
Hamburger, J. F., 'The Use of Images in the Pastoral Care of Nuns: The Case of Heinrich Suso and the Dominicans', *Art Bulletin*, 71 (1989), 20–46.
Harper, J., *The Forms and Orders of Western Liturgy from the Tenth to the Eighteenth Century* (Oxford, 1991).
Harper, S., ' "By cowntynaunce it is not wist": Thomas Hoccleve's *Complaint* and the Spectacularity of Madness in the Middle Ages', *History of Psychiatry*, 8 (1997), 387–94.
Harrison Thomson, S., *The Writings of Robert Grosseteste* (Cambridge, 1940).

Hartung, A. E., *A Manual of the Writings in Middle English 1050–1500*, 9 vols. (New Haven, 1967–93).
Harvey, E. R., *The Inward Wits: Psychological Theory in the Middle Ages and the Renaissance*, Warburg Institute Surveys 6 (London, 1975).
Harvey, P. D. A., *Medieval Maps* (London, 1991).
Haskins, S., *Mary Magdalen: Myth and Metaphor* (London, 1993).
Hawton, K., P. M. Salkovskis, J. Kirk and D. M. Clark, *Cognitive Behaviour Therapy for Psychiatric Problems: A Practical Guide* (Oxford, 1989).
Heffernan, T. J. (ed.), *The Popular Literature of Medieval England*, Tennessee Studies in Literature 28 (Knoxville, Tenn., 1985).
——, *Sacred Biography: Saints and Their Biographers in the Middle Ages* (Oxford, 1988).
Hillen, H. J., *History of the Borough of King's Lynn*, 2 vols. (Norwich, 1907; repr. Wakefield, 1978).
Hirsh, J., 'Author and Scribe in *The Book of Margery Kempe*', *Medium Ævum*, 44 (1975), 145–50.
Hogg, J. (ed.), *Zeit, Tod und Ewigkeit in der Renaissance Literatur 3*, Analecta Cartusiana 117 (Salzburg, 1987).
Holmes, T. and R. H. Rahe, 'The Social Adjustment Rating Scale', *Journal of Psychosomatic Research*, 11 (1967), 213–18.
Hourlier, J., *L'age classique 1140–1378: Les religieux*, Histoire du Droit et des Institutions de l'Église en Occident 10 (Paris, 1974).
Hughes, A., *Medieval Manuscripts for Mass and Office: A Guide to Their Organization and Terminology* (Toronto, 1982).
Hughes, J., *Pastors and Visionaries: Religion and Secular Life in Late Medieval Yorkshire* (Woodbridge, 1988).
Hunt, T., 'The Four Daughters of God: A Textual Contribution', *Archives d'histoire doctrinale et littéraire du Moyen Âge*, 48 (1981), 287–316.
Janauschek, L., *Xenia Bernardina, IV: Bibliographia Bernardina* (Vienna, 1891).
Jaouèn, F. and B. Semple (eds.), *Corps mystique, corps sacré: Textual Transfigurations of the Body from the Middle Ages to the Seventeenth Century*, Yale French Studies 86 (New Haven, 1994).
Jeffrey, D. L., *The Early English Lyric and Franciscan Spirituality* (Lincoln, 1975).
Johnson, I. R., 'The Late-Medieval Theory and Practice of Translation with Special Reference to Some Middle English Lives of Christ' (University of Bristol Ph.D. thesis, 1990).
Johnson, L. S., 'The Trope of the Scribe and the Question of Literary Authority in the Works of Julian of Norwich and Margery Kempe', *Speculum*, 66 (1991), 820–38.
——, *Margery Kempe's Dissenting Fictions* (University Park, Pa., 1994).
Jolliffe, P. S., *A Check-List of Middle English Prose Writings of Spiritual Guidance* (Toronto, 1974).

Jones, C. W., *Saints' Lives and Chronicles in Early England* (Ithaca, 1947).
Jones, D., *An Early Witness to the Nature of the Canonical Order in the Twelfth Century: A Study in the Life and Writings of Adam Scot, with Particular Reference to his Understanding of the Rule of St Augustine*, Analecta Cartusiana 151 (Salzburg, 1999).
Katz, S. T. (ed.), *Mysticism and Religious Traditions* (Oxford, 1983).
Kay, S. and M. Rubin (eds.), *Framing Medieval Bodies* (Manchester, 1994).
Kendell, R. E. and A. K. Zealley, *Companion to Psychiatric Studies*, 5th edn (Edinburgh, 1993).
Kieckhefer, R., *Unquiet Souls: Fourteenth-Century Saints and their Religious Milieu* (Chicago, 1984).
Knowles, D., *The English Mystical Tradition* (London, 1961).
Kocijancic-Pokorn, N., 'Original Audience of *The Cloud of Unknowing* (In support of the Carthusian Authorship)', Analecta Cartusiana 130.1 (1995), 60–77.
Kristeva, J., 'Stabat Mater', in *Histoires d'amour* (Paris, 1983). This essay is reprinted in T. Moi (ed.), *The Kristeva Reader* (New York, 1986), 160–86.
Kroll, J. and B. Bachrach, 'Sin and Mental Illness in the Middle Ages', *Psychological Medicine*, 14 (1984), 507–14.
Kuczynski, M. P., *Prophetic Song* (Philadelphia, 1995).
Landsborough, D., 'St. Paul and Temporal Lobe Epilepsy', *Journal of Neurology, Neurosurgery and Psychiatry*, 50 (1987), 659–64.
Lawrence, C. H., *Medieval Monasticism*, 2nd edn (London, 1989; repr. 1993).
Leclercq, J., 'Manuscrits cisterciens dans des bibliothèques d'Italie', *Analecta sacri ordinis cisterciensis*, 10 (1954), 302–8.
——, *Recueil d'études sur saint Bernard et ses écrits*, 5 vols. (Rome, 1962–92).
Lefkovitz, L. H. (ed.), *Textual Bodies: Changing Boundaries of Literary Representation* (New York, 1993).
Legge, M. D., *Anglo-Norman Literature and its Background* (Oxford, 1963).
Leroquais, V., *Les Livres d'heures manuscrits de la Bibliothèque Nationale*, 2 vols. (Paris, 1927).
Levy, S. B. (ed.), *The Bible in the Middle Ages: Its Influence on Literature and Art* (Binghamton, NY, 1992).
Leyser, H., *Medieval Women* (London, 1995).
Lishman, W. A., *Organic Psychiatry: The Psychological Consequences of Cerebral Disorder*, 2nd edn (Oxford, 1987).
Lochrie, K., *Margery Kempe and Translations of the Flesh*, New Cultural Studies Series (Philadelphia, 1991).
Lomperis, L. and S. Stanbury (eds.), *Feminist Approaches to the Body in Medieval Literature* (Philadelphia, 1993).
Loomis, C. G., 'The Miracle Traditions of the Venerable Bede', *Speculum*, 21 (1946), 404–18.

Loomis, R. S., 'The Allegorical Siege in the Art of the Middle Ages', *American Journal of Archeology*, 2nd series, 23 (1919), 255–69.

Lopes de Toro, J., *Inventorio general de manuscritos de la biblioteca nacional*, 2 vols. (Madrid, 1956).

Maaz, M. (ed.), *Kontinuität und Wandel: Lateinische Poesie von Naevius bis Baudelaire* (Hildesheim, 1986).

Mantello, F. A. C. and A. G. Rigg (eds.), *Medieval Latin: An Introduction and Bibliographical Guide* (Washington, 1996).

Margherita, G., *The Romance of Origins: Language and Sexual Difference in Middle English Literature* (Philadelphia, 1994).

Maskell, W., *Monumenta ritualia ecclesiae Anglicanae*, 3 vols. (Oxford, 1882).

McBain, W., 'St. Catherine's Mystic Marriage: The Genesis of a Hagiographic Cycle de sainte-Catherine', *Romance Languages Annual*, 2 (1990), 135–40.

McCracken, U. E., L. M. C. Randall and R. H. Randall Jr. (eds.), *Gatherings in Honor of Dorothy E. Miner* (Baltimore, 1974).

McDonnell, E. W., *The Beguines and Beghards in Medieval Culture* (New Brunswick, NJ, 1954).

McEntire, S. (ed.), *Margery Kempe: A Book of Essays* (New York and London, 1992).

—— (ed.), *Julian of Norwich: A Book of Essays* (London, 1998).

McGinn, B., *The Flowering of Mysticism* (New York, 1998).

Mc Govern-Mouron, A., 'The *Desert of Religion* in British Library Cotton Faustina B VI, pars II', *Analecta Cartusiana* 130.9 (1996), 149–62.

McGuire, B. P., 'Late Medieval Care and Control of Women: Jean Gerson and his Sisters', *Revue d'Histoire Ecclésiastique*, 92 (1997), 5–37.

McIlwain, J. T., 'The "bodelye sykenes" of Julian of Norwich', *Journal of Medieval History*, 10.3 (1984), 167–79.

McIntosh, A., M. L. Samuels and M. Laing (eds.), *Middle English Dialectology: Essays on Some Principles and Problems* (Aberdeen, 1989).

Meale, C. M. (ed.), *Women and Literature in Britain 1150–1500* (Cambridge, 1993).

Medcalf, S. (ed.), *The Context of English Literature: The Later Middle Ages* (London, 1981).

Meersseman, G. G., 'Les Frères Prêcheurs et le mouvement dévot en Flandre au xiii$^e$ siècle', *Archivum Fratrum Praedicatorum*, 18 (1948), 69–130.

—— (ed.), *Dossier de l'ordre de la Pénitence au xiii$^e$ siècle*, Spicilegium Friburgense 7 (Fribourg, 1961).

Meissner, W. W., *Ignatius of Loyola: The Psychology of a Saint* (New Haven, 1992).

*The Middle English Dictionary*, ed. H. Kurath et al. (Ann Arbor, Mich., 1952– ).

Millett, B. and J. Wogan-Browne (eds.), *Medieval English Prose for Women. Selections from the Katherine Group and Ancrene Wisse* (Oxford, 1990).

——, 'The Origins of *Ancrene Wisse*: New Answers, New Questions', *Medium Ævum*, 61 (1992), 206–28.

——, *Ancrene Wisse, the Katherine Group, and the Wooing Group*, Annotated Bibliographies of Old and Middle English Literature 2 (Cambridge, 1996).

Minnis, A., 'Langland's Theory of Ymaginatif and Late-Medieval Theories of Imagination', *Comparative Criticism*, 3 (1981), 71–103.

——, 'Affection and Imagination in *The Cloud of Unknowing* and Hilton's *Scale of Perfection*', *Traditio*, 39 (1983), 323–66.

——, *Medieval Theory of Authorship: Scholastic Literary Attitudes in the Later Middle Ages* (Aldershot, 1988).

Molho, A. and J. A. Tedeschi (eds.), *Renaissance Studies in Honor of Hans Baron* (Florence, 1971).

Morgan, N., *Early Gothic Manuscripts [I], 1190–1250*, A Survey of Manuscripts Illuminated in the British Isles 4 (London, 1982).

Neugebauer, R., 'Treatment of the Mentally Ill in Medieval and Early Modern England: A Reappraisal', *Journal of the History of the Behavioural Sciences*, 14 (1978), 158–69.

Newman, B., *From Virile Woman to WomanChrist: Studies in Medieval Religion and Literature* (Philadelphia, 1995).

Nichols, J. A. and L. T. Shank (eds.), *Distant Echoes* (Kalamazoo, 1984).

—— (eds.), *Peace Weavers* (Kalamazoo, 1987).

Oliver, J., 'Devotional Psalters and the Study of Beguine Spirituality', *Vox Benedictina*, 9 (1992), 199–225.

Ong, W. J., 'Orality, Literacy, and Medieval Textualization', *New Literary History: A Journal of Theory and Interpretation*, 16 (1984), 1–12.

Owen, D. M. (ed.), *The Making of King's Lynn: A Documentary Survey*, Records of Social and Economic History, NS 9 (London, 1984).

Parkes, M. B., *English Cursive Book Hands 1250–1500* (Oxford, 1969).

Pepler, C., *The English Religious Heritage* (London, 1958).

Persinger, M. A., 'Religious and Mystical Experience as Artifacts of Temporal Lobe Function: A General Hypothesis', *Perceptual and Motor Skills*, 57 (1983), 1255–62.

Pfaff, R. W., *New Liturgical Feasts in Later Medieval England* (Oxford, 1970).

Philippen, L. J. M., *De Begijnhoven: Oorsprong, Geschiedenis, Inrichting* (Antwerp, 1918).

Phillips, H. (ed.), *Langland, the Mystics and the Medieval English Religious Tradition: Essays Presented in Honour of S. S. Hussey* (Cambridge, 1990).

Pollard, A. W. and G. R. Redgrave, *A Short-Title Catalogue of Books Printed in England, Scotland and Ireland*, rev. edn, 3 vols. (London, 1976, 1986, 1991).

Pollard, W. F. and R. Boenig (eds.), *Mysticism and Spirituality in Medieval England* (Cambridge, 1997).

Power, E., *Medieval English Nunneries: c. 1275–1535* (Cambridge, 1922).

Raitt, J. (ed.), *Christian Spirituality 2: High Middle Ages and Reformation* (London, 1987).
Rickert, M., *The Reconstructed Carmelite Missal: An English Manuscript of the late XIV Century in the British Museum (Additional 29704–5, 44892)* (London, 1952).
Robertson, E., *Early English Devotional Prose and the Female Audience* (Knoxville, Tenn., 1990).
Robinson, P. R. and R. Zim (eds.), *Of the Making of Books* (Aldershot, 1997).
Rose, M. B. (ed.), *Women in the Middle Ages and the Renaissance: Literary and Historical Perspectives* (Syracuse, NY, 1986).
Roth, M. and J. Kroll, *The Reality of Mental Illness* (Cambridge, 1986).
Rowland, B. (ed.), *Chaucer and Middle English Studies in Honour of Rossell Hope Robbins* (London, 1974).
Saenger, P., 'Silent Reading: Its Impact on Late Medieval Script and Society', *Viator*, 13 (1982), 367–414.
Sajavaara, K., 'The Middle English Translations of Robert Grosseteste's *Château d'Amour*', *Mémoires de la Société Néophilologique de Helsinki*, 32 (1967).
Salter, E., *Nicholas Love's Myrrour of the Blessed Lyf of Jesu Christ*, Analecta Cartusiana 10 (Salzburg, 1974).
Sargent, M. G., 'Contemporary Criticism of Richard Rolle', Analecta Cartusiana 55.1 (1981), 160–205.
——, 'Bonaventure English: A Survey of the Middle English Prose Translations of Early Franciscan Literature', in *Spätmittelalterliche geistliche Literatur in der Nationalsprache*, 106.2 (Salzburg, 1984).
——, *James Grenehalgh as Textual Critic*, 2 vols., Analecta Cartusiana 85 (Salzburg, 1984).
—— (ed.), *De cella in seculum: Religious and Secular Life and Devotion in Late Medieval England* (Cambridge, 1989).
——, 'Versions of the Life of Christ: Nicholas Love's *Mirror* and Related Works', *Poetica*, 42 (1994), 39–70.
——, 'The Annihilation of Marguerite Porete', *Viator*, 28 (1997), 253–79.
Sharpe, R., *A Handlist of the Latin Writers of Great Britain and Ireland before 1540* (Turnhout, 1997).
Shields, W. J. and D. Wood (eds.), *Women in the Church*, Studies in Church History 27 (Oxford, 1990).
Shoichi, O., R. Beadle and M. S. Sargent (eds.), *Nicholas Love at Waseda: Proceedings of the International Conference 20–22 July 1995* (Cambridge, 1997).
Simons, W., 'The Beguine Movement in the Southern Low Countries: A Reassessment', *Bulletin de l'Institut Historique Belge de Rome*, 59 (1989), 63–101.
Sims, A., *Symptoms in the Mind* (London, 1988).
Sommerfeldt, J. R. (ed.), *Bernardus Magister* (Kalamazoo, 1992).

Southern, R. W., *Robert Grosseteste: The Growth of an English Mind in Medieval Europe* (Oxford, 1986).
Spearing, A. C., *Medieval Dream-Poetry* (Cambridge, 1976).
Staley, L., *Margery Kempe's Dissenting Fictions* (University Park, Pa., 1994).
Stork, N., 'Did Margery Kempe Suffer from Tourette's Syndrome?' *Medieval Studies*, 59 (1997), 261–300.
Suleiman, S. R. (ed.), *The Female Body in Western Culture: Contemporary Perspectives* (Cambridge, Mass., 1986).
Talbot, C. H., 'Some Notes on the Dating of the *Ancrene Riwle*', *Neophilologus*, 40 (1956), 38–50.
Taylor, J., and L. Smith (eds.), *Women, the Book and the Godly* (Cambridge, 1995).
Thomas, A. H. (ed.), *De oudste Constituties van de Dominicanen: Voorgeschiedenis, Tekst, Bronnen, Ontstaan en Ontwikkeling (1215–1237)*, Bibliothèque de la Revue d'Histoire Ecclésiastique 42 (Louvain, 1965).
Thompson, S., *Women Religious* (Oxford, 1991; repr. 1996).
Traver, H., *The Four Daughters of God: A Study of the Versions of this Allegory with Special Reference to those in Latin, French and English* (Bryn Mawr, 1907).
Turner, V. and E. Turner, *Image and Pilgrimage in Christian Culture: Anthropological Perspectives* (New York, 1978).
Vauchez, A., *La sainteté en occident aux derniers siècles du moyen âge, d'après les procès de canonisation et les documents hagiographiques*, Bibliothèque des Etudes Françaises d'Athènes et de Rome 241 (Rome, 1981).
Verdeyen, P., *Ruusbroec and his Mysticism* (Collegeville, Ind., 1994).
Voaden, R. (ed.), *Prophets Abroad: The Reception of Continental Holy Women in Late-Medieval England* (Cambridge, 1996).
——, *God's Words, Women's Voices: The Discernment of Spirits in the Writings of Late-Medieval Women Visionaries*, Publications of the Centre for Medieval Studies (York and Woodbridge, 1999).
Wallace, D. (ed.), *The Cambridge History of Middle English Literature* (Cambridge, 1999).
Warner, M., *Alone of All her Sex: The Myth and Cult of the Virgin Mary* (London, 1976).
Warren, A. K., *Anchorites and their Patrons in Medieval England* (Berkeley, 1985).
Warren, N. B., 'Pregnancy and Productivity: The Imagery of Female Monasticism within and beyond the Cloister Walls', *Journal of Medieval and Early Modern Studies*, 28 (1998), 531–52.
Watson, N., 'Censorship and Cultural Change in Late-Medieval England: Vernacular Theology, the Oxford Translation Debate, and Arundel's Constitutions of 1409', *Speculum*, 70 (1995), 822–64.
Watt, D. (ed.), *Medieval Women in their Communities* (Cardiff, 1997).
Waxman, S. G. and N. Geschwind, 'The Inerictal Behavior Syndrome of

Temporal Lobe Epilepsy', *Archives of General Psychiatry*, 32.12 (1975), 1580–6.

Weinstein, D. and R. M. Bell, *Saints and Society: The Two Worlds of Western Christendom, 1000–1700* (London, 1982).

Weller, M. and M. Eysenck (eds.), *The Scientific Basis of Psychiatry*, 2nd edn (London, 1992).

Wenzel, S., *Preachers, Poets, and the Early English Lyric* (Princeton, 1986).

Whitehead, C., 'Castles of the Mind: an Interpretative History of Medieval Religious Architectural Allegory' (Oxford University D.Phil. thesis, 1995).

——, 'Making a Cloister of the Soul in Medieval Religious Treatises', *Medium Ævum*, 67.1 (1998), 1–29.

Wiethaus, U. (ed.), *Maps of Flesh and Light: The Religious Experience of Medieval Women Mystics* (Syracuse, NY, 1993).

Winston, J., 'The Face of the Virgin: Problems in the History of Representation and Devotion' (University of Columbia Ph.D. thesis, 1997).

Wogan-Browne, J., N. Watson, A Taylor and R. Evans (eds.), *The Idea of the Vernacular: An Anthology of Middle English Literary Theory 1280–1520*, Exeter Medieval Texts and Studies (Exeter, 1999).

Woolf, R., 'The Theme of Christ the Lover-Knight in Medieval English Literature', *Review of English Studies*, 13 (1962), 1–16.

——, *The English Religious Lyric in the Middle Ages* (Oxford, 1968).

Yates, F. A., *The Art of Memory* (London, 1966).

Yeager, R. F. (ed.), *Fifteenth-Century Studies: Recent Essays* (Hamden, Conn., 1984).

# INDEX

Abbott, C. 217, 228, 234
Abelard, Peter 81, 93, 129n31
Aelred of Rievaulx 10, 21, 22, 82, 83, 93, 106n101, 110, 141
Aers, D. 217, 228, 232
Agatha, St 188
Agnes, St 188
Ainard 181
Alan of Lille 118
Alan of Lynn 158, 199
Albert the Great 115
Albigensian heresy 119
allegory
 in Grosseteste's *Château d'amour* 13, 109–32, 141
 in Marguerite Porete's *Mirror* 51–2, 54–7
Alphonse of Pecha 45
Ambrose, St 120
*Analecta Cartusiana* 9
anchoritic tradition
 Grosseteste and anchoritic life 121
 influence on performing body of Margery Kempe 10, 199–202, 203–4, 205–10
 spirituality in 9, 10–11, 138; *see also* Ancrene Wisse
*Ancrene Wisse* 2, 3, 45, 133, 138
 compared to *The Manere of Good Lyvyng* 10, 12, 82, 83, 84, 86, 87, 90, 93, 106n101
 and Mary as model for anchoresses 76n19, 141, 142, 202
 performative activity 200, 205
 relationship to Book of Hours 10–11, 21–40
 virginity 121, 122, 142, 174n25

Anselm, St 116, 117, 119, 125, 129n31
 and anchoritic tradition 199–202
Aquinas, Thomas *see* Thomas Aquinas, St
Aristotle 118
Arundel's Constitutions (1409) 1, 3
Augustine, St 70, 83, 85, 95n4, 164
Augustinians
 and *Liber de modo bene vivendi* 12, 84–6, 87, 92, 93
 and relationship between *Ancrene Wisse* and Book of Hours 27, 28, 31, 32, 33
autobiography
 relationship to psychological disorder 15, 217–43
 spiritual 164
*Ave regina caelorum* 115

Bakhtin, Mikhail 151n12
Bal, M. 109, 110, 126, 127
Barbara, St 14, 179, 181, 184, 187, 188
Barratt, A. 226–7
Bartholomaeus Anglicus 227
Bartlett, Anne Clark 63
Bazire, J. 45
Beckwith, Sarah 153n58, 154n67
Bede 176n36
Beguines 28, 29, 30–1, 37n52
Benedict, St 85
Benedictines 25
*Benedictus Deus* bull (1336) 154n65
Bernard, St 82, 83, 84, 93, 116, 119, 145
Bernini, Gian Lorenzo 145
Bhattacharji, S. 233
Bible 70, 91
 *see also* Song of Songs

Blanche of Castille 119
body
    feminist approaches 6
    paradox of Virgin Mary 109, 116, 123–7
    performing, of Margery Kempe 10, 15, 77nn25,27, 197–216
    representations of female body in religious lyrics 9–10, 13–14, 124, 133–54
    *see also* virginity
Boethius 55, 83
Bokenham, Osborn 181
Bonaventure 4, 115–16, 117, 170
    *see also* pseudo-Bonaventure
Book of Hours 180–1, 185, 202
    relationship to *Ancrene Wisse* 10–11, 21–40
*Book of Margery Kempe, The see* Kempe, Margery
*Book to a Mother, The* 2, 144
*Booke of Gostly Grace, The* (Mechtild of Hackeborn) 70
brides of Christ *see* mystical marriage
Bridget of Sweden, St 8, 52, 63, 166
    and *Liber de modo bene vivendi* 86–7
    *Revelationes* 43, 71–4
    as textual authority in *Speculum devotorum* 65, 70, 71–4
Bridgittines 12–13, 47, 63, 68, 71, 86, 87
Bridlington 160
Brown, Peter 140
Bugge, J. 122, 140
Burrow, J. A. 218–19, 220, 222, 233
Bynum, Caroline Walker 7–8, 84, 109, 122, 140, 143, 147, 149

Caesarius of Arles 95n4
Caesarius of Heisterbach 163
Camille, Michael 212n9, 216n44
Capgrave, John 181, 182
Carruthers, Mary 118
Carthusians 9, 11–13
    Amherst manuscript and 45–50, 53, 57
    origin of *Speculum devotorum* 63
    and *The Book of Margery Kempe* 14, 198
    and *The Manere of Good Lyvyng* 86
*Castle of Love, The* (R. Grosseteste) 113

Catherine, St, of Alexandria *see* Katherine
Catherine, St, of Siena 8, 52, 70–1
*Chastising of God's Children, The* 45
chastity, Margery Kempe 165–71, 179, 183–4
*Château d'amour* (R. Grosseteste) 2, 3, 4, 9–10
    representation of the Virgin 13, 109–32, 141
Chaucer, Geoffrey 7, 166, 215n42, 222
Christ
    representations of body in religious lyrics 13, 144–50
    *see also* mystical marriage; Passion of Christ
Cistercians 8, 81, 113, 115
Claridge, G. 219, 221, 222
Claudian 118
*Cloud of Unknowing, The* 49, 91
    author 4, 43
Colledge, E. 45
communities
    semi-religious 11, 28–32
    women's 6
community, individual and psychological disorder 232
*Complaint* (T. Hoccleve) 218, 219–24, 225
Compostela 159
Constable, G. 84
contemplative texts, compilations 11–12, 43–62
Council of Nicaea (AD 325) 141
Council of Oxford (1222) 183
Council of Paris (1212) 30
Council of Rouen (1214) 30
courtly literature
    connections between courtly romance and fortress allegory of the Virgin 119–20, 124, 126
    female body in 134–5, 137, 139

Darker, William 86
de Brailes Hours 25, 32, 191
*De calculo candido* (J. Ruusbroec translated by Jordaens) 45
*De consolatione philosophiae* (Boethius) 55, 83
*De institutione inclusarum* (Aelred of Rievaulx) 10, 21, 82, 83, 93, 141
*De laudibus sanctae Mariae* 115

*De proprietatibus rerum* (Bartholomaeus Anglicus) 227
Delaissé, L. M. J. 24
Desert Fathers 70
*Desert of Religion, The* 49
devotional lyrics *see* religious lyrics
diabology of Julian of Norwich 237–8
*Dialogo* (Catherine of Siena) 70–1
*Dialogue with a Friend* (T. Hoccleve) 218, 225
Diehl, Patrick 133
*discretio spirituum* 71, 232
*Distant Echoes* (J. A. Nichols and L. T. Shank) 8
Dobson, E. J. 27, 32
*Doctrina cordis* 90
Dominicans 27, 28, 29, 30, 31, 32, 33, 34, 133
and Virgin Mary 115
Donovan, C. 25
Doob, P. B. R. 218, 219, 227, 234
Dorothy of Montau 166, 170
Doyle, A. I. 58n10
dream-vision tradition, Marguerite Porete's *Mirror* 54–7

Eadmer of Canterbury 117, 129n31
Ebsdorf map 149
*Ego dormio* (R. Rolle) 43
Elizabeth of Hungary 52, 166
Elm, Kaspar 28
*Emendatio vitae* (R. Rolle) 43
see also *Mending of Life, The*
*Epistola solitarii* (Alphonse of Pecha) 45
Escures, Ralph d', archbishop of Canterbury 110
Evans, Ruth 6
Eve, women identified with 138
Eve of Wilton 21, 83
*Expositio in regulam beati Augustini* 82–3, 85, 92

'Fair Maid of Ribbesdale, The' 134–5
Farley, M. H. 241n28
female spirituality 44, 57
Carthusian links *see* Carthusians
*Speculum devotorum* as adaptation for female audience 12, 63–74
see also gender *and individual authors and titles*
female vernacular theology 1–5
femininity, representation of 6, 9–10, 13–14
female body in religious lyrics 124, 133–54
Virgin Mary in the *Château d'amour* 109–32, 141
feminist approach 6–7, 10, 234
*Feminist Approaches to the Body in Medieval Literature* (L. Lomperis and S. Stanbury) 6
*Feminist Readings in Middle English Literature* (R. Evans and L. Johnson) 6
Finke, Laurie 151n12
*Fire of Love, The* (R. Rolle) 43, 47, 48, 49, 51
*Form of Living, The* (R. Rolle) 43
fortress
allegory of Virgin Mary 13, 109–32, 141
virginity represented as 13, 120–2, 141, 142
Four Daughters of God allegory 112
Fourth Lateran Council (1215) 4, 83
Franciscans 27, 31, 32, 133, 154n67
association of Bishop Grosseteste with 111, 129n39
and Virgin Mary 115–16
Freeman, P. R. 242n32
*From Virile Woman to WomanChrist* (B. Newman) 7

Galenism 227
gate of heaven, virgin body as 124, 141–50
gender
changes in *Speculum devotorum* to suit female audience 12, 63–74
inversion 13, 122–3, 126–7, 147–50
and space 120–1
and spiritual friendship 63
and spirituality 6–10, 44
geography, use in *The Book of Margery Kempe* 157–60, 162–71
Gerson, Jean 95n4, 180
*Gheestelike Brulocht, Die* (Ruusbroec) 45
Gibbs, Elisabeth, abbess of Syon Abbey 86
Gilbert (Guibert) of Nogent 115, 117, 164, 170
Gilchrist, Roberta 120
Graef, H. 109, 115
Gray, Douglas 139
Grenehalgh, James 46–7, 50, 75n2

Grimestone, John 144–5, 146
Grosseteste, Robert, bishop of Lincoln
  *Château d'amour see Château d'amour*
  *Le Mariage de neuf filles du Diable* 128n13
  *Templum dei* 4, 125, 128n13
  *Tota pulchra est* 118
Guarnieri, Romana 61n43
Guibert of Nogent *see* Gilbert

hagiography
  influence on Margery Kempe 10
  internal emphases in *The Book of Margery Kempe* 14, 157–75
  veneration of virgin martyrs in *The Book of Margery Kempe* 14, 177–95
  and virginity 122
*Hali Meiðhad* 89, 103nn76,82, 120, 141, 142, 174n25
Harley lyrics 134–5, 140
Harper, S. 219, 232
Heloise 81, 93
Herebert, William 143
Hildegard of Bingen 8
Hilton, Walter 95n4
Hoccleve, Thomas, autobiography and psychological disorder 15, 217–26, 227–8, 231, 232, 233–4, 238, 239
Holloway, Julia 58n10
Holy Land 158–9
Honorius of Autun 129n31
*Horologium sapientiae* (H. Suso) 43, 45, 63, 64, 65, 66–7, 69, 70, 74
Hugh of Folieto 118
Hugh of St Victor 83, 85, 92, 118
Hull, Eleanor 2
Humbelina, prioress of Jully 83–4
Humbert of Romans 38n63
hysteria 229, 234

identity, medieval 217–39
Ignatius of Loyola 231
'In the vaile of restles mynd' 146–7
*Incendium amoris* (Bonaventure) 4
*Incendium amoris* (R. Rolle) 43
  *see also* Fire of Love
Isabella of Warwick 173n19
*Itinerarium mentis in deum* (Bonaventure) 4

Jacobus de Voragine 178, 181–2, 183, 185, 189–90

*James Grenehalgh as Textual Critic* (M. Sargent) 9
James of Vitry 28
Jane Marie of Maille 171
Jerome, St 95n4
Johnson, Ian 63, 76n20
Johnson, Lesley 6
Jordaens, Willem 45
*Judica me Deus* (R. Rolle) 5
Julian of Norwich 3
  autobiography and psychological disorder 15, 217–18, 223, 226, 228, 229, 231, 233–9
  Christ and the body 143, 146, 147, 148
  Passion of Christ 148, 201–2, 236, 237–8
  short text in the Amherst manuscript 11, 43, 44, 46, 49, 50–7, 59n23

Katherine, St, of Alexandria 14, 179, 181–3, 184, 185–7, 188, 189, 190–1
Katherine Group saints' lives 142, 181
Kempe, Margery 2–3, 10, 14–15, 46
  autobiography and psychological disorder 15, 217–18, 223, 229–33, 234, 236, 238, 239
  Christ as bridegroom and lover 145; *see also* mystical marriage
  internal emphases and spiritual growth 14, 157–76
  performing body 10, 15, 77nn25,27, 197–216
  veneration of virgin martyrs 14, 162–3, 170–1, 177–95
King and the Thrall allegory 112
Kirchberger, Clare 61n50
Knowles, D. 234
Kocijancic-Pokorn, N. 49
Kristeva, Julia 139
Kuczynski, M. P. 89

Laing, Margaret 58nn5,9, 59n19
Langland, William 143
Lateran Council, Fourth (1215) 4, 83
Latin culture and theology 3–5
Latin hymns 114–15, 133, 139
*Legenda aurea* (Jacobus de Voragine) 178, 181–2, 183, 185, 189–90
Legge, Dominica 128n17
Leroquais, Victor 23, 24, 25, 31
*Liber de modo bene vivendi ad sororem* 2, 3, 10, 12, 81–106
  *see also Manere of Good Lyvyng, The*

*Liber spiritualis gratiae* (Mechtild of Hackeborn) 70
Lille, leper-house and hospital 30
liminality, state of 178, 191
linguistic fluidity 2, 3
Little Office of the Virgin 21, 22, 23, 24, 26, 29, 30, 31, 115
liturgical influences on Margery Kempe 10, 14, 177–95, 210–11
Lochrie, K. 67, 76n25
Lomperis, Linda 6
Love, Nicholas, *Myrrour of the Blessed Lyf of Jesus Christ* 45, 77nn26,28, 78n39, 202–4, 207
*Love Rune* (Thomas de Hales) 133, 138, 142
Lucy, St 188
lullabies 144
Lydgate, John 164, 170

M.N., translator of Marguerite Porete's *Mirror* 2, 3, 46, 52, 55–6, 57
Macrobius 55
*Male regle, La* (T. Hoccleve) 218, 224
*Manere of Good Lyvyng, The* 3, 5, 12, 77n31, 81–106
manuscripts
  Beeleigh Abbey, Maldon, Essex, Foyle manuscript 75n4, 76n23
  British Library: MS Add. 22283 (Simeon manuscript) 113, 128n19; MS Add. 37049 11; MS Add. 37790 (Amherst manuscript) 11–12, 43–62; MS Add. 49999 25; MS Cotton Nero A. xiv 27, 35n5, 133; MS Egerton 927 128n20, 129n22; MS Sloane 2593 140
  California, Huntington Library MS 127 141
  Cambridge: Corpus Christi College, MS 402 22, 27, 39n66, 82; Fitzwilliam Museum MS McClean 123 113; Pembroke College MS 221 61n43; St John's College MS 71 46; University Library MS Gg. I. 6 65, 75n4
  Glasgow, University Library, MS Hunter T. 6. 18 102n62
  Oxford, Bodleian Library: MS Add. B. 107 128n19; MS Bodley 505 46; MS Canonici Liturg. 277 24–5; MS Eng.poet.a.1 (Vernon manuscript) 27, 113, 128n19, 133; MS Laud misc. 517 86, 88, 102n67
Margaret, St, significance for Margery Kempe 14, 162, 163, 164, 170, 179, 181, 183–4, 187, 188, 189, 190
Margherita, Gayle 135
*Mariale super missus est* 115
marriage 120
  in *Liber de modo bene vivendi* 88–90
  Mary as model for married women 68
Mary, Virgin
  allegorized as fortress 13, 109–32, 141
  and female body in religious lyrics 124, 138–50
  influence of iconography on Margery Kempe 189–90
  and Margery Kempe's performing body 201, 202, 206–10
  as model for religious women 76n19, 141, 202
  *Speculum devotorum* 63, 65, 66–74, 206
Mary Magdalen 179, 188–9, 194n36
  Margery Kempe as type 14, 164–5, 166, 188
Mary of Egypt 179, 194n36
'Marye mayde mylde and fre' 139–40
McDonnell, E. W. 30
McEntire, Sandra 10
McIlwain, J. T. 235–6, 238
Meale, Carol 8
Mechtild of Hackeborn 8, 52, 70, 166
Medcalf, S. 218, 219, 227
*Medieval Women in their Communities* (ed. D. Watt) 6
meditation tradition 167, 202–4, 205
*Meditationes vitae Christi* (pseudo-Bonaventure) 45, 77n26, 167, 202
*Meditations on the Passion* (R. Rolle) 204
Meech, S. B. 157, 176n33
*memento mori* verse, body in 136–8, 143
mendicants 11, 27, 28, 31–2, 133–4
  and Virgin Mary 115–16
  *see also* Dominicans; Franciscans
*Mending of Life* (R. Rolle) 43, 44, 50
militarism, association of Virgin Mary 29–30, 122–3
*Militia Beatae Virginis* 29
Millett, Bella 140
Mirk, John 178

*Mirouer des simples ames, Le* (M. Porete) 46
see also *Mirror of Simple Souls*
*Mirror of Our Lady, The* (Syon liturgy) 68
*Mirror of Simple Souls, The* (Marguerite Porete) 2, 3, 11, 43, 44, 46, 47, 48, 50–7
*Mirror of the Blessed Life of Jesus Christ, The* (N. Love) see *Myrrour*...
misogyny, medieval 5, 135
  courtly lyrics 119
  medieval devotional literature 134, 138
Misyn, Richard 43
monastic literature
  influence on female vernacular theology 5
  use of vernacular 49
Montdidier, hospital 30
Montfort, Simon de 111, 128n17
Morgan, Nigel 25, 31
Munio de Zamora 29
*Myrour of Lewd Men* (R. Grosseteste) 113
*Myrrour of the Blessed Lyf of Jesus Christ, The* (N. Love) 45, 77nn26,28, 78n39, 202–4, 207
mystical marriage
  *Liber de modo bene vivendi* 92
  Margery Kempe 14, 163, 165–9, 181–91 passim
  religious lyrics 145
mystical writing 3
  Amherst manuscript 45, 50–7
  Christ the bridegroom and lover 145–7, 149
  Christ as mother 147–8, 149, 150
  see also Julian of Norwich; Kempe, Margery

Newman, Barbara 7–8
Nicholas de Lyra 12, 70
Nichols, J. A. 16nn16,17

Oliver, Judith 31
Opicinus 212n9
*Orchard of Syon, The* 2

Passion of Christ 109
  anchoritic tradition 200–2, 205–6, 207, 208, 210

Julian of Norwich 148, 201–2, 236, 237–8
and performing body of Margery Kempe 15, 198–211
religious lyrics 133
in *Speculum devotorum* and *Horologium sapientiae* 64–70, 73–4
*Pastor of Hermas* 118
pastoral theology 4–5
  *Château d'amour* as 112
Paul, St 179, 231
*Peace Weavers* (J. A. Nichols and L. T. Shank) 8
*Pearl* 239
Pecham, John, archbishop of Canterbury 2
Pepler, C. 231, 234
Peter, St 179
Peter Comestor 12, 70
Pierre of Luxembourg 95n4
place, in *The Book of Margery Kempe* 157–60, 162–71
Plato 125
Porete, Marguerite 8
  *The Mirror of Simple Souls* 2, 3, 11, 43, 44, 46, 47, 48, 50–7
Potkay, Monica Brzezinski 125
Power, Susan 197–8
Premonstratensian canons 27, 33, 34
Price, Paul 130n52
*Prickynge of Love, The* 153–4n58
*Prophets Abroad* (R. Voaden) 8
Prudentius 123
pseudo-Bonaventure 45, 77n26, 167
psychoanalytical approaches 234
psychological disorder and autobiography 15, 217–43

*Quia amore langueo* 146–7

*Regement of Princes* (T. Hoccleve) 218, 224–5
religious lyrics, representations of female body 9–10, 13–14, 124, 133–54
religious women, regulations 81–106
*Revelationes* (Bridget of Sweden) 43, 71–4
*Revelation(s) of (Divine) Love*, see Julian of Norwich
Richard of Bardney 111
Robertson, Elizabeth 90, 138, 140, 142
Rolle, Richard 4, 5, 11, 95n4, 215n33, 238

in Amherst manuscript 43, 44, 46, 47, 48, 49, 50, 51, 53
*Ego dormio* 43
*Fire Of Love, The* 43, 47, 48, 49, 51
*Form of Living, The* 43
*Meditations on the Passion* 204
*Mending of Life, The* 43, 44, 50
*Roman de la Rose, Le* 55, 131n61
Rufo de Gurgone 29
Ruusbroec, John (Ruysbroeck, Jan van) 11, 43, 44, 45–6, 48, 49, 51, 53
Ryle, A. 219, 226

saints, veneration 14, 149, 177–95
*Salve regina* 115
Sargent, Michael 9, 11, 61n43
Sarum liturgy 14, 178, 182, 184, 185–91
satirical literature, and female body 135
Scheynton, Alicia 113
Scrope, Elizabeth 76n23
secular lyrics, female body in 134–6
self
  authorship and self-representation in *The Book of Margery Kempe* 164, 171
  autobiography and psychological disorder 217–39
*Semireligiosentum* 28–32
*Sermones super cantica canticorum* (St Bernard) 82
Sewell, Joanna 47, 75n2
sex reversal, and female spirituality in *Speculum devotorum* 63–79
Shank, L. T. 16nn16,17
Sheen Charterhouse 12, 46, 47, 63, 86
Sidonius 118
Sitwell, G. 22, 23
Smith, Lesley 9
Solterer, Helen 123
Song of Songs 5, 91, 92, 119, 141
*South English Legendary* 181
Southern, Sir Richard 111, 112
*Speculum devotorum* 2, 12, 63–79, 206
Spenser, Edmund 131n61
spiritual autobiography *see* autobiography
spiritual friendship 47, 63
*sponsa Christi see* mystical marriage
Stanbury, Sarah 6
Statius 118
*Stimulus amoris* (James of Milan) 204
Stork, N. 242n32
subjectivity, medieval 217–39
*Super lectiones mortuorum* (R. Rolle) 5

Suso, Henry, *Horologium sapientiae* 43, 45, 63–70, 74
Sylemon, Margaret 113
Syon Brigittine nuns 12, 47, 63, 68, 71, 86, 87, 206
Syon liturgy 68

*Talkying of the Love of God, A* 2, 201
Taylor, Jane 9
*Templum dei* (R. Grosseteste) 4, 125, 128n13
temporality, in *The Book of Margery Kempe* 157-8, 161–71
Tertullian 120
Theresa (Teresa) of Avila, St 145, 231
Thomas Aquinas, St 70, 115, 154n65
Thomas de Hales 133, 138, 142
Thomas of Froidmont (Thomas of Beverley) 84
translation
  importance in cultural exchange 3–4
  performance as 198–211
travel narrative, in *The Book of Margery Kempe* 158–60
*Treatise for Maidens, A* 103n76
*Treatise of Perfection of the Sons of God* (J. Ruusbroec) 11, 43, 44, 45, 48, 49, 51, 53
*Tretis of Maydenhod, A* 103n76

*Ureison of Vre Lefdi* 133

*Vanden Blinckenden Steen* (J. Ruusbroec) 43, 45, 49
  *see also* *Treatise of Perfection of the Sons of God*
Vere de, William, bishop of Hereford 111
vernacular spirituality 5
vernacular theology 1–5
Victorines 32, 33, 34
virgin martyrs, Margery Kempe's veneration 14, 162–3, 170–1, 177–95
virginity
  *Ancrene Wisse* 121, 122, 142, 174n25
  emphasized in religious lyrics 140–50
  in *Liber de modo bene vivendi* 88–90
  Margery Kempe 162–71, 179, 188–9
  represented as fortress 13, 120–2, 141, 142
visual artefacts, influence on visions of Margery Kempe 189–90, 210

*Vita Benedicti* 169
*Vita Gregori* 169
*Vita Martini* 169
Voaden, Rosalynn 8, 77n30, 232

Walsingham 159
Warner, Marina 109, 139, 140, 141, 143
Watson, Nicholas 1, 4, 46
Watt, Diane 6
widowhood in *Liber de modo bene vivendi* 88–90
William of Shoreham 139, 143, 144
Wogan-Browne, Jocelyn 120, 140, 192n15, 213n21

*Wohunge of ure Lauerd, Þe* 200–1
*Women and Literature in Britain 1150–1500* (C. Meale) 8
*Women, the Book and the Godly* (J. Taylor and L. Smith) 9
women's dance songs 136
Wooing Group of prose meditations 133, 200–1, 204, 208
Woolf, Rosemary 133, 136

York 159–60

Zimmermann, T. C. Price 228